Toward a New Art of Border Crossing

Edited by
Ananta Kumar Giri
Arnab Roy Chowdhury
David Blake Willis

ANTHEM PRESS

Anthem Press
An imprint of Wimbledon Publishing Company
www.anthempress.com

This edition first published in UK and USA 2025
by ANTHEM PRESS
75–76 Blackfriars Road, London SE1 8HA, UK
or PO Box 9779, London SW19 7ZG, UK
and
244 Madison Ave #116, New York, NY 10016, USA

© 2025 Ananta Kumar Giri, Arnab Roy Chowdhury and David Blake Willis
editorial matter and selection;
individual chapters © individual contributors

The moral right of the authors has been asserted.

All rights reserved. Without limiting the rights under copyright reserved above,
no part of this publication may be reproduced, stored or introduced into
a retrieval system, or transmitted, in any form or by any means
(electronic, mechanical, photocopying, recording or otherwise),
without the prior written permission of both the copyright
owner and the above publisher of this book.

British Library Cataloguing-in-Publication Data
A catalogue record for this book is available from the British Library.

Library of Congress Cataloging-in-Publication Data
A catalog record for this book has been requested.
2024937475

ISBN-13: 978-1-83998-638-3 (Hbk)
ISBN-10: 1-83998-638-7 (Hbk)

Cover Credit: Photographs by Prof. David Blake Willis

This title is also available as an e-book.

Dedicated to
Alexei Navalny
Fr. Stan Swamy
G.N. Saibaba
Angela Merkel
Ella Baker
Gloria Evangelina Anzaldúa

CONTENTS

Preface		vii
Notes on Editors and Contributors		ix
Toward a New Art of Border Crossing: An Introduction and an Invitation Ananta Kumar Giri, Arnab Roy Chowdhury, and David Blake Willis		xi

Part One	**Toward A New Art of Border Crossing: Reflective Horizons**	
Chapter 1	Toward a New Art of Border Crossing *Ananta Kumar Giri*	3
Chapter 2	The New Art of Crossing Borders: Pandemic Disease, Climate Crises, and Epidemic Racism as Planetary Challenges *David Blake Willis*	15
Chapter 3	Fluid Identity and Overcoming Boundaries *Soraj Hongladarom*	41
Chapter 4	Conjuring at the Margins: A Transcontinental Approach to Interpreting Border Art *Julie Geredien*	51
Chapter 5	New Arts of Border Crossing: Tagore's Engagement with Borders *Meera Chakravorty*	69
Chapter 6	Garrison—Thoreau—Gandhi: Transcending Borders *Christian Bartolf, Dominique Miething, and Vishnu Varatharajan*	83
Chapter 7	*Comparare* Philosophy Within and *Without* Borders *Agnieszka Rostalska and Purushottama Bilimoria*	97
Chapter 8	From Hegemony to Counter Hegemony: Border Crossing in Philosophical Discourse *Saji Varghese*	111

Part Two	**Toward a New Art of Border Crossing: Movements in Societies and Histories**	
Chapter 9	Between the Left, the Liberal, and the Right: Post-colonialism, Subaltern Studies, and Political 'Border Crossing' in India *Arnab Roy Chowdhury*	125

vi TOWARD A NEW ART OF BORDER CROSSING

Chapter 10	Directions: Exit, Voice, and Loyalty and the Modern History of Migration *Ronald Stade*	139
Chapter 11	Crossing the German–German Border from the End of World War II until 1990: From Escape to Alienation *Detlef Griesen*	149
Chapter 12	Overcoming the Borders in Southeast Asia? An Analysis of Transborder Collaboration in the Greater Mekong Subregion *Detlef Griesen*	165
Chapter 13	Post Oil Migration Futures in the *Khaleej*: Thinking With/Out Borders *Manishankar Prasad*	177
Chapter 14	Transnational Communities and the Formation of Alternative Sociopolitical Otherness *Abdulkadir Osman Farah*	191

Part Three   **Toward a New Art of Border Crossing: Religion, Politics, Art and Transcendence**

Chapter 15	Crossing Borders and Creolization: Creating and Negotiating New Worlds *David Blake Willis*	207
Chapter 16	Visual Construction of Borderlands: The Case of Tohono O'odham Nation at US–Mexico Borderlands [within US and Mexico] and Their Subaltern Narrative *Ahmed Abidur Razzaque Khan and Abdur Razzaque Khan*	227
Chapter 17	High Tech for the External Border *Ralf Homann and Manuela Unverdorben*	241
Chapter 18	Journeys and Myths: Transcending Boundaries in Amitav Ghosh's *Gun Island* *Amrita Satapathy and Panchali Bhattacharya*	259
Chapter 19	Transgressing Borders and Boundaries: Religion, Politics, and Art from the Pharaoh Khafra to the Work of Siona Benjamin *Ori Z. Soltes*	271
Chapter 20	Transgression, Transcendence, and Meaning Creation in Art: Mystico-Artistic Route for Re-enchanting the World *Muhammad Maroof Shah*	293
Index		305

PREFACE

[…] Ever she nurses in her sleepless breast
An inward urge that takes from her rest and peace.
—Sri Aurobindo (2021), *Savitri: A Legend and a Symbol*, p. 122.

I do not know just
What it is
Broadness open for
Us us
Unharness our days
Let all boundaries be distant
So we can wander far
In our unknowing.
—Sharmistha Mohanty (2019), *The Gods Came After Words: Poems*, p. 2.

Life is a journey with and beyond borders. Ideas germinate and travel with and beyond space and time and become part of a symphony of thinking. In November 2009, one of us, Ananta Kumar Giri, took part in a seminar on "The Politics of Boundary Maintenance," organized at the Indian Institute of Advanced Shimla where he presented a paper on "Towards a New Art of Border Crossing." He shared this as an opening invitation to interested friends to think with ideas in this paper further and now we have this humble gift with us, *Toward a New Art of Border Crossing*, to present the world as our Holi gift, a gift of colors, love, and light.

But the world has also much darkness and those who dare to challenge structures of oppression and control are cruelly treated and eliminated. We dedicate this volume to the living courage and creativity of Alexei Navalny, Fr. Stan Swamy and G.N. Saibaba. Alexei Navalny fought with courage, love, and life affirmative humor authoritarianism, corruption, and warmongering in Russia and paid this with his life in an arctic penal colony in Russia which for many is a state-sponsored murder.

Fr. Stan Swamy fought for the rights and dignity of Adivasis of India and was implicated in a sprawling case called Bhima Koregaon which many believed is a case of politically motivated arrest, and even as an 84-year-old prisoner was not given basic needed instruments such as a spoon. He collapsed in a courtroom in Mumbai on July 5, 2021. G.N Saibaba developed polio at a young age and as a result, lost his ability to walk. He had to crawl. With all the challenges of life, he got a PhD in English and taught at Ram Lal Anand College, New Delhi. He was picked up for his alleged association with the Naxalites and was imprisoned and subjected to inhuman treatment.

viii TOWARD A NEW ART OF BORDER CROSSING

Luckily the High Court of Maharashtra released him the second time on March 7, 2024. In his *Why Do You Fear My Way So Much: Poems and Letters from the Prison*, Saibaba tells us: "You cannot kill me because I love wild grass."

We also dedicate this book to Angela Merkel, Ella Baker, and Gloria Evangelina Anzaldúa. Angela Merkel welcomed vulnerable refugees to Germany where many states were closing their borders and showed a remarkable path of personal and political solidarity with those who want to cross the border in difficult circumstances including precarious conditions of life and death. Ella Baker was a transformative grassroots leader in the civil rights movement in the USA who continues to inspire many with her many border crossings of race, gender, and radical democracy. Gloria Evangelina Anzaldúa was a creative thinker whose *Borderlands/La Frontera: The New Mestiza* (1987) was one of the first deep academic studies of borders. As a scholar of borders in the Americas, as well as in cultural theory, feminism, Chicana identity, and queer theory, Gloria Anzaldúa helped us transcend borders and create multiple conditions and new movements of border crossing.

We are grateful to all the contributors to their volume for their gift of thinking, generosity, and patience. We are grateful to Anthem Press, especially Jebaslin Hephzibah and Tej P. Sood, for their kind nurturance of this project. We are grateful to our two anonymous reviewers of this book for their helpful comments and suggestions. We are also grateful to Mr Sudarshan Kcherry, Managing Director, Authors Press, New Delhi, for helping us with the index of this book. We thank Mr. Balaji Devadoss of Lumina Datamatics for his kind help.

Finally, we hope *Toward a New Art of Border Crossing* helps us all in crossing many unhelpful and destructive borders in self, society, and the world and contribute to creating a world of beauty, dignity, dialogues, and peace in our times of war and wanton destruction.

Holi, Festival of Colors, Love, and Light
March 24, 2024

Ananta Kumar Giri
David Blake Willis
Arnab Roy Chowdhury

References

Mohanty, Sharmistha. 2019. *The Gods Came After Words: Poems*. New Delhi: Speaking Tiger.
Sri Aurobindo. 2021. *Savitri: A Legend and a Symbol*. Pondicherry: Navajyoti Karyalya, Sri Aurobindo Ashram. It is in the Odia transcreation of *Savitri* by Manoj Das.

NOTES ON EDITORS AND CONTRIBUTORS

Editors

Ananta Kumar Giri is a Professor at the Madras Institute of Development Studies, Chennai, India. Email: aumkrishna@gmail.com

Arnab Roy Chowdhury is an Associate Professor at HSE (Higher School of Economics) University, Moscow, Russian Federation. Email: achowdhury@hse.ru

David Blake Willis is a Professor at Fielding Graduate University, Santa Barbara, USA. Email: dwillis@fielding.edu

Contributors

Christian Bartolf is the Founding Director of Gandhi Information Center, Berlin, Germany. Email: bartolf@snafu.de

Purushottama Bilimoria is with the Graduate Theological Union, University of California, Berkeley, USA. Email: pbilimoria@outlook.com

Meera Chakravorty taught at Jain University, Bangalore, India. Email: chakram.meera@gmail.com

A. Osman Farah is associated with Aalborg University, Denmark. Email: osmanfaraha@gmail.com

Julie M. Geredien is an independent scholar based in Annapolis, Maryland, USA. Email: jgeredien@gmail.com

Detlef Griesen teaches at Justus-Liebig-University, Gießen, Germany. Email: detlef.briesen@gmail.com

Panchali Bhattacharya teaches at the National Institute of Technology, Silchar, India. Email: pachalibhattacharya1990@gmail.com

Ralf Homann is an artist based in Munich, Germany. Email: ralfhomann@t-online.de

Soraj Hongladarom teaches at Chulalongkorn University, Bangkok, Thailand. Email: s.hongladarom@gmail.com

Ahmed Abidur Razzaque Khan teaches at the University of Liberal Arts Bangladesh (ULAB), Dhaka, Bangladesh. Email: abidur.razzaque@ulab.edu.bd

Abdur Razzaque Khan teaches at the Department of Mass Communication and Journalism, University of Dhaka, Dhaka, Bangladesh. Email: arkhanrizvi@du.ac.bd

Manishankar Prasad is completing his PhD in Geography from the University of Malay, Kuala Lumpur, Malaysia. Email: monishankarprasad@gmail.com

Agnieszka Rostalska teaches at Ghent University, Ghent, Belgium. Email: arostalska@gmail.com

Amrita Satapathy teaches at the School of Humanities, Social Sciences and Management, IIT Bhubaneswar, Odisha, India. Email: asatapathy@iitbs.ac.in

Muhammad Maroof Shah is an independent scholar based in Srinagar, Jammu & Kashmir, India. Email: maroof123@gmail.com

Ori Z. Soltes teaches at Georgetown University, Washington DC, USA. Email: orisoltes@gmail.com

Ronald Stade taught at Malmo University, Sweden. Email: Ronald.stade@mah.se

Manuela Unverdorben is an artist based in Munich, Germany. Email: Manuela-unverdorben@gmx.de

Vishnu Varatharajan is with Graduate School, Geneva, and Geneva Graduate Institute, Geneva, Switzerland. Email: vishnuvaratharajan@gmail.com

Saji Varghese teaches at North Eastern Hill University, Shillong, Meghalaya, India. Email: saji_villa@yahoo.com

TOWARD A NEW ART OF BORDER CROSSING: AN INTRODUCTION AND AN INVITATION

Ananta Kumar Giri, Arnab Roy Chowdhury, and David Blake Willis

Our lives should be measured not by how many enemies we have conquered, but how many friends we have made. That is the secret to our survival.
—Brian Hare and Vanessa Woods (2020, p. 196).

Heretic emancipation from the burden of history is also a revolution in human consciousness.
—Ramin Jahanbegloo (2021, p. xiv).

Borders and border crossings are perennial challenges for self, society, and the world. Situated in a world where questions of citizenship and cosmopolitanism loom large, border crossers critically interrogate who is a citizen and who belongs to a larger planetary history. Many of the chapters that follow touch on these questions. Two of the first forms of border crossing, religion, and commerce, dominate much of the history of humanity into the twenty-first century. Globalization is not new, as William H. McNeill and others have pointed out, and the anticipations of the crossings of trade, conquest, conversion, and colonialism have meant that borders have always had a provocative position in human history.

But something unique is now happening and needs to be reported. The speed with which border crossing is taking place today would simply be unimaginable to humans of earlier eras, not least the electronic border crossing taking place every day for most of the world's population. This book is an attempt to cover at least some of this territory. We begin this dialogue on the new art of border crossing by noting the myriad forms of border crossings and their intersections with questions of mobility, refugees, persecution, and identity politics. Violence and state and substate conflict, especially in Ukraine, Palestine, and the Congo, have deeply problematized the questions of borders and control. These topics on a planetary scale require our attention, and at least some of them show up in the chapters that follow, our effort at a transdisciplinary collection of essays from around the globe. Chapter 1 of the book by Ananta Kumar Giri presents these challenges and Chapter 2 by David Blake Willis provides the latest theoretical discourses concerning border crossing and border crossers.

In Chapter 1, "Toward a New Art of Border Crossing," Ananta Kumar Giri lays out the central conceptual thesis of the book, which deals with the notion of border crossing in an abstract (and concrete) sense. Here, he challenges the container-like conceptualization of sovereign states in postcolonial societies that have exclusionary borders surrounding them and that have led to innumerable and protracted conflicts. Giri criticizes these conceptualizations of borders and sovereignties and says that there is a necessity to "co-create and re-create" boundaries as sites of new beginnings and emergences of new ideas.

The new art of transcending borders is found not only through social scientific analysis but also conceptualized through critical politics, ethics, aesthetics, art, and spirituality of "shared sovereignties and non-sovereignties." Giri guides us to critically think about borders and divisions beyond the empirical, in an abstract and philosophical sense, in a creative aesthetic approach, where borders have a deeper significance in a cultural, social, intellectual, philosophical, and civilizational sense. Giri encourages readers to engage in meditative self-introspection to understand the location of self in a universe of plural existential forms. This pattern of thinking encourages us to think about entrenched borders and boundaries not as fixed entities but as dynamic flows. Resonating with Giri's initial poser, this book explores various empirical, intellectual, senses, and dimensions of border crossing through concepts such as non-sovereignties and shared sovereignty throughout the book. Rather than seeing the border and margins as spaces of marginal interest, Giri encourages us to see these margins as spaces of meetings and novel ideational and spatial emergencies.

In Chapter 2, "The New Art of Crossing Borders: Pandemic Disease, Climate Crises, and Epidemic Racism as Planetary Challenges", David Blake Willis argues that the Coronavirus Pandemic from 2020 to 2023 unleashed "a new normal" throughout the planet. During this period, we also saw an increasing global threat of military aggression, climate-induced environmental catastrophe, and new kinds of de-bordering and re-bordering emerge. Willis argues that we need to think about the current crises that start in one place and have the ability to affect the entire world, which is now highly integrated at a systemic level. In this scenario, we have to reconsider the meaning of border crossing at the epistemic level, through a transdisciplinary, aesthetic, and political understanding. We also need to apply and understand various phenomena through a social philosophical interpretation of the term, including not only crossing cartographic borders but also those borders of generations, races, classes, genders, ethnicities, and many more such categories.

Willis's essay is followed by Soraj Hongladarom's "Fluid Identity and Overcoming Boundaries," which primarily focuses on the notion of boundary and how that can be overcome (which he says is different from merely crossing the boundary) in an abstract sense by focusing on borders between social and ethnic groups. Hongladarom introduces the notion of fluid identity, which is connected with the possibility of overcoming a boundary, which is a pragmatic entity and is based on the identity of those who draw the line. Hongladarom makes a metaphysical analysis of social identity and social boundaries, drawing from two great occidental and oriental philosophers, Hegel and Nāgārjuna, and imagining a transcendental dialogue between them. Hongladarom concludes that imagining a fluid identity is the only way to overcome and transcend boundaries. This can be achieved through education and through an interpretive understanding of each other at an individual as well as collective level.

Hongladarom's essay is followed by Julie Geredien's "Conjuring at the Margins: A Transcontinental Approach to Interpreting Border Art," which argues that the art of border-crossing implies not only geopolitical, cultural, and philosophical boundaries but also the crossing of boundaries between the manifest and un-manifest worlds and the conscious and unconscious worlds. Through continuous planetary engagement and the practice of community hermeneutics, the divided selves participate and co-create a meaningful existence. Thus, these so-called borders or edges where the marginalized are located become spaces of the emergence of new doxa, which challenges the dogmatism and value absolutism of mainstream thoughts and practices and also the moral relativistic and nihilistic tendencies of neoliberal societies. Geredien's essay is followed by Meera Chakravorty's "New Arts of Border Crossing: Tagore's Engagement with Borders", which tells us that Tagore in his lifetime always despised boundaries and borders of all kinds. Initially, he set up a borderless school in Shantiniketan to promote universal learning and a culture of freedom. Eventually, this love and propensity for universalism and cosmopolitanism led to his argument against nationalism, borders, and restricted sovereign geographies that curb free spirit. Tagore even opposed the nationalism that Gandhi promoted and practiced during the freedom struggle in India, as he thought that Gandhi failed to take a journey to go beyond nationalism and understand universal spirit and engagement and limited himself within the notion of boundaries. He felt that there is a necessity for knowledge, culture, creativity, and the spirit of freedom to transgress the border to meaningfully engage and understand the world, which will eventually lead to the allaying of conflict and hatred through engagement and creative aesthetics.

Christian Bartolf, Dominique Miething, and Vishnu Varatharajan, in Chapter 6, titled "Garrison—Thoreau—Gandhi: Transcending Borders," argue that there are two borders that are significant in the history of nonviolent resistance. The first is the border between Mexico and the US, which has shifted on a frequent basis through annexation, war, and the increasing expansion of slavery within its boundaries. Henry David Thoreau opposed this through public speech, civil disobedience, and tax resistance. The second is the border between Natal and the Transvaal in South Africa, which Indian nonviolent resisters crossed as a non-violent act of civil disobedience and border crossing during their Epic March in November 1913 organized by Gandhi and Kallenbach. Henry David Thoreau became famous for his essay "Resistance to Civil Government," in which he refused to pay the poll taxes for six years until he was arrested for one night. This essay is a socio-historical and philosophical reflection on the act of crossing ideological borders in the process of nonviolent emancipation and struggle. It draws upon the philosophy of each of these path-breaking individuals and endeavors to bring out a mutual connection, dialogue, and understanding.

Purushottama Bilimoria and Agnieszka Rostalska, in Chapter 7, "Comparare Philosophy Within and Without Borders," argue that though within the field of studies of philosophy, there is a strict disciplinary and sub-disciplinary border that is carefully followed, comparative philosophy challenges this tendency. Comparative philosophers apply a particular method of comparative methodology by which they demolish and recreate borders around particular philosophical traditions to enable the diversification and pluralization of philosophy. One way of doing this is to hire scholars of ethnically diverse backgrounds, colors, genders, and other subject matters. Another way to do it is to diversify the curriculum content. A third position is to combine both the dimensions of subject position and shift in curriculum, which the author shows with the example of the philosophy journal *Sophia*, which diversified its tradition and scholarship.

This is followed by Saji Varghese's, "From Hegemony to Counter Hegemony: Border Crossing in Philosophical Discourse," which demonstrates that in postcolonial societies we see a new kind of border-crossing in the sphere of language practiced in philosophical discourses, where the phenomenon of "abridging language" has gained prominence. Taking the example of Gramscian traditional intellectuals and organic intellectuals, Varghese argues that for the hegemony to be formed and solidified, an act of cultural-ideological border crossing is necessary where multiple strands of ideas will be brought together in a single discourse of hegemonic formation, and language plays a central role here. At the same time, proletarian intellectuals would need to create counter-hegemonic exercises to challenge the prevailing dominant discourse. Therefore, intellectuals, opinion makers, and their cross-cultural and border-crossing discourse play a central role here.

Arnab Roy Chowdhury, in Chapter 9, titled "Between the Left, the Liberal, and the Right: Postcolonialism, Subaltern Studies, and Political Border Crossing in India," argues that late postcolonial theory in India has emerged into two distinct varieties. These two varieties of culture-centered arguments have emerged in contemporary Indian politics; he calls one the "postcolonial left" and the other the "postcolonial right." Initially, the postcolonial left emerged through border-crossing to develop a critique of colonial capitalism and then made a shift from class-based identities to caste, gender, and race-based oppressed subjectivities to transform leftist ideas and formed the basis of the "subaltern studies" school of historiography. The right very recently politically transformed its core ideologies to criticize colonialism as well as Islamic imperialism prior to that. Tracing the history of subaltern and postcolonial studies in India, he argues that it is therefore necessary not to confuse right-wing and left-wing postcolonialism, which have completely different political sources and syncs in which they operate. Chowdhury's essay is followed by Ronald Stade's who, in Chapter 10, "Directions: Exit, Voice, and Loyalty and the Modern History of Migration," applies Albert Hirschman's conceptual category of "exit, voice, and loyalty" to record three kinds of responses of the citizens quitting or leaving (exit), speaking up (voicing concerns), or staying quiet and faithful (loyalty) to understand who migrates and why in a world-historical perspective, thus establishing a direct relation between political struggle (voice) and emigration (exit). These often protracted fights for human and citizen rights resulted in the establishment of liberal democracies and welfare rights. These polities often pull people out of autocracies; the migrants in these novel political spaces often find themselves under new kinds of injustices and oppressions, such as injustice, inequality, and violence, to fight against, and the struggle for justice continues in another form. Stade uses his fieldwork experience in the Middle East to explicate these new types of political border-crossing and struggle.

Detlef Griesen, in Chapter 11, "Crossing the German–German Border from the End of World War II until 1990: From Escape to Alienation," talks about the creation and nullification of the internal border (that also became an international border) between the German Democratic Republic (GDR) and the Federal Republic of Germany (FRG) that once divided the German space. The inner German border, which for some time became a national border, has different interpretive connotations in the minds of the German-speaking people. The Germans commonly term this border "Grenze," which is a loanword from the Slavic language and means more than just a precise "border" as in English. It means limit, edge, or frontier. Although this was a political border, the imprecise connotation of "Grenze" had different interpretive meanings for the Germans on both sides, which shows an ambiguity toward the existence of such a divided space. This is followed by Griesen's other essay, "Overcoming the Borders in Southeast Asia? An Analysis of Trans-Border Collaboration in the Greater Mekong Sub-Region," in which he argues that increasingly there have been attempts to establish cross-border transnational cooperation among the Southeast Asian countries, despite the immense diversity of culture, language, religion, economy, and society that exist here. During historical antiquity, this entire region was hugely influenced by Indic civilization and culture. After World War II, however, this region came under the influence of Japan. Later, the US and its western allies tried to wield their influence in the region for some time. However, India and mainly China, to a great extent, are getting increasingly influential and establishing hegemonic power in this space, which is leading to new imaginations and interpretations of borderlands and spaces to reform and recreate the Southeast Asian region in novel ways.

Manishankar Prasad, in Chapter 13, "Post Oil Migration Futures in the Khaleej: Thinking with/out Borders," discusses the historical role played by the Khaleej or the Gulf in international trade, migration, and demographic shifts in this entire region. There was a tussle for dominance between the Persian, Ottoman, and British Empires for a long time in this region, and the Sheikhdoms of Kuwait, Muscat, and Jeddah were mostly aligned with the British. Though the oriental imaginary, frozen in time, imagines the Gulf as long stretches of desert dunes filled with nothingness and warring tribes, the truth is far from that. The Gulf has been an important center of trade from antiquity to current times, in pearls, slaves, and oil. The recent pandemic affected oil prices and made the economy somewhat stagnant, which led to a reduced flow of migrants and laborers in and out of the region. The region had to face this challenge and adapt itself to the new demographic normal through a real and conceptual "recalibration" of external and internal borders, thus partially transforming its spatial imaginaries.

This is followed by Abdulkadir Osman Farah's chapter, "Transnational Communities and the Formation of Alternative Socio-Political Otherness," in which Farah discusses how migrant and refugee parents take a dualistic linear transnational adaptation strategy, which is partly oriented to the host country and partly toward the country of origin. Though they train their children in similar strategies, often their

xvi TOWARD A NEW ART OF BORDER CROSSING

children evolve new alternative, multi-linear, and complex nontraditional adaptations by partially learning strategies from their parents but combining them with new educational and other sociocultural socialization impulses, giving rise to situational and dynamic hybridity of strategies. This gives rise to a difference between the older and new generations of migrants and a sense of migrant and refugee otherness, which is eventually overcome by border crossing.

David Blake Willis, in Chapter 15, "Crossing Borders and Creolization: Creating and Negotiating New Worlds," begins with one of the central concerns of critical social science: to provide cultural critique, especially around development theories. The 1950s–1970s focused on a theory of convergence regarding borders, that the American model was the paragon meant to be emulated, and that we were all becoming like Americans. An alternative then appeared in the 1980s, the Japanese model that resulted in much angst in the US and resulted in a focus on the opposite process: one of divergence, that we are all becoming different from each other. Rather than either of these binary opposites from the late twentieth century, however, Willis argues for a theory of emergence, where more complex processes are taking place, especially in the intermingling of peoples and cultures. This emergence is particularly highlighted by what happens at the intersections: *creolization*. Creolization reveals cultures in more complex and novel ways, literally creating new worlds where complex systems reveal new dynamics. Culture here signifies a series of past, present, and future processes that are dynamic, alive, and constantly transforming. Creolization thus both sustains and nurtures multiple cultures. For creolization to happen, it is a necessity that all borders surrounding a culture that imagines it as a static whole need to be recognized as fluid and open to transformation. Moreover, cultures need to be imagined as re-shaping, growing, and living entities and embraced in all their authenticities.

Willis' essay is followed by Ahmed Abidur Razzaque Khan and Abdur Razzaque Khan's chapter, "Visual Construction of Borderlands: The Case of Tohono O'odham Nation at US–Mexico Borderlands [within the United States and Mexico] and their Subaltern Narrative" which maps the US and Mexico border as a highly politicized zone where illegal border crossing, drugs, and human trafficking take place regularly. Khan and Khan analyze the visual representation of these activities through films and documentaries and endeavor to capture a critical view of them. A native South American Tribe, the Tohono O'odham Nation, is the central protagonist here, whose habitation and movement are illegalized and restricted as the wall that divides the US and Mexico, made by former President Trump, has been constructed to stop illegal border crossing. The authors show how the visual representation of the US–Mexico border in films and documentaries has divergent political portrayals and significance. Whereas one produces a colonial narrative, the other produces a constructivist and subaltern narrative of the marginalized.

Ralf Homann and Manuela Unverdorben's Chapter 17, titled "High Tech for the External Border," is unique in the approach that they take to present imaginary conversations between the author, who plans to cross the border, two security guards, and a drone. It is a text that depicts techno-dystopia and the act of border-crossing that takes place there, depicted through magic realism. The paper is arranged as various conversations and phone calls and registers dialogues that take place in the borders under the constant panoptical watch of a drone that is ever moving and changing positions to observe the conversation carefully. The discussions meander around issues of transnational border crossing and the political and economic intricacies that control these migratory movements. Discussing rules, laws, and lawmaking in various places in Europe, including Greece, Dublin, Munich, and many more, the paper tries to depict the vacuity and meaninglessness of border control, which in reality does not serve any purpose through an artful endeavor.

This is followed by Amrita Satapathy and Panchali Bhattacharya's chapter, "Journeys and Myths: Transcending Boundaries in Amitav Ghosh's *Gun Island*," where Satapathy and Bhattacharya argue that the very act of border-crossing is related to multiple meaning-making and interpretation, and it is a space of multiple semantic possibilities. They discuss Amitav Ghosh's book *Gun Island*, in which he elaborates on the concept of "transition zones," which are hybrid spaces near borderlands that separate two cartographic entities. These are transitional spaces where new myths, identities, cultures, languages, and traditions are forged and eventually merge into each other. This happens through cultural exchanges that challenge rigid notions of cultural and national boundaries.

Ori Z. Soltes, in Chapter 19, titled "Transgressing Borders and Boundaries: Religion, Politics, and Art from the Pharaoh Khafra to the Work of Siona Benjamin," starts with the notion of the border between sacred and profane in relation to religious inscriptions. Soltes discusses 'borders' around norms and communities such as scared-profane, process-product, and Jewish-Christian boundaries and their depiction and representation in a series of paintings, and looks into the artworks of Fujimura, Abu-Shakra, and Benjamin. Especially the work of Benjamin challenges the existing norms and definitions of borders with new art, forcing us to imagine transnational, transcultural, and interfaith realities. The idea behind this artwork is to heal the world fractured by exclusionary borders that group and separate diversity and multicultural human existence. This is followed by Muhammad Maroof Shah's chapter, "Transgression, Transcendence, and Meaning Creation in Art: Mystico-Artisitic Route for Re-Enchanting the World," which discusses the artistic route to transcendence and recovering the sacred as a bit different from the traditionally inherited and mystical-metaphysical routes. These two routes, as Shah mentions, are not completely separate but rather invoke and evoke each other. A critique of the subject from the viewpoint of mystical ontologies, transgression of ego boundaries, and a genuinely other-centric ontology and epistemology for resolving conflicts, flowing from Cartesian dualism and subjectivity and Freudian egocentrism, is possible by engaging through the works of mystical poets at the beginning of modernity. This will help us counter the pervasive nihilism of the post-modern world.

Our book engages one of the most important discourses in the world today, the enactments and impacts of border crossings on societies and individuals. This is a complex and ever-present series of meetings and movements that indicate the paths forward for humanity aesthetically, politically, culturally, economically, and socially. At the same time, they also reveal the fractures and fault lines of a world torn asunder by climate change, late-stage predatory capitalism, wars, and rampant nationalism. In-between and on the margins are those people who are victims and/or vanguards of these dramatic transformations. The chapters that follow help us discover new ways of seeing these border crossings, enabling us to conceptualize new possibilities for those arrangements of peoples, politics, and progressive ideals that may emerge from the desperate times we live in today.

References

Hare, Brian, and Vanessa Woods. 2020. *Survival of the Friendliest: Understanding our Origins and Rediscovering our Common Humanity*. London: One World.

Jahanbegloo, Ramin. 2021. In *Praise of Heresy: From Socrates to Ambedkar*. New Delhi: Speaking Tiger.

Part One

TOWARD A NEW ART OF BORDER CROSSING: REFLECTIVE HORIZONS

Chapter 1

TOWARD A NEW ART OF BORDER CROSSING[1]

Ananta Kumar Giri

Do not give me scissors,
Give me a needle to stitch
Since I do not cut.

—Baba Farid.

Postcolonial societies everywhere are caught up in the politics of borders leading to extreme sensitivity about issues of security/insecurity around the question of population settled/ unsettled in and across these borders. Added to this problem is the understanding that the ideological construction of the state is almost always weighted against ethnic, religious and other minorities who then are relegated to the borders of democracy. Democracy is affected by the sociopolitical consciousness of those who construct it. Nationalistic democracies aim at being a hegemonic form of territorial consciousness. National identity links territory to culture, language, history and memory. The process of nation-formation legitimates national identity by tracing it back to fictional common pasts of specific groups. It also simultaneously privileges/marginalizes certain territories. It is therefore crucial to reflect on how discourses of national identities are created by privileging certain spatial units, such as the borders.

—Paula Banerjee (2010), *Borders, Histories, Existences: Gender and Beyond*, pp. xi–xii.

The exclusivist or statist view is deeply flawed. This was perceived with remarkable prescience by Hugo Grotius, Francisco de Vitoria, Francisco Suarez and other seventeenth-century writers, who were committed to the idea of human unity and worried that the newly emerging states risked undermining this by setting themselves up to morally self-contained units standing between individuals and humankind in general. To say that humankind is divided into states is only partially true. The humanity of the citizen is not exhausted in the state, territorial boundaries do not negate the moral bonds that obtain between human beings, and every state remains embedded in a wider human community.

—Bhikhu Parekh (2008), *A New Politics of Identity: Political Principles for an Interdependent World*, p. 240.

If the Samaritan had followed the demands of sacred social boundaries, he would never have stopped to help the wounded Jew. It is plain that the Kingdom involves another kind of solidarity altogether, one that would bring us into a network of agape.

—Charles Taylor (2004), *Modern Social Imaginaries*, p. 66.

4   TOWARD A NEW ART OF BORDER CROSSING

Introduction and Invitation

Boundaries, borders, and margins are related concepts and realities, and each of these can be conceptualized and organized in closed or open ways with variations in degrees of closure as well as openness.[2] The existing conceptualization and organization of boundaries, borders, and margins reflect and embody a logic of *statis*, closure, and a cult of exclusivistic and exclusionary sovereignty (Agamben 1998; Maguire 2009). In this place, we need a new art and politics of boundary transmutation, boundary transformation, and border crossing. We also need a new realization of margins as spaces of creative boundary transmutation and border crossing rather than a helpless mirror of dualism between the margin and the mainstream.

In this chapter, I explore new meanings of boundaries, borders, and margins and a new art of border crossing, which can help us transform the existing politics of boundary maintenance, existing conceptualization and organization of identities and differences and help us realize, cocreate, and recreate boundaries, borders, and margins as places and times of new beginnings.[3] While the existing politics of boundary maintenance is wedded to a cult of sovereignty at the levels of state, society, and self—a sovereignty which produces bare lives, bodies, and lands—a new art, politics, and spirituality of border crossing is inspired by a new politics, art, and spirituality of shared sovereignties and non-sovereignties (cf. Dallmayr 2005; Giri 2009). This bordercrossing challenges us for creative aesthetic, ethical, political, and spiritual work not only in the field of physical borders and bounded territories but also in the fields of cultural, social, intellectual, and civilizational borders.

A new art of border crossing is also linked to a new art, politics, and spirituality of pluralization, which may be called meditative verbs of pluralization, which are different from conventional discourse and practice of pluralism. Conventional pluralism looks at pluralism as a noun and in a fixed state where identities and differences are also conceptualized in essentialized ways as nouns. Meditative verbs of pluralizations transform these nouns into multiple verbs, which are simultaneously activistic as well as meditative (Giri 2012). The "Art of Border Crossing" with meditative pluralization at the heart not only pluralizes existing conceptions of boundaries, borders, identities, and differences but also brings a process of meditation into the dynamics of interactions and interrelationships. Interaction here is not only merely reflective or action-oriented, as it is in the dominant discourse and practice of modernity but also involves meditation so that interacting individuals and groups also meditate about their selves and identities and realize the need for pluralization and bordercrossing. Meditation brings a depth dimension to action and interactions involved in border crossing.

Rethinking Boundaries, Borders, and Margins

Our borders and boundaries are usually looked at as fixed. But they are historically generated and embody dynamic flows. One epochal challenge is how do we transform entrenched borders and boundaries into dynamic flows of travels, interactions and a conjoint consciousnessness formation. Borders and boundaries are related to conceptions and organization of order. In modernity, we have been deeply preoccupied with the problem of order but we now need to realize that non-order is also an integral part of order.[4] Similarly, sovereignty has a dimension of non-sovereignty and shared sovereignties. Modern nation-states have been based upon a cult of sovereignty, but sovereignty has a dimension of limits of sovereignty. Non-sovereignty is a fact of life though states, societies, and selves that want to assert themselves through violence and war. The history of the modern world is in fact a story of the fragile sovereignty of nation-states where they have attacked each other in the name of sovereignty. In the modern world, the inability to share sovereignties has resulted again and again in wars and violence, which continue unabated when it comes to politics of boundary maintenance and border policing. In this context, there is an epochal need to realize that sovereignty has a dimension of non-sovereignty and is confronted with the challenge of practicing shared sovereignties. A new art, politics, and spirituality of non-sovereignties and shared sovereignties is crucial in zones of boundaries and borders and spaces of margins.

This also calls for understanding non-differences in the work of differences and nonidentities in the work of identities. Usually, we have monolithic, absolutist, and one-dimensional conception of identities and differences. But identity has also an integral dimension of nonidentity as differences have also an integral dimension of non-difference. If we approach the relationship between identity and difference from the reality, journey, and aspiration of nonidentity and non-difference then it can help us overcome entrenched boundaries and dualism between identities and differences. This in turn calls for and leads to a new process of identity formation and differentiation where nonidentities and non-differences play an important role.

But in this journey of creative identity formation and differentiation, the issue of closure and openness does face us squarely. Both are parts of life, they have their own necessities as well as their own in-built limitations. Life needs boundaries, but the crucial challenge is what is the nature of these boundaries? The crucial distinction here is if our boundaries are lines of death and destruction of potential or circles of generation and cultivation of lives and co-lives. The line between the two can and often is drawn deliberately thin by the powers that be. In this context, the challenge is critical contextual judgment, development of moral and spiritual consciousness as well as institutional forms, which facilitate creative boundary making and their transcendence.[5] We also need conscious work on creative boundary transmutation and border crossing and border workers, institutions, and pedagogies embodying this (see Giroux 2005)

Borders and Margins: Some Contemporary Reflections

At this point, we can invite two interesting contemporary reflections on borders and margins, one which looks at margins as spaces of meeting, building upon insights of philosopher Gilles Deleuze, and the other which challenges us to understand the limits of the discourse of margins, especially when it is posited against the notion of mainstream. The first reflection comes from Noel Parker who builds upon Deleuze and the second comes from the philosopher Mrinal Miri. In his essay, "From Borders to Margins: A Deleuzian Ontology for Identities in the Postinternational Environment," Parker argues that the idea of the "border" was "too stringent a concept for discrimination

TOWARD A NEW ART OF BORDER CROSSING

between entities in play" (Parker 2009: 28). "It suggests [...] manifest difference, *sovereign* separation, usually control, sometimes the opposition between what lies on one side of the border and what lies in the other. We need to identify the possibility of discriminating identities in much more open terms than the concept of border permits" (ibid). For Parker, the notion of margins is much more helpful than the concept of border. For him, margin is the "space of the meeting of identities. It is the space to determine provisionally shared and discriminating features" (ibid: 29). Furthermore, for him, "most openness can be captured with a notion of margins between entities [...] At their margins [...] the identities of entities are continuously being determined and redetermined" (ibid: 28).[6]

While Parker presents margins as more open than borders, with more possibilities, Miri challenges us to understand the limitation of the discourse of margins in his essay "On Mainstream and Marginality" (Miri 2003). For Miri, "It is clear that the metaphor of the mainstream is a powerful hindrance to the understanding of India, especially for those who set great store by the idea of one nation, one culture" (Miri 2003: 113).[7] For Miri, "To begin with, the idea of a margin suggests a condition beyond the limit, beyond which a thing ceases to be possible, or simply does not exist. Does this picture at all help us in understanding the cultural situation in India? If we take it seriously, culture other than what we might call the 'Indian culture' proper with its own proper margins (frame) will have to be obliterated from our view [...] Can an image of India be more distorting than this? There are cultural texts, and perhaps subtexts, which together constitute the complete text of Indian culture" (ibid).

Miri makes a distinction between boundaries and margins: "These texts may have boundaries, which [...] are fluid and frequently messy (mixed up, imprecise). None of them has margins in the above sense; nor does the 'complete' text of Indian culture have any margins. It perhaps has boundaries, but if it does, these boundaries can never be delineated. And, this is, of course, just as it should be. The margin metaphor as an aid to understanding the culture of India should, therefore, be abandoned as quickly as possible" (ibid).

It may be noted here that Miri and Parker are looking at margins from two different vantage points. While Miri looks at the limits of discourse of margins as it is produced by the discourse of mainstream in the context of a pervasive and hierarchical dualism between margins and mainstreams, Parker drawing on Deleuze looks at margins as a space in between and thus integral to any condition of life, more so in the work of identities and differences. Both Parker and Miri urge us to make borders more fluid. Parker here stresses the significance of making borderlands into spaces of margins—meeting places. For Miri, for this, we need not only abstract and intellectualized interactions among individuals and groups but also living interactions touching the poetic and intuitive level of our existence.[8]

Art of Border Crossing: Toward a Festivity of Incompleteness and An Artistic Ontological Epistemology of Participation

Our borders are governed by a logic of anxiety and the attendant rule to control and govern. The existing logic of boundary maintenance and border control is governed by what Arjun Appadurai calls, in another context, an "anxiety of incompleteness"

(Appadurai 2004: 8). This anxiety of incompleteness also governs our existing logic of identity, difference, and identity formation and differentiation. In this place, we need to cultivate and create a festivity of incompleteness.

Incompleteness is a condition of life; it is integral to any identity and difference. Post-structuralist thinkers such as Ernesto Laclau (cf. Laclau 1994) urge us to realize this, to which we can add the Buddhist perspective and realization of emptiness. Our cultivation of identity and difference can be accompanied by the cultivation of emptiness and incompleteness, and we can celebrate our incompleteness rather than be anxious about it. Our borderlands can be zones of the festive celebration of the limits of our identities rather than anxious places of anxiety-ridden security arrangements, violence, and death. Our border zones can be "zones of proximal development," to use the words of Vygotsky, where we help each other to develop our potential rather than to annihilate it (cf. Holzman 2009). At present, our border zones are not only spaces of terrorism of state and non-state actors but also zones of meetings, communication, and transcendence. One concrete policy of transcendence can be to make our borderlands places of welcome, hospitality, singing, and even dancing. When we cross borders we could be welcomed with a smile and song rather than be subjected to suspicious looks. Our border patrol officers also could be trained to sing the songs of both cultures lying on the sides of borders.[9] Both the border-crossing officers and people can dance together, too.

But for this, we need to cultivate an art of incompleteness and emptiness which is not static but dynamic. It calls for self-transformation and transformation of the existing organization of state and society. This agenda of transformation is a continuous one—any little step that we take toward a new art of border crossing can contribute to the transformation of existing consciousness, discourse, and organization.

In our anxiety of incompleteness, violence becomes an intimate mode of knowing as Appadurai (2004) tells us in his work on collective violence. We need here other modes of knowing and being. We need fluid and seeking ontologies instead of aggressive, self-certain, arrogant, and violent ontologies. We need new modes of knowing or epistemologies where knowing of or about the other is also a festive and artistic process of knowing with (cf. Giri 2013; Sundara Rajan 1998). We need an artistic ontological epistemology of participation for a new art of border crossing in which the boundary between ontology and epistemology is continuously being redrawn with emergent negotiation and creativity (cf. Giri 2006).[10]

In our contemporary reflections, we get intimations of such emergent moves in some thinkers. Parker here brings the perspective of Deleuzian ontology, which urges us to realize the distinction between "ontological" conditions of existence valid for the world and "ontic" conditions of existence of particular entities or types of entities in the world. Parker further presents us the glimpses of Deleuzian ontology that are helpful here:

> Discriminations between players are now seen to be needed, but neither fixed nor inherently hostile. Discriminations arise in political processes, broadly understood, in and among the players, whose identities are determined in the qualities that they acquire or lose over time. [We can note this point about quality of actors and then link it to the issue of artistic

8 TOWARD A NEW ART OF BORDER CROSSING

representation discussed later in the section on border crossing and a new aesthetic politics]
As the qualities of entities shift, so do the articulations of their margins, which determine
the identities they exhibit in the world and to themselves (2009: 34).

To this we can bring the perspectives of Betsy Taylor and Herbert Reid who talk
about 'ecological ontology', building upon the insights of Dewey and Merleau-Ponty.
Ecological ontology is a folded and layered ontology in which self is part of body, place
and commons (Taylor & Reid 2010). In terms of interactions among people and groups,
Taylor and Reid, building upon Dewey, talk about an aesthetic ecology of public
intelligence (Reid & Taylor 2006). While the dominant ontology and epistemology
creates a logic of fungibility where we are produced and realize ourselves as separate
and unconnected atoms which then feeds separatism and fundamentalism, ecological
ontology and an aesthetic ecology of public intelligence realizes the connections that
exist and then cultivates it in creative ways. Ecological ontology helps us have a field
view of our identities, differences and borders and realize that both the sides of borders
are part of a field. At present, this field is divided by fences but ecological ontology,
aesthetic ecology of public intelligence, and the artistic ontological epistemology of
participation urge us to build bridges by ourselves becoming bridges.

Toward a New Art of Border Crossing and a New Aesthetic Politics

The new art of border crossing is also accompanied by a new art of politics. The
predominant mode of politics in both traditions and modernities has been one of a
politics of closure rather than openness. Our politics of closure has determined our
existing politics of boundary maintenance and border crossing. Here, a new art of
politics can help us open up our politics of closure.

Bringing art and politics together is not easy, and traditionally, it has been fraught
with the danger of what David Harvey (1989) had termed long ago as "aesthetics of
empowerment." In the aesthetics of empowerment, for Harvey, as it happened in Nazi
Germany, art was used to annihilate the other. Here, we can also remember the way the
music of Richard Wagner was played to trump up the nationalistic spirit of Germany.
It is said, too, that Wagner was played by the Nazi soldiers while marching the Jews to
concentration camps. But this political use of Wagner in creating an aesthetics of hatred,
humiliation, torture, and annihilation does not exhaust the possibilities in Wagner's
music, as Daniel Barenboim shows us. Barenboim is a creative Jewish musician who has
not only played Wagner in Israel but also played with Edward Said. Together, Barenboim
and Said created a space for bringing young musicians from Israel and Palestine together
(Barenboim & Said 2002). In the context of the current war in Gaza and the genocide
of the innocent and terror of Hamas, we need more border-crossing initiatives like this.[11]

This is a new aesthetics and politics of crossing borders and building bridges by
singing songs of harmony, realizing that disunity is at the heart of the quest for harmony
itself. Historian and philosopher F.R. Ankersmit (1996) has spoken of aesthetic politics
and made a distinction between mimetic representation and artistic representation.
Politics in modernity has been imprisoned within a logic of mimetic representation

TOWARD A NEW ART OF BORDER CROSSING

in which politicians mimic the existing reality as representatives within a logic of representation. They mimic the existing logic and politics of closure and the politics of border patrol and boundary maintenance. They rarely have the courage to question the existing logic and representation itself.

But in a new aesthetic politics, politicians as representatives understand the limit of the logic of representation itself. They realize how difficult it is to represent one's constituency. In order to represent others and the public they need to develop themselves, and this is an artistic process. When they develop their own lives as a work of art, they are better able to perceive the nuances in the desires and aspirations of people, and they can give voice to some of these in their work as representatives. A new art of border crossing calls for such politics of artistic representation where political actors realize the need to go beyond the existing logic of constitutive closure and justification and create new spaces and times of conviviality and co-creation. We see this at times in the border politics of India and Pakistan when concerned actors—politicians, singers, players, and citizens—try to go beyond mimetic representation of the status quo and seek new ways of meeting, bordercrossing, and reconciliation (though such efforts are often sabotaged by forces who are prisoners of existing logic of bounded violence).

Aesthetics politics through artistic representation as different from mimetic representation is related to the aesthetics of travel rather than being imprisoned within a logic of fixed and controlled borders. The aesthetics of travel creates a "travelling identity" (Majeed 2009).[12] But the contemporary organization of nation-state and border control does not make this possible. Our borders are spaces of intense and military security arrangement, yet, despite this, borders are made fluid by the varieties of actions of actors. The politics of boundary maintenance as it revolves around nation-states needs to be transformed to make space for the aesthetics of travel and a new art of border crossing facilitated by aesthetic politics at home and the world.

This aesthetic politics and aesthetic travel also needs to go beyond the dualism between ethics and aesthetics. In the conventional understanding, while ethics is oriented to the other, aesthetics is oriented to the self. We need a border crossing between ethics and aesthetics, which nurtures the self and others simultaneously in creative ways with the additional integral cultivation of the spiritual.[13] Thus, we need an aesthetics ethics of politics and travel for a new art of border crossing which can emerge from the very space of the contemporary conditions of boundary maintenance, border controls and entrenched closures, and parochialisms of many kinds.

By Way of Conclusion: The *Sadhana* and Struggle of a New Art of Border Crossing

Our contemporary condition of border and boundary maintenance reflects deep anxiety and a military apparatus of exclusion. This is confined not only to national borders but also the borders between disciplines. While old borders are being dismantled such as that among nation-states of Europe that have become members of the European Union (EU), an impenetrable and brutal border is being created between Europe and outside which is called Fortress Europe. In the meantime, the EU itself is facing the threat of

10 TOWARD A NEW ART OF BORDER CROSSING

being pulled apart with Brexit and other moves. The condition is equally precarious in our part of the world in South Asia (cf. Banerjee 2010). It is in this space of difficulty that we would have to practice a new art of border crossing. This calls for *sadhana* (ego-transcending spiritual practice) and struggle. In this chapter, I have presented an outline of some pathways toward this. As we do this, we can draw inspiration from the following thoughts of Gilles Deleuze and Claire Parnet:

> Movement always happens behind the thinker's back, or in the moment when he blinks [...] Questions are generally aimed at a future (or a past). [...] But during this time, while you turn in circles among these questions, there are becomings which are silently at work, which are almost impossible. We think too much in terms of history, whether personal or universal. Becomings belong to geography, they are orientations, directions, entries and exits (Deleuze & Parnet 1987: 1).

References

Agamben, Giorgio. 1998. *Homo Sacer: Sovereign Power and Bare Life*. Stanford: Stanford University Press.

Ankersmit, Frank R. 1996. *Aesthetic Politics: Political Theory Beyond Fact and Value*. Stanford: Stanford University Press.

Appadurai, Arjun. 2004. *Fear of Small Numbers: An Essay on the Geography of Anger*. Durham: Duke University Press.

Banerjee, Paula. 2010. *Borders, Histories, Existences: Gender and Beyond*. Delhi: Sage.

Barenboim, Daniel & Edward W. Said. 2002. *Parallels and Paradoxes: Explorations in Music and Society*. Edited with a preface by Ara Guzeliman. London: Bloomsbury.

Bussey, Marcus. 2018. "Dancing East and West: Charting Intercultural Possibilities in the thought of Gilles Deleuze and Prabhat Ranjan Sarkar." In *Social Theory and Asian Dialogues: Cultivating Planetary Conversations* (ed.), Ananta Kumar Giri, pp. 35–48. Singapore: Palgrave Macmillan.

Dallmayr, Fred. 2005. *Small Wonder: Global Power and Its Discontents*. Lanham, MD: Rowman & Littlefield.

Deleuze, G. & F. Guittari. 1994. *What is Philosophy?* New York: Columbia University Press.

Delueze, Gilles & Claire Parnet. 2017. *Dialogues*. Tr. H. Tomlinson & B. Habberjam. London: The Athlone Press.

Gandhi, Gopal. 2010. *Dara Shhukoh: A Play*. Chennai: Tranquebar Press.

Giri, Ananta Kumar. 2007a. "Cross-Fertilizing Roots and Routes: Ethnicity, Socio-Cultural Regeneration and Planetary Realizations." *Social Alternatives* 36 (1): 5–10.

———(ed.). 2009. *The Modern Prince and the Modern Sage: Transforming Power and Freedom*. Delhi: Sage.

———(ed.). 2017a. *Pathways of Creative Research: Towards a Festival of Dialogues*. Delhi: Primus Books.

———2017b. "Poetics of Development." In *The Aesthetics of Development: Art, Culture and Social Transformations*, (eds.), John Clammer and Ananta Kumar Giri. New York: Palgrave Macmillan.

———2017c. "New Horizons of Human Development: Art, Spirituality and Social Transformations." In *The Aesthetics of Development: Art, Culture and Social Transformations*, (eds.), John Clammer and Ananta Kumar Giri. New York: Palgrave Macmillan.

———2013. *Knowledge and Human Liberation: Towards Planetary Realizations*. London et al: Anthem Press.

———2012. *Socioloy and Beyond: Windows and Horizons*. Jaipur: Rawat Publications.

———2006. "Creative Social Research: Rethinking Theories and Methods and the Calling of an Ontological Epistemology of Participation." *Dialectical Anthropology*.

TOWARD A NEW ART OF BORDER CROSSING

Giroux, Henry. 2005. *Border Crossing: Cultural Workers and the Politics of Education*. London: Routledge.

Harvey, David. 1989. *The Condition of Postmodernity: An Inquiry into Origins of Cultural Change*. Cambridge, MA: Basil Blackwell.

Holzman, Lois. 2009. *Vygotsky at Play and Work*. London: Routledge.

Laclau, Ernesto. (ed.). 1994. *The Making of Political Identities*. London: Verso.

Maguire, Mark. 2009. "The Birth of Biometric Security." *Anthropology Today* 25 (2): 9–14.

Majeed, Javed. 2009. *Muhammad Iqbal: Islam, Aesthetics and Postcolonialism*. Delhi: Routledge.

Miri, Mrinal. 2003. *Identity and Moral Life*. Delhi: Oxford University Press.

Parekh, Bhikhu. 2008. *A New Politics of Identity: Political Principles for an Interdependent World*. New York: Palgrave Macmillan.

Parker, Noel. 2009. "From Borders to Margins: A Deleuzian Ontology for Identities in the Postinternational Environment." *Alternatives*. 17–39.

Reid, Herbert & Betsy Taylor. 2006. "Globalization, Democracy and the Aesthetic Ecology of Emergent Publics for a Sustainable World: Working from John Dewey." *Asian Journal of Social Sciences* 34 (1): 22–46.

Schott, Robin May. 2007. "Introduction: Philosophy on the Border." In *Philosophy on the Border* (eds.), Robin May Schott and Kirsten Klercke, pp. 7–23. Copenhagen: University of Copenhagen, Museum Tusculanum Press.

Shikoh, Dara. 2006. *Majma-Ul-Bahrain: Commingling of Two Oceans: A Discourse on Inter-Religious Understanding*. Gurgaon: Hope India Publications.

Sundara Rajan, R. 1998. *Beyond the Crisis of European Sciences: New Beginnings*. Shimla: Indian Institute of Advanced Studies.

Taylor, Betsy & Herbert Reid. 2010. *Recovering the Commons: Democracy, Place, and Global Justice*. Urbana Champagne: University of Illinois Press.

Taylor, Charles. 2004. *Modern Social Imaginaries*. Durham: Duke University Press.

Notes

1 This builds on an essay of mine on this theme in my book *Social Healing* (Routledge 2023).

2 Here, we can think with philosopher Anindita Balslev's distinction between hard and soft meanings of the term "border." Here, what Robin May Schott writes in her introduction to her coedited book, *Philosophy on the Border*, is helpful:
In invoking the metaphor of border, we follow Anindita Balslev's distinction between the hard and soft meanings of the word. The hard meaning of the word refers to a boundary, a barrier which hinders us in crossing it, and which denies any crossing as a trespassing. The soft sense of border refers to a separating line that allows one to cross, to witness the differences that exist between life on the other side of the border, and the differences and tensions that exist on each side of the border (Schott 2007: 9–10; Schott is here referring to Balslev's Introduction to her 1996 edited book, *Cross-Cultural Conversations*, Atlanta: Scholars Press).

3 Here we can draw upon Bussey (2018) and Shikoh (2006).

4 This may be linked to contemporary discourse of chaos theory and notion of order emerging out of chaos.

5 Bhikhu Parekh's related discussion of morality of partiality and impartiality can help us to think of the difficult challenge of morality of closure and opening. For Parekh, morality is not just about impartiality: "If the principle of impartiality were to be the sole basis of morality, one would either need to avoid identity relations, or so define and structure them that they do not make moral claims" (Parekh 2008: 231).
Parekh's plea for balance here has implications for the difficult field of morality of closure and opening, boundary and boundary transmutation: "The question therefore is one of

TOWARD A NEW ART OF BORDER CROSSING

striking a balance, a and determining to what degree and kind of partiality should be allowed to enable special relations to be sustained and the basic demands of principle of impartiality to be met" (ibid: 235).

6 What Deleuze and Guattari (1994: 17, 19–20) write below about concepts is applicable to borders as well:

There are no simple concepts. Every concept has components [...]. It is a multiplicity [...] Components are distinct, heterogeneous, and yet not separable. The point is that each partially overlaps, has a zone of neighborhood [...] something passes from one to the other, something that is undecidable between them. There is an area *ab* that belongs to both *a* and *b*, where a and b "become" indiscernible.

In this context, what Bussey writes about Deleuze deserves our careful attention: "His tools are his creative disregard for boundaries, a playful approach to language and form, what Tony Conley describes as a 'consciousness of possibility'" (Bussey 2018: 2).

7 What Miri (2003) writes about Shankaradev and the tribals in Assam is helpful here: "Shankardev's Vaishnavite movement among the tribals has enriched them 'in their independent being'" "rather than blind them into walking into Hindu embrace. And this was a good thing to do" (ibid: 114).

8 As Miri writes:

At a popular level, cultures and therefore, religions have met, conversed with each other, and in many ways, made an impact on each other but such conversations and meeting took place at an intuitive, instinctive, and 'poetic' level rather than at an abstract and cerebral, intellectual level. Mutual understanding was, for the most part, unmediated by an abstract articulation of cultures in which one lived and had one's being. On the other hand, abstract articulations frequently lead to closing of boundaries and deadlocks in communication (2003: 111).

In recent works, I have also been exploring how poetics can help us in moving across entrenched and be part of creative border crossing (see Giri 2017).

9 We can consider here the following poem on how a cauliflower crosses the border between America and Canada:

With a cauliflower
We would go from America to Canada
But what would we say
On the border?
Asks the officer
Do you have anything?
Oh We have just a cauliflower
We have got it with us
We want to make a salad
While having our lunch
Under the sun and near Detroit Art Museum
With the cauliflower
We crossed the border
Smile also returned
Before the border
So much silence, so much anxiety
All smile lost
In the dreary desert
Why do our borders feel so dry
Why are they not homes of welcome
A place of affection
Oh our cauliflower
We brought it home

TOWARD A NEW ART OF BORDER CROSSING

It may have been born in a green field of America
We got this transnational cauliflower
From a Canadian supermarket
But is the cauliflower happy to come back home
America is my motherland
Am I happy to come home?
(A poem originally written in Oriya by the author and then the above is an extract from this longer poem).

10 I have discussed elsewhere ontological epistemology of participation which involves simultaneously epistemic and ontological in transformational ways. This has relevance for border crossing as it involves simultaneously work on our mode of being and mode of knowing in mutually interpenetrative and dynamic ways (Giri 2006; 2017d).

11 For example, peace activist and scholar Mohammed Dajani Daoudi has created a holocaust museum in his home in East Jerusalem, Palestine, to teach Palestinians the horror of holocaust the Jews have gone through so as to not to lose empathy even when some of the Jews now are perpetrating the same and sometimes far worse Holocaust on the innocent in Gaza, West Bank, and Palestine.

12 Majeed discusses this in the context of the work of Iqbal. He discusses Iqbal notion of creative selfhood as a dynamic process. He, at the same time, refers to Iqbal's preference for Aurangzeb over Dara Sikoh whom he killed to get the throne of the Mughal Empire. While Aurangzeb was for a bounded purity of orthodox Islam, Dara Sikoh for creative border crossing. He translated Upanishads into Arabic and has gifted us this epochal work in border crossing, *Majma Ul Bahrain: Commingling of Two Oceans, A Discourse on Inter-religious Understanding.* See Dara Sikhoh (2006) and also Gopal Gandhi's (2010) play on him.

13 Note here what Edward Said (in Barenboim & Said 2002: 11–12) writes in his dialogue with Daniel Barenboim about his work:

One of the striking things about the kind of work you do is that you act as an interpreter, as a performer—an artist concerned not so much with the articulation of the self, but rather with the articulation of other selves. That's a challenge. The interesting thing about Goethe […] was that art, for Goethe especially, was all about a voyage to the "other," and not concentrating on oneself, which is very much a minority view today. There is more of a concentration today on the affirmation of identity, on the need for roots, on the value of one's culture and one' sense of belonging. It has become quite rare to project one's self outward, to have a broader perspective.

In your work as a performer, Daniel, and in my work as an interpreter—an interpreter of literature and literary criticism—one has to accept the idea that one is putting one's identity to the side in order to explore the "other."

The above pathways reflects a primacy of the ethical and a conventional understanding of self and identity as closed in oneself. The proposed pathway of aesthetic ethics of border crossing seeks to simultaneously cultivate and transform the self and other in creative ways including cultivation of its aesthetic and spiritual reality and potential (see Giri 2017b; Giri 2017c).

Chapter 2

THE NEW ART OF CROSSING BORDERS: PANDEMIC DISEASE, CLIMATE CRISES, AND EPIDEMIC RACISM AS PLANETARY CHALLENGES

David Blake Willis

Living in the Borderlands [is] [...] a numinous experience. It is always a path/state to something else.

—Gloria Anzaldúa

The Age of the Coronavirus unleashed a new normal on the world in 2020–2023. Within the borders imposed by the disease and its variants, we witnessed locked-down humans, massive casualties, and clearer evidence of natural habitat destruction. Rapidly moving to center stage at the same time in the consciousness of sophisticated planners, whether civilian, governmental, or military, are an array of clear environmental threats that cross borders. Complex, destructive, and extractive global networks highlight the disregard and depredations of humans toward the environment and have resulted in catastrophic losses along and within borders political, ecological, and social.

"The pandemic is a portal" as Arundhati Roy has shared with us (2020), and portals are the borderlands of emergent new worlds. What we had previously thought of as a world headed inexorably toward globalization, borderlessness, and a "habitus of homogeneity" (Befu, 2001) is once again disrupted by innovation and newness as intrusions, extractions, and catastrophes challenge and pressure us for transformation. Debordering is taking place in some places and rebordering in others, particularly when invasions and war dominate the headlines.

More importantly for the long run, climate-induced catastrophes are now very real, appearing literally at our doorsteps every day, crossing borders with impunity. Nearly every indicator of climate change that was predicted appears to have been deeply underestimated. The consequences of not planning and not acting when faced with these "wicked problems" are simply unfathomable (Satterwhite, Miller, & Sheridan, 2015). The historical roots and routes of what has happened are deeply intertwined with who we are in the world and how we cross these borders: metaphoric, symbolic, literal, and spiritual.

What we discover, especially now as the Coronavirus has upended many traditional notions of structure and agency around borders, is a reimagining of the human condition that extends to the rest of our environment. We thus face a stark, existential question at the borderlands of our survival: *Can societies encourage sufficient changes in human lifestyles to avert ecological collapse?*

Pandemic disease as a planetary challenge that is crossing borders is not new. Seriously manifesting itself in dramatic ways with the first waves of imperial expansion, the Doctrine of Discovery, and Colonialism (see Barry, 2005, for the Great Influenza of 1918–1919: we have been here before), pandemics wiped out massive populations in the Americas and elsewhere. Like racism and environmental destruction, pandemic disease can be interpreted as occurring in multiple forms and multiple contexts. The Age of Colonialism or Imperialism and its Doctrine of Discovery was the beginning of what might also be called the Capitalocene (Hayman, 2018, p. 78), of a predatory capitalism that went hand-in-hand with this colonization. *"I found it, it's mine"* became the mantra. For Europeans and later Americans, colonization utilized a clear dictum in the Bible affirmed by Christians, Jews, and Muslims alike that clearly indicates and dictates human separation from and dominance over Nature: Genesis 1:28: *God blessed them and said to them, 'Be fruitful and increase in number; fill the earth and subdue it. Rule over the fish of the sea and the birds of the air and over every living creature that moves on the ground.* And yet something has changed.

What are the philosophical, spiritual, worldview, educational, and policy orientations in the borderlands that reflect where we are today? What colonialisms, external and internal, have become deeply embedded in our souls around these borders, to the extent that we are literally killing ourselves, profligately over-consuming, and over-extracting the bountiful resources of our planet? How has the crossing of borders led us to this state?

We have now begun a reimagining of what borders and boundaries mean for our world. No longer are they human alone. Nor are they exclusively national political borders. The borders and boundaries of the natural environment, as climate crises descend upon us, have become more real just as the burgeoning movements of people have meant a reappraisal of the meanings of border crossings (Shah, 2020). The COVID-19 pandemic meant reordering/rebordering on a massive scale (Radil, Pinos, & Ptak, 2020; Kenwick & Simmons, 2020), disrupting the already huge increases in human mobilities (Urry, 2007, 2016). Crossing borders into new territories can thus be seen in many ways.

As Sarah Lawrence Lightfoot has put it, these can be: "[...] crossing disciplinary boundaries, crossing the boundaries between art and science, crossing generational boundaries, crossing geographic boundaries, crossing the boundaries of race and class, crossing gender boundaries, and crossing the boundaries between work and play" (2009, p. 141).[1] We are also concerned with new politics, art, and spirituality of shared sovereignties and non-sovereignties at the intersection of many borders where mixing and hybridity takes place (Hazan 2015). As we will share later, this is about encounters that are continually redrawn through emergent negotiation and creativity (Brown, 2017). In the process of navigating these borders, we learn new skills, take on different temperaments, enlarge our repertoires and perspectives, and reinvent ourselves.

Borderlands: Identities, Mobilities, Frontiers, and Laws

The pre-eminent voice on borders in the twentieth century was Gloria Anzaldúa, whose *Borderlands: The New Mestiza = La Frontera* (1987) opened the field in ways unanticipated and eye-opening. Beginning as a poet, Anzaldúa developed her ideas of the borderland in an essay titled "Politics of a Poet" (Keating, 2022). Her contribution was to disrupt the binary ideas of oppositional borders and to focus, not on the hard edges of political borders alone, but on the processes and above all relationality at the heart of mixing. These borderlands can be psychological, spiritual, and sexual and are not confined to the original borderlands where she, Ramón Saldívar, and others lived and had their inspirations.

Borders are in a constant state of transition, too, even as they are created to define and exclude, meaning that there is no clear division of power and place. One day there is a wall, and another day there is no wall, the political demarcations being illusory. The importance of walls in border theory (Amilhat-Szary, 2012; Bissonnette & Vallet, 2020) quickly falls away. What is important is the bridge, the connection (Nederveen Pieterse, 2021) as well as border images and border narratives, what Johan Schimanski and Jopi Nyman in their edited volume of that name call "The political aesthetics of boundaries and crossings" (2017), mixing the political and the aesthetic in novel and innovative ways.

Wherever two or more cultures meet, those are the Borderlands. They include class, gender, race, ethnicity, and aesthetics. For Anzaldúa, borderlands with a small "b" meant the actual physical borderlands, whereas Borderlands with a capital "B" meant the emotional spaces associated with cultures meeting, clashing, and transforming. But they are not always distinct, the blurriness between them challenging binary and power dynamics. Feminist theory is brought to the fore early on. As Anzaldúa stated, "To carry the metaphor further, the Borderlands is representative of the female body, how it has been entered, violated, taken over, just like the physical land" (Keating, 2022, p. 92). She saw her idea of the Borderlands as a "bridge idea," a reconfiguring that could be generative and creative (p. 93). Anzaldúa thus opens the door for border theorists, border practitioners, and researchers in the Borderlands.

Following Anzaldúa, borders and border crossings have moved from the margins to the center of scholarship, as evidenced by the work of, among others, Martínez (1986, 1994), Prescott (1987), Giroux (1992), Donnan and Wilson (1994, 1999, 2010, 2012), Bhabha (1994, 1997a, 1997b, 2013), Matsuda (2001), Willis (1999, 2001, 2010, 2018), Willis and Murphy-Shigematsu (2008), Willis and Rappleye (2011), Meinhof (2002), LaDuke (2005), Appiah (2006), Saldívar (2006), Shimoni (2006), Rahimieh (2007), Schneider (2011), Margono Slamet and Josep Bambang (2013), Agier (2016), Hurd et al. (2017), Wilkinson (n.d.), Nederveen Pieterse (2004, 2019, 2021), and our co-editor here, Ananta Kumar Giri (in this volume, 2013, 2018, 2021a, 2021b, and in many other publications. See https://www.mids.ac.in/ananta/).

Theorizing on borders and borderlands at the turn of the century can be found in Van Houtum and van Naerssen's article "Bordering, Ordering and Othering" (2002), followed by Brunet-Jailly (2005) and Rumford (2006). The geographical studies of Kumar Rajaram and Grundy-Warr touched on politics and "hidden geographies" (2007) utilizing Appadurai's concept of borderscapes (1990, 2000). Critical border studies then became a topic du *jour* from the 2010s onward (Parker, Vaughan-Williams, et al., 2009; Parker and Vaughan-Williams, 2014), with a range of authors signaling a new space of border theory (Paasi, 2011; Mezzandra & Neilson, 2012), culminating in an edited volume of Amilhat-Szary and Giraut (2015).

A significant voice throughout on migration and borders has been Josiah "Joe" Heyman (1994, 2012, 2018, 2022), who has spoken of borders as the centers, not margins, of human endeavor. The critical and divisive nature of borders and border talk that touches deeply on human rights needs to also be mentioned. Joe of course follows the geographer Edward Soja, who introduced the idea of a Third Space, a space beyond the binary where the coalescing of multiple factors and players takes place (1989). Michael Rösler and Tobias Wendl shared similar thoughts on the rise and relevance of borders in anthropology (1999) along with Hastings Donnan and Thomas M. Wilson in their ethnographic account (2010), notably in terms of the construction of identities, security, law and legal concepts, political economy, communication, and policy studies in the literal and the metaphoric borderlands. Peña's narrative of border reinforcement follows in this same line of thought on the power of the law, knowledge, and communications (2019).

Chiara Brambilla further asserted such ideas in *Transnational Migration, Cosmopolitanism, and Dis-located Borders* (Riccio & Brambilla, 2010), and then in exploring "the critical potential of borderscapes" (2015). She has been especially emphatic in encouraging the cross-bordering of academic disciplines, seeing the differences as those similar to maps and the multiple representations they might create, a semiotic system for borders (Sidaway, 2007; Ferdoush, 2018; Dupeyron, Noferini & Payan, 2020). Values are a key here as "spaces that are represented, perceived and lived-in as a fluid terrain of a multitude of political negotiations, claims and counterclaims that reveals the hidden geographies that are often excluded by institutional 'visible' narratives" (2020). For Brambilla, "A focus on border-scapes will thus help reveal borders not as a mere space of 'di-vision' (space of meaning-breaking) but as one animated by multiple perceptions and representations, making it a 'pluri-vision' (zone of plural cultural production and meaning-making)" (2009), echoed later by the pluriversal work of Arturo Escobar (2017, 2020, 2021).

An impressive compilation, *The Ashgate Research Companion to Border Studies* published in 2011 and edited by Doris Wastl-Walter contains sections from multiple disciplines on border theory, geopolitics, border enforcement, territorial identities, borders in a borderless world, crossing borders, creating neighborhoods, and nature and environment. One of the features of such research is how we continue to see borders as frontiers and sites of conflict. Borders are the sites of raw contestations of power, as David Newman (2003, 2006) points out, too. Anssi Paasi examined this earlier in the context of the Finnish-Russian border (1996) and later (2009).

The journal *Border and Regional Studies* founded in 2013 in Poland also focuses on borders as zones of conflict in their essays, as do Nira Yuval-Davis, Georgie Wemyss, and Kathryn Cassidy in their deeply considered book *Bordering* (2019), framing

THE NEW ART OF CROSSING BORDERS

bordering through the lenses of governance, belonging, firewalls, citizenship, and gray zones. Citizenship appears in most discussions of borders and bordering, notably in the work of Willis and Murphy-Shigematsu (2008), Schneider (2011), Gaudelli (2016), and Longo (2017).

The Edge of the Plain: How Borders Make and Break Our World by James Crawford (2023) highlights these aspects of borders as well (see also Poole, 2022). As he says, "Borders don't just divide the landscape. They multiply it, creating a new world, new realities." (p. 24; see also Eker and van Houtum, 2013; and Redniss, 2023). Borders and their crossings are characterized by Crawford as *Making* (a line of bones, an endless margin, limitless) *Moving* (walled off, lost), *Crossing* (hostile terrain, burning borders), and *Breaking* (melting borders, a "wall of flesh," and "a green line across a great shore"). These are still the main topics when borders are considered in academic discourse, but the field is expanding into the conceptions Anzaldúa delineated in her expansive theories of the Borderlands. Like her, as Crawford discusses in an excellent chapter on the COVID pandemic and somatics, our body "is a landscape that is under constant attack and always has been. A landscape that never stops watching its perimeter for incursions or unauthorised entry." (p. 319)

This of course has echoes of Anzaldúa's own struggles with the borders of her own body and the social injustices of exclusion and difference as detailed by Keating (2022). Another living border is the "Great Green Wall" of trees across the Sahel in Africa, an attempt to stop desertification. A Cameroonian agro-forester whom Crawford met, Tabi Joda, has shared his thoughts on borders: "As Africans," he says, "we are living within lots of artificial borders, imposed borders. And I feel really not just Africa, but I think the entire world needs to redefine what we call borders. The whole world should see itself as an entire ecosystem." (Crawford, p. 364).

Human Geography, the history of borders, social construction of cross-border areas, the biometrics of border construction, deterritorialization, and reterritorialization, with the legal, territorial, economic, cultural, institutional, and governance dimensions of borders have been made explicit by Gabriel Popescu (2011). The process of border construction and the dialectical nature of borders may at first sight appear to be binary visions of order, but they quickly dissolve into multiple, polyvocal meanings. Borders are often unfinished, flexible, and changing (p. 133), and in some places, they have highly selective permeability (p. 135).

Rumford has similar thoughts, emphasizing what he calls "seeing like a border" (2011) and the necessity of being "multiperspectival" (2012) as does Laine on "the multiscalar" (2016), ambiguity (2020a), and safety (2020b). Borders have also been theorized by Thomas Nail as in between, in motion, a process of circulation, and not reducible to space (2016) as have Laine, Moyo, and Nshimbi (2020). Disciplinary locations for these approaches to borders and borderlands have included political geography, political science, political economy, and geopolitics.

The increasing prominence of borders and Borderlands in scholarship has been evidenced by the Routledge Border Regions Series (24 books) as well as the Borderlands Studies Series (10+ books) by Routledge. These generally follow the concerns of political economy, public policy, and literal borders/borderlands, which can be found also in the *Journal of Borderlands Studies* founded in 1986 (2023), the primary publication of the

Association for Borderlands Studies (2023). The primary concerns of the journal and the association have been hard borders, migration, resources, processes, and spatial dimensions of borders and their crossings.

Other important centers for border/borderlands research include the Nijmegen Centre for Border Research (2023), founded in the year 2000 by Prof. Dr. Henk van Houtum and colleagues of Radboud University in the Netherlands. The Center has sponsored 23 conferences since they began in 2000. A key center for border studies, they have an extensive site for relevant literature as well as links to other border research centers. The Centre For International Borders Research at Queen's University Belfast (2023) has also been an important research center, not surprising given its proximity to critically important borders. The Association for Borderlands Studies (2023) is now located in the School of Transborder Studies, Arizona State University, US, which reflects another borderland of considerable consequence.

Key figures in recent borders and borderlands studies, most of whom are in Europe, can be found at The Arctic University of Norway (UIT), a major center for Border Studies. These include Johan Schimanski, Chiara Brambilla, Stephen Wolfe, Tuulikki Kurki, David Newman, Henk van Houtum, Victor Konrad, and Anne-Laure Amilhat-Szary, among others. The terms of what some of these researchers call "Border poetics," echo Anzaldúa's earlier work and has been shared by scholars in a working group at the University of Tromsø in Norway led by Heidi Isaksen, Johan Schimanski, and Stephen Wolfe (2023):

Border concept
Border crosser
Border crossing
Border-crossing narrative
Border figure
Border formation
Border narrative
Border planes
Border poetics
Border studies
Border subjects
Border theory
Border zones
Bordering
Borderland
Contact
Epistemological border
Liminality
Symbolic Border
Temporal border
Textual border
Topographic border

THE NEW ART OF CROSSING BORDERS

Of special note is the work on "borderscaping" by Chiara Brambilla et al. (2016), which discusses the multilevel and multi-sited complexity of borderlands on the ground in a project supported by the EU. A major recent study in the latter series on "Border Culture" from Victor Konrad and Anne-Laure Amilhat-Szary (2023, following Konrad's earlier work, 2015, 2020, 2021) examines border cultures "on the move" with border imaginaries, narratives, and cultural production in transnational spaces (viz. Anderson, 1994). Not surprisingly, given border conflicts in Ukraine, Afghanistan, China, Turkey, the US–Mexico, and elsewhere, there is an emphasis in this book on sites of tension and conflict, which is the focus of much of the recent scholarship in the two series mentioned above as well.

Psychologists, too, are grappling with identity construction in our complicated, nomadic world, which have created "a kind of polyphony of voices" (Fontal et al., 2021; see also Marsico, Komatsu, Koji, & Iannaccone, 2013; Almond, 2016; Marsico, 2016; Das, Bhowal, Syangbo, & Roy, 2017; and Kullasepp & Marsico, 2021), earlier exemplified by the border crosser *sine qua non* Edward Said in his remarkable memoir *Out of Place* (2000). Gender and transgender spaces of border crossing are another ripe new field for border studies (Saldívar-Hull, 2000; Vila 2005; Willis & Murphy-Shigematsu, 2008; Casaglia, 2020), with Anzaldúa once again leading the way in her explorations of sexuality (Anzaldúa, 1987; Anzaldúa & Keating, 2015; and Keating, 2022).

The humanist and explanatory potential of multidisciplinary border crossings has been discussed by Tuulikki Kurki in a special journal issue titled *Writing at Borders* (2014). Kurki notes the transition from talking about borders and border crossings through territorial, semantic, ritualized, performative, and now discursive filters. Geography, anthropology, and political science perspectives are offered in this important essay, which turns to Arnold van Gennep, Victor Turner, Mary Douglas, Benedict Anderson, Homi Bhabha, and Hastings Donnan and Thomas M. Wilson.

The border in Mexican-American and Caribbean thought has been discussed by Hicks (1991), Michaelsen and Johnson (1997), and Fine-Dare and Rubinstein (2009), though they also go further afield, defining the transnational space as extending deep into the US. Stavans (2010), as well as Anzaldúa earlier (1987), Calderon and Saldívar (1991), Saldívar (1997), Saldívar-Hull (2000), Vila (2005), Saldívar (2006), Sadowski-Smith (2000, 2008), and Anzaldúa and Keating (2015), have also been concerned with the immediate borderlands and bordering spaces between the US and Mexico. They have been doing this work in the midst of art and aesthetics in their particular borderlands.

The New Art of Crossing Borders: Transdisciplinary and Aesthetic Perspectives

A border is not a noun but a verb.

—Henk van Houtum (2013, p. 174)

As the present book portrays it, too, there are many aesthetic dimensions to border crossings as well. Literature and poetics have been a major preoccupation of borders researchers, notably presented by *Border Crossings* magazine since 1977 (Walsh, 1977–Present); Anzaldúa's collection of poems titled "Borderlands" (1987); Sidaway on "the poetry of boundaries" (2007); Amilhat-Szary on the politics of art display on borders and walls (2012); and the literary work reflected in the edited volume by Hein Viljoen (2013) titled *Crossing Borders, Dissolving Boundaries (Cross/Cultures—Readings in the Post/Colonial Literatures in English)*.

One of the leaders in these studies is Johan Schimanski (2023), Head of the Border Readings Research Group, whose key essay "Borders are fundamental to our dealings with the world. How does literature help us understand borders?" examines matters of aesthetics and borders. His volume with Nyman (2017) is an eye-opener, with forms, zones, and migrations associated with borders portrayed by a series of border thinkers, including Wolfe, Amilhat-Szary, Konrad, Kurki, Brambilla, and Pötzsch.

One of the most extensive efforts to examine borders has come from The Arctic University of Norway (UiT) mentioned above and the Border Poetics and Border Culture Research Group. UiT's work on borders began as early as November 2004 with an International symposium on "Border Poetics?—A Comparative Perspective." Their stated aims have been to examine "forms of representation in the intersection between territorial borders and aesthetic works" (The Arctic University of Norway, UiT, 2023a, 2023b) with a primary interest in border-crossing narratives and symbolic representation. They also support and participate in the projects titled Border Aesthetics and EUBORDERSCAPES, a project from 2012 to 2016 (EUBORDERSCAPES, 2023). Some of the most notable contributions of this group have come from Schimanski (2006, 2019) and Brambilla (2010, 2015).

Cultural production assumed a major role in borders/Borderlands studies, with this group responsible for a steady stream of scholarship beginning in the early 2000s. As they point out on their website, they have published collaborative collections such as *Border Aesthetics* (Schimanski & Wolfe, 2017) and, earlier, *Border Poetics De-Limited* (2007) as well as special issues of *Nordlit* (2006, 2009, 2014), the *Journal of Northern Studies* and the *Journal of Borderlands Studies*, all mentioned on the website. A musical was even produced, *Chtodelat? / What is to be done? "A Border Musical,"* which premiered in 2013 and can be seen online (Border Aesthetics Project, 2013).

Contributions of the group and its associates to border studies are legion. They include Schimanski's initial thoughts in "Crossing and Reading: Notes towards a Theory and a Method" in 2006, quickly followed by his edited work with Stephen Wolfe titled *Border Poetics De-limited* (2007). Further work followed that is detailed on the bibliography located website for the Border Poetics Group, now the Migration, Borders and Identity research group at the University of Oslo (2023), Border Poetics Bibliography: Border Readings. The connections of borders and literature were then explored in a 2009 essay by Ruben Moi titled "Bordering Binarities and Cognitive Cartography: What on Earth Does Literature Have to do with Border Transactions?" in a special issue of *Nordlit* edited by Schimanski and Wolfe (2009) that featured "cultural production and negotiation of borders" (also reproduced in 2010 in the *Journal of Borderlands Studies*).

Scandinavian borders were featured in a volume of *Folklore* (Kurki & Laurén, 2012), edited by Tuulikki Kurki and Kirsi Laurén, that highlighted borders and life stories, a

THE NEW ART OF CROSSING BORDERS 23

keynote lecture by Stephen Wolfe, and an interview with him (2012). In the interview, Wolfe notes that we all bring the border with us into any place we are, into Anderson's "imagined communities" (1994) that are also "disciplined" by the ways we internalize laws and narratives, "often forcing our decisions into an algorithmic order calculated for 'threat' risk and 'terror' potential. As we resist these dominant narratives, we also live inside them, making us very aware of the provisional nature of the boundaries placed around our communities" (pp. 115–116). Borders are thus processes or *borderings*, figurative and imaginative, that intersect with our lives, including cyberspace. As Wolfe says, the spaces and places of borders have captured our imagination.

In Asia, we have many voices, including those of Das, Bhowal, Syangbo, and Roy on poetry, literature, and aesthetics in South Asia as they locate and understand global identity (2017); Sarkar and Munshi on borders and bordering in politics and poetics (2021); and in Japan, the Kyotographie Border exhibit of 2023 (Shields, 2023; Kyoto Graphie, 2023; Relations Media, 2023), joined by the Kyotophonie Borderless Music Festival (Reyboz & Nakanishi, 2023), among others.

Aesthetics features prominently from 2013 with the report of a conference on Border Aesthetics (Schimanski & Wolfe, 2013a, 2013b) and attention to poetry and writing through 2014–2016 detailed on the website. New directions can be seen in the work of Holger Pötzsch in 2015 on what he calls "ibordering" (the bordering of bodies, networks, and machines, 2015a) and "seeing and thinking borders" (2015b) in an elegant collection edited by Brambilla, Laine, Scott, and Bocchi, *Borderscaping: Imaginations and Practices of Border Making* (2015). Cristina Giudice and Chiara Giubilaro called for the reimagining of border art as "spaces of critical imagination and creative resistance" in that same year (2015), something that has long been reflected in the work of the artist Banksy and others.

This continued with a fascinating volume on *Border Aesthetics: Concepts and Intersections* edited by Schimanski and Wolfe in 2017 that included essays on the imaginary (Moi & Johannessen, 2017), in/visibility (Pötzsch & Brambilla, 2017), sovereignty (Schimanski & Görling, 2017), waiting (Wolfe & van Houtum, 2017), palimpsests (Wråkberg & Kinossian, 2017), and introduction on "concepts and intersections" (Wolfe & Rosello, 2017). These scholarly border communities in Northern Europe continue to do their work, with impressive production at the universities and research centers mentioned earlier. Aesthetics thus figures largely in academic discussion of borders.

Of course, the work of Ai Weiwei is another prominent example of an artist/ provocateur who has often focused on border crossing in his choice of materials and methods, from his Lego constructions of Human Rights Activists at Alcatraz to demonstration of the problematics of surveillance and the state. The musician Yo–Yo Ma has also been explicit in not only his border crossings with classical works from Mozart, Schubert, and so many others but also in his Silk Road and Appalachia work. The theatre director Peter Sellars is another explicit example of a border crosser, marrying Kabuki to modern opera and storytelling.

The WOMAD World Music genre from the 1980s onward, now called global music, including Putumayo and other labels, can also be considered to be border crossing, with the musician David Byrne a leading voice in these crossings, even as he disliked the term itself as ghettoizing other forms of music as different from mainstream pop or other music in the US and Europe (Kalia, 2019). Cinema has long been concerned with border crossings as a theme, with films on the nuances of intersectional encounters across time and space, not least the recent *Everything Everywhere All At Once* (2022), which became the most-awarded film of all time. Without the theme of crossing borders, there would be far less cinema, certainly far less interesting cinema. The distinctive film treatment of crossing borders is the theme of Monica Hanna's and Rebecca A. Sheehan's *Border Cinema: Reimagining Identity Through Aesthetics* (2019).

Anzaldúa's path-breaking theory extends to aesthetics in her chapter titled "Border Arte: Nepantla, ellugar de la frontera" (Anzaldúa & Keating, 2015, pp. 47–64). Indeed, it is her theory that takes us into art and the creative process. *Nepantla* is the Nahuatl word for "in-between," and is the most complex development of her theory of the borderlands (Keating, 2022, p. 156). It is "an epistemology that contains, reflects, and transforms contradictions [...] opening space for non-Cartesian epistemologies and ontologies" (Ibid., pp. 156–157). Anzaldúa used nepantla to expand the definitions of the borderlands to include the psychic and emotional. Intersectional theory here in Anzaldúa's conception is a sophisticated, playful, sometimes painful, guide for us, helping us understand our own borderlands and the crossings we undertake (see also Crenshaw, 2017; Hill-Collins, 2019). Like the borders and borderlands, nepantla "enters our lives and asks us to change" (Op.cit., p. 157). A light in the darkness.

Border Crossings and Shifting Politics: Time, Space, and Materiality

Border crossings involve time, space, and materiality and often are substantially affected by shifting policies and boundaries. How do contract or smuggled workers crossing borders see what they are doing, for example? How do host populations define them? How do they see themselves, redefine migrancy, and change those whose borders they have crossed? (Hurd et al., 2017, pp. 1–2). This is as true for internal displacement as for external mobilities. We witnessed the calamitous migrations of workers in India in 2020 with the pandemic shutdown. What are the shared narratives? How does crossing borders affect relationships "back home"? How are these experiences shaped, felt, experienced, and embodied by those of us crossing borders? (Op.cit., p. 2). Chronic liminalities, rebordering, disempowerment, and empowerment can all happen in these border-crossing spaces (Radil, Pinos, & Ptak, 2021; Kenwick & Simmons, 2020). Time–space boundaries have been critically affected by Zoom, Skype, and WhatsApp. The seeming impermeability of some borders is belied by the porosity of what emerges on the ground. Like Kimmerer's *Braiding Sweetgrass* (2015), we see the interpenetration of natural and human boundaries as border crossers weave new realities into societies.

The emphasis on connections and connectivity is especially important now that borders have moved to the centers of contemporary discourses. This has been elaborated on by Nederveen Pieterse (2021), who sees borders and connectivity through the lens of enlargement and containment, of debordering and rebordering. Other prescient commentary on borders today includes Latour on the metamorphosis

THE NEW ART OF CROSSING BORDERS

of science and technology (2018, 2021), Kimmerer (2015) and Yunkaporta (2020) on indigenous wisdom and scientific knowledge, Komatsu et al. (2019) on culture and the self, and the work of Escobar on the pluriversal (2017, 2020, 2021; also Kothari et al., 2019; Sklair, 2021).

Descriptions of borderlands have included alienated, coexistent, interdependent, and integrated borderlands (the first being the Iron Curtain and the Koreas as examples, while the last can be seen with those of the EU and Canada–US; see Martínez, 1986, 1994). As Jane Wilkinson has noted (n.d.), there has often been a discrepancy between political narratives on borderlands and the narratives of borderlands' natives. These are very different from the hegemony of atavistic social movements like the Hindutva in India and red-hatted MAGA white extremists of the US, resembling the nineteenth century Know-Nothings in the US and anti-foreigner *Sonnō jōi* movement in Japan (尊皇攘夷 Revere the Emperor, Expel the Barbarians!).

We are now in an age where crossing borders means movement and migration, refugees, and immigrants, and uncertain futures, requiring new strategies for acceptance or at least recognition). Border researchers like Ali Noorani, President and CEO of the National Immigration Forum, which promotes the value of immigrants and immigration, have been going directly to those involved in these physical and psychological border crossings (2022; see also Horsti, 2019). Following the waves of openings and closings of the Coronavirus, the oscillations of human fears and loathing (sometimes extreme, even leading to genocide) lead us to the realization of the need for others in our midst, especially medical, food, or farm workers and a reminder of our duty to our fellow human beings.

These openings can become reopenings not only physically but of the heart as well (physical, mental shifts/spaces), an altering of the Global Order is an escaping from globalization (Konrad, 2021), its conceits and hubris of focusing only on the nation-state and corporate multinational cultures. Victor Konrad and his colleagues have studied the evolution of North American borders and borderspaces (Konrad and Brunet-Jailly, 2019; Correa-Cabrera and Konrad, 2020) as well as theorizing on the borders in work mentioned earlier (2015, 2020, 2021) as well as the research agenda suggested by Scott and colleagues (2020) and the critically important edited volume titled *Border Culture: Theory, Imagination, Geopolitics* (Konrad and Amilhat-Szary, 2023). Other voices have also recently appeared on philosophical and theoretical perspectives of borders, including Demetriou and Dimova (2018) and Cooper and Tinning (2019).

A good example of what can happen with migration controls across borders is Japan following World War II and the dissolution of the Japanese Empire shared by Tessa Morris-Suzuki (2012), whose precise research connects us understandably to current dilemmas of migration policy for Japan, Korea, the UK, the US, and other countries. The past is within us in so many ways, and it should not be forgotten when looking at current policy-making around borders. South Asia is of course rife with borders of all kinds, so it is not surprising that a number of recent studies on "boundaries, borders, and beyond" Tripathi and Chaturvedi (2019), "re-imagining border studies" (Tripathi, 2022), and "sensitive space: fragmented territory" (Cons, 2016). These studies have mostly been about geopolitical realities around borders, although David N. Gellner's edited volume looks more directly at the experiences of individuals and communities through the lens of ethnography (2013).

Crossing borders now also means those of our physical being and even the possibility of becoming a Cyborg (Eken, 2022). The techno-human condition which emerged in the late twentieth and early twenty-first centuries (Allenby & Sarewitz, 2011), reflected in Fuller's "Humanity 2.0" and converging technologies (2011), as well as ChatGPT and other AI tools and the potential loss of control by humans of the narratives of boundary construction and controls, raises the question again of other borders we may be crossing as human beings, hopefully to what the great social activist Grace Lee Boggs envisioned as sustainable humanity for the twenty-first century (2011, 2012). But there are ominous dark clouds on the horizon.

Racism as a Pandemic Disease: New/Old Portals

If you are neutral in situations of injustice, you have chosen the side of the oppressor.

— Desmond Tutu

If your freedom relies on my oppression then neither of us are free.

— Ilhan Omar

Say Their Names [...] *George Floyd, Breonna Taylor, Ahmaud Arbery, Sandra Bland, Freddie Gray, Stephon Clark, Trayvon Martin, and so many more* [...] (*And not just in the United States* [...])

Linking COVID-19 and racism across borders is a shared sense of ongoing pandemics in our world. The movement for social justice represented by Black Lives Matter protests against racism thrust us into new realities as more and more borders are crossed (Garza, 2020; Buchanan, Oui, and Patel, 2020). Ibram X. Kendi has spoken of the ravages of his own cancer as paralleled by the cancer that is racism (2019). At the same time, the Shaheen Bagh protests and the Kisan Farmer's struggles of 2019–2021 in India revealed the drumbeat of similar continued oppressions and Othering. With women in the lead (Bhowmick, 2021) it is becoming clearer that we need tools, and we need examples. Common to BLM protests in America and protest movements in India has been a commitment to nonviolence (*ahimsa*), the search for truth (*satya*), and the pressure of truth force (*satyagraha*) which can be brought to bear on challenging social contexts.

One thing is certain, Black Lives Matter, the major response to this epidemic of racism, has been constructed like Gandhi's movement in the 1930s as inclusive in relation to self and others. American and Canadian Activists Angela Davis and Naomi Klein spoke in a recent webinar about the importance of taking care of each other and the planet during this precious moment we are in now, of international solidarity, and of the transformative power of crisis (Rising Majority, 2020). This is the foundation of our common dreams of human liberation, a sustainable activism that crosses borders based on love and justice. Experiencing the Coronavirus Pandemic together with "Racism as Pandemic" has been accompanied by a call for extraordinary and transformative leadership that mixes urgency and agency.

THE NEW ART OF CROSSING BORDERS

Cultural hegemony in the form of racism can only go so far. We search here for new imaginations and even more, critical interrogations, probing for new vistas and perspectives to help us understand what has been happening. As the memes of socio-cultural differences have been reactivated, they have also become new grounds for reimagining who we are and what comes next if we are the targets of those metaphors and disparagements. Our colleagues Blai Guarné and Paul Hansen note in their writings about Japan, for example, that what is especially important in opening ourselves to these new views is locating personal, close territories of challenges and conflicts (Guarné & Hansen, 2018; see also Willis, 2018). These help us illuminate something even more important: complexity, elegantly expressed by them in the case of Japanese society as "a site of increasing social and cultural exchange, where ethnic identities and national bounds are subject to paradoxical tensions in which both continuity and dislocation are involved."

We are thus moving from the vision of Nederveen Pieterse's *global mélange* (2004) to intricate, often obfuscated versions of mélanges that are often pastiches of racial identity theories from left to right across the spectrum, just as the lightning speed and amplification of the internet and social media crossing borders exacerbates and expands these racisms. The pandemic of multiple racisms that cross borders is met by resistance in the form of creolizations, hybrid identities, and cosmopolitanisms in ever-expanding forms (Willis, 2001; Bhabha, 1994, 1997a, 1997b, 2013; Hannerz 1992, 1996; Appiah, 2006; Guarné & Hansen, 2018).

The Black Lives Matter Uprising has demonstrated an emphasis on the end to violence against the poor and a broader concern with human development, not just identity and nationalism. It is a new age where the new art of crossing of borders includes anti-racism and decolonization as exemplified by Ibram X. Kendi, Layla F. Saad, Tarana Burke, Michelle Alexander, Cornel West, and others who led the resistance to these transnational pandemics (Kendi, 2019). The goal is an equity-focused global health agenda that crosses borders in the fight against the pandemics of disease and racism in Jensen, Kelly, and Avendano (2021). The origins of this resistance can be found in the crossing of borders represented by creolizations and *créolité*. More on these later in our book.

Crossing Borders: The Common Sense of Resolving Old Wounds

> If the problem of the twentieth century was the problem of the color line, as Du Bois said, then the problem of the twenty-first century is the problem of the border line.
> —(Oks and Williams, 2022, p. 25)

There is a great need to connect with the powerful scholarship of today in these active Borderlands (Nederveen Pieterse, 2021).[2] The transformation of peripheries to centers/ centers to peripheries, the idea of the margins of societies becoming the signposts for what is next, is now becoming apparent. Marginality is now seen as conveying power and originality, as helping societies to move forward. The margins are now becoming the centers, but how and why are the transactions taking place? The recognition of the impacts of these orientations is reflected in the founding of the journal *Anthropocene* in 2013, whose editors noted at the time that "Virtually no place on Earth is left untouched now by human activity" (Chin, Fu, Harbor, Taylor, & Vanacker, 2013), as well as by creation of *The Anthropocene Review* in 2014. We now need to do some serious soul-searching for the causes, consequences, and possible solutions for our behavior as *anthropos*, as humans, that can move beyond a singular focus on ourselves at the center. What does Anthropocentrism mean for crossing borders?

What, moreover, of the planetary? Recent discourse has moved, thanks to Chakrabarty (2021) and others, away from globalization, a project of neoliberalism and its emphasis on commodities and profits, to the planetary. The hubris of humans in much of the discussion and assumptions of the universal is revealed by the planetary. Creolization, instead, places us in relationality to crossing borders, creating and negotiating new worlds (Smith, 2013; Willis, 2001; 2010; Stewart, 2007). How we construct our narratives is negotiated at the wider intersections of identities, historical consciousness, representations, and justice. Racism is a central, driving force itself, an ongoing pandemic from 1492 onward (and even earlier) in the midst of all this, as discussed earlier.

What intersections and cross-learnings might be ahead for those of us who study borders and Borderlands? One thing is certain, the cross-fertilizations are only beginning, with the Europeans discovering more of Anzaldúa and New World border issues, scholars in the Americas discovering more from Europe and the rich traditions in Spanish and other languages, and everyone learning more from the discussions of borders from Asia and Africa. The dawn of the pluriversal has begun, but it also brings up old wounds and difficult, long-standing, if hidden until now, issues. Many of the problems of borders can be attributed to language and translation (Arteaga, 1994), something explored by Gambier and van Doorslaer in an edited volume (2016) on translation studies. With the advent of AI and more precise translation, if not interpretation, one wonders if devices will change this landscape of the borders of languages.

Many of the problems we encounter with borders come from colonization, especially of indigenous peoples. It may be time to decolonize our studies of borders, following Tuhiwai Smith (1999), Mohanty (2003), Tuck and Yang (2012), Hayman 2018, Bhambra et al. (2018), Alonso et al. (2019), and Tuhiwai Smith, Tuck, and Yang (2019). The critical work of Walter Mignolo is especially important here on border thinking and the need for decolonization (2000, 2012, 2021; see also Mignolo and Walsh, 2018, Agnew, 2008), which is also reflected in the controversial presidential address in 2021 to the AAA American Anthropological Association by Akhil Gupta (2022).

Turning to indigenous wisdom and approaches to heal divides and restore balance may be helpful here (Villanueva, 2018), and we are already seeing this with regard to such topics as fire suppression, and control, community welfare, and sharing economies, as Kimmerer and others have been gently pointing out to us. A more gentle model for agriculture such as perma-gardening could limit the damage wrought by the industrialization and commodification of all resources. Wahinke Topa (Four Arrows) and Darcia Narvaez argue for "restoring the kinship worldview," that we really are not so divided and that there are ways to rebalance what we are doing with our divide and rule (again, borders, setting up borders) tactics for "conquering" the world (2022; see also Yunkaporta, 2018).

THE NEW ART OF CROSSING BORDERS 29

Our authors in our book here are inveterate border crossers from nine countries. Many of us are multiple in our residencies and citizenships and well-traveled in not only geographical but also cultural, psychological, and aesthetic realms. Our topics on border crossings range from pandemic disease to climate crises to the sacred and profane. Our contexts include India, Germany, the US, Kashmir, Delhi, Chennai, Bangkok, Singapore, Appalachia, the Haleej (Persian/Arabian Gulf), Indigenous Nations, Mexico, Wolastoqey, Southeast Asia, Appalachia, Transnational Communities, and Denmark.

We encompass concerns with High Tech, Capitalism, Energy, Migrants and Refugees, Gender, Sexuality, Mysticism, Religion, Comparative Philosophy, Spiritual Activism, Literature and Borders, Art and Artists, and the Epidemic of Racism. Our topics include Hegel and Nāgārjuna, the Great Sphinx, the Church and the Triune, *tikkun olam*, transgressions and transcendence, Globalectics, flux, Salutogenesis, Dis/Ability, and Creoles and Creolization. This panoply of voices brings much to the table of transnational, border-crossing scholarship.

However, we may look at borders and the Borderlands, it is important that we address the sources of our problems directly. It is only common sense to resolve old wounds. We now face an uncommon and possibly existential question of our future on the planet. What happens next is up to us. In the chapters of this book, we aim to address some of these wounds. What can we learn from our colleagues and their research?

References

Agier, Michael. (2016). *Borderlands: Towards an Anthropology of the Cosmopolitan Condition*. Cambridge UK: Polity Press.

Agnew, John. (2008). Borders on the Mind: Reframing Border Thinking. *Ethics and Global Politics* 1, no. 4: 175–91. doi: https://doi-org.fgul.idm.oclc.org/10.3402/egp.v1i4.1892.

Allenby, Braden R., & Sarewitz, Daniel. (2011). *The Techno-Human Condition*. Cambridge: MIT Press.

Almond, Brenda. (2016). Border Anxiety: Culture, Identity and Belonging. *Philosophy* (London, England) 91, no. 4: 463–81.

Alonso Bejarano, Carolina, Lopez Juarez, Lucia, Mijangos Garcia, Mirian A., & Goldstein, Daniel M. (2019). *Decolonizing Ethnography: Undocumented Immigrants and New Direction in Social Science*. Durham: Duke University Press.

Amilhat-Szary, Anne-Laure. (2012). Walls and Border Art: The Politics of Art Display, *Journal of Borderlands Studies*, 27: 2, 213–28, DOI: 10.1080/08865655.2012.687216.

Amilhat-Szary, Anne-Laure, & Giraut, Frédéric. (2015). *Borderities: The Politics of Contemporary Mobile Borders*. New York: Palgrave Macmillan.

Anderson, Benedict. (1994). *Imagined Communities*. London: Verso.

Anzaldúa, Gloria. (1987). *Borderlands: The New Mestiza = La Frontera*. San Francisco: Aunt Lute Books. 2.

Anzaldúa, Gloria, & Keating, AnaLouise (ed.) (2015). *Light in the Dark/Luz en lo Oscuro: Rewriting Identity, Spirituality, Reality*. Durham NC: Duke University Press.

Appadurai, Arjun (1990). Disjuncture and Difference in the Global Cultural Economy, *Public Culture*. 2 (2) Spring: 1–24.

_____(2000). Guest Editor. Globalization. Special Issue of Public Culture, Millennial Quartet, 12 (1) Winter.

TOWARD A NEW ART OF BORDER CROSSING

Appiah, Kwame Anthony. (2006). *Cosmopolitanism: Ethics in a World of Strangers*, New York: W.W. Norton.

Arctic University of Norway (UiT). (2023a). Border Poetics and Border Culture Research Group, https://en.uit.no/forskning/forskningsgrupper/gruppe?p_document_id=344750.

Arctic University of Norway (UiT). (2023b). Links, Border Poetics and Border Culture Research Group, https://en.uit.no/forskning/forskningsgrupper/sub?p_document_id=344750&sub_id=344769.

Arteaga, Alfred. (ed.). (1994). *An Other Tongue: Nation and Ethnicity in the Linguistic Borderlands*. Durham NC: Duke University Press.

Association for Borderlands Studies. (2023). Home page for ABS, School of Transborder Studies, Arizona State University, https://absborderlands.org Also, Useful Links (For Border Studies): https://absborderlands.org/resources/

Balibar, Etienne, & Wallerstein, Immanuel. (1993). *Race, Nation, Class: Ambiguous Identities*. London: Verso.

Barry, John M. (2005). *The Great Influenza: The Epic Story of the Deadliest Plague in History*. New York: Penguin.

Befu, Harumi. (2001). *Hegemony of Homogeneity: An Anthropological Analysis of Nihonjinron*. Tokyo: Trans Pacific Press.

Bhabha, Homi (Guest Editor) (1997a). 'Front Lines/Border Posts,' *Critical Inquiry*, Spring, Volume 23, Number 3.

———(1997b). 'Life at the Border: Hybrid Identities of the Present,' *New Perspectives Quarterly*, Vol 14, Number 1.

———(1994). *The Location of Culture*, London: Routledge. 3.

———(2013). In Between Cultures, in New Perspectives Quarterly, Fall, pp. 107–109.

Bhambra, Gurinder K., Gebrial, Dalia, & Nişancıoğlu, Kerem. (2018). *Decolonizing the University*. London: Pluto Press.

Bhowmick, Nilanjana. (2021). 'I Cannot Be Intimidated. I Cannot Be Bought.' The Women Leading India's Farmer Protests, Time, March 4, https://time.com/5942125/women-india-farmers-protests/

Bissonnette, Andréanne, & Vallet, Élisabeth. (2020). *Borders and Border Walls: In-Security, Symbolism, Vulnerabilities*. London: Routledge.

Boggs, Grace Lee, with Kurashige, Scott. (2011, 2012). *The Next American Revolution: Sustainable Activism for the Twenty-First Century*. Berkeley: University of California Press.

Border Aesthetics Project. (2013). Chtodelat? / What is to be done? "A Border Musical," première at Barents Spektakel 2013, 6 February, http://chtodelat.org.

Border and Regional Studies (https://czasopisma.uni.opole.pl) – Journal of political science from Poland since 2013.

Border Poetics Group (now the Migration, Borders and Identity research group at the University of Oslo) (2023). Border Poetics Bibliography: Border Readings, https://www.hf.uio.no/ilos/english/research/groups/migration-borders-and-identity/border-poetics-bibliography/readings/

Brambilla, Chiara. (2009). Borders: Paradoxical Structures Between Essentialization and Creativity. *World Futures* 65 (8): 582–88.

Brambilla, Chiara. (2010). "Borders Still Exist! What Are Borders?", in Riccio B., Brambilla C. (eds), *Transnational Migration, Cosmopolitanism and Dis-located Borders*, Guaraldi, Rimini, pp. 73–85.

Brambilla, Chiara. (2015). "Exploring the Critical Potential of the Borderscapes Concept", *Geopolitics*, 20(1), pp. 14–34.

Brambilla, Chiara, Laine, Jussi, Scott, James W., & Bocchi, Gianluca (eds). (2016). *Borderscaping: Imaginations and Practices of Border Making*. London: Routledge.

Brown, Adrienne Maree. (2017). *Emergent Strategy: Shaping Change, Changing Worlds*. Oakland: AK Press.

THE NEW ART OF CROSSING BORDERS 31

Brunet-Jailly, Emmanuel. (2005). Theorizing Borders: An Interdisciplinary Perspective. *Geopolitics* 10: 633–49. doi: https://doi-org.fgul.idm.oclc.org/10.1080/146500405003 18449 4.

Buchanan, Larry, Bui, Quoctrung, & Patel, Jugal K. (2020). Black Lives Matter May Be the Largest Movement in US History, *New York Times*, July 3, https://www.nytimes.com/interactive/2020/07/03/us/george-floyd-protests-crowd-size.html.

Calderón, Héctor, & Saldívar, José David. (eds.). (1991). *Criticism in the Borderlands: Studies in Chicano Literature, Culture, and Ideology.* Durham NC: Duke University Press.

Casaglia, A. (2020). Pornography at the Borders: Ethnosexual Borderscapes, Gendered Violence, and Embodied Control. *Geopolitics.* doi:https://doi-org.fgul.idm.oclc.org/10.1080/14650045.2020.1755266.

Centre For International Borders Research. (2023). Home Page, Queen's University Belfast, https://www.qub.ac.uk/research-centres/bordersresearch//.

Chakrabarty, Dipesh. (2021). *The Climate of History in a Planetary Age.* Chicago: University of Chicago Press.

Chin, Anne, Fu, Rong, Harbor, Jon, Taylor, Mark P., & Vanacker, Verle. (2013). Anthropocene: Human Interactions with Earth Systems, *Anthropocene*, Vol. 1, September, pp.1–2.

Cons, Jason. (2016). *Sensitive Space: Fragmented Territory at the India-Bangladesh Border*, Seattle, Washington: University of Washington Press.

Cooper, Anthony, & Tinning, Søren. (eds.). (2019). *Debating and Defining Borders: Philosophical and Theoretical Perspectives.* Abingdon: Routledge.

Correa-Cabrera, Guadalupe, & Konrad, Victor. (eds.). (2020). *North American Borders in Comparative Perspective.* Tucson: University of Arizona Press.

Crawford, James. (2023). *The Edge of the Plain: How Borders Make and Break Our World.* New York: W.W. Norton & Co.

Crenshaw, Kimberlé W. (2017). *On Intersectionality: Essential Writings*, New York: New Press.

Das, Sukanta, Bhowal, Sanatan, Syangbo, Sisodhara, & Roy, Abhinanda, eds. (2017). *Border, Globalization and Identity*, Newcastle-upon-Tyne: Cambridge Scholars Publishing, 2017.

Demetriou, Olga, & Dimova, Rosita. (2018). *The Political Materialities of Borders: New Theoretical Dimensions.* Manchester: Manchester University Press.

Donnan, Hastings, & Wilson, Thomas M. (eds.). (1994). *Border Approaches. Anthropological Perspectives on Frontiers.* Lanham, MD: University Press of America. 5.

———(1999). *Borders: Frontiers of Identity, Nation and State.* Oxford: Berg.

———(2010). *Borderlands: Ethnographic Approaches to Security, Power, and Identity.* Lanham, MD: UPA. Accessed December 23, 2022.

———(2012). *A Companion to Border Studies*, Malden & Oxford: Wiley-Blackwell.

Dupeyron, Bruno, Noferini, Andrea, & Payan, Tony. (2020). *Agents and Structures in Cross-Border Governance: North American and European Comparative Perspective.* Toronto: University of Toronto Press.

Eken, Sylvia Antoinette Maria. (2022). *On Being a Cyborg – Crossing Borders and Negotiating Perspectives.* Baltimore: University of Maryland, Baltimore County and ProQuest Dissertations Publishing.

Eker, M. & van Houtum, H. (eds.). (2013). *Borderland: Atlas, Essays and Design. History and Future of the Border Landscape.* Eindhoven: Blauwdruck.

Escobar, Arturo. (2017). *Designs for the Pluriverse: Radical Interdependence, Autonomy and the Making of Worlds.* Durham: Duke University Press.

———(2020). *Pluriversal Politics: The Real and the Possible.* Durham: Duke University Press.

———(2021). Reframing civilization(s): from critique transitions, Globalizations, to DOI: 10.1080/14747731.2021.2002673.

EUBORDERSCAPES. (2023). Border Crossing and Cultural Production, https://en.uit.no/prosjekter/prosjekt?p_document_id=344773; Final Workpackage *Report* (2016): https://en.uit.no/Content/476862/EUBORDERSCAPES-Final-Workpackage-Report-WP10.pdf.

Ferdoush, Md. Azmeary. (2018). Seeing Borders Through the Lens of Structuration: A Theoretical Framework. *Geopolitics* 23, no. 1: 180–200. doi: https://doi-org.fgul.idm.oclc.org /10.1080/14650045.2017.1341406.

Fine-Dare, Kathleen S., & Rubenstein, Steven L., eds. (2009). *Border Crossings: Transnational Americanist Anthropology.* Lincoln: University of Nebraska Press.

Fontal, Andrew, Marsico, Giuseppina, Ossa, Julio César, Millán, Juan David, & Prado, Alexander. (2021). The Dynamic Functionality of Borders: A Study from a Cultural Perspective. In Kullasepp, K., & Marsico, G. (eds) *Identity at the Borders and Between the Borders. SpringerBriefs in Psychology.* Cham, Switzerland: Springer. https://doi-org.fgul.idm.oclc. org/10.1007/978-3-030-62267-1_4.

Four Arrows, & Narvaez, Darcia. (2016). Reclaiming our indigenous worldview: A more authentic baseline for social/ecological justice work in education. In N. McCrary & W. Ross (Eds.), *Working for social justice inside and outside the classroom: A community of teachers, researchers, and activists* (pp. 91–112). In J. Miller & L.D. Burns, Eds., Social justice across contexts in education. New York, NY: Peter Lang.

Fuller, Steve. (2011). *Humanity 2.0: What It Means to Be Human Past, Present, and Future.* Basingstoke: Palgrave.

Gambier, Yves, & van Doorslaer, Luc van (eds). (2016). *Border Crossings: Translation Studies and Other Disciplines.* Amsterdam: John Benjamins Publishing Company.

Garza, Alicia. (2020). *The Purpose of Power: How to Build Movements or the 21st Century.* New York: Random House.

Gaudelli, William. (2016). *Global Citizenship Education: Everyday Transcendence.* London: Routledge.

Gellner, David N. (ed.). (2013). *Borderland Lives in Northern South Asia,* Durham: Duke University Press.

Giri, Ananta Kumar, (ed.) (2013). *Philosophy and Anthropology: Border Crossing and Transformations.* London: Anthem Press.

———(ed.) (2021a). *Pragmatism, Spirituality, and Society: Border Crossings, Transformations, and Planetary Realizations.* Singapore: Palgrave Macmillan, Singapore.

———(ed.) (2021b). *Roots, Routes and a New Awakening Beyond One and Many and Alternative Planetary Futures.* Singapore: Palgrave Macmillan.

———(ed.) (2018). *Social Theory and Asian Dialogues: Cultivating Planetary Conversations,* New York: Palgrave Macmillan.

Giroux, Henry A. (1992). *Border Crossings: Cultural Workers and the Politics of Education.* New York: Routledge.

Giudice, Cristina, & Giubilaro, Chiara. (2015). Re-Imagining the Border: Border Art as a Space of Critical Imagination and Creative Resistance, *Geopolitics,* 20: 1, 79–94, DOI: 10.1080/14650045.2014.8967917.

Guarné, Blai, & Hansen, Paul. (2018). *Escaping Japan: Reflections on Estrangement and Exile in the Twenty-First Century.* Routledge.

Gupta, Akhil. (2022). Decolonizing US Anthropology, AAA Presidential Lecture, The American Anthropological Association, Nov 2022, available at https://anthrosource.onlinelibrary. wiley.com/doi/10.1111/aman.13775.

Hanna, Monica, & Sheehan, Rebecca A. (eds). (2019). *Border Cinema: Reimagining Identity Through Aesthetics.* New Brunswick: Rutgers University Press.

Hannerz, Ulf. (1992). *Cultural Complexity.* New York: Columbia University Press.

———(1996) *Transnational Connections.* London: Routledge.

Hayman, Eleanor, James, Colleen, & Wedge, Mark. (2018). Future rivers of the Anthropocene or Whose Anthropocene is It? Decolonising the Anthropocene! Decolonisation: Indigeneity, *Education, and Society.* 6, 2, 77–92.

Hazan, Haim. (2015). *Against Hybridity: Social Impasses in a Globalizing World.* Cambridge UK: Polity Press.

THE NEW ART OF CROSSING BORDERS

Heyman, Josiah. (2018). Borders, Michael Kearney Honorary Lecture, Society of Applied Anthropology Annual Conference, Philadelphia, USA, April 5.

———(2012). Culture Theory and the US-Mexico Border, in Thomas M. Wilson & Hastings Donnan (eds), *A Companion to Border Studies*, Wiley-Blackwell: Malden & Oxford.

———(1994). The Mexico-United States Border in Anthropology: A Critique and Reformulation, *Journal of Political Ecology*, 1, 43–66.

———(2022). Rethinking Borders, *Journal of Borderlands Studies*, DOI: 10.1080/08865655. 2022.2151034.

Hicks, D. Emily. (1991). *Border Writing: The Multidimensional Text*. Minneapolis: University of Minnesota Press.

Hill Collins, Patricia. (2019). *Intersectionality as Critical Social Theory*. Durham: Duke University Press.

Horsti, Karina. (ed.). (2019). *The Politics of Public Memories of Forced Migration and Bordering in Europe*. Cham: Palgrave Pivot.

Hurd, Madeleine, Donnan, Hastings, & Leutloff-Grandits, Carolin (eds.). (2017). Introduction, Crossing borders, changing times, in *Migrating borders and moving times: Temporality and the crossing of borders in Europe*. Manchester: Manchester University Press. Chapter DOI: https://doi.org/10.7765/9781526116413.00007.

Isaksen, Heidi, Schimanski, Johan, & Wolfe, Stephen. (2023). Key terms, border poetics project, http://borderpoetics.wikidot.com/about-border-poetics-key-terms/p/1.

Jensen, N., Kelly, A.H., & Avendano, M. (2021). The COVID-19 pandemic underscores the need for an equity-focused global health agenda, Humanities and Social Sciences Communications | 8:15 | https://doi.org/10.1057/s41599-020-00700-x.

Journal of Borderlands Studies. (2023). Primary publication of the Association for Borderlands Studies, 1986–2023 https://www.tandfonline.com/toc/rjbs20/25/1.

Kalia, Ammar. (2019). 'So flawed and problematic': why the term 'world music' is dead, The Guardian, 24 Jul, https://www.theguardian.com/music/2019/jul/24/guardian-world-music-outdated-global.

Keating, AnaLouise. (2022). *The Anzaldúan Theory Handbook*. Durham NC: Duke University Press.

Kendi, Ibram X. (2019). *How to Be an Antiracist*. New York: One World.

Kenwick, Michael R., & Simmons, Beth A. (2020). Pandemic Response as Border Politics. *International Organization*, 1–23. doi: https://doi-org.fgul.idm.oclc.org/10.1017/80020818320000363.

Kimmerer, Robin Wall. (2015). *Braiding Sweetgrass: Indigenous Wisdom, Scientific Knowledge and the Teachings of Plants*. Minneapolis: Milkweed Editions.

Komatsu, Hikaru, Rappleye, Jeremy, & Silova, Iveta S. (2019). Culture and the Independent Self: Obstacles to Environmental Sustainability? *Anthropocene* 26, pp. 1–13.

Konrad, Victor. (2015). Toward a Theory of Borders in Motion. *Journal of Borderlands Studies* 30, no. 1: 1–18. doi: https://doi-org.fgul.idm.oclc.org/10.1080/08865655.2015.1008387.

Konrad, Victor. (2020). Belongingness and Borders. In *A Research Agenda for Border Studies*, ed. James W. Scott, 107–26. Oxford: Edward Elgar.

Konrad, Victor. (2021). New Directions at the Post-Globalization Border, *Journal of Borderlands Studies*, 36: 5, 713–26, DOI: 10.1080/08865655.2021.1980733.

Konrad, Victor, & Amilhat-Szary, Anne-Laure, eds. (2023). *Border Culture: Theory, Imagination, Geopolitics*. London: Routledge.

Konrad, Victor, & Brunet-Jailly, Emmanuel. (2019). Approaching Borders, Creating Borderland Spaces, and Exploring the Evolving Borders Between Canada and the United States. *The Canadian Geographer / Le geographecanadien* 63, no. 1: 4–10.

Kothari, Ashish, Salleh, Ariel, Escobar, Arturo, Demaria, Federico, & Acosta, Alberto. (2019). *Pluriverse: A Post-Development Dictionary*. New Delhi: Tulika Books.

Kullasepp, Katrin, & Marsico, Giuseppina. (eds.). (2021). *Identity at the Borders and Between the Borders. Springer Briefs in Psychology*. Cham, Switzerland: Springer. https://doi-org.fgul.idm.oclc.org/10.1007/978-3-030-62267-1_4.

Kumar Rajaram, Prem, & Grundy-Warr, Carl. (eds.) (2007). *Borderscapes: Hidden Geographies and Politics at Territory's Edge*, Minneapolis and London: University of Minnesota Press.

Kurki, Tuulikki. (2014). Borders from the Cultural Point of View: An Introduction to Writing at Borders, in Culture Unbound, Volume 6: 1055–1070. Hosted by Linköping University Electronic Press: http://www.cultureunbound.ep.liu.se.

Kurki, Tuulikki, & Laurén, Kirsi (Guest Editors). (2012). Borders and Life-Stories, Folklore, vol. 52 (On Scandinavian borders). Includes keynote lecture by Stephen Wolfe at "In, Out and In-Between: Dynamics of Cultural Borders", V. from the Autumn Conference of the Centre of Excellence in Cultural Theory, University of Tallin, October 17–19.

Kurki, Tuulikki, & Laurén, Kirsi (2012). Borders and Borderlands, Interview with Associate Professor Stephen Wolfe, in Borders and Life-Stories, *Folklore*, vol. 52 (On Scandinavian borders), pp. 109–17.

Kyoto Graphie, International Photography Festival. (2023). Border. https://www.kyotographie.jp/editions/2023/.

LaDuke, Winona. (2005). *Recovering the Sacred: The Power of Naming and Claiming*. Chicago: Haymarket Books.

Laine, Jussi P. (2016). The Multiscalar Production of Borders. *Geopolitics* 21, no. 3: 465–82. doi: https://doi-org.fgul.idm.oclc.org/10.1080/14650045.2016.1195132.

Laine, Jussi P. (2020a). Ambiguous Bordering Practices at the EU's Edges. In *Borders and Border Walls: In-Security, Symbolism, Vulnerabilities*, A. Bissonnette & E. Vallet, eds., 69–87. London: Routledge.

Laine, Jussi P. (2020b). Safe European Home – Where Did You Go? On Immigration, B/Ordered Self and the Territorial Home. In *Expanding Boundaries, Borders, Mobilities and the Future of Europe-Africa Relations*, 216–36, eds. Jussi P. Laine, Inocent Moyo, & Christopher Changwe Nshimbi. London: Routledge.

Laine, Jussi P., Moyo, Inocent, & Nshimbi, Christopher Changwe. (2020). *Expanding Boundaries, Borders, Mobilities and the Future of Europe-Africa Relations*. London: Routledge.

Latour, Bruno. (2021). *After Lockdown: A Metamorphosis*. Cambridge, UK: Polity.

―――(2018). *Down to Earth: Politics in the New Climatic Regime*. Cambridge, UK: Polity.

Lawrence-Lightfoot, Sara. (2009). *The Third Chapter: Passion, Risk, and Adventure in the 25 Years After 50*. New York: Sarah Crichton Books.

Longo, Matthew. (2017). *Politics of Borders: Sovereignty, Security and the Citizen After 9/11*. Cambridge: Cambridge University Press.

Margono Slamet, & Yosep Bambang. (2013). *Stories of crossing borders: Identities, place and culture.* Iowa City: The University of Iowa and ProQuest Dissertations Publishing, https://fgul.idm.oclc.org/login?url=https://www.proquest.com/dissertations-theses/stories-crossing-borders-identities-place-culture/docview/1494496260/se-2?accountid=10868.

Marsico, Giuseppina. (2013). Moving Between the Social Spaces: Conditions for Boundaries Crossing. In *Crossing Boundaries: Intercontextural Dynamics Between Family and School*, eds. G. Marsico, K. Komatsu, & A. Iannaccone, 361–74. Charlotte: Information Age.

Marsico, Giuseppina. (2016). The Borderland. *Culture and Psychology* 22, no. 2: 206–15.

Marsico, Giuseppina, Komatsu, Koji, & Iannaccone, Antonio. (2013). *Crossing Boundaries: Intercontextural Dynamics Between Family and School*. Charlotte: Information Age.

Martínez, Oscar, (ed). (1986). *Across Boundaries: Transborder Interaction in Comparative Perspective*. El Paso: Texas Western Press.

Martínez, Oscar. (1994). *Border People: Life and Society in the U.S.-Mexico Borderlands*. Tucson: The University of Arizona Press.

Matsuda, Takeshi. (ed.). (2001). *The Age of Creolization in the Pacific: In Search of Emerging Cultures and Shared Values in the Japan-America Borderlands*. Hiroshima: Keisuisha.

Meinhof, Ulrike Hanna. (ed). (2002). *Living (with) Borders: Identity Discourses on East-West Borders in Europe*. Aldershot: Ashgate.

Menchú, Rigoberta. (1998). *Crossing Borders*. London: Verso.

Mezzandra, Sandro, & Neilson, Brett. (2012). Between Inclusion and Exclusion: On the Topology of Global Space and Borders. *Theory, Culture and Society* 29, no. 4–5: 58–75.

Michaelsen, Scott, & Johnson, David E. (1997). *Border Theory: The Limits of Cultural Politics*, University of Minnesota Press.

Mignolo, Walter D. (2000, 2012). *Local Histories/Global Designs: Coloniality, Subaltern Knowledges, and Border Thinking*. Princeton: Princeton University Press.

Mignolo, Walter D. (2021). *The Politics of Decolonial Investigations (On Decoloniality)*. Durham: Duke University Press.

Mignolo, Walter D., & Walsh, Catherine E. (2018). *On Decoloniality: Concepts, Analytics, Practice*. Durham: Duke University Press.

Mohanty, Chandra Talpade. (2003). *Feminism Without Borders: Decolonizing Theory, Practicing Solidarity*. Durham: Duke University Press.

Moi, Ruben. (2009). "Bordering Binarities and Cognitive Cartography: What on Earth Does Literature Have to do with Border Transactions?". *Nordlit* 24: 53–64.

Moi, Ruben, & Johannessen, Lene M. (2017). "Imaginary". *Border Aesthetics: Concepts and Intersections*. Eds. Johan Schimanski & Stephen F. Wolfe. New York: Berghahn, pp. 50–67.

Morris-Suzuki, Tessa. (2012). *Borderline Japan: Foreigners and Frontier Controls in the Postwar Era*. Cambridge: Cambridge University Press.

Nail, Thomas. (2016). *Theory of the Border*. London: Oxford University Press.

Nederveen Pieterse, Jan. (2021). *Connectivity and Global Studies*. London: Palgrave Macmillan.

———(2004, 2019). *Globalization & Culture: Global Mélange*. Lanham, MD: Rowman & Littlefield.

Newman, David. (2003). On borders and power: A theoretical framework, *Journal of Borderlands Studies*, pp.13–25. 12.

Newman, David. (2006). "The Lines that Continue to Separate Us: Borders in Our "Borderless" World," *Progress in Human Geography* 30.2: 1–19.

Nijmegen Centre for Border Research. (2023). NCBR, https://www.ru.nl/nsm/imr/research-facilities/research-centres/vm/nijmegen-centre-border-research/; Relevant literature(https://www.ru.nl/nsm/imr/research-facilities/research-centres/vm/nijmegen-centre-border-research/border-portal/relevant-literature/); and links to other border research centers (https://www.ru.nl/nsm/imr/research-facilities/research-centres/vm/nijmegen-centre-border-research/border-portal/links/).

Noorani, Ali. (2022). *Crossing Borders: The Reconciliation of a Nation of Immigrants*. Lanham, MD: Rowman & Littlefield.

Oks, David, & Williams, Henry. (2022). The Long, Slow Death of Global Development, *American Affairs Journal*, Winter, Vol. VI, No. 4, https://americanaffairsjournal.org/2022/11/the-long-slow-death-of-global-development/.

Paasi, Anssi. (1996). *Territories, Boundaries and Consciousness: The Changing Geographies of the Finnish-Russian Border*. New York: Wiley.

Paasi, Anssi. (2009). Bounded Spaces in a 'Borderless World': Border Studies, Power and the Anatomy of Territory. *Journal of Power* 2, no. 2: 213–34.

Paasi, Anssi. (2011). A 'Border Theory': An Unattainable Dream or a Realistic aim for Border Scholars? In *A Research Companion for Border Studies*, ed. D. Wastl-Walter, 11–31. Aldershot: Ashgate.

Parker, Noel, Vaughan-Williams, Nick, et al., (2009). Lines in the Sand? Towards an Agenda for Critical Border Studies, *Geopolitics*, 14 (3), pp. 582–87.

Parker, Noel, & Vaughan-Williams, Nick (eds.). (2014). *Critical Border Studies: Broadening and Deepening the 'Lines in the Sand' Agenda*. New York: Routledge.

Peña, Sergio. (2019). Narratives of Border Reinforcement: The Role of Knowledge and Communications Power. *Estudio Fronterizos* 20: e027.

Poole, Steven. (2022). Review: The Edge of the Plain by James Crawford review – beyond borders, The Guardian, https://www.theguardian.com/books/2022/aug/11/the-edge-of-the-plain-by-james-crawford-review-beyond-borders.

Popescu, Gabriel. (2011). *Bordering and Ordering the Twenty-first Century: Understanding Borders.* Lanham, MD: Rowman & Littlefield Publishers.

Pötzsch, Holger. (2015a). The Emergence of iBorder: Bordering Bodies, Networks, and Machines, *Environment and Planning D: Society and Space* 33.1: pp. 101–18.

Pötzsch, Holger. (2015b). *Seeing and Thinking Borders, in Borderscaping: Imaginations and Practices of Border Making.* Chiara Brambilla, Jussi Laine, James W. Scott & Gianluca Bocchi, (eds.). Aldershot: Ashgate, pp. 217–27.

Pötzsch, Holger, & Chiara Brambilla. (2017). "In/visibility". *Border Aesthetics: Concepts and Intersections.* Johan Schimanski & Stephen F. Wolfe (eds.). New York: Berghahn, pp. 68–89.

Prescott, J.R.V. (1987). *Political Frontiers and Boundaries.* London: Allen & Unwin.

Radil, Steven M., Pinos, Jaume Castan, & Ptak, Thomas. (2021). Borders Resurgent: Towards a Post-Covid-19 Border Regime? *Space and Polity* 25 (1), pp. 132–140. doi: https://doi-org.fgul. idm.oclc.org/10.1080/13562576.2020.1773254.

Rahimieh, Nasrin. (2007). Border crossing, in Comparative Studies of South Asia, *Africa and the Middle East*, Volume 27, Number 2, 2007, pp. 225–32.

Redniss, Lauren. (2023). Can Borders Work? In "The Edge of the Plain," the journalist James Crawford asks whether good fences really do make good neighbors. *New York Times*, Jan 8.

Relations Media. (2023). Festival Kyotographie 2023 – BORDER – https://www.kyotographie. jp/editions/2023.

Reyboz, Lucille, & Nakanishi, Yusuke. (2023). KYOTOPHONIE Borderless Music Festival, https://kyotophonie.jp/en/.

Riccio, Bruno, & Brambilla, Chiara (eds). (2010). *Transnational Migration, Cosmopolitanism and Dislocated Borders.* Rimini: Guaraldi, https://www.academia.edu/26278429/Transnational_ Migration_Cosmopolitanism_and_Dis_located_Borders.

The Rising Majority. (2020). Movement Building in the Time of the Coronavirus Crisis – Angela Davis and Naomi Klein, April 2, https://therisingmajority.com/events/movement-building/.

Rösler, Michael, & Wendl, Tobias. (1999). *Frontiers and borderlands. The rise and relevance of an anthropological research genre, in Frontiers and Borderlands: Anthropological Perspectives.* Frankfurt am Main: Peter Lang, pp. 1–30.

Roy, Arundhati. (2020). 'The Pandemic Is a Portal," *The Financial Times*, April 3. 14.

Rumford, Chris. (2006). Theorizing Borders, *European Journal of Social Theory*, 9 (2), pp. 155–69.

Rumford, Chris. (2011). Seeing Like a Border. *Political Geography* 30, no. 2: 67–68.

Rumford, Chris. (2012). Towards a Multiperspectival Study of Borders. *Geopolitics* 17, no. 4: 887–902.

Said, Edward. (2000). *Out of Place – A Memoir.* New York: Vintage.

Sadowski-Smith, Claudia. (2000). *Globalization on the Line: Culture, Capital, and Citizenship at U.S. Borders* (Palgrave, 2002).

Sadowski-Smith, Claudia. (2008). *Border Fictions: Globalization, Empire, and Writing at the Boundaries of the United States.* Charlottesville: University of Virginia Press.

Saldívar, José David. (1997). *Border Matters: Remapping American Cultural Studies.* Berkeley: University of California Press.

Saldívar, Ramón. (2006). *The Borderlands of Culture: Américo Paredes and the Transnational Imaginary.* Durham: Duke University Press.

Saldívar-Hull, Sonia. (2000). *Feminism on the Border: Chicana Gender Politics and Literature.* Berkeley: University of California Press.

Sarkar, Jayajit, & Munshi, Auritra. (2021). *Border and Bordering: Politics, Poetics, Precariousness,* Stuttgart: Ibidem Verlag.

Satterwhite, Rian, Miller, Whitney McIntyre, & Sheridan, Kate. (2015). Leadership for Sustainability and Peace: Responding to the Wicked Challenges of the Future, pp. 59–74, in Sowcik, Matthew, Adenaro, Anthony C., McNutt, Mondy, & Murphy, Susan Elaine (Eds.), *Leadership 2050: Critical Challenges, Key Contexts, and Emerging Trends.* Bingley, UK: Emerald Group Publishing.

THE NEW ART OF CROSSING BORDERS 37

Schimanski, Johan. (2006). Crossing and Reading: Notes towards a Theory and a Method". *Nordlit* 19: 41–63.

Schimanski, Johan. (2019). 'Migratory angels: The political aesthetics of border trauma,' in K. Horsti (ed.), *The Politics of Public Memories of Forced Migration and Bordering in Europe*. Cham: Palgrave Pivot.

Schimanski, Johan. (2023). Border Readings Research Group (Borders are fundamental to our dealings with the world. How does literature help us understand borders?), https://www.hf.uio.no/ilos/english/research/groups/border-readings/index.html.

Schimanski, Johan, & Stephen Wolfe, eds. *Nordlit 24* (2009). Special issue with papers from the 2008 European Conference of the Association of Borderland Studies.

Schimanski, Johan, & Stephen Wolfe, eds. (2010). Special dossier on "Cultural Production and Negotiation of Borders" (papers from the 2008 European Conference of the Association of Borderland Studies), *Journal of Borderlands Studies* 25.1.

Schimanski, Johan, & Stephen Wolfe. (2013a) "The Aesthetics of Borders". In: *Assigning Cultural Values*. Ed. Kjerstin Aukrust. New York: Peter Lang, pp. 235–50.

Schimanski, Johan, & Stephen Wolfe. (2013b). "Border | Aesthetics: REPORT: The final conference of the Border Aesthetics research project University of Tromsø, Tromsø. 5-8 September 2012". La Frontera: Association for Borderlands Studies Newsletter 33.2: 7–9. Also published in EUBORDERSCAPES Newsletter 2 (2013): 7–8.

Schimanski, Johan, & Wolfe, Stephen F. (eds). (2017). *Border Aesthetics: Concepts and Intersections*. New York: Berghahn.

Schimanski, Johan, & Wolfe, Stephen F. (2017). "Intersections: A Conclusion in the Form of a Glossary". In *Border Aesthetics: Concepts and Intersections*. Eds. Johan Schimanski & Stephen F. Wolfe. New York: Berghahn, pp. 147–69.

Schimanski, Johan & Görling, Reinhold. (2017). "Sovereignty". In *Border Aesthetics: Concepts and Intersections*. Eds. Johan Schimanski & Stephen F. Wolfe. New York: Berghahn, pp. 111–28.

Schimanski, Johan, & Nyman, Jopi (eds.). (2017). *Border Images, Border Narratives: The Political Aesthetics of Boundaries and Crossings*. Manchester: Manchester University Press.

Schimanski, Johan, & Wolfe, Stephen F. (eds) (2017). *Border Aesthetics: Concepts and Intersections*. New York: Berghahn.

Schneider, Dorothee. (2011). *Crossing Borders: Migration and Citizenship in the Twentieth-Century United States*. Cambridge: Harvard University Press.

Scott, James W. (ed.) (2020). *A Research Agenda for Border Studies*, Oxford: Edward Elgar.

Shah, Sonia. (2020). *The Next Great Migration – The Beauty and Terror of Life on the Move*. London: Bloomsbury Publishing.

Shields, Fiona. (2023). Crossing the lines: photography without frontiers at Kyotographie 2023 – photo essay, The Guardian, https://www.theguardian.com/artanddesign/2023/apr/21/kyotographie-2023-borders-international-festival-photography-japan-photo-essay 16.

Shimoni, Baruch. (2006). Cultural Borders, Hybridization, and a Sense of Boundaries in Thailand, Mexico, and Israel, *Journal of Anthropological Research* 62, no. 2: 217–34. http://www.jstor.org/stable/3630899.

Sidaway, James D. (2007). The Poetry of Boundaries, in: Kumar Rajaram, P., Grundy-Warr, C. eds., *Borderscapes: Hidden Geographies and Politics at Territory's Edge*, Minneapolis and London: University of Minnesota Press, pp. 161–81.

Sklair, Leslie. (2021). Development, post-development, and the pluriverse, Globalizations, DOI: 10.1080/14747731.2021.1917870.

Smith, Christopher J. (2013). *The Creolization of American Culture: William Sidney Mount and the Roots of Blackface Minstrelsy*. Bielefeld: University of Illinois Press. Accessed December 23, 2022. ProQuest Ebook Central.

Soja, Edward. (1989). *Postmodern Geographies: The Reassertion of Space in Critical Social Theory*. London: Verso.

Stavans, Ilan (ed.). (2010). *Border Culture.* Santa Barbara: Greenwood.

Stewart, Charles (ed.). (2007). *Creolization: History, Ethnography, Theory.* London: Routledge.

Todorov, Tzvetan. (1982). *The Conquest of America: The Question of the Other.* Trans by R. Howard. New York: Harper Collins.

Todorov, Tzvetan. (1993). *On Human Diversity: Nationalism, Racism, and Exoticism in French Thought.* Cambridge: Harvard University Press.

Tripathi, Dhanajay (ed.). (2022). *Re-imagining border studies in South Asia,* London and New York, Routledge.

Tripathi, Dhananjay, & Chaturvedi, Sanjay (2019). South Asia: Boundaries, Borders and Beyond, *Journal of Borderlands Studies,* pp.173–81.

Tuck, Eve, & Yang, Wayne. (2012). Decolonization is not a metaphor, in Decolonization: Indigeneity, *Education & Society,* Vol. 1, No. 1, 2012, pp. 1–40. 17.

Tuhiwai Smith, Linda. (1999). *Decolonizing Methodologies: Research and Indigenous Peoples.* London: Zed Books.

Tuhiwai Smith, Linda, Tuck, Eve, & Yang, K. Wayne. (2019). *Indigenous and Decolonizing Studies in Education: Mapping the Long View.* London: Routledge.

Urry, John. (2007). *Mobilities.* Cambridge: Polity.

Urry, John (ed.). (2016). *Mobilities: New Perspectives on Transport and Society.* New York: Routledge.

van Houtum, Henk. (2013). "The border as a moral design: 'Over there lies a land, another land,'" in M. Eker & H. van Houtum (eds.), *Borderland.* Eindhoven: Blauwdruck, pp. 172–83.

van Houtum, Henk, & van Naerssen, Tone. (2002). Bordering, Ordering and Othering, *Tijdschrift voor Economicheen Sociale Geografie,* 93 (2), 2002, pp. 125–36.

Vila, Pablo. (2005). *Border Identifications: Narratives of Religion, Gender, and Class, on the U.S.-Mexico Border.* Austin: University of Texas Press.

Viljoen, Hein (ed.). (2013). *Crossing Borders, Dissolving Boundaries (Cross/Cultures – Readings in the Post/ Colonial Literatures in English).* Amsterdam: Rodopi.

Villanueva, Edgar. (2018). *Decolonizing Wealth: Indigenous Wisdom to Heal Divides and Restore Balance.* Oakland: Berrett-Koehler.

Wahinke Topa (Four Arrows), & Narvaez, Darcia, eds. (2022). *Restoring the Kinship Worldview: Indigenous Voices Introduce 28 Precepts for Rebalancing Life on Planet Earth.* Berkeley: North Atlantic Books.

Walsh, Meeka. (1977- Present). Border Crossings magazine, https://bordercrossingsmag.com – "Since 1977: If you love art and you want to be taken to unexpected places, if you want to know about the most challenging contemporary artists and issues." Winnipeg, Manitoba, Canada.

Wastl-Walter, Doris. (2011). *The Ashgate Research Companion to Border Studies,* London: Routledge.

Wilkinson, Jane. (n.d.). Turning Border Theory 'Inside Out.' (Ms.).

Willis, David Blake (2001). 'Creole Times: Notes on Understanding Creolization for Transnational Japan-America,' in Takeshi Matsuda (Ed.) *The Age of Creolization in the Pacific: In Search of Emerging Cultures and Shared Values in the Japan-America Borderlands,* Hiroshima: Keisuisha.

———(2010). *Creolization in Transnational Japan-America, in The Creolization Reader: Studies in Mixed Identities and Cultures,* edited by Robin Cohen and Paola Toninato. London: Routledge.

———(2018). Resist and Relearn: Comments on Circulations and Escapes in a Barbaric Age, Afterword in Blai Guarné & Paul Hansen, (Eds.), *Escaping Japan: Reflections on Estrangement and Exile in the Twenty-First Century* (2018). London: Routledge.

Willis, David Blake, & Murphy-Shigematsu, Stephen (Eds.) (2008). *Transcultural Japan: At the Borderlands of Race, Gender, and Identity.* London: Routledge.

Willis, David Blake, & Rappleye, Jeremy (Eds.). (2011). *Reimagining Japanese Education: Borders, Circulations, and the Comparative.* Oxford: Symposium Books.

Willis, David Blake, & Rappleye, Jeremy. (2011). Education in Japan: Testing the Limits of Asian Education, *Foro de Educación* (Spain), vol. 9, núm. 13, 2011, pp. 19–35.

Wolfe, Stephen, & Schimanski, Johan. (2007). *Border Poetics De-limited.* Hannover: Wehrhahn.

THE NEW ART OF CROSSING BORDERS   39

Wolfe, Stephen F., & Henk van Houtum. (2017). "Waiting". In *Border Aesthetics: Concepts and Intersections*. Eds. Johan Schimanski & Stephen F. Wolfe. New York: Berghahn, pp. 129–46.

Wolfe, Stephen F., & Mireille Rosello. (2017). "Introduction". In *Border Aesthetics: Concepts and Intersections*. Eds. Johan Schimanski & Stephen F. Wolfe. New York: Berghahn, pp. 50–67.

Wråkberg, Urban, & Nadir Kinossian. (2017). "Palimpsests". In *Border Aesthetics: Concepts and Intersections*. Eds. Johan Schimanski & Stephen F. Wolfe. New York: Berghahn, pp. 90–110.

Yunkaporta, Tyson. (2020). *Sand Talk: How Indigenous Thinking Can Save the World*. New York: Harper One.

Yuval-Davis, Nira, Wemyss, Georgie, & Cassidy, Kathryn. (2019). *Bordering*. Cambridge: Polity.

Notes

1 Some readers will recognize with titles as reflecting that of the autobiography of Nobel Prize winner Rigoberta Menchú (1998). We are honored to be in such illustrious company. We also acknowledge Schneider (2011), Margono Slamet and Josep Bambang (2013), Hurd and Leutlloff-Grandits, and Noorani (2022) with title associated with crossing borders. Menchu's work of crossing borders concerns the interior world of the Maya and other Guatemalans, of time and space in the Yucatan Peninsula, of severe political and social repression, and ultimately of the hope that can come out of activism. This book, too, is about hope, for all those crossing borders.

2 Early examples include Gloria Anzaldúa (1987), as mentioned earlier; Tzvetan Todorov (1982, 1993); Etienne Balibar and Immanuel Wallerstein (1993); and especially Benedict Anderson (1994).

Chapter 3

FLUID IDENTITY AND OVERCOMING BOUNDARIES

Soraj Hongladarom

What I would like to do in this paper is to look at an analysis of the concept of "overcoming boundaries." What do we mean when we see that we are overcoming boundaries? Is overcoming boundaries the same as crossing boundaries? And what actually are boundaries? We can look at the issue at various levels, but in this paper, I will tend to focus more on the abstract level of the meaning of the term "boundary" itself, both in the context of physical objects and, more interestingly, a social entity such as a social or an ethnic group. The latter obviously depends on the former for their metaphysical analysis. A boundary is what separates one thing from another. There is a boundary, and it is supposed to divide one thing, one entity, from another. However, as we are focusing on overcoming a boundary, this implies a further analysis of the concept of "a thing" or in other words its identity. I would like to introduce the notion of fluid identity as a corollary to the notion of boundary. If the identity of a thing is fluid, then a possibility exists for a boundary to be overcome. An implication of this is that "boundary" is always a pragmatic concept. There is no way to separate out one thing from another objectively; instead, it depends on us who do the separating and creating a boundary. Afterward, I will discuss this metaphysical analysis in the context of *social* identity and social boundaries. Then, toward the end of the paper, I will discuss what this pragmatic consideration means for the more practical acts of crossing or overcoming the existing cultural, social, political, and other forms of boundaries.

A Metaphysical Analysis of Identity and Boundary: Hegel and Nāgārjuna

We begin by undertaking a metaphysical analysis of the concept of identity first. This is because identity is a counterpart concept of the boundary. There can be no boundary if there is no identity and vice versa. If all things completely dissolve into one another, then we can draw no boundaries between them. Furthermore, creating boundaries in an unspecified object in effect creates more objects whose identities are defined by those boundaries themselves. Imagine cutting a cake into eight pieces. The boundaries are created through the cutting, and the identity of each of the eight smaller pieces is created as a result. This metaphor is also apt. We can also cut the cake into four bigger pieces; this seems to show that it is the boundary that creates the identity, and more importantly, it is us who cut up the cake, thereby defining the boundaries and creating the identity of either the eight or the four pieces.

An obvious objection to this line of thinking is to maintain that objects have their own *objective* existence. Cake can be cut up into smaller or bigger pieces, and so are rocks and stones, which can be broken down into smaller pieces, or even melted together to create one large rock. Other objects, on the contrary, especially biological ones such as animals seem to have their own objective identity in that they maintain their identity as what they are with their internal constitution. We just cannot cut up a cat and thereby produce more cats. But even then, some ambiguities exist. How do we count a cat pregnant with a litter of kittens inside her womb? Is there only one cat or more? Even though the boundary of a cat is defined by its skin–what is inside the skin is the cat and what is outside is not—a cat is still what it is through its relationship with other objects. In other words, the fact that a cat is defined through the outermost layer of its body shows that there must be something else beyond the layer. A cat cannot simply be a cat if we cannot find this outermost layer. Imagine a cat so big as to lack any boundary, that would not be a cat at all, not least because we would not be able to make out its shape. The shape is defined through the boundary, and the boundary presupposes that there are other things beyond it.

Hegel saw through this problem quite clearly. In his *Phenomenology of Spirit*, he discusses the epistemological status of sense-certainty (see Taylor 1977: 142–144). *Prima facie*, it seems that sense-certainty is the most certain piece of the belief that one can have. It is immediate, the object presenting itself to the subject barely and directly, and the subject can perceive it through her own sensory faculties, which are supposed to provide a direct connection with the object itself. However, according to Hegel, the knowledge obtained through direct sense perception is necessarily mediated by other forms of knowledge. It is this relation to the other forms that provides the subject with the knowledge that she believes she has gained through direct perception. For example, the subject sees a cat lying on a mat. The knowledge that she apparently gains through direct perception, that the cat is on the mat, is only possible through its relation to a whole system of conceptual relations which enables the subject to know that what she sees is a cat from the beginning. Without this prior knowledge, she would not be able to recognize it as a cat. And she cannot obtain this conceptual knowledge of a cat through prior perception either, because that would simply repeat the process one step further, engendering a regress. Learning what a cat is part of a holistic process of language learning in general.

According to Venanzio Raspa, quoting Hegel's *Encyclopedia of the Philosophical Sciences in Basic Outline,* "This means, [...], that, '[i]n the opposition, what is differentiated has not only *an* other but *its* other opposite it'." We usually tend to consider different things as indifferent in comparison to each other. Instead—Hegel writes in one of his rare examples— "one says: I am a human being, and around me are air, water, animals, and other things generally" (quoted from Hegel 2010: 185 in Raspa 2016: 357). The idea is that in defining the identity of an object, not only as another object required but also the whole system of things that surround the object itself. Hegel's example is that of a human being, who is surrounded by air, water, and so on. The surroundings of the human being together help define the identity of the human being in question, because without these

FLUID IDENTITY AND OVERCOMING BOUNDARIES

surroundings the human being would have no *boundary*, and as a result would explode up to the whole universe, ceasing to be an individual object, a human being. What is opposite is not one object standing against the object, but *its* other, namely everything surrounding it, and the point is that it is everything surrounding the object that gives it its identity. Identity is not constituted through the internal constitution alone.

The idea is that the identity of a human being, or a cat, its conceptual understanding, already depends on a host of other factors. We cannot let in a stream of data coming in through our senses and thereby gain knowledge of the world without any prior knowledge. The boundary of a cat, as an individual object, is also established through the conceptual understanding of the cat, which in turn is part of the holistic understanding of language and its use. An implication of this is that the identity, even that of a cat, is conceptually dependent on others. We can imagine a scenario where there are certain animals that look quite like a cat but are not exactly the same. In that case, the conceptual boundary becomes rather blurry. Then we would need, if necessary, to locate what exactly is a cat and find certain "essential" marks for it. But then it would be a rather ad hoc one, made up for the purpose of distinguishing one animal from another. In any case, the idea is that the identity of a cat is something that we language users make up. Surely there are genetic markers of a cat, but then we need to know what a cat is to be able to identify the markers as that of a cat, in the same way as we need to know what a cat is before knowing that it is lying on the mat. Genetic markers display very minute differences among each individual organism, and one needs to have a conceptual understanding of, say, a cat, before being able to identify which set of markers comprise those of a cat. We seem to be located in the conceptual space discussed by Hegel in this sense too.

The identity of a thing that depends for its being on its relation to others and on our conceptual use through language means that it is fluid. Another way of explaining how identity can be fluid is through a look at its putative essence. Essence is what is supposed to fix the identity of an entity. According to Aristotle, the essence of a thing is the "what-it-is-to-be" thing (Aristotle, *Metaphysics* Book Z, Chapter 4). It is the property that defines a thing to be the thing it is. Thus, a human being is defined as "a rational animal"; being rational is what defines an animal so that it has the property of being a human being and none other. On the contrary, "a featherless biped" is not an essential property because we could imagine some biped animals, chickens perhaps, being bred so that it has no feathers. In that case, it would not become a human being. The essence, thus, is internal to an entity and gives that entity its identity as the thing it is.

However, it is doubtful whether essences do really exist beyond our pragmatic consideration in day-to-day language use. As Wittgenstein has famously said in *Philosophical Investigations* (Wittgenstein 2009), things are more familiarly grouped according to "family resemblances" rather than strict essential property. Even Aristotle's property of being rational does not seem to be well defined. Is a newborn infant a rational being? It does not seem so, but the infant is a human being nonetheless. Instead of property with strict criteria of application, what we normally do in everyday circumstances is to define things more or less as they resemble one another according to aspects that we find interesting. I resemble my mother a little bit; my mother resembles her father a little bit, and so on. But there is no one essential property defining the

44 TOWARD A NEW ART OF BORDER CROSSING

property of the Hongladarom family. This implies that identity is defined more in terms of pragmatic considerations—what we deem to be interesting—rather than in terms of essence. This implies further that the boundary of a thing is more or less defined in pragmatic terms also because boundary and identity are counterpart concepts as we have seen. The conceptual boundary between two entities is always porous—we can pick and choose what criteria we deem to be important according to changing circumstances. This does not mean that we can jumble all identities as haphazardly as we wish; that would make mutual understanding impossible, but it means that the objective, mathematical property or boundary that neatly separates one thing from another is lacking in objective reality.

The idea of fluid identity and fluid boundary is also found in Buddhist philosophy. Nāgārjuna has the following to say in his masterpiece, *The Fundamental Wisdom of the Middle Way* (Nāgārjuna 1995):

> If things did not exist
> Without essence,
> The phrase, "When this exists so this will be,"
> Would not be acceptable (Nāgārjuna 1995: Chapter I, Verse 10).

The argument is a *modus tollens*. If things were not to exist without an essence, it would not be possible for change or transformation to take place. The phrase "When this exists, so this will be" would not be acceptable because if things were to have an essence, the essence would be fixed (since if it were not fixed it would not be able to function as an essence, properly so-called), but then things cannot change either, prevented from doing so by the fixed essence. Since things obviously are changing, there are no fixed essences. The idea bears a certain similarity to Hegel's view that we have seen. Without a fixed essence, things have no fixed boundaries either. This makes it possible for one thing to become another, thereby making change possible. Let us look at one of Nāgārjuna's favorite examples, the changing of milk into yogurt. The point of contention is, if there were essences, the essence of the milk must change into the essence of the yogurt because the milk itself changes into the yogurt. The question is, at what point does the milk become the yogurt? Where do we draw a line, a boundary, clearly demarcating the milk on one side, and the yogurt on the other? Those who believe in fixed essences have to posit that the essence of the milk is replaced by the essence of the yogurt, but that borders on something mysterious. How can the essence of one thing be replaced by the essence of another? Since there is no clear boundary between milk and yogurt, it is indeed a mystery how change can happen if one insists on the existence of a fixed essence identifying the milk and the yogurt in question.

Nāgārjuna goes on in the next verse immediately following the earlier one:

> In the several or united conditions
> The effect cannot be found.
> How could something not be in the conditions
> Come from the conditions? (Nāgārjuna 1995: Chapter I, Verse 11).

FLUID IDENTITY AND OVERCOMING BOUNDARIES

In Buddhist terminology, change is affected by both causes and conditions. "Causes" are what actually become something else. In this case, the Buddhist says that milk is the cause of yogurt because the former is transformed into the latter. Another example is that of a seed of a mango tree, which is the cause of the tree. The change cannot be affected without a number of conditions. Milk cannot turn into yogurt if there are no bacteria to ferment it, for example. The appropriate temperature which would allow the bacteria to grow is another condition, and so on. In this verse, Nāgārjuna is saying that if there were fixed essences, they must become the effects (such as the yogurt) and could not be found in the conditions that make the transformation possible. They could neither be found in the bacteria nor the temperature, or any other conditions. Thus, it seems like the effect miraculously happens–the milk ends; its essence disappears, and then suddenly a new essence comes into being, that of the yogurt, which is not found in any or more of the conditions. However, since it is the milk that changes into the yogurt, something in the milk must carry over to the yogurt, which means that the effects must be available in the cause or the conditions, but it is nowhere to be found. This leads to the denial of the premise that there is a fixed essence. Nāgārjuna's rhetorical question in the last two lines: "How could something not in the conditions come from the conditions?" is meant to present a *reductio* argument against the premise that there is an essence. If there is an essence, then it must come from somewhere, and it could not come from anywhere else except for the conditions, but as we have seen the effect or its essence does not come from the conditions, so the premise must be rejected.

Social Identity

The preceding rather lengthy analysis of the concepts of identity and boundary serves to provide a robust foundation for the idea of how boundaries could be overcome in the sociocultural and political domains. Though broadly speaking, the notions of identity that appear in the metaphysical analysis as in the above section and as appear in the social scientific literature belong to the same family of meanings (after all, they both talk about "identity," that is, as what it means to be the same), the notion of identity in the sociocultural and political domains have assumed so much charged meaning and contention. This is understandable because much of the political contentions we are facing nowadays have their roots in the different conceptions of different groups of people as to what it means to be the same. One group wants to assert their identity vis-à-vis that of other groups, and when there are issues of imbalance of power involved, the issue can become political and volatile. Nonetheless, it is my contention that a way toward a fuller understanding of the issue, known broadly as "identity politics," should be based on a clear understanding of the metaphysics as discussed in the previous section.

A complete understanding here can be achieved through a realization that all identity, social or otherwise, is essentially fluid. Any boundaries that are imposed on groups to create identities are necessarily pragmatic, based on the expediency of the moment, or on some criteria which when analyzed in depth are found to be anything but objective. In the context of social identity, however, talks about identity being fluid might invite an objection that when identity is fluid its strength is thus weakened. For groups that are fighting to maintain their identities, such talks might not be powerful enough: If identities are fluid, then what are these groups fighting for? The motivation for the fight to maintain the group's identity would perhaps be made stronger if the underlying belief were such that their identity is essential and objective. Then the fight would be to maintain such an objective essence.

However, the problem with the belief in the objective essence of identity is that it cannot be maintained philosophically, as I have shown earlier. Furthermore, the notion of fluid identity could in fact strengthen the case for maintaining one's own identity better than the belief in the objective essence, because when identity is fluid, all that matters is the argument purporting to show that the identity must be maintained, safeguarded, and fought for. Various pragmatic reasons can be brought on to do the job, and these reasons are normally those that the groups already use to argue their case anyway. For example, a group could argue that their identity must be maintained because it is their right of expression as guaranteed by the constitution of the country to which they belong. Or because doing so creates a situation where there is diversity within the country, and diversity is better than pure homogeneity where everywhere is the same. Or other arguments along this line. The point is that none of these arguments relies on the idea that the identity the group is arguing for is objective and exists *in perpetuo*.

The upshot, then, is that fluid identity seems to function more effectively than its competitor when it comes to providing a foundation for a successful overcoming of boundaries. This points to some practical considerations, which I will take in the following section.

Practical Implications

The conclusion one gets from the discussion above is that the identity of an object is always fluid, meaning that it is not fixed objectively and is dependent on a variety of factors. This conclusion has a lot of practical implications. In the call for chapters that comprise this book, Prof. Ananta Kumar Giri wrote: "In this place, we need a new art and politics of boundary transmutation, boundary transformation, and border crossing. We also need a new realization of margins as spaces of creative boundary transmutation and border crossing rather than a helpless mirror of dualism between margin and the mainstream." The new art and the new politics of "boundary transmutation" would not be possible if identity and boundary are not fluid in the sense discussed here. The transmutation and the crossing mentioned in the call for chapters are pertinent not only in the rarefied realm of metaphysics but in concrete, lived experiences of people all around the world, border crossing and boundary transmuting have become part of everyday life.

We find them everywhere. In Thailand where I live there have been lively debates about same-sex marriage. This is a highly visible case of boundary transmuting. There is the traditional gender line–the one between male and female–and this line is being challenged by those who believe that the traditional gender line is too restrictive and does not reflect the new reality (Thailand Edges Closer to Legalising Same-Sex Unions, 2022). It used to be believed as part of the objective, bedrock world that there are men and women and that marriages must consist of a union between a man and a woman. But the arguments in support of same-sex marriages upturn all that. Those who are in favor of changing the law to support same-sex marriages in Thailand (and elsewhere) argue that the desire to live together, to build a family, can be found also in couples who are of the same biological sex. The only reason why a couple of different biological sexes are required for marriage is the belief that marriage is necessary for procreation. But if we change that belief—and in fact, the belief is indeed changing—then marriage comes to be understood as something whose sole purpose is not to procreate, but something else such as companionship. Even the desire to build a new family can be possible within same-sex couples because technology has made it possible for them to have children who are genetically related to either one of the couples, not to mention the more traditional method of adoption. In any case, this is a clear example of boundary crossing and reflects what Prof. Giri said to be "a new realization of margins." The identity of being a man and being a woman, together with the belief system that accompanies it, is being challenged. The same-sex couple knows full well that they are of the same biological sex, but they believe that being of the same biological sex is not a deterrence against living together and building a loving family.

What the idea presented in this paper can contribute is emphasizing the fact, through philosophical argumentation and theorization, that identity and boundary are fluid. This also includes sexual identity. The argument makes it clear that the belief in fixed gender roles based on biological sex is too restrictive and does not reflect the fluid nature of sexual identity.

Another example concerns the boundary between two nation-states. If there is anything as objective as it can be, perhaps that is nothing but the national boundary. This is so because the national boundary is protected by force and in many cases, heavily patrolled by armed personnel. All these seem to make it clear that the national boundary is as objective as it can be. Wars can be fought because of this type of boundary. Nonetheless, it is also clear that national boundaries do not exist in nature. Looking at a photo of the planet Earth taken from space, we cannot see any national boundaries, but the actual terrain of the planet itself. So what explains the paradox? The example of the national boundary also shows that the boundary is man-made. It is only that it is supported by the forces of sovereign national states that national boundaries look very real and objective as they are. But the forces are products of the social and national convention, and it is through this type of convention and agreement that national or political boundaries are created in the first place.

The implication is that even national boundaries are fluid. This does not mean that a country can invade another and claim a territory as one's own without any regard to international law, but one should bear in mind that national boundaries are only creations of humans. As John Searle says, it is part of "social reality" (Searle 1997). The idea of fluid national boundaries can lead to many practical solutions. For example, the problem of hatred of people belonging to different religions and backgrounds, the problem made known worldwide by the treatment of the Burmese government against the Rohingya people (see, e.g., Islam 2018; Hung 2022; Ansar 2020), could be solved eventually by starting at the realization that all boundaries, religious, political, cultural and others, are by nature fluid and are not fixed forever in stone. The Buddhist Burmese fear that the Muslim Rohingyas would threaten their identity and their culture—we are coming back to identity again. This fear can be diminished by programs of mutual understanding where people from both sides talk and listen to each other, where everyone trusts each other in an atmosphere of trust and openness. This would be a tangible example of the "new realization of margins" that Prof. Giri talks about; it is where the boundary between the margins and the centers merge together, both of which are fluid by nature.

The talk about margins and centers merging together, however, might be taken to give rise to neglecting the importance of political or cultural pluralism, or the need for minority groups to maintain their distinct identity. In fact, the notion of fluid identity and fluid boundary that I introduce here, instead of dissolving the lines between groups, nonetheless could be seen to strengthen them further. This ironic situation is explained by the fact that identity is not part of objective reality, but is socially constructed. And as such the construction can be as strong as we wish it to be. When we consider how national boundaries are strongly defended and how national identities are naturally taken as almost sacrosanct, it is a small step to the conclusion that ethnic identities and other forms of traditionally excluded identities can be strongly defended too. One might object that these traditionally excluded groups are not accorded the same status as nation-states, thus the force defending them is not as strong. However, this is essentially a political decision, and it is the proposal of this paper that, since the deliberations regarding pluralism and the identity of minority groups are political in nature, they need to be done through a democratic process informed by values such as respect for human rights and the rule of law, in order that all voices are respected and can be heard, and that no one voice can dominate.

Apart from the example of the treatment of the Rohingyas by the Burmese authorities discussed earlier, another example that illustrates the point above can be found also here in Thailand. There has been a long-standing conflict between the Buddhist majority and the Muslim minority in the country, especially in the south of the country where the Muslims form the majority. The Muslim Thais in the southernmost provinces of the country want more autonomy so that they can live in accordance with their religious belief, and sometimes this spills over into a demand for more political autonomy, thus exacerbating the conflict with the central authority in Bangkok. The disagreement has turned into a long-lasting, though at a rather low level, conflict sometimes resulting in violence. Discussions on how to achieve a breakthrough have been stalled due to mistrust and the refusal of the authority in Bangkok to recognize the status of Muslim representatives as negotiating partners of equal footing (see, e.g., Bakhshi 2021). The recognition that identities and boundaries are fluid could help with this situation by helping both sides, but especially those in power, to see that the minority groups need to maintain their identity as they understand it, not as the kind of identity that has been imposed on them from outside. The idea that identity is fixed objectively, on the contrary, could lead to detrimental consequences. The reason is that, when identities are seen to be fixed, they are either fixed by one party or another and when the identity of the Muslim minority is fixed in the mindset of the power wielders in Bangkok, the mindset would be very hard to change.

Any attempt to change this fixed identity, such as the attempt to establish a new political status for the people in the three southernmost provinces, would then be seen as a threat. This situation is thus not very conducive to any kind of peaceful resolution. Furthermore, when the identity is seen to be fixed by the minority, it can lead to stringent demands with few possibilities for accommodation. Negotiation can arrive at an impasse. In the end, fluid identities and boundaries appear to accommodate reconciliation, resolution, and agreement better than the view that identities are fixed objectively.

Overcoming Boundaries

It should by now be clear that the only way to overcome boundaries is that identities, especially social ones, need to be seen to be fluid. The opposite notion of fluid identity is that of fixed identity, and we have seen that the latter notion could lead to rigidization and unwillingness or inability to accommodate change, which could lead to detrimental consequences as we have seen. Admittedly, this is not an easy thing to accomplish. People are naturally attached to their identity, whether it be their national identity, their professional identity, or any other form. Calls for rethinking the notion of identity could lead to a sense of loss, as identity can be necessary for a person to hold on to as their sense of self or sense of security. But it does not have to happen this way. Realizing that identity is fluid is not the same as experiencing a loss of identity altogether. The latter can be traumatic, but the former does not have to be. As we have seen, fluid identity is not incompatible with the idea that identity can be very strongly felt and defended. When a group of people cheers on a national sports team, they have a sense of identity together as belonging to the same team, the same nation. There is nothing inherently wrong with that, but when this sense of identity is rigidified, it can lead to stereotyping, and marginalization, creating the sense that those who do not belong are enemies that must be destroyed. All these are elements that fuel division, hatred, and violence rather than their opposite.

There are many ways to achieve this sense of fluid identity in society. One thing is through education. The younger generation must be educated in a way that hatred and divisive mindsets be a thing of the past and the concepts of inclusiveness and loving-kindness be cultivated instead. Another factor is government policy, which must reflect the views presented here rather than those views that are based on fixed identities, which only create more boundaries rather than overcome them. Finally, it should be emphasized that overcoming boundaries means that people get closer to one another, not only in the literal sense but also in the sense that they understand one another and can see through one another's eyes. That would be the ideal condition that we should always strive toward in our policies.

References

Ansar, A. 2020. The Unfolding of Belonging, Exclusion, and Exile: A Reflection on the History of Rohingya Refugee Crisis in Southeast Asia. *Journal of Muslim Minority Affairs*, 40(3), 441–456.
Bakhshi, U. 2021. 'The Apparent Stalemate in Thailand's Deep South', *The Diplomat December 20, 2021* (https://thediplomat.com/2021/12/the-apparent-stalemate-in-thailands-deep-south/) (accessed on July 11, 2022).

Hegel, G. W. F. 2010. *Encyclopedia of the Philosophical Sciences in Basic Outline. Part I: Science of Logic*. K. Brinkmann and D. O. Dahlstrom transl. Cambridge University Press.

Hung, A. H. C. 2022. Exploring the Root Causes of the Persecution Policy Against Rohingya People: A Study Based on Three Constitutions of Burma/Myanmar. *Asian Journal of Law and Policy*, 2(2), 75–97.

Islam, M. T. 2018. The Stateless Rohingya: Victims of Burma's Identity Politics and Priority for R2P. *Unpublished Thesis of Master of Security and Development, University of Bradford*, 22–31.

Nāgārjuna. 1995. *The Fundamental Wisdom of the Middle Way; Nāgārjuna's Mulamadhayamakakārikā*. Jay Garfield transl. Oxford University Press.

Raspa, V. 2016. What Makes a Thing What It Is?: Aristotle and Hegel on Identity. *Acta Analytica*, 31: 345–361.

Searle, J. 1997. *The Construction of Social Reality*. New York: The Free Press.

Taylor, C. 1977. *Hegel*. Cambridge University Press.

'Thailand Edges Closer to Legalising Same-Sex Unions.' 2022. *Reuters, June 17, 2022* (https://www.reuters.com/world/asia-pacific/thailand-edges-closer-legalising-same-sex-unions-2022-06-15/) (accessed on July 11, 2022).

Wittgenstein, L. 2009. *Philosophical Investigations*. 4th Edition. G. E. M. Anscombe, P. M. S. Hacker, and Joachim Schulte Transl. and Ed. Wiley-Blackwell.

Chapter 4

CONJURING AT THE MARGINS: A TRANSCONTINENTAL APPROACH TO INTERPRETING BORDER ART

Julie Geredien

The subaltern creativity that directs border thinking may be said to begin "from a point of breakage"—a point from which, unrectified potentials, and the symbols of the unconscious, can assert themselves over or against unifying ideologies, "fictive ethnicities," or arbitrary, standardized expectations (Keating 2012: 11; Merçon 2014). In the freedom space created by the breakage, border artists often surprisingly access dimensions of the "whole self" that are suppressed or simply lost and unknown in more mainstream cultural contexts. Although artists' border thinking may begin from a place of difference and distinction, their creative work often awakens a mediating intelligence that can potentially support more differentiated integrations as it challenges false universals.

In his opening essay in this volume, Ananta Kumar Giri helpfully distinguishes Mrinal Miri's approach to the subject of margins (2003) from that of Noel Parker (2009). The contrast between the two perspectives, and their possible complementarity, is useful for framing my arguments regarding the nature of subaltern creativity and the artist's border-crossing intelligence. As Giri explains, Miri views "the limits of discourse of margins" as a product of mainstream discourse and thus something that leaves the individual and society subject to a "point of breakage" because they are positioned "in the context of a pervasive and hierarchical dualism between margins and mainstreams." Parker's work, however, which is based in part upon Deleuzian philosophy, affirms the liminal nature of marginality as "integral to any condition of life," noting that the is-and-is not, in-between position can be particularly helpful in negotiating identities and differences.

This chapter considers the possibility of negotiating between these two positions: it applies an oscillating approach that engages both the limits and the possibilities of margins and their discourses. I develop the oscillating strategy by exploring culture itself as a holistic reality, and by distinguishing margin-mainstream dualisms from the inner conflicts and hierarchies that beset in-group members within a given marginalized group. While conceptualizing culture as the totality of all things may enrich our appreciation of Parker's view, the complex tension existing between margin and mainstream dualisms and in-group conflicts generates what Theophus Smith calls a "double-sidedness" that brings to the fore Miri's point regarding the limits of discourse of margins. For the border artist whose thinking begins from a "point of breakage," double-sided afflictions or tensions function as a limit which may nevertheless provoke a more transformation-focused way of handling toxicities—one that reflects an intuitive respect for conjure, agency, and nonviolent social change.

"Conjuring at the margins" refers to a process whereby "negatives" (harms or barriers) become a means of bringing into the world a new moral order. Rather than contributing to further divide or cultural schism, the breakage point and resulting autonomy space help to access the creative life within a transcendent or liminal subjecthood. "Negations" may then become "antidotal," and experience of the negative and marginality may provoke a new agential ontology (Smith 1995, 218). Engaging an intercultural method and transcontinental perspective on this subject—one that spans geopolitical boundaries, cultural traditions, and philosophical frameworks—can create intellectual conditions that invite into contemporary Western theories of human development and social change, a much-needed poetic, intuitive dimension.

As we consider the "limits of discourse of margins" dialectically, we can see how the emergent points of breakage are not bound by the limits of identity imposed upon a group by a nation's politically idealized construction of that group's "pre-existing unity" or by its absorption of the group's "ethnic" differences (Mercon 2014: 85); instead, those breakage points, when acknowledged as such, may become potential points of connection and expansion that can then link dignity-making to place, historical materialisms, and the inner conditions for ancestry.

To justify the chapter's oscillating approach to the art of border crossing, I begin by defining discourse, its implications for agency, and its relevance to the pharmaconic worldview. I argue that the border artist's agent-centered morality empowers a mode of participatory reasoning that can debunk false universals and thus create a visionary space for change. I present engagement in discourse and the practice of community hermeneutics as keys to unlocking the oscillating approach.

Next, I turn to an example from the social history of Appalachia which highlights the power of discourse, coupled with community hermeneutics, to uproot the dogmatisms underlying racialized knowledge systems. This example shows how activists with a pharmaconic worldview may heroically draw upon a life-affirming response, known as salutogenesis. To further develop the mediating logic of oscillation, I introduce concepts from Dis/ability Studies which demonstrate how the ethical conjuror's agent-centered morality can identify meta patterns of relationship that contribute to symbolic reproduction and thus overcome barriers created by the margin-center construction. To underscore the importance of identifying those patterns, I discuss how the industrial era's treatment of "livestock" distorts the human relationship to both animal and deity. Later in the chapter, I provide examples from Gunnar Myrdal's *An American Dilemma*, Ralph Ellison's *The Invisible Man*, and Mary Chase's *Harvey*, to support my points about the relevance of border art to critical consciousness and social change.

The chapter closes by considering how genocidal practices, like ghettoization, bring moral finality to what Miri called the "pervasive and hierarchical dualism between margins and mainstreams"; yet in some instances, it is out of the finality of

CONJURING AT THE MARGINS

these enclosures, chasms, and toxicities that border artists like Gloria Anzaldúa, and members of First Nations reclaiming cultural heritage, access the knowledge to heal themselves and the world. I conclude that the oscillating approach and transcontinental perspective facilitate the conversion of allopathic modes of social healing, into vitalist ones. By affirming communion and the poetic and intuitive dimensions of our humanity, while also remembering the limits of margin-center discourse, we promote the human spirit's movement toward responsible self-determination.

Discourse and Community Hermeneutics

According to Stuart Hall, a discourse is "a kind of receptive perception or stance" that provides "an overall view of human conduct as always meaningful" (2017: 31). Terms like "wilderness," "homosexual," or "disabled" are constructed categories or apparatuses that function in particular historical ways to maintain civil society norms (Tremain 2017a; ibid: 31). Without consciousness-raising efforts, like discourse, these classifications go unnoticed. Furthermore, discursive realities—like social and economic circumstances or the availability of emotional and intellectual resources at a given point in political history—function as "tactical elements" or "blocks" that impact how power manifests. Those influencing factors also organize relationships and knowledge formation (Tremain 2017a: 48; Barad 2008: 137; Foucault 1978: 101–102). Challenging how power organizes disciplinary learning and maintains the force relations behind the apparatus of dis/ability, for example, requires discerning the deeper tactical elements at work and identifying those that inevitably reproduce borders and margins.

Because discourse is "a kind of receptive perception or stance" that grants access to the inner meaning of human conduct, it maintains an ambiguous relationship to power (Balibar 1995). By itself, discourse does not posit a constructive response, alternative imagining, or "right" way. Instead, Nature distributes differences in the material realm with an infinite variety. We can name and identify these material differences through the practice of discourse, but nevertheless, they have no inherent or absolute meaning in and of themselves. Consequently, discourse, in itself, can never represent a given ethical direction. However, it makes possible modes of comprehension through which hermeneutic rationality can restore a collective connection to the *unitas intellectus*. In this regard, discourse liberates and conduces to wisdom. Without a healthy dose of self-negating activity, the worldly and apathetic forget the ultimately arbitrary "so what" nature of their meaningful associations with material differences. Discourse's ultimate neutrality, and the ambiguity of material world differences and significations, do not condone ambivalence toward life decisions. Instead, reimagining discourse in terms of an opening for creative possibility and the reclamation of moral agency can change how we practice it. Put simply, it affirms that *"the choice is yours."*

Those who engage organically with Indigenous lifeways or wisdom practices based on folk or religious tradition have long sensed and intuited this creative dimension of the moral obligations implied by the material world's ambiguity. They recognize that the pharmaconic worldview offers extraordinary possibilities for moral agency and

54 TOWARD A NEW ART OF BORDER CROSSING

coherence-making. In Bakongo culture, for example, Afro-American conjurors draw from both lines of their spiritual and moral inheritance, and they are figures who can both "help" and "harm." A conjuror's help protects defensively while her harm may offend for the sake of her "client," and Afro-American sorcerers are "socially distinguished" based on their specialization or orientation toward either operation. In qualifying this social difference, Theophus Smith warns against collapsing the distinction between that which defends and that which offends so that these categories simplistically correspond to a good–evil moral binary. Instead, both offensive and defensive conjure can be benevolent or malignant. To avoid the epistemic flaws and social ills that come with fixed categorization and the will to power, one must understand this duality in "morally neutral terms" (Smith 1995: 43). Creative ethical conjurors, however, abide in the immediacy and volitional purity of an inner "freedom space": their active reasoning counters all rigid essentialisms as it engages the epistemic value of uncertainty, liminality, and multivalent logic.

One way they achieve consistency and steadiness despite the inherent dynamism of this ethical creativity is by honoring the "distinctively moral traits" cited by Dewey— including "wide sympathy, keen sensitiveness, persistence in the face of the disagreeable," and a "balance of interests." These traits help cultivate the communal conditions and hermeneutic capacities needed to apprehend subaltern creativities and to integrate the multifaceted insights they offer (Dewey *MW* 1920: 173–174).

Adequately thorough and detailed reasoning within communities dedicated to the search for truth makes possible the kinds of revelatory experiences that clarify how and why the social order must change. Attention to particularity and commitment to participatory reasoning facilitates the opening of the "mystical world of *mundus imaginalis*." Free from the constraints of invariant top-down representations, one recognizes primal motifs, usually obscured from consciousness. This embodied, revelatory experience of the images and symbols in cultural events becomes significant and interpretable (Glock 2008: 49). When supported by the inter-related, "distinctively moral traits," community hermeneutics further invites observation of "disguised and discarded" shadows hidden within cultural happenings and complexes (ibid: 50).

The Symbolic Reproduction of Racism and the Emergence of Salutogenesis

Let us now consider examples of center-margin dynamics and discourse. How do those spiritual and political activists who resist mainstream hegemonies encourage engagement in community hermeneutics through their work as ethical conjurors, and as border artists? Consideration of racism's "inversion" in the late nineteenth century— which was enabled by the symbolic construction of the Appalachian as "white trash"— exposes how the race concept functions problematically as a will to power in the US. Discourse coupled with community hermeneutics can tend to this "disguised and discarded" shadow aspect of race as trope (Hall 2017). Employed by activists these tools can address the racialized hierarchizations that constitute what Theophus Smith calls a "negative homeopathy of violence" (Smith 1995: 198).

In this instance, the negative homeopathy functioned to expel the "real" source of social pollution—the alleged "filthy and uneducated" white Appalachian. Cast as offending or polluting margins, these constructed "white trash" people give reality to the "symbolic purification" of the national mainstream (Taylor 2020). Collective construction of an Other, empowers "mechanisms of security" that then hide or submerge the society's other sources of tension and violence (Tremain 2017b). The cultural scapegoat (*pharmakos*) then serves the dominant group's interests by suppressing or distracting from other kinds of tension or hostility (Smith 1995: 198). Designating a group of people as "waste" ultimately served to sanction the coal industry and justify its exploitation of the region's peoples and resources to achieve economic stabilization (Holtman 2004: 55). It also helped elide the country's history of anti-Black racism, which troubles professed national ideals of inclusivity and racial harmony. Appalachian activist and cultural anthropologist Betsy Taylor aptly describes the rapid production of the "Appalachian" as a "laboratory experiment in how rapidly political economic contradictions within the Center can whip up a social psychology that needs an Other and will therefore make an Other" (Taylor 2020: 80).

The negative homeopathy of violence draws attention to itself over time because of its socially complex consequences. And in recognizing its insidious mechanistic structures, the moral agent accesses the wisdom and resolve to transform it homeopathically. The justice-maker awakens a life-affirming response to the crisis, known as salutogenesis (Antonovsky 1979). Arising as an emergent healing potential that manifests through resilience and adaptivity, salutogenesis fosters internal coherence. Appalachian mothers, organizers, and activists, like Julia "Judy" Thompson Bonds, the "godmother of the anti-mountaintop removal movement," provide an example of this affirmative life response. Bonds actively and publicly resisted the presence of a toxic Massey coal slurry dam and storage silo near a West Virginia elementary school. She manifested her dream of a "thousand hillbilly march" in Washington, D.C., in September 2010, just three months before her premature death at age 58. By resisting negative homeopathy, such leaders initiate activists into the radical possibility of becoming vessels for the promulgation of *nonviolent* homeopathy, thus disrupting the human-constructed discursive systems that permit the will to power to harm the vulnerable or scapegoated.

Like Afro-American conjuring, in a nonviolent homeopathy, people cannot simplistically categorize each other into simple moral binaries of good (that which defends) and evil (that which offends) (Smith 1995: 43). Women like Judy Bonds defy cultural conventions and habitual ways of seeing the world; they touch the deeper fabric of reality and experience its creative moral power (Davenport 2015). The emboldened individual's tactics and intentions align with the forces of resilience within salutogenesis and reflect the play of a greater evolutionary intelligence.

Challenging the Limits of Centrist Elements: The Cultural Model of Dis/ability

Dis/ability Studies affirm an agent-centered approach to morality and can directly address the blocks or barriers created through a margin-center construction. The cultural model of dis/ability purposefully shifts the epistemological perspective. Rather than permitting a perception of the margin as the source of disease, scholars explore the psychological and ethical limitations at play within centrist elements of society and culture (Waldschmidt 2006: 26). They do not problematize the category of the Other; instead, the focus turns to how normalcy and deviancy, regularity and aberration, interact with one another. Center-margin interfaces—like acceptable/damaged, or "clean" (and racially inclusive) national mainstream/Appalachian "white trash" (and excluded non-American fringe)—provide a way to understand the histories, paths of development, and critical moments of change that continue to influence a range of factors that impact human development, like how power manifests in relationships, organizes disciplinary learning, and maintains the force relations behind the apparatus of "disability" (ibid). Studying these processes of interaction reveals the dichotomies and social insecurities that continually induce both a Center and its Others by maintaining the symbol-making mechanisms that underlie a patterned way of relating. Focusing on the specificity and multiplicity of those schisms further exposes how over-arching discursive and systemic patterns reproduce these symbolic meanings (Taylor 2020, Mignolo and Walsh 2018, Wood 2018).

The dialectical consciousness fostered by a Dis/ability Studies framework provides valuable insights into race-related issues. Words and texts convey the oppressive symbolic meanings race produces, which allow the racial concept to stand in for multiple varieties of Otherization. But racialized meanings also constitute *systems* in which the relationship between that held in common and that deemed meaningfully different can never exceed the merely human constructed. And the reproduction of these meanings over time, through bio-power, marginalizes and stigmatizes the Others, turning them into a veritable "problem" in society. To perceive how that history has unfolded, anti-racist work—work that contends with the history of Otherization—must integrate an anti-materialist component.

Consider, for example, how Enlightenment-era thinking reified reason as the attribute that most distinguished human from animal, thus fortifying the agricultural era's ability to assert dominion over animals and harness their labor. But to maintain the force relations required for the political and economic order, this thinking also politically relegated people of color, women, and children to the culturally and intellectually inferior status of animals, reifying male reason over community-based hermeneutic rationality. Without having to respond in the community to different perspectives and ways of knowing, early industrialists could easily rationalize their systematic breeding and killing of "livestock" for mass consumption. Without a critical anti-materialist component in our discourse and justice-making practices, perspectives on social transformation remain subject to profound bias in their understanding of the human relation to animal and deity.

Increased economic freedom or the attainment of politicized civic rights alone cannot address how broader systems of symbolic meaning influence human relations and development. Consider how those economic and political remedies also conceal institutionalized cruelty to animals and foster apathy. Only a more nonmaterialist approach can address the deeper oppression caused by systems of symbolic meaning that racist ideology reproduces.

Invisible Men are Not America's Dilemma: Gunnar Myrdal and Ralph Ellison

To investigate the problem of symbolic reproduction using the cultural model of dis/ability, which directly identifies and challenges the limits of centrist elements, we can look at the ways modern rationality takes shape in the work of Gunnar Myrdal, the leading credited author of *An American Dilemma*. This 1944 study on race reflects the European philosophical tradition's dehumanizing elements, which problematize and bias knowledge formation by discriminating against any non-disinterested or subject-based mode of evaluation. Myrdal remains uncritically within an American universalist paradigm when he describes "Negroes" as lacking the capacity for self-determination and offering "only a fluid mass of all sorts of embryos of thoughts" (Mrydal 1962: 146). He is not only blind to the limitations of that moral framework—one shaped by Alexander Hamilton's papers, (which focused dominantly on a paradigm of national economic growth), and by the U.S. Constitution and the Federalist papers, (which supported a liberal democracy instituted by a mostly elite class of white males.) Myrdal is also himself steeped in Euro-centric and imperialist discourses. He blames the "immaturity" he perceives in the development of Black thinking on the fact that the Black population had simply not experienced a white, and therefore "normative," national identity. In *An American Dilemma*, underlying racist ideologies conceal themselves under the guise of a more liberal and "forgiving" paternal acceptance of the racialized "Other" (Singh 2021: 146). The moral blindness needed to continue to reproduce the appearance of national unity functions socially, not as a "handicap" in the conventionalized sense but as a "favor" to the dominant group.

Nikhil Pal Singh observes that "modernizing racial liberalism" may have arguably produced a more insidious form of racist tactical blocking than even "imperial discourse." In *An American Dilemma*, "Black thinking" was deemed "not merely childlike but fetal" due to Blacks' "prior exclusion from the public sphere (the denial to Blacks of normative national identities)." But that new explanation for "mental incapacity" was hardly more progressive than the view that "deficient" Black thinking reflected relatively poor inherent capabilities (ibid: 147).

Unable to denaturalize and question the social and historical conditions that made whites' exclusion of Blacks from public life socially acceptable, the prevailing conception of rationality normalizes racism and serves as the default moral framework for public discourse. Myrdal fails to question the rationality of the initial exclusion. He also allows this exclusion to determine the intellectual grounds of his inquiry and set the parameters of meaningful, collective identity-forming discourse. He relies upon the "racial definition" and the foundationalist assumptions supporting the formation of disciplinary knowledge in Western institutional life, which ultimately strengthened centrist ideas about normativity and the universality of national belonging (ibid: 21).

With this in mind, Ralph Ellison's 1952 novel, *Invisible Man*, reads as a critical literary response to the kinds of biases found in Myrdal's work, an exemplary artistic communication from within borderlands that plays, on the one hand, with the oscillation between the limits of discourse of margins and, on the other, with the affirmation of

58 TOWARD A NEW ART OF BORDER CROSSING

creative life from within the liminality of margins. The "scientists" in the novel, who subject the protagonist to electro-convulsive shock therapy and treat him as an "object" of study, play the part of the "villain." They are not blatantly racist, however. Instead, they are villainous because they are "progressive and liberal whites who purport to be anti-racist, while nonetheless harboring unconscious assumptions about 'the Negro' and framing him as a problem to be compartmentalized and solved" (IM 1). The scientists function largely through satire, and they serve as a critique of the dehumanizing effects modernist ideologies and technocracy wreak on knowledge formation. They induce the subject under their treatment to produce actions that are merely reactions. As any advertisement guru knows, however, reactions within objectifying contexts can be controlled and predicted, so the protagonist's humanity becomes questionable. In this scenario, conventional practices and top-down constructs organize the scientists' thinking and feeling. They manipulate the perception that the subject under their "control" has any capacity for moral agency or self-determination. Those entrained perceptual faculties then feed the scientists' biases and thought patterns. It is the astute reader who perceives that the scientists are the ones with an issue problematizing their cognitive order and intuition.

Cut off from the Hippocratic tradition's real origins, practitioners of Western medicine cannot perceive how their historical implication in cruelty to animals, eugenic experimentations, and practices like dissection theater—which all rely on notions of "objective detachment" based upon apathy, Otherizing, and the reproduction of violence-based forms of mass "entertainment"—has profoundly harmed the internal relations between animal, human, and deity crucial for the just unfolding of deep comprehension and ethical innovation (Federici 2004).

In *Invisible Man*, Ellison disrupts the dehumanizing cycles perpetuated by medicalizing subjective life and preserving the emotionally distanced stance evident in Myrdal's diagnosis of America's dilemma. "American Negroes" do have a subjectivity of their own, Ellison asserts, but it remains imperceptible to white men because they cannot recognize how, despite the pervasiveness of white supremacy, the marginalized do find ecological niches for survival and creativity. "Men have made a way of life in caves and upon cliffs," he writes famously, "why cannot Negroes have made a life upon the horns of the white man's dilemma" (1995/1952)? In converting the white man to a beast while still affirming the habitation he provides as a "normative-enough" ecological niche in which to survive, Ellison reveals the soundness of his own intimate connection to the animal–human–deity worlds and becomes a defending-offending social healer capable of reclaiming his people's remarkable resilience, moral agency, and matrixial powers of transformation.

The Pooka and the Black Nationalist: Community Hermeneutics and Mary Chase's Harvey

The margins can provide access to political and legal power in that they intensify creative insecurity and foster wisdom-making capacities. Ellison's *Invisible Man* supports anti-oppression endeavors by contributing culturally to the larger struggle by the marginalized to participate in the realization of a common humanity or, in the making of borderlands into what Miri calls "spaces of margins—meeting places." Out

CONJURING AT THE MARGINS

of the "forcible enclosures of racial stigma," community hermeneutics generate "new universals" with political and legal importance (Singh 2021: 44). For Ellison's invisible narrator, enclosure entails social disappearance and life underground.

Mary Chase's 1945 play, *Harvey*, written just a year after *An American Dilemma* was published, likewise engages the co-creative relation of animal, human, and deity, developing themes of invisibility, scientific rationality, and norms of sociality that Ellison would explore seven years later in his own novel. Chase's protagonist, Elwood P. Dowd, sees and befriends a six-foot-tall pooka. His conformist, white family members perceive him to be socially unacceptable and insane, a complete embarrassment. After a comical mix-up in which Elwood's "doctors" become confused about who actually needs treatment, he is institutionalized and told to submit to a "cure" for his "delusions" (Chase 1971). *Harvey* explores the social construction of mental illness as "impairment" and "disability," and it glances sideways, with light but pointed significance, at the effects modernist ideology has on those in the US' white mainstream.

The eponymous "invisible" pooka (or *puca*) is a Celtic version of the African Br'er Rabbit figure that was popularized in written stories in the late nineteenth and early twentieth centuries that were based on hybrid oral traditions in the antebellum South. The rabbit, a hero in these traditions though not necessarily an exemplary figure, provides unique insight into survival intelligences, and his often troublesome or immoderate behaviors express the struggle of staying alive in oppressive or contradictory circumstances. Like the marginalized who are continually subjected to double binds, Br'er Rabbit finds a way out of no way.

That a similar figure would "appear" in Chase's Pulitzer Prize-winning play at a time when the "problems" of the racially marginalized were being studied from a centrist standpoint is perhaps not surprising. In his relationship with the pooka, the receptive Elwood (a name based on a place in England that translates to "old noble wood") finds only friendship, social gracefulness, and a spirit of hospitality. But Harvey has far more disruptive effects on Elwood's family and broader social system. The "invisible rabbit" thus raises questions about social values and norms that exceed simple moral polarities. The universal power of the mythopoetic imagination arises and speaks the truth about the human psyche in times of crisis when a culture thirsts for renewing energies and creative insights into a social predicament.

The ways in which the play's setting and themes draw upon symbolic meanings within center–margin interactions indicate that, although it does not directly allude to the country's racial tensions, it still tacitly acknowledges them. Chase, through her use of art as social commentary, challenges racial concepts by engaging with the discursive system in a more critical or heightened way. Considering the contents of the cultural unconscious, one may ask, for example: In the liminal space created on stage by the presence of Harvey (an actual absence), is a creative social alliance being made—through the unconscious musicality of rhyme and the proximity of alphabetical ordering—between *Harvey* and Marcus Moziah *Garvey*, the Black nationalist and Pan-Africanist who had died just five years before Chase's play appeared?

While in prison, Garvey boldly proclaimed his pervasive spiritual presence in the world. Overcoming the enclosures of jail and embracing a spiritual politics of Nature

60 TOWARD A NEW ART OF BORDER CROSSING

that exceeds every human-constructed limit maintained by centrist modes of thinking, he wrote, "Look for me in the whirlwind or storm." He furthermore prophesied his spiritual return and role in a global movement of liberation:

> look for me all around you, for, with God's grace, I shall come and bring with me countless millions of Black slaves who have died in America and the West Indies and the millions in Africa to aid you in the fight for Liberty, Freedom and Life. (Garvey 1969: 237–238)

In terms of Chase's own involvement with racial politics, her husband, Robert, worked to fight the Ku Klux Klan in state and local politics in Colorado. Garvey was an unlikely friend of the racist organization in that he, too—though from a different direction—was interested in ideas of preserving "racial purity." Garvey's "friendship" toward the KKK, an unexpected orientation for a Black man, may be interpreted as a manifestation of survival intelligence and Br'er Rabbit, trickster-like energy in that it functions counterintuitively to dominant modes of allyship and valuation. It is a prime example of "complex personhood" as defined by Avery Gordon, in which people are understood to be naturally "beset by contradiction" (2008). Due to the double bind they are placed in, the need-fulfillments, and the racialized constructions for advancing "progress," which are naturalized for the privileged, often become seemingly exceedingly contradictory in relation to oppressed people's physical needs, ethical cultural requirements for dignity, and social and political creative desires.

Associations like the echoes between "Harvey" and "Garvey"—which would be more resonant, at least subliminally, with theater audiences in the 1940s—may nevertheless offer a path today to recovering mental health, through greater respect for "haunting," a way of knowing Gordon describes in *Ghostly Matters: Haunting and the Sociological Imagination*. In Gordon's framework, a person uncovers the ways in which "history and subjectivity" constitute social reality by increasing receptivity to "that which appears to be not there" but which is nevertheless "a seething presence" that acts on and often meddles with "taken-for granted realities" (2008: 195). Such associations—and others, like the homophonic pairing of the white, privileged Myrdal, credited author of *An American Dilemma*, and Chase's character Myrtle Mae, Elwood's image-obsessed niece who is determined to protect her family's normalcy in order to establish her own marriageability—encourage engagement with the liminality of the imaginal realm (and perhaps with the pharmacopeic potentials of the "old noble wood" that provides a home for the myrtle plant). By affirming the internal dynamism of salutogenesis, those actively engaging in community hermeneutics can explore sociality and relationality from a much broader and more inclusive viewpoint, one capable of exposing the wide-ranging connections linking center–margin interactions, public mental health, and racialized knowledge systems.

Social and Cultural Perspectives on the Pharmacopeic Project

Dis/ability theorists such as Shelley Tremain do not view culture in isolation. Instead, communications transpire fluidly, interweaving natural, cultural, and symbolic-imaginal realms as a unity. Consequently, culture itself encompasses "the totality of 'things'" physical, intellectual, or spiritual that people make and use to maintain their way of life. This includes "objects and instruments, institutions and organizations, ideas and knowledge, symbols and values, meanings and interpretations, narratives and histories, traditions, rituals and customs, social behavior, attitudes and identities" (Waldschmidt 2018: 71). This approach to culture resonates with the aims of decoloniality and emphasizes coexistence and the necessary interrelationship of all entities (Mignolo and Walsh 2018). It resembles the logic of friendship and psychic struggle found in Elwood's fluid structural relation to the invisible pooka in *Harvey*.

This perspective on culture also foregrounds Parker's point concerning how liminality itself is an important psychological condition for creative life. Transitional border states release people from a fixation upon categorical factors and a reliance upon the value absolutism those factors produce. In contrast to psychiatry's rigid, nonreflective categorizing and reliance upon established codes for naming, which Elwood encounters when his sister and niece commit him to a "sanitorium," a dynamic nominalist philosophical stance addresses the inclusive totality, movement, interactivity, and liminality that is involved in creating "kinds" of anything.

Because dis/ability theorists internalize the dynamic nominalist stance and do not view culture in isolation, when they apply anti-oppression analysis—whether to a seemingly "children's play" like *Harvey* or any other timely cultural entity or social practice—they include a more thorough investigation of how "the relations between symbolic (knowledge) systems, categorization and institutionalization processes, material artifacts, practices and 'ways of doing things',", impact the "social positions, relations and ways of subjectivation" of those in the national mainstream and outside of it, of those with dis/abilities and without, and of those with racialized identity or not (Tremain 2017b: 22). In other words, for critical dis/ability theorists, anti-oppression analyses call for a cultural hermeneutics with transformative potentials so that people can participate individually and communally in creative social change movement. They require both an acknowledgment of Miri's point about the limits of center-margin discourse and an appreciation of Parker's affirmation of margins as places of creative renewal.

Toxins with Tonic Powers: BIPOC Social Change Movement, Nepantleras, and the Wolastoqey Nation

Theophus Smith asserts that acknowledging "the spectacle of a European nation that had attempted systematically to exterminate its minority population" helps us assess the real value of the Black freedom movement's achievements. Exposing people to the horrible realities of cultural scapegoating sensitizes the white mainstream to the significance of the indictments[1] made by people of color—that the government and dominant cultural forces enacted "genocidal and oppressive" institutional policies against them (Smith 1995: 213). In terms of human development, this sensitization and comprehension process leads to the transformation of a group's dependence upon nationalist narratives and bio-power for a sense of normativity. When activists imitate and eventually internalize a nonviolent model, their scapegoated status awakens the

62 TOWARD A NEW ART OF BORDER CROSSING

conscience and serves as a "homeopathic" cure rather than a further accentuation of their victimization.

Here, acknowledging the totality that constitutes culture makes possible the "magic" of cultural evolution. The strategic practice of negation distinguishes Black thinkers' ability to "authenticate" or translate their "pharmacopeic wisdom tradition" and to manifest a Western logocentricity with persuasive communicative power. Smith explains this practice has its functional equivalent in Indigenous "malign" or "offensive aggressive" conjure. Preserving "toxic pharmacopeia" skill—that is, "negative" or "poisoning, toxifying, harmful, or destructive practices"—and generating the meta-awareness needed to reverse that harm and produce a "cure" helps Black theologians, for example, make critical, transformational significations related to the interpretation and value meanings within Biblical scripture (Smith 1995: 213). They can then express these significations within Western culture's traditional modes of discourse as that mode makes its own borders permeable and receptive to diverse perspectives, through engagement in transcontinental philosophizing and other forms of interculturality.

One major instance of harm that qualifies as cultural genocide is the enclosure of Blacks in major cities after their migration North generally between World War I and the 1960s, which was directed and enabled in part, by local real estate agencies and government agencies, including the Home Owners Loan Corporation (HOEC) and the Federal Housing Administration (FHA). Critical theorists have compared the oft-ignored ghettoization in the US to neocolonialism because ghettos are "internal colonies" from which it is increasingly difficult to escape. For people who live there, options include premature death and prison. Furthermore, the internalizing of neo-colonialist practices creates such a potent contradiction between nationalist ideals and historical practices that, from the subject's viewpoint, the "normative" idea of "common" citizenship becomes completely delegitimized.

The term "ghetto" is itself haunted not only by the unreported history of suicide and self-harm that occurs within them in the US but also by the history in Italy, from over 400 years ago, in which Jews, who lacked a real homeland, were restricted to partitioned-off neighborhoods. In order for minority groups to avoid the problems of homogenization and conformity consciousness as they seek transformation and solidarity with one another, it is necessary for each person to know "the history of their struggle" and the unique aspects of their history of resistance (Anzaldúa 1987: 86).

Speaking to this point, Smith suggests that African Americans co-participate in "a contemporary, global configuration of all Abrahamic communities currently experiencing Diaspora" (1995: 252). He adds that whether or not they perceive themselves within their "host cultures" as "rooted" or "captive," these dispersed and displaced communities can actualize new modes of social change and forms of solidarity. Because estranged from their host nation, they are auspiciously positioned to achieve "prophetic distance" from nationhood. Facilitating a diasporan approach to the poisonous ideologies and "fictive ethnicities" of the nation-state, the inherent liminality of an emergent transcendent subjecthood, can conjure cultural well-being and health (ibid; Balibar 2002). The creativity, passion, and self-organizing structure of the contemporary *Black Lives Matter* movement today testify to the truth of Smith's observation over 25 years ago. So too, does that of other Black, Indigenous, People of Color (BIPOC) social change organizations committed to the pharmaconic worldview.

But in this discussion of subjecthood and the possibility of conjuring at the margins, we must consider that often, the most intense harms for the marginalized derive from their relationships with racial or ethnic in-group members, including family, or from power struggles within political activist groups. Therefore, we need to ask more general questions about power. For example, in a particular context, who is getting stigmatized, and who is recognized? Power differentials arise naturally in all groups and persist unless practices are in place to respect the interpsychic nature of exchange in the community. Transforming in-group toxicity requires, among other things, reconnection to the conditions of ancestry and to the kinds of moral traits that Dewey recommends.

Furthermore, when the need to transform in-group toxicity is erased or minimized, and a person belongs to more than one cultural group, then unhealthy power dynamics more readily intensify across the groups. Speaking to this phenomenon in *Borderlands: La Frontera*, Gloria Anzaldúa describes the aggressive nature of "cultural collision" or "*choque*":

> Within us and within *la cultura chicana*, commonly held beliefs of the white culture attack commonly held beliefs of the Mexican culture, and both attack commonly held beliefs of the Indigenous culture. Subconsciously, we see an attack on ourselves and our beliefs as a threat and we attempt to block with a counterstance. (1987: 78)

Minorities are endangered "from within" when members internalize the use of Othering as a negative homeopathic remedy by seeking higher status, for example (Smith 1995: 218); or by using strategies like shunning to create a center that organizes values and priorities in the group through social power, rather than through a shared commitment to realize human moral and spiritual potential.

The latter commitment involves transforming social power into primordial legal and political power and then re-engaging sociality in a decentered way. In her politically meaningful discussion of spiritual activists who participate in this transformation of power, Anzaldúa engages with the Nahuatl word *nepantla*—signifying an in-between space that is also a psychic chasm within which the spiritual activist finds pharmacopeic remedies. She speaks of these activists as *nepantleras*, and describes their wisdom path, called *conocimiento* (1987). But we must always remember the destructive tendency to defensive "counterstance": even when *nepantleras* fully pursue spiritual activism, or when minority groups do affirm their internal solidarity and relation-to-coalitional networks, majority groups still threaten "from without" when they perceive the individual's or the minority democratic movement's vital materiality as a socially destabilizing force. And some of those threats—like the idealized politics of nations that create "fictive ethnicities"—are disguised and conceal the true meaning of culture.

Countermanding both internal and external toxic harms requires embracing social healing that reverses the hazardous potentials of the defensive "counterstance," without succumbing to tacit acceptance of mainstream or more dominant group political and social norms. According to Theophus Smith, that countermanding remains "the major pharmacopeic project of Black America." He foresees that recovering from the toxicity of Black America's own "traditions, institutions, and social practices" will require more informed practices and discourses that can turn around those harms most dangerously affecting its communities.

Because of this assortment of simultaneous toxic-tonic realities subaltern groups face, a "double-sided view" makes possible "a convergence" between the "curative, healing interests of Black culture" (hinting at Parker's stance) and its "negative tasks" (a reminder of Miri's position). And just as "homeopathic medicines are curative," it is also true that "negations can become antidotal" (Smith 1995: 218). We need both sides of the oscillating approach to appreciate how and why creative moral potentials within margins either do or do not, manifest. Comprehending "double-sidedness" helps people avoid essentialism, recognize the historical roots of tension, and cultivate a mediating intelligence, to navigate disease and friction. This approach invites participation in social healing within and across groups and contexts.

Border artist and scholar Gloria Anzaldúa, who "juggles" Indigenous, Mexican, and Anglo cultures herself, exemplifies the spirit of salutogenesis in this regard. She finds new ways to respect the "plural personality" that arises through *mestiza* consciousness as a person becomes tolerant of contradictions and ambiguities and learns "to be an Indian in Mexican culture, to be Mexican from an Anglo point of view"—thus always remembering the point of breakage as well as the possibility of it converting to a point of growth and connection (1987: 79).

For the *mestiza*, culture itself is a liminal reality. The most successful cultural reclamations by First Nations peoples seem to link that liminality to salutogenesis. Today, for example, members of the Wolastoqey Nation, who have been affected by cultural genocide,[2] have moved beyond reconciliation work with the government, social workers, and the white population. They embrace the totality of their cultural heritage and seek to reclaim the "intellectual, political energy" of Indigeneity as self-governance, knowledge, and identity. Uncovering "a new and fluid way of being," Wolastoqey people work with the liminality of borders to expand the temporal dimension within and between worlds. As they engage in "seven-generation thinking," they carry peace and redemption forward to unborn generations by awakening ancestral spirits (*Ktuhkelokepon*) (Perley 2015). Wolastoqey kinship, *Wetapeksi*, encompasses "history, ceremony, land, language and all that lives," and forms the foundation of "relationality, holism and synergy within" (Kress, Perley, I., Perley, D., Plaice & Sabattis-Atwin 2019). It therefore obliterates the colonizing nation-state's fictive conceptualization of Indigeneity and shakes up the staid, reductionistic notion of culture as something made up of only surface objects and bodies.

Like the non-Native people who are generating "new universals" out of stigma and forced enclosure, the Wolastoqey and countless other First Nations peoples are countermanding the many toxic forces wielded against them historically—like forced schooling, for example—to participate in a larger, less visible process of forming public consciousness at the global level, where the primordial basis of their political and legal power can transform the trajectory of international politics (Lightfoot 2016). They may initiate listening projects, archive primary source materials relevant to justice issues, and initiate new partnerships for building trust and understanding that integrate arts-based

CONJURING AT THE MARGINS

expression. The effort's theoretical conclusions become a transcendent source of wisdom to guide what Smith calls "the consummate human project of our time and all history." The "cascading impact" of those committed to that greater praxis can then enkindle cultural and spiritual awakenings in other Indigenous communities.

And as these—and "rationalist"—technical approaches to progress grow increasingly virtuosic and interactive with non-Indigenous communities receptive to practices like community hermeneutics, a fruitful marriage of seeming oppositions may yield a new "ethnocentric view of rationality," through which a more nuanced perspective on the Subject as social actor may animate the "modulations or transmutations of Indigenous traditions" and subvert passive acceptance of their atrophy, so that cultural evolution may flourish (Smith 1995: 217). This ethnocentric rationality can lead to material remedies of past harms. But even more importantly for the long term, it can challenge and transform "cultural narratives, practices, and histories," to offer a debunking counternarrative to civic nationalism and a critical realist contrast to "fictive ethnicities" (Balibar 2002: 96).

Practicing the emptiness at the heart of critical dis/ability theory's anti-materialistic attitude and dynamic nominalist stance, participants convert allopathic approaches to maintaining "stable" order into vitalist approaches to social health, that empower people to transform relationship to structural and ideological conflicts. The promise of the evolutionary transmutation of Indigenous wisdom, and the practice that Theophus Smith refers to, lives in the ability of those with a "rational-ritualistic" and "pharmaconic" world perspective to enact these conversions and to thrive continually as new converts themselves.

References

Antonovsky, A. (1979). Health, Stress, and Coping. *New Perspectives on Mental and Physical Well-being*, (The Jossey-Bass Social and Behavioral Science Series) First Edition, 12–37.

Anzaldúa, G. (1987). *Borderlands/la frontera*. na.

Balibar, E. (1995). Ambiguous Universalism. *Differences: A Journal of Feminist Cultural Studies*, 7(1): 61–62.

Barad, K. M., Alaimo, S., & Hekman, S. (2008). Post-humanist performativity.

Chase, M. (1971). *Harvey: Comedy in Three Acts*. Dramatists Play Service, Inc.

Davenport, A. K. (2015). *Place, space, and family: A rhetorical analysis of the resistance rhetoric of Judy Bonds*.

Davis, E. (1999). "Trickster at the Crossroads: West Africa's God of Messages, Sex, and Deceit," *Gnosis* 14 (1991): 26, http://www.levity.com/figment/trickster.htm.

Dewey, J. (1980/1920). "The middle works of John Dewey, 1899–1924." Compiled by Jo Ann Boydston Southern Illinois University Press.

Ellison, R. (1995). *Invisible man*. 1952.

Federici, S. (2004). *Caliban and the Witch*. Autonomedia.

Foucault. (1978/1990). *The History of Sexuality: Volume 1*. New York: Vintage.

Garvey, M. (1969). First Message to the Negroes of the World from Atlanta Prison. *Philosophy and Opinions of Marcus Garvey*, 2, 237–239.

Glock, Michael. (2008). *Cultural Futuristics: A Social Science Foresight Methodology* (copyright on content held by author).

Gordon, A. F. (2008). *Ghostly Matters: Haunting and the Sociological Imagination*. University of Minnesota Press.

66 TOWARD A NEW ART OF BORDER CROSSING

Hall, S. (2017). *The Fateful Triangle: Race, Ethnicity, Nation.* Harvard University Press.

Holtman, J. M. (2004). *"White trash" Discourses: Literature, History, Social Science and Poor White Subjectivity.* The Pennsylvania State University. *Proquest Dissertations Publishing.* Web.

Jacobs, M. D. (2014). *A Generation Removed: The Fostering and Adoption of Indigenous Children in the Postwar World.* University of Nebraska Press.

Keating, A. (2012). *Transformation Now!: Toward a Post-oppositional Politics of Change.* University of Illinois Press.

Kress, M., Perley, I., Perley, D., Plaice, E., & Sabattis-Atwin, A. (2019). "Ktuhkelokepon" Awakening our Indigeneity: A Wabanaki Story of Truth, Justice and Reconciliation. *Antistasis,* 9(1), 1–12.

Lightfoot, S. (2016). *Global Indigenous Politics: A Subtle Revolution.* Routledge.

Merçon, J. (2014). Fictive Ethnicity, Language and Race: A Brief Start for a Longer Discussion on Schooling and Identity. *Das Questões,* 1(1), 85.

Mignolo, Walter D., and Catherine E. Walsh. (2018). *On Decoloniality: Concepts, Analytics, Praxis.* Duke University Press.

Miri, Mrinal. (2003). *Identity and Moral Life.* Delhi: Oxford U. Press.

Myrdal, G. (1962). An American Dilemma. In Hughey, M.W. (eds) *New Tribalisms* (pp. 61–72). Palgrave Macmillan, London.

Parker, Noel. (2009). "From Borders to Margins: A Deleuzian Ontology for Identities in the Postinternational Environment." *Alternatives, 34(1),* 17–39.

Perley, I. (November 16, 2015). Personal Conversation with Margaret Kress. Mi'kmaq Wolastoqey Centre. (Cited in Kress et al. 2019.)

Singh, N. P. (2021). *Black is a Country.* Harvard University Press.

Smith, T. H. (1995). *Conjuring Culture: Biblical Formations of Black America.* Oxford University Press.

Taylor, Betsy. (2020). Pollution, Subsistence, Sustainability in USA Nationalism: The Symbolic Construction of 'Appalachia' as America's 'trash' People. In Frederique Apffel-Marglin, Sanjay Kumar, and Arvind Mishra (eds). *Interrogating Development: Insights from Margins* (pp. 62–82). New Delhi: Oxford University Press.

Tremain, S. (2017a). *Foucault and Feminist Philosophy of Disability.* University of Michigan Press.

Tremain, S. (2017b). Knowing Disability, Differently. In Ian James Kidd, José Medina & Gaile Pohlhaus (eds). *The Routledge Handbook of Epistemic Injustice* (pp. 124–126). New York: Routledge.

Waldschmidt, Λ. (2006). Normalcy, Bio-Politics and Disability: Some Remarks on the German Disability Discourse. *Disability Studies Quarterly,* 26(2). Available online https://doi.org/10.18061/dsq.v26i2.694 .

Waldschmidt, A. (2018). Disability–Culture–Society: Strengths and Weaknesses of a Cultural Model of Dis/ability. *ALTER – European Journal of Disability Research / Revue Européenne de Recherche sur le Handicap,* 12(2): 65–78.

Wood, D. A. (2018). *Epistemic Decolonization: A Critical Epistemography of the Anticolonial Politics of Knowledge.* Villanova University.

Notes

1   Article II of the United Nations Convention on Genocide clarifies that the term pertains not only to the eradication of a group by killing but also, acts done to harm it, either in part or in whole, including the intent: to cause serious bodily or mental harm to members of the group; to inflict conditions of life calculated to bring physical destruction; to impose measures intended to prevent births within group; to transfer children of the group to another group. By recognizing that culture encompasses "the totality of 'things'" and that it includes, more broadly, those intellectual and spiritual traditions, habits, beliefs, and practices that maintain ways of life, the violations experienced by marginalized peoples can finally be perceived and addressed by the dominant group.

CONJURING AT THE MARGINS 67

2 One can still perceive how cultural genocide was enacted in the center-margin power dynamics of the Indian Adoption Project. The Civilization Fund Act of 1819 funded boarding schools for Indian children that prevented them from speaking their native language, practicing their traditions, and living with siblings. Having disrupted the ways of living in Native community and family, the U.S. government created the Indian Adoption Project in 1958. The Bureau of Indian Affairs and the Child Welfare League of America, would address the "Indian problem." Government sanctioned notions of "normalcy" were to be imposed on Native American children as they were relocated into white foster families. In the 1970s, the government terminated the Indian Adoption Project, but it continued adoptions and performed involuntary sterilizations on Native American women through the Indian Health Service. The U.S. General Accounting Office numbers these at over three thousand. Margaret D. Jacobs, author of A Generation Removed, writes that this U.S. campaign ultimately "undermined the image of good-hearted American families." White Americans who seem to benefit socially and economically from their identification with the universalized "norm" must question their complicity in these oppressive practices. "The moral of this story," Jacobs concludes, "depends on who is telling the story" (2014: xxviii).

Chapter 5

NEW ARTS OF BORDER CROSSING: TAGORE'S ENGAGEMENT WITH BORDERS

Meera Chakravorty

The Idea of Border

Concerned with the mounting tension at international borders, where countries often deploy their troops in anticipation of a possible conflict, it is hard to think of an analysis of this phenomenon that is matched by decisiveness. Wars and the politics of conflicts in democracy and civil society ignore the sensitivity to social justice in general and people in particular. War, for a long time, used to be considered a feature of earlier history. Still, in the not-very recent past, the phases of global trends have brought more tough competition with various forces, leading to unexpected revivals of many conflict zones. Such situations often give vent to the feeling that we live in a world where people suffer within their boundaries and have no hope that anything or anyone can make a difference. Any analysis of war, at first, appears as an organized hostility against most of the people who are grouped into abstract categories; however, the intricate collaboration between people who suffer most and those who cause the suffering often becomes inventive, which does not bring any sense of relief to the already problematic situations leading to more conflict. It was the vision of statesmanship when the late Prime Minister A. B. Vajpayee, in February 1999, took the historic Lahore Bus visit, crossing the border with the message of peace from India, which the people gratefully remembered of Pakistan in later years: "In Pakistan, it seems Vajpayee will be remembered for a Nixonian diplomatic gamble in 1999 when he undertook a historic bus trip to Pakistan's Lahore."[1] One might argue that one can cross borders anytime as they are deliberately created, as are the boundaries and the margins. These are constructs created often for convenience and are supposed to be widely held; while the reality might be that though these may not have popular legitimacy to support, they still have constitutional support, which is not enough to contain the eruptions of tension and disaffection. As can be seen in a report of a recent incident in August 2019 in Islington, London, journalist Owen Jones of the Guardian was brutally assaulted by, as he said, the far-right supporters for his left-oriented views on several issues. More brutal earlier was the attack on Julian Assange, Wikileaks founder, and Australian editor, for practicing investigative journalism that exposed the war crimes reported by various news agencies

70 TOWARD A NEW ART OF BORDER CROSSING

in 2010. It is also noteworthy how the protestors in Hong Kong against the extradition bill marched in large numbers demanding their democratic rights in recent times. It has been going on since March 2019, bringing people's demonstration opposing the bill into focus. It is exactly this kind of a situation that had occurred during the independence struggle in India and which shows what happened in the British regime in India, as Tagore pointed out in his letter of protest to Edwin Montagu, the then Secretary of State for India which says: "As far as we can judge, the men who represent the British people in India are extremely reluctant to concede to us any power which now they fully enjoy themselves; and it seems it deeply hurts their susceptibilities to form any relationships with us based on equality" (Tagore 1918: 45–49).[2]

This view of Tagore tells us something important about the destructive capability of being bound by any coercive power, even if it appears to be great. He found Gandhi's concept of "Charka" resentful as Gandhi wanted to make it binding on people. Tagore opposed it, as it happened when Gandhi came to Santiniketan to discuss the relation of Swaraj (self-governance) and Charka (the spinning wheel). Tagore needed to be convinced. In response, he wrote elaborately (in an article) how essential it was to note that people's poverty would not be solved by spinning Charka and producing clothes: "My complaint is that by the promulgation of this confusion between swaraj and Charka, the mind of the country is being distracted from swaraj. To give the Charka the first place in our striving for the country's welfare is only a way to make our insulted intelligence recoil in despairing action" (Tagore 1925: 112).[3] The idea and act of spinning should define a community appeared as a commonplace boundary to identify a country's ontological aspiration, which was, in fact, the expression of the poet's agony. He, therefore, suggested the alternative, which would be a strategy to cross narrow margins. He said: "I think it to be primarily necessary that, in different places over the country, small centers should be established in which expression is given to the responsibility of the country for achieving its swaraj that is to say, its welfare as a whole and not only regarding its supply of homespun thread. We must have before us, in various centers of population, examples of different types of revived life abounding in health and wisdom and prosperity."[4] Tagore contributes to the view that instead of a boundary limiting the understanding of people, the concept or idea must intend to be peripatetic, quite in the style of peripatetic philosophers who would travel with their scholarship, crossing different boundaries and attracting students on their way. The poet's tone in his response to Gandhi seems to emphasize the message that borders are like "disciplines" meant to be followed by a cadre; however, people are not a controlled group; they have "imagination" which is not a particular "thing" to be kept static in someplace, it must be allowed to flourish and therefore, crossing and recrossing does not become a matter of offense. Tagore says: "It may be argued that spinning is also a creative act. But that is not so: for, by turning its wheel, a man merely becomes an appendage of the Charka; that is to say, he but does himself what a machine might have done: he converts his living energy into a dead turning movement. The machine is solitary because being devoid of mind, it is sufficient and knows nothing outside itself."[5] By such observations, Tagore implied Gandhi's "instruction" to spin as a compulsory act for the Congress members and other people as authoritative and, hence, a boundary

NEW ARTS OF BORDER CROSSING

that would confine people to inhibiting the same unwillingly. This was totally against any act of freedom, and it was not thrilling for Tagore. On the other hand, through his critical oeuvre, he must have felt that people's intellectual generosity must have paved the way for people's contradictory imagination, which resists any boundary.

This has a lot of implications for the relation of the border to the practice of freedom. In the Indian context, we can see how the lacunae of perception occur when we see people tagged on to a set of myths like a border or a boundary constructed by the colonial perception, which took a firm root in consequent interpretations of people's history especially. In short, an opaque view is given legitimacy. To propose a clearer picture, we may note how, in the Indian subcontinent, the colonial regime, not being aware of the local language and culture, had still taken the liberty to impose lock, stock, and barrel the imposed label on an ancient civilization like that of the Indian subcontinent as "history-less" despite the works of the Indigenous scholars like Kalhana's Rajtarangini. Evidence from other sources such as inscription from monarchs of different dynasties besides numismatic and archeological ones, also contributed to this. Despite this evidence, the British colonizers' inhibitions about India made them construct her history according to their fancies. The historian Romila Thapar commented on the ramifications of such a construction by the British when she said: "In the course of investigating what came to be called Hinduism, together with various aspects of its belief, ritual, and custom, many were baffled by a religion that was altogether different from their own. It was not monotheistic; there was no historical founder, single sacred text, dogma, or ecclesiastical organization" (Thapar 2002: 3).[6] In such a context, Thapar continues: "There was much discussion at the meetings of the Asiatic Society in Calcutta, focusing largely on the origins and reconstruction of language and religion and custom. Unfortunately, but curiously, membership in society was not open to Indians for many years, even though Indian scholars were training those presenting their findings."[7] The idea of a history-less India did continue even when the missionaries crossed their borders and came to India; however, they imagined while interacting with people that perhaps the Indian language Sanskrit had some European connection. A new border was thus created, and William Jones, a member of the Asiatic Society, thought of exploring this idea. Thapar commented on this: "A son of Noah was said to have migrated to India to establish Indian population, but the evidence for this was found wanting!" (Thapar 2002: 3).[8] From this reflection of Thapar, it is possible to see how border crossing, a construct yet used to relate vigorously, further creates another construct of European civilization as the source of history-less subcontinent.

Arguing further, Thapar clarifies: "The so-called 'discovery' of India was largely through selected literature in Sanskrit. This interpretation tended to emphasize non-historical aspects of Indian culture, such as the idea of an unchanging continuity of society and religion over 3000 years. It was believed that the Indian pattern of life was so concerned with metaphysics and the subtleties of religious belief that little attention was given to the more tangible aspects" (Thapar 2005: 3).[9] This indeed lacked evidence. India never had a monocultural landscape. Neither did she suffer from a lack of richness in possessing vivid linguistic and other landscapes representing diverse communities, their faith, and their ways of living. Metaphysics was part of this vividness. This fact has been established rigorously

72 TOWARD A NEW ART OF BORDER CROSSING

and meticulously by historians through their study and research after exploring how many kinds of habitats continued to cross and re-cross, how they lived their lives sometimes by dominating other groups, and at times being subdued by stronger communities. Thapar thus clarifies the ambiguity that permeated the colonialists: "The Indian subcontinent has been the habitat of many societies ranging from those with a relatively simple organization to others with more complex organizations, the range disallowing easy generalizations. Complex societies were the more dominant and elbowed their way into history. Others were forced to be more reticent, but they did not disappear. It is often in the interface of such differing societies that the patterns of Indian culture were forged" (Thapar 2005: 54).[10] This shows how crossing and recrossing borders happened as a continuous process, whether one liked it or not, or whether any gain and loss were of concern, the journey continued. However, one may argue that borders are strictly followed as a measure of discipline and further emphasize that it is also ethically critical. But others may unrepentantly reiterate this claim as absurd, wishing to dissociate themselves from getting into such disciplines that exclude borderless journey rationales. Tagore belongs to the latter.

Resistance to Border

His initial resistance was to the schooling system, which always reminded him of a kind of regimentation in the name of discipline, about which he says: "So long as I was forced to attend school, I felt an unbearable torture. I often counted the years before I would have my freedom. My elder brothers had finished their academic careers and were engaged in life, each in his way; how I envied them when, after a hurried meal in the morning, I found the inevitable carriage that took us to school. I wished that, by some magic spell, I could cross the intervening fifteen or twenty years and suddenly become a grown-up man" (Tagore 1925: 24–30).[11] Later in life, this experience must have helped him when Tagore found a school in Santiniketan, Bengal, where any regimentation would not be a factor in teaching students. Tagore also mentioned how he felt tormented at that young age. He felt exasperated and wondered why his teacher could not fall sick. "When my English teacher used to come in the evening, with trepidation, I waited! I would yearn to go to my mother and ask her to tell me a fairy story. Still, instead, I had to go and get my textbook with its unimpressive black binding and chapters of lessons, followed by rows of separated syllables with accent marks like soldier's bayonets. As for the teacher, I can never forgive him. He insisted on coming every evening, and his family never seemed to have illness or death" (Tagore 1901: 18).[12]

This view of Tagore tells us something important about the destructive capability of being bound by any idea of coercive power, even if it appears to be a great one. He found Gandhi's concept of "Charka" resentful as Gandhi wanted to make it a binding act on people. He opposed it, as happened when Gandhi came to Santiniketan to discuss the relationship of Swaraj (self-governance) with Charka (the spinning wheel). Tagore was not convinced. In response, he wrote elaborately (in an article) how essential it was to note that people's poverty would not be solved by spinning Charka and producing clothes: "My complaint is that by the promulgation of this confusion between swaraj and Charka, the mind of the country is being distracted from swaraj. To give the

Charka the first place in our striving for the country's welfare is only a way to make our insulted intelligence recoil in despairing action" (Tagore 1925: 112).[13] The idea and act of spinning should define a community appeared as a commonplace boundary to identify a country's ontological aspiration, which was, in fact, the expression of the poet's agony. He, therefore, suggested the alternative, which would be a strategy to cross narrow margins. He said: "I think it to be primarily necessary that, in different places over the country, small centers should be established in which expression is given to the responsibility of the country for achieving its own swaraj—that is to say, its own welfare as a whole and not only in regard to its supply of homespun thread."[14] Tagore appears to contribute to the view that instead of a boundary limiting the understanding of people, the concept or idea must intend to be peripatetic, quite in the style of peripatetic philosophers who would travel with their scholarship, crossing different boundaries and attract students on their way. In his response to Gandhi, the poet's tone emphasizes the message that borders are like "disciplines" meant to be followed by a cadre. However, people are not a regimented group; they have "imagination," which is not a particular "thing" to be kept static in someplace; it must be allowed to flourish, so crossing and recrossing does not become a matter of offense. Anticipating a thesis that spinning may be posed as an act of creativity, Tagore says: "It may be argued that spinning is also a creative act. But that is not so: for, by turning, its wheelman merely becomes an appendage of the Charka; that is to say, he but does himself what a machine might have done: he converts his living energy into a dead turning movement. The machine is solitary because being devoid of mind, it is sufficient unto itself and knows nothing outside itself."[15] By such observations, Tagore implied Gandhi's "instruction" to spin as a compulsory act for the Congress members and other people as authoritative and, hence, a boundary that would confine people to inhibiting the same unwillingly.

Even when so young, Tagore had decided to free himself after experiencing the strict implementation of the daily routine imposed on him as painful and demeaning as they were. In later years, he must have realized the irony of such institutions, which, on the one hand, systematically try to throttle freedom and talk, on the other hand, of freedom being imperative to every human being, presenting instances of personalities from history who strived and struggled to death like Ram Mohan Roy and others to save freedom and liberty of people. To young students, this creates a sense of obscurity, added to the great inconvenience the children face while studying in colonial institutions through a foreign language. In the Indian context, it was English. This kind of mechanism of designing borders may be seen as a "force" that propels rebellion against the system, compelling people to cross borders.

Borders, be it geographical, cultural, linguistic, or any other, represent tension and war. Since institutions construct borders with leaders who have a hegemonic relation with their creation, it then necessarily follows that leadership stands for the centralization of power, as is evident in all institutions and systems. Experiencing and reviewing the war histories, women have always felt something fundamentally disturbing and disgusting about the war theories related to liberation. They have shown unhappiness with war, causing the disappearance of their folks. Women have vigorously made this point that they are not just beings but are sensible beings and that they not only feel but are rational

74 TOWARD A NEW ART OF BORDER CROSSING

to decide that war cannot simply be another word for human relations. If politics, economics, and religion could not easily shelve themselves from such a disappointing comparison, why should arms and war history be able to? It is important to note that any theory centering on the significance of liberation or emancipation of people through war does not appear to be rational. Women are often taken as the subject of war study or theory. They are used as tableaus or models to be associated with the war "glamour." The war that affects them is daunting and undreamt of ways.

Being fully aware of the nature of centralization of power that the borders are associated with, Tagore would largely try to remain unattached to any idea of boundaries as he believed that boundaries emerged from certain assumptions which were then imposed in the name of rules to be followed or duties to be performed. As mentioned above, ideas of boundary symbolize a centralization of power that the imperial regime would always like to use against the subject—colonized to enslave and labeled by the administration as "natives" and treated as slaves like any African native similarly colonized. Critical here is to draw attention to Ngugi wa Thiong'o's, the African scholar who opposed centralization in any form and, like Tagore, welcomed the system of inter-participation by the term "globalectics," which would not confine people within any border. In his book on "Globalectics [...]" Thiongo'o says: "Globalectics is derived from the shape of the globe. On its surface, there is no one center; any point is equally a center. As for the internal center of the globe, all points on the surface are equidistant to it—like the spokes of a bicycle wheel that meet at the hub. Globalectics combine the global and the dialectical to describe a mutually affecting dialogue, or multi-logue, in the phenomena of nature and nurture in a global space that's rapidly transcending that of the artificially bounded, as nation and region" (Ngugi 2012: 8).[16] That this inter-participation can be abundantly found, especially in the oral literature, was revealed to Tagore quite early in life as his home was welcoming many talents well established in storytelling music, poetry, proverbs, and so on. He needed to find the boundaries more distinct and coherent in their presentation. He would remember how he enjoyed his young-age freedom with courage, acquainting himself with a kind of resistance to welcome the reading of the wandering litterateur: "If you ask me what gave me boldness when I was young, I should say that one thing was my early acquaintance with the old Vaishnava poets of Bengal, full of freedom of meter and courage of expression. I think I was only twelve when these poems were first reprinted. I surreptitiously got hold of copies from the desks of my elders. For the edification of the young, I must confess that this was not right for a boy of my age. I should have been passing my examinations. I must also admit that the greater part of these lyrics was erotic and not quite suited to a boy just about to reach his teens. But my imagination was fully occupied with the beauty of their words, and their breath, heavily laden with voluptuousness, passed over my mind without distracting it" (Tagore 1925: 38).[17]

A Different Ontology

Boundaries are always opposed, at least not when they are treated like the Buddhist concept of "flux." To embrace categories and boundaries as monolith would stop the growth of "Being" as a fixed entity. Allowing it's "Becoming" by proposing a different ontology, it is possible to rearticulate the Being. The Buddha did not emphasize a fixed entity; instead, he pointed out "Anatta" (or Non-Being) as an important dynamic to understand the freedom from boundaries or bondages leading to universal humanism without the distinctions of caste and class ethnicity or any other constructs. The concept of flux helps us understand how things have an ongoing interaction. He implied that things in the world must be seen as ongoing interactions and not as static projects to work with. Such ongoing interactions attempt to resist static boundaries, borders, colonial hierarchies, or any hegemonic and centralized system. This is why Ngugi's globalectics aim to "transcend the artificially bounded [...] nation and region" (Ngugi 2012: 8)[18] can help the process of re-negotiation, which is yet another way of denying borders. Hence, as a non-static process like the flux referred to earlier, it is possible through the re-negotiation to make the epistemic subject realize that constructing the subject has to be a continuous part of the process. The deep insight that Tagore expresses regarding the absence of such a process is impressive: "One need not dive deep, it seems to me, to discover the problem of India; it is so plainly evident on the surface. Our country is divided by numberless differences—physical, social, linguistic, and religious. I need not cite modern instances of animosity which divide white men from negroes in your own country and exclude Asiatics from European colonies. At the sacrifice of her own political welfare, she has, through long ages, borne this great burden of heterogeneity, patiently working all the time to evolve out of these warring contradictions a great synthesis. Now is when she must begin to build, and dead arrangements must gradually give way to living construction and organic growth. All the illustrious names of our country have been those who came to bridge over the differences of colours and scriptures and recognize all that is highest and best as the common heritage of humanity. Our emperors Asoka and Akbar, our philosophers Shankara and Ramanuja, our spiritual masters Kabir, Nanak, Chaitanya, and others belong to various sects and castes, some of them of the very 'lowest', but still they occupy the ever sacred seat of guru, which is the highest honour that India confers on her children. This shows that even in the darkest of her days, the consciousness of her true power and purpose has never forsaken her" (Tagore 1910: 184–187).[19]

In the same context, Tagore's music plays an important role in supporting the re-negotiation through the idea of new "borders" through the "absence of borders" and creating alternative borders to cross again. This process does not render a center or a periphery. On the contrary, it becomes an alternative way of being both borders, an absence of borders and new borders, and keeps evolving thus through dialectical processes. While it is also interesting to find out how this perspective of Tagore resembles the notion of Edouard Glissant (1928–2011), a French writer, poet, and philosopher from Martinique and an influential figure in the Caribbean thought, who in his "Poetics of Relation" has done away with the idea of center and periphery, as he says: "The poet's words lead from periphery to periphery, and, yes, it reproduces the track of circular nomadism; that is, it makes every periphery into a centre; furthermore, it abolishes the very notion of centre and periphery" (Glissant 1997: 29).[20] Tagore's denial and acceptance of the conventional border idea had the profundity as the process helped him to create and recreate according to his artistic demands. Sociologist and writer Dhurjati Prasad Mukerji (1894–1961) explains how a re-orientation by Tagore becomes an artistic production when he crosses the boundary of folk like baul and other forms of music to go into the classical arena or vice versa. Mukerji points out: "The introduction of baul, bhatial and kirtan in the classical compositions marked a notable departure. In a sense, this kind of introduction always registered a crisis, a great divide. The folk tunes had been there, but whenever the classical melodic pattern was attenuated, it entered them again and formed a new vogue" (Mukerji 1961: 180–186).[21] As music is a kind of expression of an inner voice, it brings the spontaneous mode of expression to the forms of aesthetics, which in turn helps to liberate one from opposition or subordination by directing the subject toward an imagination of alienation, bringing contradictory feelings of both pain and joy which is critical for aesthetic enjoyment, when the poet sings, "O my beloved Lord, [...] may my pain of separation from you caused by the distance between you and me be a melodious joy" (Tagore 1831: 95).[22] That alienation can be a source of joy is clearly very un-Marxian, as can be seen in the context of Marxian discourse on labor theory. Tagore's poetic imagination would bring a blending of different musical compositions and yet attribute independence to them by crossing the traditional borders. Mukerji explains in detail about this independence thus, "The structure of the peculiar property of Tagore's music was the fact that each song was an independent entity with the result that each entity carved out a kingdom fit for itself in its own ways, and each rule formulated its own regulations. Instead of one 'chhayanat',[23] developing all or nearly all the forms of chhayanat, there would be many forms of chhayanats, each framing its character according to each song of the genus chhayanat. Leaving aside the combination of Chhaya and nat and taking them as one, this chhayanat would mix with chhayanats and become *sui generis*. The result was that any raga became many songs with each raga's special properties" (Mukerji 2010: 182–183).[24]

However, this kind of dislodging and re-engaging or transgressing can also create anxiety for those who believe that the spirit of 'dislodging' creates an uncomfortable zone and, therefore, becomes incomprehensible as the denial of traditional approach becomes an attempt toward violating a fixed border and consequently, people feel threatened. This is what exactly happened with Ludwig Wittgenstein (1889–1951), the brilliant German philosopher. In his review of the newly published book titled *Wittgenstein's Family Letters: Corresponding with Ludwig*,[25] Jonathan Ree reveals how he was misrepresented by Russell, who initially liked him for his views, feeling overwhelmed though gradually began to oppose him as he disagreed with his dynamic viewpoints. For example, Wittgenstein had in his "book Der Satz (a word that evokes not only 'sentence' but also 'set' or 'musical movement'), combined philosophical boldness of a kind that Russell appreciated, with ingenious literary experimentation, which Russell didn't like at all" (Ree 2018: 7).[26] Wittgenstein could not publish the book. Continuing, Ree mentions the source of Russell's misunderstanding and how Wittgenstein was rebuffed. Referring to his view that "Philosophy is not a theory but an activity, and hence: 'Whereof one cannot speak, thereof one must be silent', Ree explains that "Russell had taken pity on his abandoned book and got it published in 1922, though with a rebarbative title—Tractatus Logico Philosophicus—and a ponderous introduction in which he claimed that Wittgenstein's aim was to 'prevent non-sense' by constructing a 'logically perfect language'. This may be what Russell would have liked Wittgenstein to say, but it was a spectacular misrepresentation of what he had actually written" (Ree 2018: 7).[27] A distance was created between Wittgenstein and Russell. It appears that Russell could no more appreciate Wittgenstein's independent philosophical approach and insisted on what he thought should be the one to such an extent that in the introduction of the book, as Ree mentions, "He concluded by sniping at his former pupil for relapsing into 'mysticism', joking with supreme self-satisfaction that 'Mr. Wittgenstein manages to say a good deal about what cannot be said. Wittgenstein was appalled to discover a band of philosophical enthusiasts who believed that the Tractatus justified in treating religion as a joke and morality as no more than an expression of raw emotion" (Ree 2018: 8).[28] The idea of this re-negotiation should also be true in cases of other art forms.

As a fundamental critic of the idea of boundaries as a monolith, Tagore points out how, from a structured boundary, it is a joy always for him to experience aesthetic delight and peace of mind by joining the non-monolith Nature that is borderless and boundless yet creates temporary boundaries sometimes very aesthetic in appearance and at other times rugged and unapproachable but attractive in a different way. It is a kind of structural change that an individual realizes that occurs only when it appears as a revelation to him/her. In fact, Nature's crucial dimension of freedom is rarely appreciated by human beings who are always bound and bordered and, hence, unable to comprehend and engage themselves with Her. Tagore says: "From the first time that I can remember, I was passionately fond of Nature. Oh, it used to make me mad with joy when I saw the clouds come up in the sky one by one. Even in those early days, I felt that a very intense and intimate companionship surrounded me, though I do not know how to name it. I had such exceeding love for Nature, that I cannot think in what way to describe it to you; but she was a kind of loving companion, always with me, and always revealing to me some fresh beauty" (Tagore 1912: 22).[29] He expressed this feeling of intensity when he says he felt as if he became the part of Nature herself. He said: "The sky seemed to bring to me the call of personal companionship, and all my heart my whole body, in fact—used to drink in at a draught the overflowing light and peace of those silent hours. I was anxious never to miss a single morning because each one was precious to me, more precious than gold to a miser. I am certain I felt a larger meaning of myself when the barrier vanished between me and what was beyond myself" (Tagore 1931: 98).[30] This idea of the vanishing of barriers remains oriented in all his reflections on his literary ventures and political activism. Using violent methods to gain the objective or to reach the goal was never the solution, felt Tagore. He expressed displeasure regarding the lack of insights into such behavior because, as he says, "The most important fact of the present age is that all the different races of men have come close together. And again, we are confronted with two alternatives. The problem is whether the different groups of people shall go on fighting with one another or find out some true basis of reconciliation and mutual help; whether it will be interminable competition or cooperation" (Tagore 1917: 97–101).[31] It's important to see how Tagore's engagement to go beyond the barriers without being self-assertive brings in a theoretical dimension of a people-oriented and non-colonial project that facilitates recognition of people's rights to resort to political action but not in a hegemonic way, which the nation-state generally does to make people powerless, obvious in this insightful remark, "India has never had a real sense of nationalism. Even though from childhood I had been taught that the idolatry of a nation is almost better than reverence for God and humanity, I believe I have outgrown that teaching, and it is my conviction that my countrymen will truly gain their India by fighting against that education which teaches them that a country is greater than the ideals of humanity" (Idem).[32]

Further, it is also important to see how Tagore appears to suggest a resultant identity of Nature and Human beings, which, besides rendering a sense of aesthetic joy, also implies that we, too, become unbound and without barriers like her, "The sky is free, the fields limitless and the sun merges them into one blazing whole. Amid this, man seems so trivial [...]." The intellectual concerns generally miss this perspective, though young children can instantly communicate with Nature and animals. It's not a matter of conjecture that the intellectual concerns generally attempt to essentialize Nature. Besides reducing her to an object of enjoyment only, it also fails to perceive the relationship of human beings with her as an act of inclusivity, which necessarily affects the creative faculty of humans. The human being does not realize that by keeping Nature at a distance or alienating her, one loses the capability to be ever a creative being. As a creative writer, Tagore introduces this challenge for a serious reflection. He says, "When I became one with the universe when the green grass grew on my very Being, and the autumn light-drenched me when the pores of my youthful body were aroused by the fragrance of the mother earth all green with vegetation, when I lay under the bright sky, spreading myself over distant land and waters. I can even now remember the sensation of those moments when the autumn sun cast unspoken happiness over me, and a larger-than-life creative power enter my subconscious. It is as if that consciousness passed from me into every blade of grass and the roots of every tree, causing the mustard fields and the leaves of the coconut palm to quiver with the outburst of life's passion" (Tagore 1400: 73).[33] This is exactly why the literature and philosophy in Indian tradition refer to Nature as a person with the terms like Prakriti, Prithivi, Vasudha, and so on, because she sustains everyone and in Tagore's words, "In these I recognized the ministrations of a Mother" (Tagore 1933: 208).[34] These terms are indicative of the feminine gender. Besides, this perspective points out the relationship between human beings and Nature as a confirmation of inclusivity and calls for a critique of the theory of alienation and colonial perception.

Conclusion

In this context, it is necessary to understand that the advent of colonialism impacted the cultures of many lands, including India, seriously, one effect of which is uprooting the resources of those lands by treating them as commodities to pursue the administration's interest. This is bound to be the experience of any country which has been colonized. Such an administration demonstrated that there could only be a power relationship between it and the rest of the country with its natural resources. Under such circumstances, it is interesting to see how Tagore's engagement with Nature could be considered an anti-colonial critique, bringing home the point that the mechanics of trade relations pursued by the colonial administration could never be a means for its sustenance of any relationship whatsoever which is intended to pursue, not to mention how trivial it is. Tagore says, "I sat wondering: Why is there this deep shade of melancholy over the fields and river banks, the sky and sunshine of our country? I came to the conclusion that it is because, for us, nature is the most important thing. In the midst of this, man seems so trivial [...] Where Nature is ever hidden and cowers under mist and cloud, snow and darkness, there man feels himself master; he regards his desires, his work as permanent; he wants to perpetuate them, [...] he raises monuments, he writes biographies, [...] so busy he is that he has not the time to consider how many monuments crumble, how often names are forgotten" (Tagore 1921: 27–30).[35] It's significant to note how the perspective of Tagore regarding Nature has become a part of global consciousness mediated by especially the younger generation members. They also demand the de-politicization of environmental issues to cross barriers and borders to find a solution to save the environment by addressing the fundamental dimensions of the problem. These movements in many parts of the world regarding environmental issues symbolize the relationship that Tagore implied, and that which the vested interests are ignoring would efface both the interests of earth and of human history. The participators of this movement are making us aware that we, the elderly generation, are responsible for bringing back slavery as we have become slaves to the market economy, that we are equally responsible for bringing back colonialism by colonizing earth and, we are, therefore, responsible for neo-colonialism today. We must become aware that by treating earth or Nature as something inferior to us is the typical characteristic of any colonial relationship. Further, we must also become aware of the behavior and attitude of many of the cultures that treat Nature on par with humans and thus try their best to save natural resources. Can we possibly reflect on the fact that nature or the environment does not need us and does not depend on human beings, but we, human beings, clearly depend on her? This singularity, therefore, in a genuine sense, should be the rationale that we should draw to acknowledge that the tension that we have created between Nature and us needs to be dissolved not on our terms but on Nature's terms. Tagore's approach, in this sense, is crucial that the transformation must come from within the subject, that our idiosyncrasy and self-assertion must be challenged in our approach to Nature, which need not bring any anxiety whatsoever. "I have no anxiety about the world of Nature," says Tagore. "The sun does not wait to be trimmed by me. But from the early morning, all my thoughts are occupied by this little world of myself. Its importance is owing to the fact that I have a world given to me. It's great that I have the power to make it worthy of its relationship with me." (Tagore 1929: 30).[36] Can we not build such a new relationship landscape?

Notes

1 www.indiatoday.in Accessed on August 20, 2019. U.S. President Richard Nixon's 1972 visit to the People's Republic of China was an essential diplomatic overture.

2 Rabindranath Tagore to Edwin Montagu, April 6, 1918, Calcutta. Ms Accession No. 350. pp. 45–49, in English. (Rabindra Bhavana Archive). Edwin Samuel Montagu (1879–1924), British Liberal Politician, Secretary of State for India, 1917–1922. Ref. Uma Dasgupta, 2010. Ed. *My Life in My Words*. New Delhi, Penguin Books.

3 Bhattacharya, S., 1997. "The Cult of the Charka" in Ed, *The Mahatma and the Poet: Letters and Debates Between Gandhi and Tagore 1915–1941*, New Delhi, National Book Trust.

4 Idem.

5 Idem.

6 Thapar, Romila. 2002. *The Penguin History of Early India*. New Delhi, Penguin Books.

7 Idem.

8 Idem.

9 Idem.

10 Idem.

11 Tagore, Rabindranath. 1925. "Autobiographical," Talk in China. Calcutta, Viswa-Bharati.

12 Tagore, Rabindranath. 1901. "A Poet's School," Santiniketan Vidyalaya. 1901, 2000. Calcutta, Viswa-Bharati.

13 Bhattacharya, S., 1997. "The Cult of the Charka" in Ed, *The Mahatma and the Poet: Letters and Debates Between Gandhi and Tagore 1915–1941*, New Delhi, National Book Trust.

14 Idem.

15 Idem.

16 Thiong'o, wa Ngugi. 2012. *Globalectics: Theory and the Politics of Knowing*. New York, Columbia University Press.

17 Tagore. 1925. Talk in China.

18 Ngugi. 2012.

19 Tagore. 1910. "The Problem of India," A Letter to Myron H. Phelps Kolkata, Santiniketan, January 4, 1909, in *the Modern Review*, August 1910.

20 Glissant, Edouard, and Betsy Wing. (1997. Print). *Poetics of Relation*. Ann Arbor. University of Michigan Press.

21 Mukerji, D.P. 1961. *Tagore's Music in Rabindranath Tagore: A Centenary Volume 1861–1961*. Delhi, Sahitya Akademi.

22 Tagore, R.1932. *Gitabitan (Bengali Original)*. *Kolkata, Vishwabharati, Santiniketan*. (The above translation is by the author of this paper).

23 A composition (called Raga) in Indian classical music.

24 Mukerji. 2010.

25 McGuinness, Brian. 2018. Ed. *Wittgenstein's Family Letters: Corresponding with Ludwig*, Trans Peter Winslow. London, Bloomsbury, quoted in London Review of Books, November 21, 2019, by Jonathan Ree.

26 Ree, Jonathan. 2018. "The Young Man One Hopes For" in *London Review of Books*. London. November 21, 2019.

27 Ree, 2018.

28 Ree 2018

29 Tagore 1912, to C.F. Andrews, in conversation, London, September 1912. Letters to a Friend.

30 Tagore, R. 1931. The Religion of Man: The Hibbert Lectures for 1930. London, George Allen and Unwin.

31 Tagore, R. 1917. "Nationalism in India," *Nationalism*, New York, Macmillan.

NEW ARTS OF BORDER CROSSING

32 Tagore, R. 1917.

33 Tagore, R. 1400. *Atmaparichay, Reprint, Calcutta, Visva-Bharati (1993)* Trans. (*Knowing Oneself*) Uma Dasgupta.

34 Tagore,R. 1933. *My Reminiscences.* London, Macmillan.

35 Tagore, R. 1921. *Glimpses of Bengal: The Letters of Sir Rabindranath Tagore 1885–1895.* London, Macmillan.

36 Tagore, R. 1929. "Thoughts from Rabindranath Tagore," *English Writings*, Volume III. London, Macmillan.

Chapter 6

GARRISON—THOREAU—GANDHI: TRANSCENDING BORDERS

Christian Bartolf, Dominique Miething, and Vishnu Varatharajan

Introduction

Two political borders are remarkably significant for the history of nonviolent resistance:

1. The border between Mexico and the USA, which shifted by annexations and wars, resulting in the expansion of the exploitation system of slavery to the newly conquered territories. Henry David Thoreau (1817–1862) opposed slavery and war: by public speeches and civil disobedience through tax resistance.
2. The border between Natal and Transvaal in South Africa, which Indian nonviolent resisters crossed as an act of civil disobedience during the Epic March in November 1913, organized by Mohandas Karamchand Gandhi (1869–1948) and Hermann Kallenbach (1871–1945), the owner of Tolstoy Farm (1910–1913).

Both Thoreau and Gandhi, contributed to the emancipation struggle against slavery and war by example: Thoreau's resistance was individual civil disobedience, and Gandhi's border crossing was a collective act of defiance against degrading and oppressive legislation—after he had introduced the notion Satyagraha in the year 1908, emphasizing not only "firmness in Truth" (satyāgraha), but awareness, heart and spirit: courage, equanimity, fearlessness, humility, persistence, righteousness—soul-force. Or in the words of American abolitionist, friend of the New England Transcendentalists, and poet James Russell Lowell (1819–1891):

They are slaves who fear to speak
For the fallen and the weak;
They are slaves who will not choose
Hatred, scoffing, and abuse,
Rather than in silence shrink
From the truth they needs must think;
They are slaves who dare not be
In the right with two or three. (Lowell 1843, p. 211f.)
—James Russell Lowell: *Stanzas. Sung at the Anti-Slavery Picnic in Dedham, on the Anniversary of West-India Emancipation, August 1, 1843*

84 TOWARD A NEW ART OF BORDER CROSSING

We comprehend the transcending of borders as an overarching motto for all those who strove for the abolition of slavery, aimed at establishing cooperative settlements to find alternatives to private property, and denounced racist discrimination, human rights violations, violence, and war. Thus, we demonstrate that the evolution of nonviolent resistance itself is deeply entrenched within the history of human emancipation and pacifist ethics—from the American abolitionists William Lloyd Garrison (1805–1879), Adin Ballou (1803–1890), and Ralph Waldo Emerson (1803–1882) to the Russian writer Leo Tolstoy (1828–1910).

Underground Railroad

Not by the sword shall your deliverance be
Not by the shedding of your masters' blood;
Not by rebellion—or foul treachery,
Upspringing suddenly, like swelling flood:
Revenge and rapine ne'er did bring forth good.
God's time is best!—nor will it long delay
Even now your barren cause begins to bud,
And glorious shall the fruit be!—Watch and pray,
For, lo ! the kindling dawn, that ushers in the day! (Garrison 1852, p. 65)
—William Lloyd Garrison: *Universal Emancipation*

Abolitionism denotes the social movement to end slavery. In northern America, abolitionism has taken many different forms. Illegally crossing the border to Canada for freedom was one of them: during the early to mid-nineteenth century in the USA, the Underground Railroad emerged as a clandestine network of hidden pathways and secure havens. "The origin of the term 'Underground Railroad' has several versions. One story [...] places the origin in Washington, DC, in 1839, when allegedly a fugitive slave, after being tortured, claimed that he was to have been sent north, where 'the railroad ran underground all the way to Boston'." (Blight 2004, p. 3). It seems that the concept was implied in an editorial by Hiram Wilson (1803–1864) in the anti-slavery newspaper *The Liberator*, who asked: "Could a great republican railroad be constructed from Mason to Dixon's to the Canada line, upon which fugitives from slavery might come pouring into this province, at the rate of five hundred per day, its entire length would have the smile of heaven by day, and freedom's great *polar lamp* to guide, and the northern lights to cheer the nightly train." (Vol. IX, No. 41, October 1, 1839, p. 1. Emphasis in the original) An explicit reference to the verbatim term "the underground railroad" in *The Liberator* can be found in the October 11 issue of 1842 (Vol. XII, No. 41, p. 163).

Driven by the belief that slavery contradicted the ethical teachings of Jesus, the Religious Society of Friends (Quakers), Congregationalists, Wesleyan Methodists, and Reformed Presbyterians, along with the antislavery groups clashed with mainstream Christian denominations on the crime of slavery.

Those who sought freedom from slavery in the south traveled on a route leading up the Appalachian Mountains. Abolitionist Harriet Tubman (c. 1820–1913), for instance,

GARRISON—THOREAU—GANDHI

passed through Harpers Ferry, West Virginia, onto northeastern Ohio and Lake Erie from where a boat took her to Canada. A smaller group of those fleeing slavery opted for a route starting in New York or New England. They passed through Syracuse, which was notable as the residence of social reformer Samuel Joseph May (1797–1871), and then proceeded to Rochester, New York, the home of the well-known orator and writer Frederick Douglass (c. 1817–1895). Crossing either the Niagara River or Lake Ontario, they finally found sanctuary in Canada. For those who took the path through the New York Adirondack Mountains, sometimes passing through Black communities like Timbuctoo, New York, their route led them into Canada via Ogdensburg on the St. Lawrence River, or through Lake Champlain with the assistance of Joshua Young (1823–1904), a Unitarian minister, who led the ceremony for the abolitionist John Brown (1800–1859). Brown was executed for an armed assault on the United States Armory and Arsenal at Harpers Ferry, Virginia, in 1859, hoping to incite a revolt against slavery. Years before, Brown himself had frequented yet another route in the Underground Railroad network, leading from western Missouri to Kansas and Iowa to Chicago and the Detroit River.

William Lloyd Garrison

One of the oftentimes overlooked champions of the abolitionist movement was William Lloyd Garrison, a typesetter, journalist, and social reformer. Indicative of Garrison's place in the cultural memory of the USA is the site of his former home on today's 17 Highland Park Street, Roxbury, Boston. The William Lloyd Garrison House was designated a National Historic Landmark in 1965. According to an official Study Report by the Boston Landmark Commission, Garrison "lived in the house from 1864 until his death in 1879. The property, affectionately named 'Rockledge,' remained in the ownership of the Garrison family until 1900. The Garrison House was maintained for a brief period between 1900 and 1904 by the Rock Ledge Improvement Association, an organization of black men and women who intended to preserve the house in Garrison's memory." (Loveday 2015, p. 5; see pp. 32ff. for more information on the Rock Ledge Improvement Association's continued involvement with the cause of the early civil rights movement and links to the Boston branch of the National Association for the Advancement of Colored People [NAACP]). Since 2012, the House has become a part of Emmanuel College's Notre Dame Campus.

In 1829, in Baltimore, Maryland, Garrison began contributing to the Quaker newspaper *Genius of Universal Emancipation*, before eventually taking on the editorship together with Benjamin Lundy (1789–1839). Initiating a recurring column, the "Black List", Garrison reported on and denounced the latest atrocities committed by collaborators with the system of slavery. In 1831, Garrison, together with his friend Isaac Knapp (1804–1843), established a weekly newspaper, *The Liberator*, and continued its publication in Boston until the Thirteenth Amendment brought an end to slavery in the USA in 1865. Garrison's debut article contained a confession and a statement of intent:

TOWARD A NEW ART OF BORDER CROSSING

> In Park-street Church, on the Fourth of July, 1829, in an address on slavery, I unreflectingly assented to the popular but pernicious doctrine of *gradual* abolition. I seize this opportunity to make a full and unequivocal recantation, and thus publicly to ask pardon of my God, of my country, and of my brethren the poor slaves, for having uttered a sentiment so full of timidity, injustice, and absurdity. A similar recantation, from my pen, was published in the Genius of Universal Emancipation at Baltimore, in September, 1829. My conscience is now satisfied.
>
> I am aware, that many object to the severity of my language; but is there not cause for severity? I *will* be as harsh as truth, and as uncompromising as justice. On this subject, I do not wish to think, or speak, or write, with moderation. No! no! Tell a man whose house is on fire, to give a moderate alarm; tell him to moderately rescue his wife from the hands of the ravisher; tell the mother to gradually extricate her babe from the fire into which it has fallen;—but urge me not to use moderation in a cause like the present. I am in earnest—I will not equivocate—I will not excuse—I will not retreat a single inch—AND I WILL BE HEARD. The apathy of the people is enough to make every statue leap from its pedestal, and to hasten the resurrection of the dead. (Garrison 1831, p. 1. Emphasis in the original)

Initially, Garrison stood firmly against violence, upholding Christian pacifism in the face of evil. While deeply impressed by his fellow Bostonian David Walker (1785–1830) (Newman 2018, p. 57), who less than a year before his death penned an *Appeal, in Four Articles; Together with a Preamble, to the Coloured Citizens of the World, but in particular, and very expressly to those of the United States of America* (written in Boston, State of Massachusetts, September 28, 1829, third and last edition with additional notes, corrections, &c., 1830), Garrison disagreed with the use of violence as a means of emancipation.

When the American Civil War erupted in 1861, however, Garrison underwent a significant transformation, forsaking some of his former beliefs and embracing both armed conflict and support for the Lincoln administration. Not only did Garrison play a pivotal role in establishing the American Anti-Slavery Society but also actively advocated for immediate and uncompensated emancipation, opposing the gradual and compensated approach. As early as December 6, 1833, in his "Declaration of Sentiments of the American Anti-Slavery Convention" in Philadelphia, Pennsylvania, Garrison went as far as demanding reparation payment to be made to all those dehumanized, exploited, and hurt by the system of racism and slavery:

> We maintain that no compensation should be given to the planters emancipating the slaves:
>
> Because it would be a surrender of the great fundamental principle that man cannot hold property in man:
>
> Because slavery is a crime, and therefore is not an article to be sold:
>
> Because the holders of slaves are not the just proprietors of what they claim; freeing the slaves is not depriving them of property, but restoring it to its rightful owner; it is not wronging the master, but righting the slave—restoring him to himself:
>
> Because immediate and general emancipation would only destroy nominal, not real property; it would not amputate a limb or break a bone of the slaves, but by infusing motives into their breasts, would make them doubly valuable to the masters as free labourers; and
>
> Because, if compensation is to be given at all, it should be given to the outraged and guiltless slaves, and not to those who have plundered and abused them.

We regard as delusive, cruel, and dangerous, any scheme of expatriation, which pretends to aid, either directly or indirectly, in the emancipation of the slaves, or to be a substitute for the immediate and total abolition of slavery. (Garrison 1852, p. 69f.)

Following this 1833 Declaration, Garrison was among the first people to organize abolitionism more forcefully and systematically. For this purpose, he founded two influential organizations:

First, the New England Anti-Slavery Society (1832–1835), reorganized in 1835 as the Massachusetts Anti-Slavery Society (Boston), an auxiliary of the American Anti-Slavery Society (since 1833), with Garrison as editor of the society's journal *The Liberator*. Among the journal's readers was Frederick Douglass, who initially joined forces with Garrison, going on lecture tours with him in 1843 (Newman 2018, pp. 71 and 85), with Garrison also distributing the autobiographical memoir *Narrative of the Life of Frederick Douglass, an American Slave* (1845).

Second, the New England Non-Resistance Society was founded in September 1838. Its members refused to pledge allegiance to human government and favored secession from the slaveholding American South (Brock 1968, pp. 523–615). Merging the ethics of nonviolence with the cause of abolitionism, Garrison's "Declaration of Sentiments adopted by the Peace Convention, held in Boston, September 18, 19 and 20, 1838" (printed in *The Liberator*, September 28, 1838, p. 2, reprinted in Garrison 1852, pp. 72–77) was directed against nationalism, racism, and sexism, and refused any participation in acts or institutions of violence, for instance, even opposition to individual acts of self-defense. Among the Society's members were Adin Ballou, the transcendentalist Amos Bronson Alcott (1799–1888), and Maria Weston Chapman (1806–1885). Together with Edmund Quincy (1808–1877) and Garrison, Chapman co-edited the Society's journal *The Non-Resistant* (1839–1845) for several years, while also serving on the executive committee of American Anti-Slavery Society as an elected member.

The Non-Resistance Principle

A distinctive characteristic of Garrison's efforts to bring about the destruction of slavery is the underlying principle of nonresistance, i.e., the rejection of the use of force in resisting violence in war, in jurisdiction (death penalty), and self-defense. The term's meaning may also encompass "the practice or principle of not resisting authority, even when it is unjustly exercised" (Oxford English Dictionary 2023). Sometimes also spelled nonresistance, this principle is integral to nonviolent pacifism, for it rejects all physical violence at the individual, group, state, or international level. Those practicing nonresistance do so, because of their refusal to retaliate. Especially Christian adherents refer to Jesus' Sermon on the Mount in their opposition to any kind of revenge (cf. Matthew 5: 38–42)

Among the better-known proponents of nonresistance were Leo Tolstoy and Mahatma Gandhi. As we will highlight below, Gandhi's application of the principle on a mass scale, however, entailed a much more active approach to nonviolent resistance than the connotation of the term nonresistance itself and its original usage may suggest, for instance, in the life and work of Garrison's contemporary Adin Ballou.

Ballou, an experienced Universalist and Unitarian minister, presided over the New England Non-Resistance Society from 1843 onward. Hoping to convince a wider audience of his ideal, he disseminated tracts such as "Catechism of Non-Resistance" (first published in his own journal *The Practical Christian. Devoted to Truth and Righteousness*, Vol. 5, No. 5, July 20, 1844, p. 22 and in Garrison's *The Liberator*, Vol. XIV, No. 34, August 23, 1844, p. 132) and *Christian Non-resistance, in All Its Important Bearings, Illustrated and Defended* (1846). Remembered today as the founder of the Hopedale Community (1843–1857) in Milford, Massachusetts, he attempted to put his ideals for an egalitarian society into practice and reflected upon this in his book *Practical Christian Socialism: A Conversational Exposition of the True System of Human Society* (1854). Ballou's community emphasized several progressive causes such as abolitionism, education, spiritualism, temperance, and women's rights.

Nonresistance and civil disobedience are closely related and of significance to North American abolitionists. Their circles strongly intersected with the Transcendentalist movement in New England.

Abolitionism and Transcendentalism: Emerson, Alcott, and Thoreau

It is within the context of the New England transcendentalist movement since the 1830s that civil disobedience as a deliberate transgression of an unjust law emerged as a new concept of nonviolent resistance. Transcendentalism is associated with one of its foremost writers, Ralph Waldo Emerson and with Concord, Massachusetts, where Emerson lived from 1835 onward. The city was a hotbed for both, Abolitionism and Transcendentalism—of course, Henry David Thoreau, one of the city's best remembered natives, comes to mind—but also a city of former enslaved people such as Brister Freeman (1744–1822), whose lives at the literal fringes of society were still stricken by poverty and racism(see *Walden; or, Life in the Woods*, Chapter 14: "Former Inhabitants; and Winter Visitors" in: Thoreau 1854, p. 277; and esp. Lemire 2009 and also today's The Robbins House, 320 Monument Street, Concord Massachusetts, where the city's African American and antislavery history from the seventeenth through the nineteenth centuries is represented).

Transcendentalism, a spiritual movement to reform and renew society, developed out of a variety of sources. Of prime importance for its formulation were Emerson's essays such as "Self-Reliance" and "The Over-Soul" (first published in 1841) as well as his lecture "The Transcendentalist" given at the Masonic Temple in Boston, Massachusetts, in January 1842. Growing out of Unitarianism and inspired by Greek and Indian philosophies and Romanticism, transcendentalist philosophy emphasizes the freedom of conscience and the value of intellectual reason.

Prompted by the murder of the abolitionist publisher and Presbyterian minister Elijah Parish Lovejoy (1802–1837) on November 7, 1837, in Alton, Illinois—where Lovejoy shortly before had co-founded a chapter of Garrison's American Anti-Slavery Society (see reports of the murder in the November and December 1837 issues of *The Liberator*)—Emerson admitted to his admiration of Lovejoy's bravery: "[he] gave his breast to the bullets of a mob, for the rights of free speech and opinion, and died when

GARRISON—THOREAU—GANDHI

it was better not to live" (Emerson 1841, p. 217). Emerson's lecture, entitled "Heroism," delivered at the Masonic Temple in Boston, on January 24, 1838 (Emerson 1964, p. 327), may be regarded as his first public statement against slavery, albeit much less impressive and outspoken compared with his fiery address before the citizens of Concord on May 3, 1851, entitled "The Fugitive Slave Law," in which he claimed that it is a moral duty to break immoral laws such as the one in question, "on the earliest occasion" (Emerson 1911, p. 192f.).

Here, Emerson echoed his friend Henry David Thoreau's earlier call for "Resistance to Civil Government," first published by Elizabeth Palmer Peabody (1804–1894). She was a writer, teacher, and business manager of *The Dial*, the chief magazine of the Transcendentalists, edited by Margaret Fuller (1810–1850) since 1840. Peabody requested Thoreau's essay for her anthology *Aesthetic Papers* (Thoreau 1849). The text that Thoreau eventually submitted was most likely composed from his two-part lecture delivered before the members of the Concord Lyceum, convening on Wednesday evenings at the vestry of the Unitarian Church in Concord, Massachusetts. While Thoreau spoke about "The Relation of the Individual to the State" on January 26, 1848, the focus of the second part probably shifted quite considerably on February 16, 1848, when he reflected upon "The Rights and Duties of the Individual in Relation to the State" (Dean & Hoag 1995, pp. 153–155). These lectures addressed the question of why the author had refused to pay poll taxes for several years until he was arrested and spent a night in a prison cell. This was during the time when he lived in a small self-built cabin at the shore of Walden Pond between 1845 and 1847 when Thoreau wanted to deepen his understanding of the "over-soul" (Emerson) of ecology and humanity.

Today, the essay has become famous, circulating under the title "Civil Disobedience," a term neither appearing in the text, nor chosen by Thoreau himself, but applied to it only four years after his death by the editors, his sister Sophia Elizabeth Thoreau (1819–1879) and his friends William Ellery Channing II (1817–1901) and Ralph Waldo Emerson, of a fresh collection of some of Thoreau's writings (Thoreau 1866). Thoreau's essay became the blueprint for Mahatma Gandhi and Dr. Martin Luther King Jr. in their nonviolent emancipation struggles.

While certainly the most well-known example of public protest—Thoreau's refusal to pay the poll tax and his voluntary time in jail—was not singular, and one of his immediate role models was Amos Bronson Alcott, another member of Garrison's Non-Resistance Society (Broderick 1956). Alcott moved to Concord in April 1840 and deliberately had paid no poll tax to withdraw all cooperation with the state before his own arrest in January 1843. His prison time only lasted a few hours, for the anti-slavery lawyer and politician Samuel Hoar (1778–1856) paid what Alcott owed. Thus, it becomes clearer why Alcott, sitting in the audience of Thoreau's first lecture, rejoiced about the content in his diary entry of January 26, 1848: "Heard Thoreau's lecture before the Lyceum on the relation of the individual to the State—an admirable statement of the rights of the individual to self-government, and an attentive audience. His allusions to the Mexican War, to Mr. Hoar's expulsion from Carolina, his own imprisonment in Concord Jail for refusal to pay his tax, Mr. Hoar's payment of mine when taken to prison for a similar

90 TOWARD A NEW ART OF BORDER CROSSING

refusal, were all pertinent, well considered, and reasoned. I took great pleasure in this deed of Thoreau's." (as cited in Dean & Hoag 1995, p. 154).

Alcott was a philosopher and teacher. He founded and worked at the Temple School, Boston, Massachusetts, together with Elisabeth Peabody and Margaret Fuller. Alcott's interactions with students focused less on teacher-centered lectures and more on engaging in conversation with the class, avoiding corporal punishment, and deliberating upon consequences for rule infractions with his students. An abolitionist and advocate for women's rights, Alcott befriended Emerson and engaged in Transcendentalist debates on perfecting the human spirit and in practical experiments to reform society. Together with fellow tax-resister Charles Lane (1800–1870), Alcott advocated a vegan diet and in 1843 established an agrarian community, called Fruitlands, in Harvard, Massachusetts, where today the Fruitlands Museum is located.

Leo Tolstoy, the Abolitionists, and the Emancipation Struggle in South Africa

Leo Tolstoy admired the writings of Ballou, Garrison, and Thoreau. One tenet uniting these Americans and the Russian Count was the assumption that all governments inherently rest on violence or the permanent threat of the same—as long as these institutions prevail, they will present a major cause for war between human beings. Since the resort to violence was antithetical to the Christian ethics of non-retaliation, Tolstoy could easily invoke the American abolitionists to bolster his own philosophy of nonviolence. For this purpose, he corresponded with the family of Adin Ballou and funded Russian translations of some of his works.

Tolstoy repeatedly introduced these abolitionists' ideas to a wide readership in his books, letters, and pamphlets. For instance, in his *For Every Day* (in German: 1906; in English: 1909), but much more influential in his *The Kingdom of God Is Within You* (1893). This book is considered today a foundational treatise for Christian anarchism and canonical within the Tolstoyan nonviolence movement as evidenced by, for example, the Doukhobors (Spirit Wrestlers) and their representative Peter V. Verigin (1859–1924). Immediately banned in Russia, Tolstoy published the book one year later in German and English languages. Alluding to Luke 17:21, the subtitle already announces that Tolstoy set out to establish *Christianity not as a mystical doctrine but as a new understanding of life*. Throughout, Tolstoy reaffirms Jesus' teaching of non-retaliation found within the Sermon on the Mount, thereby countering all apologies of violence by Roman and medieval scholars, because God's commandment "Thou shalt not kill" is clear and applies to defensive violence, too.

Tolstoy discussed, praised, and quoted Garrison's 1838 "Declaration of Sentiments" and Ballou's "Catechism of Non-Resistance" originally published in 1844 (e.g., Tolstoy 1936, pp. 1–23) at length. When, in 1904, Tolstoy's secretary Vladimir Chertkov (1854–1936) together with Florence Holah (date of birth and death unknown) published a book-length biography of Garrison, Tolstoy happily provided an introductory appreciation:

GARRISON—THOREAU—GANDHI

Garrison, as a man enlightened by the Christian teaching, having begun with the practical aim of strife against slavery, very soon understood that the cause of slavery was not the casual temporary seizure by the Southerners of a few millions of negroes, but the ancient and universal recognition, contrary to the Christian teaching, of the right of coercion on the part of certain people in regard to certain others. A pretext for recognising this right has always been that men regarded it as possible to eradicate or diminish evil by brute force, *i.e.*, also by evil. Having once realised this fallacy, Garrison put forward against slavery neither the suffering of slaves, nor the cruelty of slaveholders, nor the social equality of men, but the eternal Christian law of refraining from opposing evil by violence, i.e., of 'non-resistance.' Garrison understood that which the most advanced among the fighters against slavery did not understand: that the only irrefutable argument against slavery is the denial of the right of any man over the liberty of another under any conditions whatsoever.

[...] the principle of non-resistance is not a principle of coercion but of concord and love, and therefore it cannot be made coercively binding upon men. The principle of non-resistance to evil by violence, which consists in the substitution of persuasion for brute force, can be only accepted voluntarily, and in whatever measure it is freely accepted by men and applied to life—i.e., according to the measure in which people renounce violence and establish their relations upon rational persuasion—only in that measure is true progress in the life of men accomplished. (Tolstoy 1904, p. vi f. and xi; reprinted also in Tolstoi 1924)

Tolstoy also recommended reading Thoreau's essay "Civil Disobedience" as early as 1896 in his letter to the editor of the German-language journal *Ohne Staat. Organ der idealistischen Anarchisten* (literally: Without the State. Organ of the Idealistic Anarchists), Eugen Heinrich Schmitt (1851–1916), who resided in Budapest, Hungary:

It is now fifty years since a not widely known, but very remarkable, American writer—Thoreau—not only clearly expressed that incompatibility in his admirable essay on 'Civil Disobedience,' but gave a practical example of such disobedience. Not wishing to be an accomplice or supporter of a government which legalized slavery, he declined to pay a tax demanded of him, and went to prison for it.

Thoreau refused to pay taxes to government, and evidently the same motives as actuated him would prevent men from serving a government. As, in your letter to the minister, you have admirably expressed it: you do not consider it compatible with your moral dignity to work for an institution which represents legalized murder and robbery.

Thoreau was, I think, the first to express this view. People paid scant attention to either his refusal or his article fifty years ago—the thing seemed so strange. It was put down to his eccentricity. Today your refusal attracts some attention, and, as is always the case when new truth is clearly expressed, it evokes a double surprise—first, surprise that a man should say such queer things, and then, surprise that I had not myself discovered what this man is saying; it is so certain and so obvious.

Such a truth as that a Christian must not be a soldier—*i.e.* a murderer—and must not be the servant of an institution maintained by violence and murder, is so certain, so clear and irrefutable, that to enable people to grasp it, discussion, proof, or eloquence are not necessary. For the majority of men to hear and understand this truth, it is only needful that it should be constantly repeated.

The truth that a Christian should not take part in murdering, or serve the chiefs of the murderers for a salary collected from the poor by force, is so plain and indisputable that

92   TOWARD A NEW ART OF BORDER CROSSING

> those who hear it cannot but agree with it. And if a man continues to act contrary to these truths after hearing them, it is only because he is accustomed to act contrary to them, and it is difficult to break the habit. Moreover, as long as most people act as he does, he will not, by acting contrary to the truth, lose the regard of the majority of those who are most respected. (Tolstoi 1902, p. 358f. Emphasis in the original)

The principle of nonresistance—aside from playing an important role in the nonviolent resistance movement led by the Tolstoyans during the Russian Revolution of 1905 (Gordeeva 2019)—was transmitted from Tolstoy to Gandhi. Let us remember that Henry David Thoreau's "Resistance to Civil Government" or "Civil Disobedience," translated into Gujarati by Gandhi for his *Indian Opinion* in 1907, became the basis (not only for the civil rights movement guided by Dr. Martin Luther King, Jr.) for Satyagraha in January 1908 with the fearless follower of the wisdom of Truth, Socrates, as role model (Bartolf, Miething & Varatharajan 2021). Gandhi emphasized the principle in the formative stages of the development of his nonviolent philosophy while at Tolstoy Farm, where he resided with Hermann Kallenbach, a German-Jewish architect, and friend of Gandhi (Bartolf & Sarid 1997).

Tolstoy Farm, near Lawley Station close to Johannesburg in South Africa, was founded as a cooperative settlement, with resemblance to an ashram, by Kallenbach and Gandhi during their South African Satyagraha campaign and movement between 1908 and 1914 (Bhana 1975). In 1910, Kallenbach purchased the land spanning 1100 acres and then donated Tolstoy Farm to serve as the campaign's center which aimed at combating discrimination against Indians in Transvaal. Approximately 80 people lived on the property permanently, more visited and stayed during daytime. The community's members refused to rely on outside help or servants for the preparation of meals or other daily chores. Thanks to his training as an architect, Kallenbach designed and built an additional three building: living quarters, a workshop, and a school (Bartolf & Sarid 1997, pp. 19ff.)

Following the establishment of his first farm in South Africa in 1904—Phoenix Settlement at Inanda near Phoenix and Durban in Natal—this second communal experiment honored the name of Russian novelist Leo Tolstoy, whose *The Kingdom of God Is Within You* profoundly influenced Gandhi's critique of violence. As Gandhi remarked, the book "overwhelmed me. It left an abiding impression on me. Before the independent thinking, profound morality, and the truthfulness of this book, all the books given me [...] seemed to pale into insignificance." (Gandhi 1927, p. 322)

The period from 1910 and 1913 stands out as one of the most intense phases of Indian struggle against injustice in South Africa, epitomized by "The Epic March" or "The Great March" (South African History Online n.d.). On October 29, 1913, under the leadership of Gandhi, several hundred men, women, and children embarked on a historic demonstration from Newcastle in the Natal Colony (today: KwaZulu-Natal) to the Transvaal. Their purpose was to publicly defy the Immigrants Regulation Act of 1913. Two additional groups of protestors followed Gandhi, one led by Thambi Naidoo (1875–1933), the other by the barrister Albert Christopher (1885–1960). The following day, the police arrested Gandhi at Palm Ford.

Naidoo, an early collaborator of Gandhi, served as an organizer of the Indian community at Newcastle, where he initiated the Satyagraha campaign. Gandhi himself laid out the satyagrahi's rules of conduct: patient submission and no retaliation to insult, flogging or arrest. For Gandhi, refusing to back down in the struggle against the discriminatory law, a series of arrests, releases on bail and re-arrests ensued during yet another march on November 6, 1913, with the participation of 127 women, 57 children, and 2037 men. At the height of the struggle, there were about fifty thousand so-called indentured laborers on strike and several thousand other Indians in jail. The Government resorted to armed repression, resulting in many deaths. A spontaneous strike by Indians in Natal came as a decisive turn when the violent clash with the police led to the killing and injury of several strikers. By the end of November 1913, produce markets and sugar mills in Durban and Pietermaritzburg stopped operating. Domestic workers at hotels, restaurants and homes refused to perform their tasks. Upon his release from prison in January 1914, Gandhi negotiated with General Smuts over the Indian Relief Bill, a law that nullified the discriminatory £3 tax on ex-indentured workers. The successful end of this Satyagraha campaign, marked by the agreement with Smuts, became a key moment for Gandhi's future recognition as a political authority in India still ruled by the British Empire. Here, more Satyagraha campaigns were to com: Gandhi continued to organize acts of civil disobedience, tax resistance, and nonviolent non-cooperation campaigns, reaching a climax with the 24-day Salt March from Sabarmati to Dandi, Gujarat, India, in 1930.

Epilogue

Recalling Niagara Falls as a crucial border crossing point for the Underground Railroad and a symbol for abolitionist efforts in the nineteenth century, the Niagara Movement (1905–1910) continued the struggle against racism and disenfranchisement in the USA in the post-Civil War era and paved the way for the nascent civil rights movement. The Niagara Movement preceded the NAACP (since 1909). Among the latter's founding members were activists such as the investigative journalist Ida Bell Wells (1862–1931) and William Edward Burghardt Du Bois (1868–1963), author of *The Souls of Black Folk* (1903) and advocate of Pan-Africanism.

While engaged in ideological conflict with Du Bois and opposed to the Niagara Movement's approach to emancipation, Booker Taliaferro Washington (1856–1915) and his Tuskegee Institute, established 1881 at Tuskegee, Alabama, had a notable influence on Gandhi (e.g., in his 1903 article "From Slave to College President," see Gandhi 1979). Washington also inspired John Langalibalele Dube (1871–1946) and Nokutela Dube (1873–1917) at Ohlange High School in Inanda, KwaZulu-Natal, founded in 1901, who were neighbors of Gandhi at Phoenix Settlement in South Africa.

Du Bois, in turn, who founded and edited the NAACP's monthly *The Crisis*, corresponded with Gandhi, "the greatest colored man in the world, and perhaps the greatest man in the world" (*The Crisis*, Vol. 36, No. 7, July 1929, p. 225), who, as per request of Du Bois, sent him a programmatic message (facsimile reproduced in ibid.), written. May 1, 1929, from India:

94 TOWARD A NEW ART OF BORDER CROSSING

Let not the 12 million Negroes be ashamed of the fact that they are the grandchildren of slaves. There is no dishonour in being slaves. There is dishonour in being slave-owners. But let us not think of honour or dishonour in connection with the past. Let us realise that the future is with those who would be truthful, pure, and loving. For, as the old wise men have said, truth ever is, untruth never was. Love alone binds and truth and love accrue only to the truly humble. (Gandhi 1929)

—Oppression! I have seen thee, face to face,
And met thy cruel eye and cloudy brow;
But thy soul-withering glance I fear not now—
For dread to prouder feelings doth give place,
Of deep abhorrence! Scorning the disgrace
Of slavish knees that at thy footstool bow,
I also kneel—but with far other vow
Do hail thee and thy herd of hirelings base :—
I swear, while life-blood warms my throbbing veins,
Still to oppose and thwart, with heart and hand.
Thy brutalizing sway—till Afric's chains
Are burst, and Freedom rules the rescued land,
Trampling Oppression and his iron rod :—
Such is the vow I take—so help me, God! (Garrison 1852, p. 64)
                —William Lloyd Garrison: *Commencement of The Liberator*,
                                    Boston, January 1, 1831

Sources

Bartolf, Christian, Dominique Miething and Vishnu Varatharajan. 2021. Thoreau—Tolstoy—Gandhi: The Origin of Satyagraha. In: *Roots, Routes and a New Awakening. Beyond One and Many and Alternative Planetary Futures*, edited by Ananta Kumar Giri, 133–148. Singapore: Springer Nature: Palgrave Macmillan.

Bartolf, Christian and Isa Sarid. 1997. *Hermann Kallenbach – Mahatma Gandhi's friend in South Africa*. Berlin: Gandhi-Informations-Zentrum.

Bhana, Surendra. 1975. The Tolstoy Farm: Gandhi's experiment in "Co-operative Commonwealth". *South African Historical Journal*, Vol. 7, No. 1: 88–100.

Blight, David W. (ed.). 2004. *Passages to Freedom: The Underground Railroad in History and Memory*. Washington, DC: Smithsonian Institution.

Brock, Peter. 1968. *Pacifism in the United States, from the Colonial Era to the First World War*. Princeton, N.J.: Princeton University Press.

Broderick, John C. 1956. Thoreau, Alcott, and the Poll Tax. *Studies in Philology*, Vol. 53, No. 4 (October): 612–626.

Dean, Bradley P. and Ronald Wesley Hoag. 1995. Thoreau's Lectures before Walden: An Annotated Calendar. *Studies in the American Renaissance*: 127–228.

Emerson, Ralph Waldo. 1964. *The Early Lectures of Ralph Waldo Emerson. Volume II: 1836–1838*. Cambridge: Harvard University Press.

Emerson, Ralph Waldo. 1911. The Fugitive Slave Law. In: *The Complete Works of Ralph Waldo Emerson: Miscellanies. Volume XI*, edited by Edward W. Emerson, 177–214. Boston/New York: Houghton Mifflin Company.

Emerson, Ralph Waldo. 1841. *Essays. First Series*. Boston: James Munroe and Company.

Gandhi, Mohandas Karamchand. 1979. From Slave to College President [*Indian Opinion*, 10 September 1903]. In: *The Collected Works of Mahatma Gandhi, Volume 3*, edited by The Publications Division, Ministry of Information and Broadcasting, Government of India, 529–532. Ahmedabad: Navajivan Trust.

Gandhi, Mohandas Karamchand. 1929. Message from Mahatma Gandhi, ca. May 1, 1929. *W. E. B. Du Bois Papers* (MS 312). Special Collections and University Archives, University of Massachusetts Amherst Libraries. https://credo.library.umass.edu/view/full/mums312-b181-i614 (access: 23.08.2023).

Gandhi, Mohandas Karamchand. 1927. *An Autobiography or The Story of My Experiments with Truth, Volume 1*. Translated from the original in Gujarati by Mahadev Desai. Ahmedabad: Navajivan Trust.

Garrison, William Lloyd. 1852. *Selections from the Writings and Speeches of William Lloyd Garrison*. Boston: R.F. Wallcut.

Garrison, William Lloyd. 1831. To the Public. *The Liberator* (Boston), Vol. 1, No.1 (January 1): 1.

Gordeeva, Irina. 2019. The Evolution of Tolstoyan Pacifism in the Russian Empire and the Soviet Union, 1900–1937. In: *The Routledge History of World Peace since 1750*, edited by Christian Philip Peterson, William M. Knoblauch and Michael Loadenthal, 98–108. London/New York: Routledge.

Lemire, Elise. 2009. *Black Walden. Slavery and Its Aftermath in Concord, Massachusetts*. Philadelphia: University of Pennsylvania Press.

Loveday, Tonya M. 2015. *William Lloyd Garrison House. Boston Landmarks Commission. Study Report*. Petition #243.11, Boston Landmarks Commission, Environment Department: City of Boston.

Lowell, James Russell. 1843. *Poems*. Cambridge: John Owen.

Newman, Richard S. 2018. *Abolitionism. A Very Short Introduction*. New York: Oxford University Press.

Oxford English Dictionary. 2023. Non-resistance, n. & adj. July 2023. https://doi.org/10.1093/OED/1010157305.

South African History Online, n.d. Mohandas Karamchand Gandhi. https://www.sahistory.org.za/people/mohandas-karamchand-gandhi (access: 23.08.2023).

Thoreau, Henry David. 1866. Civil Disobedience. In: *A Yankee in Canada, with Anti-Slavery and Reform Papers*, edited by Sophia Thoreau, William Ellery Channing and Ralph Waldo Emerson, 123–151. Boston: Ticknor and Fields.

Thoreau, Henry David. 1854. *Walden; or, Life in the Woods*. Boston: Ticknor and Fields.

Thoreau, Henry David. 1849. Resistance to Civil Government; a Lecture delivered in 1847 [sic!]. In: *Aesthetic Papers*, edited by Elizabeth P. Peabody, 189–213. Boston: The Editor.

Tolstoy, Leo. 1936. The Kingdom of God is Within You. Christianity Not As a Mystical Doctrine But As a New Understanding of Life. In: *The Kingdom of God and Peace Essays*, edited, translated and with an introduction by Aylmer Maude. London: Oxford University Press.

Tolstoi, Leo. 1924. What I Owe to Garrison. In: *William Lloyd Garrison on Non-Resistance. Together with a Personal Sketch by His Daughter Fanny Garrison Villard and a Tribute by Leo Tolstoi*, edited by Fanny Garrison Villard. New York: The Nation Printing Press, pp. 47–55.

Tolstoi, Lyof N. 1902. Letter to Dr. Eugen Heinrich Schmitt. In: *Essays, Letters, Miscellanies. The Works of Lyof N. Tolstoi*, edited by Nathan Haskell Dole. *Vol. XX*, 358–361. New York: Charles Scribner's Sons.

Tolstoy, Leo. 1904. Introduction. In: *A Short Biography of William Lloyd Garrison. With an Introductory Appreciation of His Life and Work by Leo Tolstoy*, edited by Vladimir Tchertkoff and Florence Holah. London: Free Age Press.

Chapter 7

COMPARARE PHILOSOPHY WITHIN AND *WITHOUT* BORDERS

Agnieszka Rostalska and Purushottama Bilimoria[1]

Introduction: The Curse of Borders

There is a tendency to demarcate Western philosophy from all other alleged pedigrees of the discipline of philosophy, where the borders are anything but porous or in smooth communicative dialogue. Comparative philosophy has always been suspected of stealth border-crossing; however, if that attempt is intrinsic to the methodology of the comparative or cross-cultural enterprise, without which the exercise would all but collapse, then why should there be this suspicion, almost bordering on accusation. (Pun unintended; henceforth, 'comparative' and 'cross-cultural' will be used interchangeably, unless otherwise specified, and sometimes aligned with World Philosophy.)

It is believed by the practitioners of 'comparative philosophy' that their endeavour consists in developing and realising a particular comparativist methodology in philosophical studies. A depiction of this approach using a metaphor of 'removing borders' was made by Arindam Chakrabarti and Ralph Weber (2015: 1–2):

> A border, literally, is a line, often conventional, seldom natural, that separates two regions of space. Borders connect what is separated and separate what is connected. In principle, borders can be crossed [...] Comparative philosophy is all about the erecting, detecting, smudging, and tearing down of borders, borders between philosophical traditions coming from different parts of the world, different time periods, different disciplinary affiliations, and even within a single period and pedigree, between opposite or at least distinguishable persuasions. Philosophical comparisons, more often than not, separate and connect at the same time what are very likely or unlikely pairs of, or entire sets *of comparanda* (that which is set out to compare).

The objective of removing 'borders' is to enable the diversifying and pluralisation of philosophy, hitherto practiced in narrower cloisters, especially in Western (i.e., Anglo-American-European-Australasian) professionalized departments of philosophy, and aped some professional fraternities in India, Japan, Israel, UAE and Brazil. But what exactly is this strategy of 'diversification' or diversity and what does it entail? In responding to these questions, the chapter will focus on the 'border-problems' and certain encumbrances faced in the effort to achieve the strategic goal of diversity.

98 TOWARD A NEW ART OF BORDER CROSSING

Now there are two ways of looking at the strategy for 'diversity' in philosophy in a higher institutional setting.

The first one entails changing the colour and gender of the faculty by appointing scholars of colour and ethnically divergent background, but – and here is the rub – expect, indeed demand, of them that they continue to be compliant with the status quo, and therefore in heavily analytic departments do just that and not stray outside of the Anglophone perimeters or be lured into divergencies. And female and non-binary appointees are not expected nor encouraged to stray into feminist and deconstructive fads current and perpetrated by what are seen as mostly French feminist philosophers and a few Australian and North American women philosophers.

The second approach takes as its objective to diversify the curriculum content so that there is increasingly a recognition of the diversity of the contemporary world we live in and this moves away from what in politics might be called 'partisan lines'. Here, the philosophical academy recognizes that systems of thinking and reasoning, in short, philosophising, is not the ones confined to the alleged roots of Greece and developed in Europe and the West.

There might be a third position that combines both approaches and diversifies in terms of both colour, ethnicity, gender as well as the subject matter(drawn from across several globally representative traditions). This is how the journal *Sophia* has diversified (as will be showcased later). Although this case only impacts on the diversification of philosophy journals – still a vital instrument for the dissemination of knowledge and for shaping particular disciplines – an exemplary model has been carved out which the world of philosophy might just wish to take note of. And to consider as a possible response in the face of various threats from without that face philosophy departments in these trying times when questions of application, as well as global relevance, are asked.

Comparative Philosophy

The objective to diversify philosophy in terms of content is frequently supported by the thesis that philosophising is not an intellectual practice confined to the alleged roots of the 'ancient' philosophy of the Greeks. This has subsequently developed in Europe and the West over the last two millennia – which as Heidegger ([1959] 1982: 15) implied – is linked to the gradual thrust towards 'the complete Europeanization of the earth and of man'.[2] Many departments in the Humanities and Social Sciences recognize that our human world presents a much larger tapestry with diverse and varied histories and sociopolitical systems; the same, one could argue, ought to apply to the systems of thinking and knowledge-making. In philosophy, this diversifying objective was (and continuously is) for nearly 100 years promoted under the umbrella of an enterprise known as comparative philosophy, or recently, cross-cultural (and sometimes 'intercultural' or 'fusion') philosophy.

The label 'comparative philosophy' is frequently used in two ways. First, in a broader sense, it stands for an attempt to make the discipline of philosophy a more universal, and cosmopolitan[3] intellectual inquiry. Ronnie Littlejohn (2005) characterises this appeal as both aspiration and challenge 'to include all the philosophies of global

COMPARARE PHILOSOPHY WITHIN AND WITHOUT BORDERS 99

humanity in its vision of what is constituted by philosophy'. Probably the first influential scholar[4] to use the term 'comparative philosophy' was Paul Masson-Oursel in his 1923 doctoral dissertation entitled *La Philosophie Comparée* (published in English translation as *Comparative Philosophy* 1926):

> We only plan to extend our knowledge in order that the more we know, the better we may understand; we only peer more distantly in order that we may see more plainly and more clear[ly] (sic). Both ends are secured when we discern fundamental likeness beneath apparent dissimilitude. All judgement is comparison: every comparison an interpretation of diversity by way of identity. (p. 31)
>
> [...] whilst the positive philosopher insist that all variety should revel before his eyes, if not a systematization of hard and fast laws, at any rate the constancy of certain conditions and some generality of certain facts.
>
> In support of the assertion that positive philosophy must be comparative philosophy, we would in the first place make deliberate appeal to some assumptions based upon analogy. One after another, the different "moral sciences' are becoming positive in being comparative. (p. 32)
>
> This philosophy, which ought to be comparative, should not take man, or human reason, but the different types of humanity or reason, for its subject: and, the more these types differ, the more fruitful can we hope their confrontation will show itself to be. (p. 39)

Masson-Oursel and McCarthy evoke 'comparative philosophy' in the opening words of the first volume of the journal *Philosophy East-West* (1951: 8):

> Comparative philosophy can furnish to each nation or people resources that others conceived, the knowledge of which can be humanizing.

Wilhelm Halbfass (1985) was probably the first prominent scholar who has made a remark on the understanding of the practice of comparison in the first sense, still ambiguously understood in philosophy:

> Comparison means different things to different people; this is obvious when we compare its applications in India and in Europe. It is done for different reasons, based upon different cultural and historical conditions, and pursued with different methods. [...] "Comparative philosophy" as an open-minded, methodically rigorous, hermeneutically alert, and yet existentially committed comparative study of human orientations is still in a nascent stage.

This brings us to the second, narrower sense of 'comparative philosophy', which refers to a subfield or a subdiscipline of philosophy broadly understood. Such an endeavour consists of executing a particular comparative methodology in philosophical studies. Jay Garfield (2015: 3) addresses the first understanding and moves forward to the second one:

> I have previously used the term 'cross-cultural philosophy' to characterize my own enterprise, and I still like that term. Mark Siderits prefers to think in terms of 'fusion philosophy' (2003: xi). I like that phrase as well, but I think that it can be misleading. I intend

not to fuse philosophical traditions, but rather, while respecting their distinct heritages and horizons, to put them in dialogue with one another, recognizing enough commonality of purpose, concern and even method that conversation is possible, but still enough difference in outlook that conversation is both necessary and informative. This may well be what Siderits has in mind as well, and I have no quarrel with his project, but the term suggests a project that is not my own. I am trying to build bridges, not to merge streams.

The Methods of Comparative Philosophy

One may wonder, how is 'comparative philosophy' done? And what distinguishes its method from the regular ones applied to the standard philosophical canon? In his later essay, Halbfass[5] (1997: 301–302) gives an example of how one could execute the aforesaid comparative approach. While commenting on the paper of Scharfstein, he points out some features of the method:

> Scharfstein discusses the reasons for, and the practical and didactic feasibility of, studying the three philosophical traditions together (p. 240ff.). He asks whether the concept of philosophy is the same in all three traditions and focuses on a number of exemplary issues as they arise within these traditions. Cross-cultural correlations are chosen carefully; familiar generalizations are supplied with some less familiar, but necessary caveats (see, for instance, p. 276ff.).

More recently, Mark Siderits (2017: 76) characterises comparative philosophy as the interrelation of two distinct traditions or cultures:

> [...] there is another sort of scholarship, one that proceeds from the assumption that a given Indian text or author is sufficiently well understood that we can bring it into dialogue with something from Western philosophy. In the past much of this was done under the banner of something called "comparative philosophy."

Siderits (ibid.) coins the term 'fusion philosophy' understood as a form of a dialogue (related to the terms 'engagement' and 'confluence') not restricted to only comparison and contrast of the two distant cultures, but rather stands for deliberate cross-cultural philosophising:

> [...] when we set out to solve some philosophical problem we should look at how others have approached the issue, regardless of whether they belong to "our" philosophical lineage or not. What to call this way of doing philosophy is would not matter once the practice took hold. We wouldn't after all, classify a paper as an instance of "classical-contemporary fusion philosophy" just because it discussed Aristotle in the course of developing a new approach to the problem of incontinence. We'd just call it "philosophy".

A practical consequence of this framework would be to incorporate cognate 'non-Western' philosophical theories and problems into university curricula, still dominated by 'Western' thought (Jay Garfield & Bryan Van Noorden 2016).[6]

COMPARARE PHILOSOPHY WITHIN AND *WITHOUT* BORDERS

Another and more recent model developed is the *Saṃvāda* project attributed to Daya Krishna (1991) calling to go beyond mere platitudinal dialogue among contemporary Indian philosophers and modern philosophers, and instead return to the classical texts (Sanskrit: *Śāstra*), albeit as living traditions – and engage in intense discursive dialogue and debates (Sanskrit: *vāda*) with (*sam-*) traditional pandits versed in the ancient and classical texts. In this encounter, the parties may have to concede to what might be called 'counter-positions', consistent with the logical (Nyāya[7]) school's dialectic of *vāda*, *jalpa* and *vitaṇḍā*, that is confrontational cavil with a view to defeating the opponent's standpoint and arriving at the truth of the problem at hand. *Saṃvāda* is further propelled by K. C. Bhattacharyya's ([1928] 2011) manifesto of 'Svarāj in ideas' (echoing Gandhi's idea of *swarāj*, self-determination, in national politics to disrupt colonial domination), advocating freedom in the spaces of thinking[8] with a preparedness to accept a synthesized outcome or a 'reasoned rejection' of the other's or one's own position as the case may be. However, this exercise should at the same time lead to expanding the horizons beyond the limited purview of the traditions in dialogue so that the work of *conceptual* re-tooling for the benefit of global *borderless* philosophy – crossing borders, visiting the other as curious stranger ('strangification') – would be advanced a step further. To this end, Daya Krishna accompanied a group of colleagues – philosophers (trained in Indian and Western philosophy) and linguists (trained in Sanskrit, Arabic and Persian) in the early1980s, and travelled to different parts of India in pursuit of just such intellectual encounters (Daya Krishna et al. 1991; Mayaram 2014; Freschi, Coquereau, & Ali 2017).

There is yet one other intervention in this attempt to find the best possible model for engaging the diverse traditions of philosophy without being hampered by the problems that beset the narrow (revisionist) or broad (progressive)approaches of comparative philosophy.[9] In his 'What Is Comparative Philosophy Comparing?' Panikkar (1988) develops his own methodology wherein he places emphasis on what he calls the 'imparative hermeneutic'. He explains that in this method a real space of mutual criticism and fecundation is opened up for genuine encounters between different philosophical and religious traditions. One 'enters' into another's dimensions of intellectual or spiritual 'meaning', and allows that to speak to, and reappraise, one's own convictions in a dialogical situation. One then assumes a more nuanced vantage point from which an assessment is made of the comparative worth of the aspects investigated.

Not one for 'global philosophy', Panikkar views the larger objective of the Imparative-hermeneutic program to draw into dialogue different perspectives from among the various traditions to address real-life and global issues in such a way that dialogue can become relevant to the human condition, to the problems and crises that face humankind regardless of whether religions are implicated or not. To the question Why is there a need for 'imparative hermeneutics?', Panikkar offers these intriguing insights. First, in regards to the motivation: because comparative philosophy is problematic for the reason that the self-other encounter will never allow itself the luxury of comparison. As philosophy pretends to the universal itself, it would appear that any neutral point from which to compare philosophies is a fantasy. There is no context-free point of departure: 'any effort at comparing philosophies starts consciously or unconsciously from a concrete philosophical position'. (1988: 127) Panikkar suggests in this regard that we forego the *comparative* project for the *imparative* one. Panikkar in the quote below suggests in this regard that we forego the *comparative* project for the *imparative* one(from the nonverb *in* + *parare*, to prepare, furnish, provide). Imparative philosophy proposes that 'we may learn by being ready to undergo the different philosophical experiences of other people' (ibid., 127–128), even strangers to us. He also calls this diatopical hermeneutics (ibid., 130):

> Diatopical hermeneutics is the required method of interpretation when the distance to overcome, needed for any understanding, is not just a distance within one single culture (morphological hermeneutics), or a temporal one (diachronic hermeneutics), but rather the distance between two (or more) cultures, which have independently developed in different spaces (topoi) their own methods of philosophizing and ways of reaching intelligibility along with their proper categories.

Here, diatopical hermeneutics has a functional role of forging a common universe of discourse in the dialogical form taking place in the very encounter. Panikkar does seem to echo the methods from 'fusion philosophy' but argues for recognition of the distinctiveness of the tradition as well. Thomas B. Ellis, picking up on a close analogue with J. L. Mehta's postcolonial-Hindu hermeneutics (Mehta 1985), suggests that Panikkar's diatopical hermeneutics insists on the deconstructability of all traditions, for as Panikkar writes: 'we need, further, to be ready to contest our own conclusions'. (Mehta 1985).[10] Again, the encounter with the other is not always edifying. From a colonialist's perspective, this may seem misconstrued; from a colonial subject's position, it is obvious.

In 'What Is Comparative Philosophy Comparing?' (Op.cit., pp. 125–126), Panikkar suggests that there is a phenomenology implicit in this cross-cultural enterprise, and this calls upon the researcher's conscious engagement with empathy and a preparedness to bracket-out belief in the truth of one or the other position that does not allow for a possible third position suggested in the *imparare* encounter which takes into account the universal range of human experience in as much as it is possible to do so in any concrete situation. Imparative philosophy as an alternative to comparative philosophy may be the antidote to overring parochialism ('provincially chauvinist views'), as well as to cultivating tolerance and understanding of the richness of human experience. And here diatopical hermeneutics has a functional role of forging a common universe of discourse (not a common ground through assumed equivalences) in the dialogical form taking place in the very encounter. So Panikkar basically argues that comparative philosophy should not parade itself as an independent, autonomous, discipline but rather see itself as a 'mature *ontonomic* activity of the human spirit, contrasting everything, learning from everywhere, and radically criticizing the enterprise itself'? (ibid., 136) But for his time as a 'Hindu in the ghāts of Varanasi, mingling with traditional Mīmāṃsaka and modern-day hermeneuticians such as J. L. Mehta, Panikkar would have easily acquiesced to the temptations of what we would now call classical comparative philosophy and comparative religion (even comparative theology), believing that comparisons happen naturally as in comparative ethnology, without much concerns about methodological niceties, such as of intranslatability across conceptual schemas and the spectre of value-judgements.

COMPARARE PHILOSOPHY WITHIN AND *WITHOUT* BORDERS   103

Instructively, an area in which a nexus of Daya Krishna's *saṃvāda* strategy and the ideal of 'Imparative' philosophy developed by Raimon Panikkar is being fruitfully applied is in the global-critical and postcolonial philosophy of religion, wrenching the subdiscipline of philosophy of religion away from the dominant preoccupations with proofs for the existence of God, the problem of evil (or theodicy),[11] and other remnants from pre-Enlightenment natural theology as prevalent in the Western academy (Bilimoria & Irvine 2009, Loewen & Rostalska 2023).

After this brief description of what comparative philosophy's endeavour amounts to, we now turn to the staple examples of pursuing comparative philosophy which incorporate Western philosophy with Indian philosophy as its counterpart. The important influence on the recent engagements of comparative philosophers specializing in Indian and Indian Buddhist philosophy with the analytical thinkers were the numerous publications of Bimal Krishna Matilal – especially his widely read masterpiece *Perception. An Essay on Classical Indian Theories of Knowledge* (1986) – and with the continental thinkers the works of Jitendra Nath Mohanty, especially his widely read *Reason and Tradition in Indian Thought* (1992). Comparative philosophy with Indian and analytical philosophy as its focus developed mostly through academic publications. Likewise, and in a parallel pursuit, modern scholars of Chinese philosophy have had similar training within their own contexts and have made sterling strides in reconstructive cross-traditional engagement with modern philosophy (see: Bo Mou 2010, Roger T. Ames & Henry Rosemont Jr. 1999, Roger T. Ames & David L. Hall 2003, Chung-Ying Cheng 2020, among others).

The versions of comparative philosophy discussed so far are problematic for the reasons Bo Mou identifies in the introductory theme to the journal *Comparative Philosophy*. In his explanation (2010: 3, 16) of 'the constructive-engagement goal and methodological strategy'), he elaborates on the constructive-engagement:

> […] is to inquire into how, via reflective criticism and self-criticism, distinct modes of thinking, methodological approaches, visions, insights, substantial points of view, or conceptual and explanatory resources from different philosophical traditions and/or different styles/orientations of doing philosophy (within one tradition or from different traditions) can learn from each other and jointly contribute to our understanding and treatment of a series of issue, themes or topics of philosophical significance, which can be jointly concerned through appropriate philosophical interpretation and/or from a broader philosophical vantage point. This strategic goal and basic methodological strategy might as well be called the 'constructive engagement' goal and methodological strategy of comparative philosophy ('constructive-engagement strategy' for short).

Mou specifies further (2010: 16) that the 'constructive-engagement strategy' consists of critical engagements, constructive contributions and philosophical interpretations. He stresses the 'philosophical-issue-engagement orientation', the aspect of comparative philosophy directed at common philosophical concerns:

> The primary purpose of this orientation in studies of ancient or contemporary thinkers is to see how, through reflective criticism (including self-criticism) and argumentation, these thinkers could constructively contribute to the common philosophical enterprise and/or a

104 TOWARD A NEW ART OF BORDER CROSSING

series of issues, themes or topics of philosophical significance that can be jointly concerned through appropriate philosophical interpretation and/or from a broader philosophical vantage point [...] rather than focus on providing a historical or descriptive account (or on interpreting some ideas historically developed in a certain tradition or account) merely for the sake of being aware of them.

Mou's aim stands in line with Siderits' purpose of 'deliberate cross-cultural philosophising', as both encourage conversations between various philosophical orientations. However, with the view to forging a novel hybrid vista, as endeavoured by fusion philosophers, here the challenge is to embrace multiple viewpoints while acknowledging their distinctive approaches to common philosophical issues. In other words, Siderits wants to advance philosophy, whereas Mou only wants to know many perspectives but does not want to propose a new concept or build a new framework, but to clarify existing positions. Comparison and contrast are employed not as sole ends in themselves, but rather used explicitly to widen the perspective, and improve clarity about philosophical matters and as yet unresolved issues. Engaging more substantively with different traditions, while maintaining the acknowledgement of their differences, may not only improve one's understanding of philosophical problems but also prove useful towards critical examination of the definitions, analysis of philosophical notions and the evaluation of the validity of arguments.

As Comparative Philosophy developed in the later twentieth century, the focus shifted towards the removal of misconceptions, overgeneralisations and false stereotyping (e.g. 'Hegelian echoes' that the 'focus of philosophical attention' for the West is *concepts*, for the Indian *intuition*, for the Chinese *action*) and, by the same token, the general ignorance persistent among narrowly – specialized researchers and scholars (Chakrabarti & Weber: 8). Consequently, in response to this problem of exclusion, they proposed inclusiveness, that is when investigating a particular philosophical problem, for example a focus on knowledge, belief and our capacities to track these states in ourselves and others – one ought to examine the theories from the history of epistemology broadly understood: both in the Western traditions, dating back to the ancient Greeks, and the non–Western – departing from the Classical Indian, Chinese, African, etc.

Journals, Book Series and Associations Dedicated to Comparative Philosophy

For the establishment of 'comparative philosophy' as a field, or subdiscipline, the vital role has played in the thematic and general conferences, research journals, associations and publishing series. The *East-West Philosophers' Conferences* (since 1939) have been bringing together comparative philosophers from around the world to present times (Shaner 1986). The conference resulted in the founding of the journal *Philosophy East and West* in 1951, which still remains active today. Other top research journals that ensure the continuous development of the comparative enterprise include: *Sophia. International Journal of Philosophy and Traditions* (since 1962), *Asian Philosophy. An International Journal of the Philosophical Traditions of the East* (from 1991), *Dao: A Journal of Comparative Philosophy* (since 2001), *Comparative and Continental Philosophy* (since 2009),[12] *Comparative Philosophy. An International Journal of Constructive Engagement of Distinct Approaches towards World Philosophy* (from 2010) *and Journal of World Philosophies* (since 2016, earlier: *Confluence: Online Journal of World Philosophies*). Occasionally, comparative articles appear in the *International Philosophical Quarterly, History of Philosophy Quarterly, Journal of the American Philosophical Association, The Philosophical Quarterly, American Philosophical Quarterly, Argument: Biannual Philosophical Journal, Australasian Journal of Philosophy, Philosophy and Phenomenological Research, Monist* and *Mind*, to name a few.[13]

An active role in the promotion of comparative thought is played by the *Society for Asian and Comparative Philosophy* (SACP)established in by Karl H. Potter,[14] Chung-ying Cheng and Eliot Deutsch, and annually gathering philosophers[15] specializing in 'Non-Western' and comparative philosophy. It is also present during the central American congresses like the *American Philosophical Association* (APA) Regular Meetings and the Annual Meetings of the *American Academy of Religion* (AAR), to name a few. The *SACP* has collaborated with its counterpart in Oceania-Asia, the *Australasian Society for Asian and Comparative Philosophy* (ASACP),[16] in co-hosting conferences with both the *East-West Philosophers' Conference* and the *Australasian Association of Philosophy* (AAP). This has included contributions on Indigenous Aboriginals, Māori, Pacific Islanders or 'Rainbow Philosophy' (Bilimoria 1995).[17] Additionally, SACP has The Society for Asian and Comparative Philosophy (SACP) Monograph Series with the University of Hawaii Press (launched in 1974) publishing books in the Asia-Comparative field. Books on 'Non-Western' philosophy that include Indian, Chinese, Indo-Tibetan Buddhist, Japanese, Korean, African, Persian, Arabic, Native American Philosophy and Latin American philosophy, are published more and more frequently by reputable academic publishers, including Springer, Lexington Books, Routledge, Bloomsbury, De Gruyter, Brill, Blackwell and recognized university presses: Oxford University Press, State University of New York Press and Princeton University Press.

Diversity of Journals and the Example of Sophia

In October 2018, the American Philosophical Association (APA) working group on *Diversity and Philosophy Journals: Practices for Improving Diversity in Philosophy Journal Publishing*, made key recommendations for Philosophy Journals:

- Diversify representatives – editors, editorial board members, referees, trustees, staff, etc. – to include more people from under-represented groups and on important but neglected topics of interest to a diverse range of philosophers, utilizing a diverse range of methods;
- For under-represented groups, long-term targets might include publishing and promoting their work at least in proportion to their presence in the part of the discipline that your journal covers.
- Solicit submissions of promising work by members of under-represented groups (*PhilPeople* might be a useful resource).

106 TOWARD A NEW ART OF BORDER CROSSING

- Reserve more space for articles by members of under-represented groups to help meet specific targets.
- Publish more papers of interest to under-represented groups in philosophy and on important but neglected topics of interest to a diverse range of philosophers.

Perhaps not uncoincidentally, *Sophia,* under the inspiration of similar mandates towards diversity in Philosophy entertained in Australasia and supported by AAP and ASACP, has been a pioneer of this trend. In the *Diversity and Philosophy Journals: Practices for Improving* blog article on 'Sophia's History of Encouraging Diversity', Bilimoria (2018) reports:

> This modest-sized journal that began Downunder in 1962 in a cyclostyle format as a discussion point for small group of philosophers interested in the dialogue between philosophy and religion/theology, has become a prominent and poignant platform for philosophers and budding scholars, graduates, and students to engage more intensely in sophisticated areas of the discipline that cross a few borders and boundaries which are of relevance in the current critical age. [Moreover] The success of Sophia in taking this bold direction and blazing a trail is testified by the dramatic growth-rate of submissions, concomitant with the high rejection rate, the exponential increase of global readership and calibrated matrix (e.g. 12,500 articles are downloaded in this year to-date alone). Sophia also sees itself moving towards engagement with issues in "mainstream" Anglo-American philosophy, albeit from the critical perspectives of Cross-cultural, Continental, Feminist, Post-secular Political, Postcolonial and Indigenous traditions of thinking. There is no looking back.

We have drawn for our commentary from a range of approaches: in main, classical comparative, or cross-cultural philosophy, philosophy east and west, imparative hermeneutics, *saṃvāda* fusion philosophy, crossing boundaries and borders. The range speaks to the diversity within the comparative platform itself: it is not a monolithic (in the words of an Australian analytic philosopher) 'eastie-westie' thinking. Without dismissing any one approach, we have been disposed to highlight how each one undergirds certain insights and makes a significant contribution to the unfolding prospectus for what the great cross-culturalist, Ninian Smart (2008), had dubbed World Philosophy.

Bibliography

Ames, Roger T. and Henry Rosemont Jr. (1999). *The Analects of Confucius: A Philosophical Translation. A New Translation Based on the Dingzhou Fragments and Other Recent Archeological Findings.* New York: Ballantine Books.

Ames, Roger T. and David L. Hall (2003). *Daodejing "Making this Life Significant": A Philosophical Translation.* New York: Ballantine Books.

Bhattacharyya, Krishna C. ([1928] 2011). 'Svaraj in Ideas', In: Bhusan, Nalini and Jay L. Garfield (eds.) *Indian Philosophy in English. From Renaissance to Independence,* 103–111, Oxford, New York: Oxford University Press.

Bhusan, Nalini and Jay L. Garfield (eds.) (2011). *Indian Philosophy in English. From Renaissance to Independence,* Oxford, New York: Oxford University Press.

COMPARARE PHILOSOPHY WITHIN AND WITHOUT BORDERS 107

Bilimoria, Purushottama (1995). 'Introduction to the Special Issue: Comparative and Asian Philosophy in Australia and New Zealand'. *Philosophy East and West* 45(2): 151–169.

———(2008). 'Nietzsche as 'Europe's Buddha' and 'Asia's Superman (Pitfalls of Bad Comparative Philosophy)'. *Sophia* 47(3): 359–376.

———(2015). 'Philosophical Orientalism in Comparative Philosophy of Religion: Hegel to Habermas (&Zîzêk)', *Cultura Oriental, Capa* 2(2): 47–53.

———(2018). 'Diversity and Philosophy Journals: Sophia's History of Encouraging Diversity', Blog of the APA. Diversity and Inclusiveness, 6 September. Available online: https://blog.apaonline.org/2018/09/06/diversity-and-philosophy-journals-sophias-history-of-encouraging-diversity/ (accessed 15 July 2021).

———(2021). '*After* Comparative Philosophy: Discussion of "Wilhelm Halbfass and the Purposes of Cross-Cultural Dialogue," by Dimitry Shevchenko', *Philosophy East & West* 71(3), 815–829.

Bilimoria, Purushottama and Andrew B. Irvine (eds.) (2009). *Postcolonial Philosophy of Religion*. Dordrecht: Springer Netherlands.

Bilimoria, Purushottama and Agnieszka Rostalska (2023). 'Diversity in Philosophy', In: Sarah Flavel and Chiarra Robbiano (eds.) *Key Concepts in World Philosophies: A Toolkit for Philosophers*, 369–379. London: Bloomsbury Academics.

Bilimoria, Purushottama and Devasia Anthony (2019). 'Raimon Panikkar: A Peripatetic Hindu Hermes', *European Journal of Humanities and Social Sciences* (online), 3(2): 9–30.

Bilimoria, Purushottama, Monima Chadha, Jay Garfield, and Karyn Lai (2014). 'Asian Philosophy', In: Graham Oppy and Nick Trakakis (eds.) *The Companion to Philosophy in Australia and New Zealand*, 32–36. Clayton, Victoria: Monash University Publishing, 2nd edition.

Chakrabarti, Arindam and Ralph Weber (eds.) (2015). *Comparative Philosophy without Borders*. London: Bloomsbury Publishing.

Cheng, Chung-Ying (2020). *The Primary Way. Philosophy of Yijing*. New York: State University of New York Press.

Freschi, Elisa, Elise Coquereau, and Muzaffar Ali (2017). 'Rethinking Classical Dialectical Traditions. Daya Krishna on Counterposition and Dialogue', *Culture and Dialogue* 5(2): 173–209.

Ganeri, Jonardon (2017). 'Freedom in Thinking: The Immersive Cosmopolitanism of Krishnachandra Bhattacharyya', In: Jonardon Ganeri (ed.) *The Oxford Handbook of Indian Philosophy*, 718–736. New York: Oxford University Press.

Garfield, Jay L. (2015). *Engaging Buddhism: Why it Matters to Philosophy*. Oxford University Press.

Garfield, Jay and Bryan W. Van Norden (2016). 'If Philosophy Won't Diversify, Let's Call It What It Really Is', *The New York Times*, 11 May. Available online: https://www.nytimes.com/2016/05/11/opinion/if-philosophy-wont-diversify-lets-call-it-what-it-really-is.html (accessed 15 July 2021).

Halbfass, Wilhelm (1985). 'India and the comparative method', *Philosophy East and West* 35(1): 3–15.

———(1988). *India and Europe: An Essay in Understanding*. State University of New York Press.

———(1997). 'Research and Reflection: Responses to my Respondents. III. Issues of Comparative Philosophy', In: Franco, Eli, and Karin Preisendanz (eds.) Beyond Orientalism: The Work of Wilhelm Halbfass and Its Impact on Indian and Cross-cultural Studies, 297–314, Poznań Studies in the Philosophy of the Sciences and Humanities 59, Amsterdam, Atlanta: Rodopi.

Heidegger, Martin ([1959]1982). 'A Dialogue on Language', In: Peter D. Hertz (trans.) On the Way to Language, 1–54. New York, Cambridge: Harper and Row. (Original: *UnterwegszurSprache*, Pfullingen: Verlag GüntherNeske, 85–155).

Jackson, William J. (ed.) (1992). *J. L. Mehta on Heidegger, Hermeneutics and Indian Tradition*. 267–277, Leiden: E. J. Brill.

Kirloskar-Steinbach, Monika (2019). 'Diversifying Philosophy: The Art of Non-Domination', *Educational Philosophy and Theory* 51(14): 1490–1503.

Krishna, Daya (1988). 'Comparative Philosophy: What it Is and What it Ought to Be', In: Gerald J. Larson and Eliot Deutsch (eds.) *Interpreting Across Boundaries. New Essays in Comparative Philosophy*, 71–83. Princeton Legacy Library 889, Princeton: Princeton University Press.

108 TOWARD A NEW ART OF BORDER CROSSING

Krishna, Daya, M. P. Rege, R. C. Dwivedi, and Mukund Lath (eds.) (1991). *Saṃvāda, a Dialogue between Two Philosophical Traditions*, Indian Council of Philosophical Research, Delhi: Motilal Banarsidass Publishers.

Littlejohn, Ronnie (2005). 'Comparative Philosophy', *Internet Encyclopedia of Philosophy*. Available online: https://iep.utm.edu/comparat/ (accessed 15 July 2021).

Loewen, Nathan and Agnieszka Rostalska (eds.) (2023). *Diversifying Philosophy of Religion: Critiques, Methods, and Case Studies*. London: Bloomsbury Academics.

Masson-Oursel, Paul (1923). *Comparative Philosophy*. London: K. Paul, Trench, Trubner & Co., New York: Harcourt, Brace & Co. (Originally published as: (1923) *La philosophiecomparée*, Paris: Alcan).

Masson-Oursel, Paul. and Harold E. McCarthy (1951). 'True Philosophy Is Comparative Philosophy', *Philosophy East and West* 1(1): 6–9.

Matilal, Bimal K. (1986). *Perception. An Essay on Classical Indian Theories of Knowledge*.

Mayaram, Shail (ed.) (2014). *Philosophy as Saṃvāda and Svarāj: Dialogical Meditations on Daya Krishna and Ramchandra Gandhi*. New Delhi: SAGE.

Mehta, J. L. (1967). *The Philosophy of Martin Heidegger*. Varanasi: Centre for Advanced Studies, Banaras Hindu University; (1971) New York: Harper and Row; Re-issued as (1976) Martin Heidegger: The Way and Vision. Honolulu: The University of Hawaii Press.

———(1985). *India and the West: The Problem of Understanding. Selected Essays of J. L. Mehta*. Chico: Scholars Press.

———(1988, 1992). 'Problems of Understanding', In: Jackson, William, J. (ed.) *J. L. Mehta on Heidegger, Hermeneutics and Indian Tradition*. Leiden: E. J. Brill.

Mohanty, J. N (1986). *An Essay on Classical Indian Theories of Knowledge*. Oxford: Clarendon Press.

———(1992). *Reason and Tradition in Indian Thought*. Oxford: Clarendon Press.

Mou, Bo (2010). 'On Constructive-Engagement Strategy of Comparative Philosophy: A Journal Theme Introduction', *Comparative Philosophy* 1(1): 1–32.

Panikkar, Raimondo (1988). 'What is Comparative Philosophy Comparing?', In: Gerald J. Larson and Eliot Deutsch (eds.) *Interpreting Across Boundaries: New Essays in Comparative Philosophy*, 116–136, New York: Princeton University Press.

Shaner, David E. (1986). 'Interpreting across Boundaries: A Conference of the Society for Asian and Comparative Philosophy', *Philosophy East and West* 3(2): 143–154.

Shevchenko, Dimitry (2021). 'Wilhelm Halbfass and the Purposes of Cross-Cultural Dialogue', *Philosophy East & West* 71(3): 793–815.

Siderits, Mark (2003). *Personal Identity and Buddhist Philosophy: Empty Persons*, London: Ashgate.

Siderits, Mark (2017). 'Comparison or Confluence in Philosophy?', In: Jonardon Ganeri (ed.) *The Oxford Handbook of Indian Philosophy*, 75–92, Oxford: Oxford University Press.

Smart, Ninian (2008). *World Philosophies*, Revised 2nd ed., Oliver Leaman (ed.), Abingdon Oxon, New York: Routledge.

Glossary and Index

comparative philosophy – (i) narrow sense: exploring similarities and dissimilarities between philosophical systems from different traditions; (ii) broad sense: opening up philosophy to be inclusive of different systems of rational and creative thinking.

constructive engagement – engaging more substantively with different traditions through critical-constructive interpretations of philosophical problems drawn from a wide range of traditions.

fusion philosophy – is a form of dialogical engagement not restricted solely to comparing and contrasting distant cultures, but rather makes for cross-cultural philosophizing to result in solutions to a concrete question.

COMPARARE PHILOSOPHY WITHIN AND *WITHOUT* BORDERS

Imparative hermeneutic – involves contrasting everything through dialogue while radically criticizing the enterprise during genuine encounters between differing traditions. Allowing one to reappraise one's own convictions.

saṃvāda – engages in intense dialogue and debates with traditional exponents of ancient or classical texts so as to expand the horizons beyond the limited purview, and permit *conceptual* re-tooling for *borderless* philosophy.

Notes

1 Acknowledgment: the shorter version of this paper is published as: Bilimoria, Purushottama and Agnieszka Rostalska (2023), "Diversity in Philosophy," in Sarah Flavel and Chiarra Robbiano (eds.), *Key Concepts in World Philosophies: A Toolkit for Philosophers*, 369–379, London: Bloomsbury Academics.

2 Although the adage is taken from Husserl, Heidegger intended to signal both a cautionary note to his followers in Asia (mostly fledgling philosophers from Japan who became prominent in the Kyoto school), and a certain inevitability, which justified his reticence to pay much attention to Asian philosophies. In fact, he marginalized Indian philosophy from his main concerns on the basis that it did not provide a radical departure from Western thinking but was in fact part of the same exploration of Being carried to its fulfilment in Greek thought. He thus looked further east to China (and especially Japan) for a way of thinking founded on completely different grounds. Thus Heidegger, following Hegel and to an extent Nietzsche, attempts to think the Greek "more Greek," transcend the Greek through Greek; except for Schopenhauer with his pessimistic bent, Merleau-Ponty, Foucault, Derrida, and Rorty likewise ignored the East; as have Habermas and Zîzêk (who has been vitriolic in his criticism of Buddhism). See: Purushottama Bilimoria 2008: 360–361 (+fn) and 2015: 47–63—with Response to Critics by Robert B. Pippins (Chicago); Mehta 1967 and 1985; Jackson 1992.

3 As Ganeri justly points out, "cosmopolitanism" does not mean here the "cosmopolitan universalism which is the legacy of Kant so problematically entangled with the emergence of European modernity, but rather a notion more akin to what Mignolo describes as 'decolonial cosmopolitan localism' (Walter Mignolo, 'Cosmopolitan localism: A decolonial shifting of the Kantian legacy', *Localities* 1 (2011): 11–45)." See: Ganeri's reply to the blogpost: https://indianphilosophyblog.org/2014/09/24/towards-an-institute-for-cosmopolitan-philosophy/

4 W. Halbfass (1985: 5) estimates that the first author who presented the term and project of comparative philosophy was the Bengali scholar and educator Brajendra Nath Seal in *Comparative Studies in Vaishnavism and Christianity*, Calcutta, 1899 and suggests that Masson-Oursel may have been familiar with his publications. See also: Bhusan and Garfield (2011: 464). The book of Seal is unavailable to us.

5 On some specific reservations on Halbfass's own hermeneutic of comparative philosophy and criticisms thereof (specially from his friend, and partner-in-dialogue; J. L. Mehta), see Mehta 1988, 1992; Mohanty 1992; Bilimoria 2021, and Shevchenko 2021. But also anticipated in: Daya Krishna 1988, and Raimundo Panikkar 1988.

6 The exemplary cases of such intercultural programs are: "Global and Comparative Perspectives" (BA, MA) and "Philosophy in World Traditions" (MA) offered at Leiden University, The Netherlands. Partly because of this, the number of students has increased by 60 percent in recent years. Recently, The Vrije Universiteit Amsterdam appointed Prof. Monika Kirloskar-Steinbach as professor by special appointment of "Diversifying Philosophy" with a purpose of increasing the diversity, for example within the field by paying more attention to Indian and African philosophical traditions to break the "white-male-European" cannon pattern of philosophical education. With this focus, the Chair is a pioneering attempt in Europe. See also: Kirloskar-Steinbach 2019.

7 Nyāya's threefold division of debate (*katha*) includes: 1. debate for truth, discussion (*vāda*), 2. disputation, wrangling (*jalpa*), and 3. destructive debate, cavil (*vitaṇḍā*).

8 See: Ganeri (2017).

9 This section is drawn generously from Bilimoria and Anthony (2019: 9–30).

10 Ellisis citing from Panikkar (1988) p. 135.

11 Present examples of fruitful scholarly collaborations in this direction are pursued by the researchers of.

(1) the "Global-Critical Philosophy of Religion" project (supported by the Wabash Foundation and the National Endowment for the Humanities) led by Tim Knepper, Drake University, Gereon Kopf, Luther College and Nathan Loewen, University of Alabama (https://globalcritical.as.ua.edu/about-the-project/).

(2) "The Global Philosophy of Religion Project" team [funded by the *John Templeton Foundation* and the Dynamic Investment Fund (DIF)] led by Yujin Nagasawa (September 2020–May 2023) at the University of Birmingham https://www.global-philosophy.org/.

12 Launched by *The Comparative and Continental Philosophy Circle* (since 1995).

13 American Academy of Philosophy's blog hosts a discussion dedicated to the issue of diversity and inclusiveness, including coverage of these trends in the academic peer-reviewed journals. See: https://blog.apaonline.org/category/diversity/

14 His edition of *Encyclopedia of Indian Philosophies* published from 1977 onward recently counts 25 volumes (26th in preparation) https://www.reddit.com/r/hinduism/comments/shy97x/encyclopedia_of_hindu_philosophy/?rdt=44935.

15 50th SACP Annual Conference in Cracow gathered over 150 participants.

16 Which co-hosted meetings with regional groups also in Singapore and Hong Kong. Other regional associations are: *Iranian Society of Intercultural Philosophy, Society for Intercultural Philosophy* (GIP) in Germany, and *Vienna Society for Intercultural Philosophy* (WIGIP) in Austria.

17 See also: Bilimoria, Chadha, Garfield, and Lai (2014).

Chapter 8

FROM HEGEMONY TO COUNTER HEGEMONY: BORDER CROSSING IN PHILOSOPHICAL DISCOURSE

Saji Varghese

Subaltern: A Site of Border Invasion

In line with the Post-Marxian tradition, in a revolutionary approach to the same at the hands of Antonio Gramsci has a theme of a possible border crossing. The Subaltern, a social class is seen as a locus of border invasion in this section of the chapter. The invasion here is in a psychological sense where the mental makeup of the members is tried to be influenced through their own 'objects of interest'. I shall return to these means or objects, later in the chapter. The notion of the subaltern was first used by the Italian political activist, Antonio Gramsci in his article 'Notes on Italian History' which appeared posthumously in his most widely known book, Prison Notebooks written between 1929 and 1935. Gramsci's standpoint is that the section of society who are termed as oppressed are not actually are given the right to determine their own history or even to participate in legislations of what is to determine their future. The understanding of the origin of the notion of the subaltern is not also theoretical rather needs some experiential wisdom from having lived in the midst of such groups. They tend to detach themselves from the mechanistic and economistic aspects of societal life as psychologically there is a large amount of discrimination that they have been subjected to.

The term 'subaltern class' is used to refer to any low-rank person or group of people in a particular society who are under the control or direction of another dominant group.They are suffering under the hegemonic domination of a ruling elite class that denies them the basic right to participate in the making of local history and culture. They in actuality are active individuals of the same nation. Gramsci's intentions when he first used the concept of the subaltern are clear enough to be given any other far-fetched interpretations. The only groups Gramsci had in mind at that time were the workers and peasants who were oppressed and discriminated against by the leader of the National Fascist Party of Benito Mussolini. Gramsci took an interest in the study of the consciousness of the subaltern class as one possible way to make their voice heard instead of relying on the historical narrative of the state. The consciousness, a vital element here with regards to the class in general, is not evolved out of their own efforts but is rather shaped by the conscious practices and

TOWARD A NEW ART OF BORDER CROSSING

conditioning done by the elite members of the other group. Here is a mental invasion that is consciously shaped by the others.

Subaltern historiography treats people as belonging to an autonomous domain that originates neither from elite politics nor depends on them. Therefore, whereas the mobilisation in the domain of elite politics is achieved vertically, in that of subaltern politics it is achieved horizontally. With all the candidness that is often associated with a Marxist, Ramachandra Guha believes that the task of historiography is to interpret the past in order to change the present world and that such a change involves a radical transformation of consciousness. He, therefore, warns social scientists and history writers not to view peasant or tribal insurgents merely as 'objects' of history but to treat them as 'makers' of their own history-endowed with a transformative consciousness of their own. The focal point which is consciousness, again is in a flux that in great measure makes the border crossing a likely phenomenon in this group. There are arguments among classical historians that the common experiences being in the group such as common suffering, common efforts, common administrative setup, and so on have led to the creation of such consciousness. In describing his 'subaltern' approach Guha makes a natural attack on the conventional discourses on peasant/tribal insurgencies which hitherto have served in the colonialist historiography as merely a stumbling block to the maintenance of 'law and order'. The subaltern for Guha is that clearly definite entity, which constitutes 'the demographic difference between the total Indian population and all those whom we have described as the "elite"' (Guha 1982). This is the foundational view relating to the subaltern as a group, being influenced by this view of Guha, the group members tried to analyse the subaltern groups as an "objective assessment of the role of the elite and as a critique of elitist interpretations of that role" (Ibid).

Border crossing as a possible phenomenon initiated by academics or elites becomes a reality only if the efforts are made by the intellectuals of both the dominant groups. For this to happen, the literature from their respective groups would play a great role. An erosion of the conventional boundaries is the fundamental requirement in this effort to reach their objective. Is there an effort in contemporary times, in societies to include the interests of all the social groups? In multicultural societies where pluralism is in practice, we find patterns of state support for some social groups over others. The scholars who defend multiculturalism have attempted to make arguments supporting the efforts of the state. There are dominant groups whose customs are more valued than those of other groups. The core and the domain of every nation and the fundamentalist attitude to develop them alone is leading to the attitude of absolutism within. The need to go to the peripheries and make them accessible, as the borders are no longer speaking the ideologies of what is unique of the centre. The concept of a whole as it has its volume been determined by each and every part including the corners, in the same way, every society needs to go beyond the core to each and every corner so as to include the interests and concerns of every group, no matter however small it is number. Thus these words of the last volume of Subaltern Studies 'beyond conventional boundaries', and 'beyond the discipline of history' are relevant even in contemporary India. Thus, an integrative or assimilative approach to include every concern within a consecrated whole is the ideal method to take forward the society.

FROM HEGEMONY TO COUNTER HEGEMONY

Intellectuals and Their Role

In the words of Gramsci, intellectuals are those active individuals with leadership qualities in any field of profession. Intellectuals are, therefore, leading workers in economic, political, and cultural fields. They are 'technicians of knowledge' in a profession. Intellectuals may not be conscious of their class roles. They may think that their ideas are neutral and universal. Actually, their positions are partisan and they promote the hegemony of a particular class. Hegemony also connotes indirectly the active consent of subaltern classes, this in actuality is a camouflaged consent. Thus, hegemony maintains the domination over subaltern classes with the aid of their active consent. That is why Gramsci calls hegemony as containing both the elements of domination and consent. Hegemony is not to be confused with domination or with consent manufacturing. It is simply uncritical consciousness, willingness to render support to the existing or the present form of governance. However, It constitutes critical consciousness simultaneously. Counter-hegemony begins with a resolution of common sense in its contradiction. This, I refer to as border crossing in consciousness, allegiance being with a rival group or class. Gramsci is usually understood as a theoretician of super-structure. If hegemony refers to a moral/intellectual function and civil society to a moral/ intellectual sphere, it does not automatically follow that Gramsci equates hegemony with power in civil society only. Several passages in Gramsci, where he talks about the ethical aspect of the state as also partly constituting hegemony. And both these entities are not part of civil society in Gramsci's own perspective. For Gramsci, ethical and intellectual functions differ from the economy, civil society and the state. Thus, hegemony is to be located in all these three sites, though in different senses.

The post-colonial theories have this feature of 'subaltern' in them which is taken up by modern Indian historiography, specifically by the group known as the Subaltern Studies Collective (Sarkar 1984; Spivak, 2005). In this appropriation of Gramsci's political struggle, the idea of the subaltern was used to call into question the elitism of historiography (Guha 1988). A lot of emphasis is on the basic fundamentals of power, domination and subordination in this area of studies named subaltern studies (Sarkar 1984), the term came to connote a 'space of difference' (Spivak 2005: 476). Most famously, in Ranajit Guha's (1988: 44) formulation, the subaltern was the 'demographic difference between the total Indian population and all hose [...] described as the "elite".' Thus, subalternity, here, is understood as the situation of the people in which they live and survive the pressures faced in their socio-political set up. There is, a general attribute of subordination which is felt among the existential predicament faced by this group (ibid. 35). The term 'subaltern' was closely associated with the idea of the popular, the general. Thus, politics is what is popular and what is among the popular culture. In the attempt of the leaders, much is felt as though they want to be closer in most practices of the subaltern groups. In the works of the Subaltern Studies Collective, the agency of change is also located in this sphere of subaltern politics.

Subalternity, thus, became more than the 'general attribute of subordination'; it also became a theory of agency, that of the 'politics of the people' (Guha 1988: 40). Organic intellectuals are understood here as allied to and serving the interests of an emergent

114 TOWARD A NEW ART OF BORDER CROSSING

social class. The notion of the intellectual as an active cultural producer also opens up the opportunity to recover a much broader range of groups and individuals – in particular, the self-educated artisan – who have historically been effective as cultural producers and reproducers in the proletarian public sphere. It is also necessary to clarify the historical forms taken by the mediation of border crossings in terms of historically specific cultural practices that can be empirically researched. When we focus on intellectuals and their active mediating practices in managing the cross-cultural mediation involved in border crossing, it becomes clear that activity is not one-sided. Vovelle (1982) has formulated the notion of cultural mediation in terms of both the objects – such as texts – and the people that establish relationships between different cultures. This is formulated in terms of the distinction between cultural mediation on the basis of material and non-material cultural resources. Hake and Marriott develop this distinction between material and non-material cultural resources in cultural mediation as involving a variable focus on cross-cultural learning that came from reading the printed word, the recorded history of the cultural groups.

More pervasive (and of course overlapping with the symbolic word) was what one might call mediated influence, impact through the advocacy of individuals and groups who adopted exotic ideas and made them accessible to their followers (Hake 1994). Such a distinction enables us to establish the basis for the primary focuses of empirical research into historical manifestations of these two forms of active cultural practices involved in border crossings. On the one hand, the cultural resources are a matter of some body of ideas or accounts of practices from elsewhere. This leads to the analysis of the specific positions of intellectuals as cultural intermediaries in the mode of mediating border crossings by means of books, journals, newspapers, pamphlets, social media, theatres and so on. A personal cross-cultural encounter with the other is willingness of adaptation of the other and their practices into one self and one's practices in both private and public spheres. These can be of great significance in shaping our historical understandings of border crossings and the encounter with the ideas, institutions and practices in other nations.

Hegemony As Intrusion into and Beyond Borders

Hegemony is understood as a form of class rule linked to social forces, as the core collective actors, engendered by the social relations of production (Overbeek & Chase-Dunn 1994, Cox 1981). Under the capitalistic mode of product and wealth 'non-political' relations associated with different forms of social power are given importance. In capitalist social forms, the owners of the means of production, are under no governance. The direct producers are thus no longer in possession of their own means of subsistence but are compelled to sell their labour power for a wage in order to gain access to the means of production (Wood 1995). The manufacturers, the direct producers create the products through their means of production by making a sale of their labour power in exchange for a wage. The market thus, becomes not an opportunity but a compulsion to which the farmers are subjected. These factors such as the imperatives of competition, profit maximisation and survival control the life in the market (Wood 2002). Class is a historical category and is employed in a heuristic way rather than as an analytical

FROM HEGEMONY TO COUNTER HEGEMONY

category. Thus, class identity emerges within and through historical processes of economic exploitation within the mode of production in a capitalistic paradigm.

The task of the working class in every sphere of life especially in its political constitution requires the guidance of a group of intellectuals. Although rooted in the work of the Ordine Nuovo to develop certain forms of new intellectualism and to determine its new concepts corresponded to latent aspirations and confirmed to the development of the real forms of life, once Gramsci is in prison, the political question of the intellectuals is intertwined with the whole process of the transition to socialism. Intellectuals and forms of intellectualism that are practical and go beyond the abstract, rationalistic schemes which Gramsci so often attacked as cut off from real life. The aim was a balance between intellectual and manual work in which the intellectual capacities of the population are developed and practical activity becomes the basis of a new conception of the world.

The efforts and the skills of individual workers are the instruments of capital in a market driven society, however in an industrial economy it is the technology and the means of production that form the foundation of economy. These can become the foundation of a new freedom within the conditions of market driven economy. They provide the basis for a new rational, social control which implies a new unity between the specialised skills and the task of the political direction of society. Gramsci's work in Prison Notebooks is, in a way, the possibility of overcoming a series of divisions and differences where they do not disappear but are negotiated in creative ways: between leaders and led, between mental and manual labour, between politics and society, between philosophy and science. The expansion of knowledge with its corresponding complexity and the consequent necessity of specialisation – which mirrors an increasing social complexity and differentiation – challenges, however, the very possibility of generalisation and with it the traditional role of the philosopher. The traditional philosophers were engaged in generalisation or they attempt to comprehend the whole while analysing a particular issue or a particular society. The long-term organic crisis which Gramsci says is undermining traditional humanistic education also sets enormous problems for any generalising philosophy, including Marxism, and these are problems which will increase rather than diminish in the transition to socialism. Lenin's concept of revolutionary intellectual is anachronistic. Technocratic solutions of any sort which are the result of a rationalistic, deductive abstract process, that is one typical of pure intellectuals are bound to be inadequate before the enormously complex needs of society. The cognitive aspect of any hegemonic structure of power is for a specific role in a particular context, the function of the present structure of power is to keep the civilians or citizens ignorant of their historical role.

Border Crossing between Social Groups and Beyond

The description given for social groups within a society do not apply to all the nations across the globe. The politics of subaltern classes in India both in the colonial period and post-colonial times do not actually match the characteristics of the rural groups described by Gramsci. Specifically, in Subaltern studies volume, Guha disagreed with one of the descriptions that, subaltern groups are always subject to the activity of ruling groups, even when they rebel and rise up (Guha 1982). The subalterns demonstrate a section of the population which gathers around the larger interest of survival in the big pluralistic society. In the few decades after the declaration of independence from the colonial Britain, it went through a stage of coming together as a conglomeration to protect their rights. Here, the elite politics too was free from the interests of the subalterns. Guha stated that the domain of subaltern politics was autonomous from elite politics. He writes, 'It neither originated from elite politics nor did its existence depend on the latter' (Ibid, 4). The colonisation period witnessed a revolutionary stage as the elites and the ideologies relating to the freedom movement completely won over the good will of the subalterns and influenced them to participate in the movements leading to the freedom. However, in the post-colonial and the contemporary times, there is big resistance to elite domination both in economic and political and social activities of their everybody lives. However, it is the organic intellectual of different social groups which make the border crossing a possibility. In the initial volumes of Subaltern Studies, there are instances of peasants and artisans joining the freedom struggle in their way without the influence of the elites or the upper class in India. Thus, political mobilisation is not a fact as has been claimed by many scholars earlier. The present-day subaltern movement is a struggle to protect their rights as has been enshrined in the laws of the land, a reaction to the fear of legislation in favour of the upper class and caste also the majority section (Guha 1983). Gramsci elaborated on the functioning of the dominant groups mainly created for the subjugation and ensuring the continuity of the subaltern, this refers to how hegemony functions within and beyond the borders of social groups. The limited rights of the groups are made to be within a structural limit which maintain the subaltern groups, those formations which may help to affirm their entire autonomy (Gramsci 1971). There is deplorable state of affairs in the case of the marginalised social groups as there is limited resources being utilised by them, there is also absence of access to the higher resources of the state. The state control of their own representation and consequently lack access to the social and cultural institutions of their state.

Border crossing as a phenomenon is associated with the movement of forces of hegemony in a variety of ways beyond the borders of a group. For Antonio Gramsci in this journey of the ascendancy the factors that play their roles include ideology, the attitude of the elites of both the groups, awareness of the members within a group and their level of education and so on. Cultural mediation in the broad field of communication and learning associated with the proletarian public sphere during the process of modernisation especially in the continents of Asia, Latin America, and Africa. It has become clear that the cross-cultural mediation of border crossings during the period of modernisation did not remain the prerogative of intellectuals associated with dominant social groups. Given the development of the class structure of industrial capitalism as a basic feature of modernisation, a very significant degree of cross-cultural mediation in border crossings was increasingly undertaken by intellectuals allied to movements and groups related to the organised working class. The analysis here has focussed on those instances of border-crossings that were mediated by intellectuals as cross-cultural intermediaries with particular reference to subaltern movements. As there

FROM HEGEMONY TO COUNTER HEGEMONY

is cross-cultural mediation, the emphasis has been placed upon cultural formations and the roles of intellectuals associated with these formations. There has to be a dismantling of the rigid structure which is the result of a strong ideology of the ruling class. However, there is an element of intended camouflaged willingness to transform the other affected groups of the society. This is within a stipulated plan of the ruling class. Here, there is an element of border crossing, though vicious as welfare as ideal is not intended but as an intended definite plan to win the consent of the marginalised groups. Somewhere Gramscian scholars term it as a cultural hegemony as culture, traditions, customs, other forms of art are a means to turn the context to their favour by the elite groups. The consciousness which is subordinated is shown to be unconvincingly tolerated and given accommodation.

Both the historical description and analysis of border crossings have made use of a distinction between material and non-material forms for the mediation of border crossings. Material resources involved the management of border crossings in cross-cultural mediation through cultural artefacts such as arts and artefacts. Significant in this regard was the importance of the translation of key texts. Non-material forms include the act of border crossings involved in travel overseas by the migrant workers, emigres, refugees, and the development of diaspora. This examination has focussed on these two categories of the mediating cultural practices of intellectuals in the actively selective processes involved in the mediation of border crossings. But the question that arise are, what are we to make of the vast volume of all this cross-cultural communication and learning built around border crossings? In the first place, the organisations operating in the proletarian public sphere made significant contributions to the establishment of an internationalist proletarian culture.

Throughout the period of modernisation, the proletarian public sphere made a very significant contribution to a cross-cultural process based upon critical learning about the existential struggles of workers at home and abroad. Second, through the selection, translation, publication and distribution of literature from a vast array of foreign languages, cultures and social circumstances, the proletarian public sphere contributed to a cosmopolitan proletarian culture. The intended purpose was to disseminate an awareness of the alternatives available for the organisation of society, and to enable working people to analyse their own situation and to take collective action. Third, the proletarian public sphere manifested important ventures that constituted the formation of working-class opinion directed towards both a critical citizenship and international solidarity.

In the common parlance the internationalism and class comradeship, solidarity was seen as class-based rather than based on nationalism. There are particularly important questions of historical analysis, however, with regard to intellectuals and their cultural work in oppositional cultural formations that became relatively well established as trans-national organisations. This applies, for example, to the cultural organisations and intellectuals aligned with oppositional movements that sought to fundamentally transform, indeed to replace, the dominant social order by revolution. As with the socialist and communist movements, parties and unions during the 1920s and 1930s, there were very important problems in the relationships between those who were not

TOWARD A NEW ART OF BORDER CROSSING

as yet a governing class and the cultural production conducted by movement, party and union intellectuals.

The analysis here suggests the need to examine In more detail the unsettled and changing relationships in oppositional movements between 'intellectual leaders', 'movement intellectuals', 'intellectuals serving the same interests as the movement', and the worker as an autonomous producer of cultural meanings. These relate to the relationships in cross-cultural mediation that are between the traditional Comintern and the cultural traditions of communist parties in different other countries. The 'centralist direction' of the management of border crossings and cultural mediation in this context might be appropriate euphemisms here.

Theoretical Notes on Cross-cultural Mediation and Border Crossing

The phenomenon of cross-cultural mediation, the management of border crossings between different societies and cultures has long been a significant theme in the literature of transcendental politics. From the early reports of individual travellers, writers, journalists, teachers, adult students and artisans, we can find that there had been considerable amount of interest in these related fields. Here the border crossing is more in the sense of moving on to other professional fields other than on which one had his/her formal education on. However, in humanities and social sciences, the border crossing attained a different connotation due to certain demand of time. This has long been dominated by the pragmatic interest in what could be learned from other theoreticians. The historical processes involved in this cross-cultural mediation of ideas, institutions and practices are in themselves legitimate phenomenon for research by social scientists (Hake 1989). Such processes involved in the cultural mediation of ideas, institutions and practices among members of different societies cannot be studied in isolation from structured social relationships. These relationships of cross-cultural mediation suggest that the patterns of cultural mediation are socially structured both within and among societies. Cultural dissemination, reception, adaptation and integration are sometimes undertaken by dominant groups with the direction and influence of their elites. This enables crossing of a line or the border of what is called a group, at other times they are carried out by alternative or indeed oppositional, even revolutionary, groups. Here, even there are elites of a different groups that influence the cultural mediation. This brings in the need to examine the social organisation of the processes of cultural mediation. The term 'social organisation' is used here to refer to the complex range of institutions, groups and individuals involved in historically specific processes of border crossings and cultural mediation. Research on the period of modernisation has indicated in particular that the roles played by artisan and workers' movements, working-class organisations and proletarian cultural formations are very significant in the management of border crossings.

There are varieties of cultural mediation, cultural processes of communication and learning involving the working class, whether formal, non-formal or informal where one elevates to the ideological arenas of a different group and make a commitment to be a part of the same (Williams 1961). It can be found in such processes leading to

FROM HEGEMONY TO COUNTER HEGEMONY

the transcending of one's boundaries in space and time. In the field of communicative education, the notion is understood in terms of the social organisation of deliberate, systematic and sustained activities undertaken by youth for the purposes of communicating and acquiring knowledge, skills and sensitivities (Hake 1987). In this the central focus is directed towards such learning activities in the context of border crossings and cross-cultural mediation in the historical development of the proletarian public sphere. Research on the development of ideas, institutions and practices associated with the organisation of learning by the youth provokes the proposal that the period of modernisation was the fundamental formative period (Hake 1994). This was indeed a period characterised by a high level of innovative activity, the establishment of a wide variety of new institutions and practices, while participation in organised communication and learning. These practices contributed in a significant way to the modernisation of the social institutions involved in the production and reproduction of cultural meanings by way of socially organised learning. Furthermore, the period of modernisation was characterised by a significant level of activities involving border crossings that were manifested both in travel and the cross-cultural exchange of ideas, institutions and practices among working-class organisations throughout the world. Given the focus on the contribution of working-class movements and organisations to the proletarian public sphere, the focus here is on intellectuals, or opinion-makers, and their contribution processes of border crossings and cross-cultural mediation.

There are a few five key questions significant for the development of a programme on the cross-cultural mediation of border crossings in relation to the development of the proletarian public arena. The preliminary one is the identification of the historical formations and movements that the groups were involved in. These can be recognised as working-class educational activities with the involvement of their own intellectuals within the group who lead them and enable a cross cultural assimilation. Second, an analysis of these movements in terms of their relationships to broader movements, institutions and groups in society at large, would reveal that they are historically specific relations to more general programmes of economic, political, social and cultural reform. This would reveal both universal and specific locale value factors in the movements. Third, it relates to the multiple level of interests and positions assumed by those individuals involved in such movements.

This can provide a basis for the identification of the class factions that were involved, the trans-national, national, regional and local leadership of working-class movements. At the same time, such analysis can facilitate the identification of those who played a prominent role in the leadership of managing border crossings through organised learning activities. Fourth, to locate individuals who contributed as intellectuals or opinion-makers to the dissemination, reception and adaptation of ideas, institutions and practices involved in border crossings. Lastly, it is of some importance to examine the processes involved in the forming of the common mass who were addressed by cross-cultural intermediaries in the proletarian public sphere. It is of vital importance here to examine the social identity of the audiences addressed and the social relations between the disseminators and their influential public space. De Sanctis (1984) reflects on the creation of a proletarian public within its own struggle against the larger scenario of the dominant groups. Thus, the cross-cultural mediation and its assimilation in the larger public space with its practices is a hybridisation which in a way integrates two apparently antagonistic groups and their practices as in their traditions.

The studies on social movements within a class or beyond the class cannot be reduced to an analysis of their specialised roles within the specific institutions identified with their historical manifestations. Williams (1977) argues that it is important to analyse the role of intellectuals in terms of their variable social relations to social institutions with an emphasis upon cultural practices. The broader cultural formations which manifest more general tendencies in cultural production and dissemination need to be given more emphasis. This demands a historical analysis of the relationships between emergent cultural formations, together with an understanding of the oppositional relationships of intellectuals associated with such formations in relation to dominant cultural formations. This use of the term intellectual involves a rejection of the exclusive notion of intellectuals as referring only to a specific and restrictive notion of writers, philosophers and thinkers. Such an understanding of the intellectual is no more than a very specific and limited historical cultural formation more generally recognised as the intelligentsia. This understanding of intellectuals actively excludes a wide range of other cultural producers and reproducers and in particular those many other kinds of intellectual workers who are directly and indirectly involved in the cultural production and reproduction carried out by working-class organisations.

Gramsci talks about such intellectuals of subaltern groups who are endowed with the task of organising the members within a group. Every human being external to his professional life, is engaged in some intellectual activity. Gramsci treats every individual as a philosopher, an artist, a man of taste, he participates in a particular conception of the world. Gramsci opines that every human being is an intellectual, but he adds that not all men have, in society, the function of intellectuals (Gramsci 1971). While demystifying the intellectual activity assigned by idealist philosophy, Gramsci, at the same time gives a fixed role to the intellectuals by pointing out that all men do not perform the function of the intellectuals, although, everyone apart from being capable of excelling in one's own professional field may have a conception of the world and may be a man of taste. With reference to the analysis here, a limiting definition also excludes an important group of intellectuals who take oppositional positions with regard to the ideological apparatuses of the dominant social order. This is to come close to Gramsci's formulation of an understanding of intellectuals as traditional and organic intellectuals, that effectively moved the analysis of intellectuals into these areas which are external (Gramsci 1957).

A possible thought that remains unexplored is with regards to the border crossing in a privative way, the possibility of a crossing from the dominant class to the working-class consciousness. What the intellectuals performs in the civil society is helping to maintain the realm of hegemony of a dominant class parallel to the hegemony established by the state in political society. In the case of the working class under capitalism, it is fighting for an alternative hegemony without the aid of state apparatus. Thus, for the working class the political party is the mechanism both for the elaboration of its

FROM HEGEMONY TO COUNTER HEGEMONY

own organic intellectuals prepared in the ideological and political fields, and for the establishment of hegemony before it reaches state power (Schumpeter 1950). Once it has achieved state power the working way of travel and reading upon the learning activities that were independently undertaken by working-class men and women. However, there is a difference between the roles of bourgeois intellectuals and the intellectuals of the proletariat (working class). In Subalternists' own words 'beyond conventional boundaries', 'beyond the discipline of history' make it the most appropriate about the border crossing. It sounds in the most appropriate manner as mentioned in Hegelian terms about the historical process of transcending the antithesis to the synthesis. Further, Spivak and Chatterjee in their own way as poststructuralists talking in terms of the twenty-first century forms of imperialism and globalisation on the subaltern classes (Partha Chatterjee 2004). Apart from a move that takes one's allegiance from a class to another, there is a need to transcend the notion of class itself. This requires a higher level of understanding and the need of returning to values. The political exigency of today demands the necessity for a return to understanding of the impact of a new mode of power associated with pure ideology and values.

References

Chatterjee, P. 2004. *The Politics of the Governed: Reflections on Popular Politics in Most of the World*. New York: Columbia University Press.

Cox, R. W. 1981. 'Social Forces, States and World Orders: Beyond International Relations'. *Millennium: Journal of International Studies*, 10(2): 126–155.

Cristi, R. 1998. *Authoritarian Liberalism*. Cardiff: University of Wales Press.

De Sanctis, F. 1984. 'Problems of Defining the Public in the Context of Lifelong Education". *International Journal of Lifelong Education*, 4(3), pp. 265–277.

De Ste. Croix, G. E. M. 1981. *The Class Struggle in the Ancient Greek World from the Archaic Age to the Arab Conquests*. London: Duckworth.

Gramsci, A. 1957. 'The Formation of Intellectuals'. pp. 3–23, In *The Modern and Other Writings*, A. Gramsci (ed), New York: International Publishers.

———1971. *Selections from the Prison Notebooks*, Quintin Hoare and Geoffrey Nowell Smith (eds). London: Lawrence and Wishart.

Guha, R. 1982. 'On Some Aspects of the Historiography of Colonial India'. In *Subaltern Studies I*, Ranajit Guha (ed). Delhi: Oxford U Press.

———1982. *Subaltern Studies*. Vol. VII. Delhi: Oxford.

———1983. *Elementary Aspects of Peasant Insurgency in Colonial India*. Delhi: Oxford University Press.

———1988. 'On Some Aspects of the Historiography of Colonial India'. In *Subaltern Studies Selected*, R. Guha and G. C. Spivak (eds). New York: Oxford University Press.

Hake, B. J. 1987. *Patriots, Democrats and Social Enlightenment: A study of political movements and the development of adult education in the Netherlands, 1780–1813*, Hull University, Dissertation, 419pp.

———'The English Connection in the Historical Development of Dutch Adult Education: A Reconsideration of the Role of Social Movements in the Organisation of Ccross-cultural Communication'. In *Adult Education, Public Information, and Ideology: British-Dutch Perspectives on Theory, History and Practice*, B. J. Hake and W. J. Morgan (eds). Nottingham: Department of Adult Education, 61–75.

———1994. 'Formative Periods'. In *Cultural and Intercultural Experiences in European Adult Education: Essays on Popular and Higher Education Since 1890*, S. Marriott and B. J. Hake (eds). Leeds: Leeds Studies in Continuing Education, no. 3, 10–36.

122 TOWARD A NEW ART OF BORDER CROSSING

————1999. 'Lifelong Learning in Late Modernity: The Challenges to Society, Organisations and Individuals'. *Adult Education Quarterly*, 49(2): 79–90.

Overbeek, H., and Chase-Dunn, C. 1994. 'Hegemony and Social Change'. *Mershon International Studies Review*, https://www.academia.edu/17723605/Hegemony_and_Social_Change.

Sarkar, S. 1984. 'The Conditions and Nature of Subaltern Militancy: Bengal from Swadeshi to on-co-operation'. In *Subaltern Studies III*, R Guha (ed). New York: Oxford University Press.

Schumpeter, J. A. 1950. *Capitalism, Socialism and Democracy*. New York: Harper and Brothers.

Spivak, G. C. 2005. 'Scattered Speculations on the Subaltern and the Popular'. In *Postcolonial Studies* vol.8. No.4, New York: Routledge.

Vovelle, M. 1982. 'Les intermediaires culturels', pp. 498–500. In *Ideologies et mentalites Volvelle*, pp. 498–500. Paris: Maspero.

Williams, R. 1961. *The Long Revolution*. London: Penguin Press.

————1977. *Marxism and Literature*. Oxford: Oxford University Press.

Wood, E. M. 1995. *Democracy against Capitalism: Renewing Historical Materialism*. Cambridge: Cambridge University Press.

————2002. *The Origin of Capitalism*. London: Verso.

Part Two

TOWARD A NEW ART OF BORDER CROSSING: MOVEMENTS IN SOCIETIES AND HISTORIES

Chapter 9

BETWEEN THE LEFT, THE LIBERAL, AND THE RIGHT: POST-COLONIALISM, SUBALTERN STUDIES, AND POLITICAL 'BORDER CROSSING' IN INDIA

Arnab Roy Chowdhury[1]

Introduction

The project of post-colonial thought and theory in Indian academia (through the Global scene) emerged as a critique and extension of left-wing thought, mainly through subaltern studies[2] and its offshoots in the discipline of Historiography (and also in English language and literature studies), in the early 1980s (Roy Chowdhury, 2016). Indian version of post-colonial theory is aligned with the ideas of the new European left mainly Gramsci (and his Southern question) and blends it with poststructuralist ideas and notions of the power of Michel Foucault, and applies it to study history from below (Dhanagare 1988). Though largely emerging from new left consciousness, within the Indian cultural context it inhabits a nuanced 'political' position between liberals, the left, and the religious right, and it is deeply critical of Hindutva and that agenda (Chatterjee 1992; 2019).

Subaltern studies, a heterodoxy of the new left, primarily emerged from international experience of the imperialist aggression and orthodoxy of the international left, mainly the former Soviet Union that disenchanted many communist party members in India, who eventually left the party line.

In the Indian context, it criticises the left-wing orthodoxies of neglecting culture, tribes, caste, religiosity, gender and ecology thus bringing in a 'cultural turn' (Roy Chowdhury 2014).

However, in the last two decades and recently, post-colonial thought has been accused of making possible a right-wing argument and imagination about neo-traditionalist cultural revival in India mainly led by Hindu right-wing party such as Bharatiya Janata Party (BJP), by creating a discursive space and clearing the political field by making revisionist history possible by closing the gap between positivist/empirical history and interpretive/mythical history by questioning the archival documents and power invested in it through a post-structuralist reading of history 'against the grain' (Sarkar 2000).

Certainly, that is an anachronistic argument, as right-wing Hindu political discourses emerged much earlier during British rule in religious reform and anti-colonial movements (Pennington 2001). So the right-wing cultural arguments have longer lineages than the new left ideas, obviously. However, since the 1990s, some cultural dimensions and 'exceptionalism of Indian culture' arguments from both the new-left and the right have appeared to be similar in logic, at least on the surface level, giving the impression that the post-colonial/subaltern studies school and right-wing politics are feeding off each other. On various social media platforms, eminent scholars (mostly orthodox Marxists) have pointed this out more. The argument gained credence when Swapan Dasgupta, a prominent member of the 'subaltern studies' collective (he wrote a single paper in the series), joined the Bharatiya Janata Party, and stood for the Bengal election in 2021 (The Wire 2021).

This has occurred because, I argue, that indeed two varieties of culture-centred arguments have emerged in contemporary Indian politics. I call one the 'post-colonial left' and the other the 'post-colonial right'. Right-wing politicians use labels such as 'western', or 'culturally alien' for concepts such as human rights (Scroll 2019; The Hindu 2019), 'democracy' and 'secularism' (Bhatt 2001; The Indian Express 2022) and increasingly talking about 'decolonization' (The Hindu PTI 2017) in a narrow specific sense of criticising the British and mainly the Muslim era epistemology (Truschke 2022), mostly limiting itself to changing Islamic names of places into Hindu names etc. They 'creatively' borrow these concepts for rhetorical purposes, strategically downplay the epistemological and ethical considerations these concepts emerged from, and use these concepts out of context. The right wing's misappropriation of the ideas of the 'post-colonial left, in recent times to gain public and intellectual credibility, has led to a semblance of the acceptableness of those ideas within the Indian academia, where the left still has a stronghold because many outstanding scholars oriented towards left ideology. Because both the post-colonial left and right emerge from the colonial experience and the background of post-colonial critique, their ideas overlap, but there are crucial differences.

The question, then, this paper raises and tries to resolve is: did post-colonialism, subaltern studies, or generally the cultural left pave the way for the Indian cultural right? Has post-colonialism made both left-wing and right-wing ideas closer to each other or equally credible?

The Evolution of the Post-colonial Left and Right

Post-colonial left (the heterodox left parties and subaltern studies) thought and theory criticises several groups and belief systems:

> the dominance without hegemony of a particular form of colonial as well as anti-colonial leadership of the Indian National Congress (Congress) and the shallowness, exclusiveness, and elitism of its 'liberal' politics and postcolonial legacy in India (Guha 1998);

The traditional communist parties, because they neglect the institutional, cultural and communitarian dimensions of colonial societies and caste, gender, ethnic and racial identities, and ecology and instead focus too much on the dimension of the class struggle; and also, the right-wing religious parties, for their elitist and communal approach to politics.

BETWEEN THE LEFT, THE LIBERAL, AND THE RIGHT

The 'post-colonial left' (that is closely related to subaltern studies academically) posits its academic discourse somewhere in between the left, the right, and the liberal and, in that sense, transcends a border in imagination and looks for an alternative in history and politics; however, the postcolonial left has not formed a political party in India yet. On the other hand, conservative, right-wing, religious majoritarian Hindutva – which promotes a culturally majoritarian, militarised and politicised version of 'Hinduism' – has been rising in the Indian political scene since the 1990s (Jaffrelot 1996).

The BJP won the national elections in 2014 and formed the central government. The BJP, an ardent votary of Hindutva, strives to conserve and reinforce the exploitative 'traditional' (neo-traditionalist) caste, class and gender hierarchies. The BJP considers the ideas of the Indian National Congress liberal and elitist and along with those of the communists, alien, and uses the rhetoric of 'culture' and 'nationalism' to posit itself against both (Roy Chowdhury & Lahiri-Dutt 2021).

The politicians and ideologues of the BJP have increasingly been using ostensibly post-colonial arguments. They have been criticising ideas, practices and interests that emerged from the west and, hence, are antithetical to Indian 'culture' and against the interests of the Indian community and traditions. The Hindutva groups claim that the 'diversity' of religions, communities and cultures in India arrived from 'outside' – although there was no political/sovereign India before 1947, when India won independence from the British, BJPs' view on Indian culture is 'civilizational' and 'sacred geographical' in nature (Savarkar 1923).

The Indian subcontinent and Hindu 'religion' has always been composed of a diversity of cults, beliefs, languages, ethnicities, tastes, food habits, sartorial habits and worldviews. People have arrived and settled here in the longue durée for trade, war, conquest and migration.

However, diversity does not imply an 'equal and multicultural' community; rather, hierarchies and inequalities – along the lines of caste, class, gender, language and ethnicity – have always existed within and across religions in India. In imperial and pre-modern politics, hierarchy and inequality characterised the modality of imperial ethnocracies, social organisation and governance and religion played a central role in state legitimacy, hegemony, war and conquest (Malesevic 2017). Colonial and decolonial powers imposed the nation-state as a political organisation in India and South Asia.

The current new conservative and partly reactionary regime in India deploys the idea of Hindutva politically. The practitioners of political Hindutva deploy a hybrid of neo-traditionalist ideas in their discourse. The discourse is a pastiche of reactionary facets that emerged as a reaction against the following: Colonial modernity or modernisation through the strands of the anti-colonial movements in India (Chatterjee 1993); around the trend of identity politics, religion and the cow protection movement (van der Veer 1994); and through the consolidation of a long-fragmented tradition of religious reform movements within Hinduism such as those of Arya Samaj and Swami Vivekananda (Chatterjee 1993), and Hindutva emerged through an eclectic and creative misappropriation of these ideas.

128 TOWARD A NEW ART OF BORDER CROSSING

Politicians of the right-wing majoritarian and conservative Hindutva regime have recently been drawing on arguments that sound increasingly 'post-colonial' in the South Asian context. They have been striving to develop a somewhat coherent ideology and nurture their own 'right-wing intellectuals', but it is unlikely to become so as Indian never had a strong conservative tradition and philosophical writings because of the hiatus/rupture of experience created by colonial modernity (Kaviraj 2018). They critique everything 'western' in thought and practice and consider it the same as 'foreign' – any idea not Indian and not amenable to the Indian tradition.

By that same neo-imperialist logic, right-wing politicians term the discourse of 'human rights' 'western', neo-colonial and 'liberal'. They claim that even so long after decolonisation the west – the 'white' Anglo-American world, the erstwhile colonisers – promotes their discourse to maintain control over the political narrative of the former colonies. This ploy denies the former colonies full socio-political and cultural sovereignty and independence. The west does not want India to become 'strong'; they want to make India a weak nation-state, internally divide its people, and make them socio-politically indecisive. Hence, we need a religion-based 'nationalism' (religio-culturally conservative ideas) that unites the Hindus, who make up the majority of the population, against these conspiracies. By that logic, Muslims, who constitute 15.5 per cent of the population in India, represent a 'challenge' to that Hindu unity (Detsch 2015).

Some nation-states may well be striving to become powerful through imperial manoeuvres and reset the geopolitical world order through belligerent aggression, war, or pushing liberalisation through and opening up markets in various parts of the world. However, what we see now in India is a majoritarian religious politics of the Hindu class and caste elites who initially use the democratic electoral mechanism to win power but then capture all democratic institutions and centralise power and resources to subvert democracy (Yadav 2020). They adapt a jingoistic model of nationalism (Malesevic 2017) in which they practise repression at home, at the same time, maintain the image of a 'powerful' strongman leadership regime, to 'unite' India but for their image abroad curate an alternative spiritual and benevolent (through Gurus and Yoga) (Business-Standard 2022), and fast development through the adaptation of neoliberal growth model (Ghosh 2020).

This right-wing regime uses the mildly imperial rhetoric of a mythical golden age and a once powerful, liberal, and open Hindu empire that was invaded initially by the Muslims and later colonised by the British (Blom Hansen 1999). The regime argues that there is a lot to learn from the Indian civilisation and its people (read 'the elites'). India – once a powerful civilisation known for its culture, knowledge, spirituality and philosophy – should emerge again as the world power in these times of the knowledge economy, through a post-colonial reverse gaze of the once subjected to imperialism and colonialism to become the *Vishwaguru* (Modi himself as world/cosmopolitan teacher) and hegemon by institutionalizing ascetic mode of power in politics, would be a perfect revenge and a poetic justice. India should take centre stage in the production of knowledge and epistemology and teach everybody Hindu culture by promoting soft-power categories like yoga (Singh 2001), vegetarian food and ayurveda through merchandising spirituality, all of which would establish India as a 'brand' and some sought of world liberator (from the shackles of modernity and its violence) (Maitra 2022).

BETWEEN THE LEFT, THE LIBERAL, AND THE RIGHT

But that rhetoric distorts and rewrites history at the same time—and its concepts, categories and meaning (Jain & Lasseter 2018)—and inflates India's capability to look important on the world stage and creates a religious enemy through 'othering'. The project of Hindutva represents a somewhat 'emasculated imperialism', which emerged from an imperial and colonial sense of humiliation, lack, inferiority, insecurity and resentment against that. Because, although imperial at its core and in its ideas, it lacks both the capacity and power to inflict global imperialism through war-like aggression. So, at the geopolitical level, it projects itself as a subaltern of world politics, now standing shoulder to shoulder with the world powers and enthralling the world with ideas that are against violence, for love, equality, cosmopolitanism and against all forms of colonialism and imperialism (they often talk about *Vasudhaiva Kutumbakam* meaning 'the world is one family' taken from ancient Indian scripture, Upanishad) (Lakshman 2014).

That makes the matter complex, perhaps because the Indian (national) elites, while doing repression at home, claim a post-colonial or decolonial subaltern status at the geopolitical level and in international relations, also making it contradictory. The truth of the matter is that once the elite has spoken to history and shown their political agency and economic and social power, they cannot again claim the status of subaltern (though subalternity is a relational term), no matter how relatively deprived they might feel in comparison to a more developed country or more privileged global elites (Spivak 1988).

The post-colonial right argues in terms of culturally conservative dimensions. During the time the British ruled India, an armed anti-colonial struggle emerged in Bengal, Punjab and Maharashtra. Various kinds of religious reform, sports and physical education movements and mobilisations gave it credence. The post-colonial right ideas emerged out of these legacies' anti-colonial mobilisations, however, the Hindu Mahasabha and Rashtriya Swayamsevak Sangh (pre-cursor organisations of BJP) members did not participate in much of the anti-colonial mobilisations or had brief stints (Kulkarni 2018) and their main enemy were the INC liberals, Communists and the Muslims not the British (Bapu 2012). The BJP party name and a coherent ideology and literature would emerge only much later – the practice preceded the discourse.

It would be grossly wrong; therefore, to claim that post-colonial theory – 'a variety of the neo-Marxist cultural left' – cleared or paved the way for cultural right-wing nationalist thinking just because they claimed culture, context and history are important and universalising theories have to reconfigure itself in a new context. At that time in India, the left was not even remotely thinking about anti-colonialism, nationalism, or culture; they were planning a revolution, although later it failed. The theoretically rich ideas of the Orthodox left had a long tradition. However, when looking at class analysis in India, orthodox Marxist theory did not consider important issues such as caste, peasant production, ecology, gender, religion or culture (Omvedt 1993). As Marxism faced new challenges, the heterodox Marxists, the new-left (and the subaltern studies) took those issues up as part of their "progressive research programme" (a term initially used by Imre Lakatos can be applied to Trotsky's Marxist analyses about Russian revolution, in a retroactive manner as demonstrated by Burawoy) – rather than terming these issues exceptional cases and bracketing these out of the sphere of theory (Burawoy 1989) – in the late 1970s and early 1980s.

130 TOWARD A NEW ART OF BORDER CROSSING

Influenced by the overall cultural turn in social science, the critical theories of post-structuralism and post-modernism, and their experiences worldwide and in India, the post-colonial left recontextualised and adapted these ideas to the complex realities of various cultures, institutions and temporalities in South Asia. The left followed what is known as 'positive heuristics' in the 'Lakatosian framework' and laid more of an emphasis on the 'culture' of the poor, subaltern poor, marginalised, and the proletariat (following Burawoy 1989). These ideas came to be understood as the neo-Marxist theories collective, including Gramscian theories, and their academic discourse gained coherence – although the orthodox Marxists somewhat pejoratively termed these ideas as 'revisionist theories and histories' because they postponed the immediacy of revolution.

In the Indian context, subaltern studies can be understood as the neo-Marxist theory that draws from Gramsci, Foucault and the history of the below school of the UK. However, the eclecticism of strands of ideas, forming discourses and changing narratives – of history and hegemonic formations – is somewhat by design (Dhanagare 1988).

Unlike in communism, where the theory and the party lead and guide the masses, political dimensions and urgencies – no theory or research – lead the vision of the politics of the post-colonial right in India and political contingencies and urgencies lead the path, making the path unpredictable, anti-intellectual and populist.

Interestingly the nodal points of the discourse of Hindutva are never fully closed or made coherent; a part of the nodes are always kept open so that a realpolitik based on new identities, ideas, discourses and interests can be appropriated by the current Hindutva regime (it is always ready to compromise). The structure of the discourse is – amoeba-like – shapeless, protean and somewhat ambiguous; because it is the realpolitik and sociopolitical contingencies (spontaneous or politically created) that matters, identities and 'interests' are more important, than any ideology. The discourse of Hindutva embraces whichever discursive and non-discursive dimension suits itself.

And even they are ready to sacrifice their own core principles such as the 'ban on beef meat' for making political alliances (Panicker 2017; One India 2018).

To form its discourse of eclecticism of ideas and around nodal discourses, the BJP creates a syncretic and 'modern' 'elitist' political discourse from above. The discourse serves the need for monopsony, and neoliberal capitalism under Big 'Indian/national' corporate houses to grow and maintain the hegemony and control of the class and caste elites in India.

The magnificent 'slyness' and chicanery of the technique are intriguing, and its unique strength, utility and structure should be understood. 'Hindutva' is a political idea, which creates a sense of structural isomorphism between its discourses and the other eclectic strands brought together from Indian traditions by hiding its intent and nodal, or real, content. The goal is to always present Hindutva together with or similar to 'something else' from the 'Indian tradition'. The public has accepted it, and the technique has gained legitimacy. Therefore, critics risk being branded communist, liberal or an enemy of the Hindus or the state and anti-national. The technique cannot be rejected because of its cultural spiritual attributions, contributions to Indian society, or its cultural historical legacy that is ambiguous or considered sacred and has mass appeal. At the same time, it hides the elite class-caste character/position of the party.

Hindutva and the post-colonial left both consider 'culture and tradition' important and use the similar logics (apparently) to criticise the so-called 'west', but they differ in intent, directionality of critical vectors, and content.

The left has a particular ontology of the lower class, proletariat or subaltern – and its cultural legacy. The culture that the post-colonial left talks about is the culture of the people, the poor, and the subalterns or the hegemonised. Also, the postcolonial and subaltern studies school are essentially post-nationalist in vision, which talks about the rights of myriad subaltern nations hidden in the womb of the Indian nation, and not nationalist (Chatterjee 1993).

But the post-colonial right uses cultural arguments merely as rhetoric, to create a sense of legitimacy through posturing and faking a structural isomorphism to win public electoral support. A closer look at their neo-traditionalist cultural discourse shows that the culture they love to talk about is essentially an "elite" culture, the culture of the ruler, the hegemon and the caste-class dominant. The Dalits, the Muslims or other diversities do not feature there (Venugopal 2020).

Therefore, their cultural arguments serve to mask their own upper-caste, upper-class elite interests. In electoral politics; they claim leadership for the subaltern in the name of nationalism, somehow by spinning new myths and fake narratives in history (*India Today* 2014).

Their nationalist ideas allow for the relatively peaceful appropriation and neoliberal accumulation of resources from above without any mass dissensus or uprising. Nationalist post-colonial and religious discourses help to create an ambiguous situation and a temporary smokescreen that partially hides this process of resource accumulation and renders it some legitimacy till the maximum national resources can be usurped (Roy Chowdhury & Lahiri-Dutt 2021).

The post-colonial new-left in India opposed Soviet imperialism and revolutionary objectivity. But sticking to their left origins and genealogy, they also argued that the poor, the subaltern and trade unions must wage a Gramscian war of positions from below and launch spontaneous movements through their existing cultural moorings and subjectivities because that would not bracket out or sanitise their 'culture' or unsophisticated expressions. The post-colonial left preferred not to wait for the revolution to come through the order of the Politburo and the party line because it would take time and it would not be spontaneous, as Indian society has many cultural blocks and stasis, if we wait for too long nothing is going to transform.

Imposed from above as an alien ideology in India, democracy helped some of the marginalised gain political power, but the liberal elites and the Indian National Congress monopolised democracy. The poor needed to understand democracy in its structural and substantive senses; to develop their democratic awareness, the post-colonial left thought it would be a good strategy to radicalise democracy every day, eventually, which would bring 'revolution' about. So, when the post-colonial left spoke of 'culture', they did not mean the dominant culture of the colonising elites or of the colonised native elites who eventually became the post-colonial national elites; they meant the culture of the people, the poor citizens and the subaltern populations.

The cultural dimension of the post-colonial left is a culture from below, a culture of the poor that has been hegemonised. The post-colonial left intended not to freeze it in time but to change it slowly. It wanted to sharpen the progressive and secular dimensions of the culture of communitarian societies and amplify it to make it counter-hegemonic so that hegemonic cultural rule can be ended by selectively deploying subaltern culture and its progressive dimensions.

The post-colonial left experiences and traditions which co-evolved with subaltern studies school in academia (indeed most of the subaltern studies founding school members such as Guha were communist party members and activists) encountered the neo-Marxist and Euro-Marxist movements. And it became inspired by Michel Foucault's methodology of writing genealogical history and also by the British School of Writing History from below. Slowly, the post-colonial left turned Gramscian and tried to operationalise Marxist class struggles and their ideas in rural Indian society. But society in India was fundamentally different than elsewhere in context and history. 'Colonial' history and its interventions had set Indian society in a certain direction of 'path dependency' in terms of cultural and discursive formations. As the post-colonial left encountered the 'traditional' and cultural issues associated with Indian society — religion, caste, gender, and, much later, environment and ecology – it realised that in India social change would not come about in exactly the same way as in Europe, or through similar understandings of the 'class struggle', or an understanding of 'civil society' in the same ways.

The post-colonial left connected the misery in India to the alien British colonial rule that transformed Indian society. The Battle of Plassey (1757) and the adoption of the Permanent Settlement Act (1793) transmogrified the agrarian landscape in colonial Bengal.

The non-settler colonialism of the British was a project of extraction for the burgeoning Industrial Revolution and Capitalism; the modernisation was a result of the setting up of extractive infrastructure and logistics. The external capitalism that came with British colonialism siphoned wealth from India and the other colonies to the UK and brought about discursive, legal, institutional and organisational transformations in the indigenous universe.

The post-colonial left and right both criticise things that originated 'outside' Indian culture (the left criticises it on a more scholarly and critical basis), but the post-colonial left does not regress beyond British colonialism, to criticise or demonise the imperial Muslim rulers, dynasties, or invasions. Nadir Shah and others were conquerors and plunderers. But beyond the initial moment of violence the rest of the imperialist Muslim adventurers – the Mughals and the Khiljis, whom the Hindutva brigades demonise – made India their home. They used the wealth they extracted to develop trade routes, infrastructure and cities in India; they did not send it back to their home country. They rarely tried to transform the cultural sphere of the Hindus, and there was never a project of mass-scale religious conversion (Kaviraj 2005 a, 2005 b).

The post-colonial left criticises the real British 'colonialism' and the modern imperialism associated with the industrial revolution, racism, and the associated ills of

BETWEEN THE LEFT, THE LIBERAL, AND THE RIGHT

expanding global capitalism that emerged therein and continues, and form the core of Marxist ideas and its lineages. So cultural critique is necessary, but the Marxist idea of the political-economic dimensions of exploitation is a more important dimension here.

The post-colonial right is not actually 'post-colonial' in thought in that sense. It takes the argument of cultural revival too seriously and runs a historical regression, going back to the past to criticise not only the colonisers (which is not so strong) but mainly the Islamic rulers, their main 'shadow enemy'. The post-colonial right uses the idea of criticising alien cultures and not only of the British colonisers but mainly the Muslim rulers and 'invaders' who ruled India for about 700–800 years. The post-colonial right argues in terms of religious and culturally conservative dimensions to argue in 'cultural and communitarian', or dominant-elite-religious, terms that the Muslims imposed their ideas and religion on the Hindus. And they invaded Hindu culture and sacred geography and the community by killing and converting Hindus and forcefully marrying women and defiling and raping them and then ruled the Hindu majority by force. They argue this happened partially because the Hindus were not a united force as a national 'community' under a sovereign/national authority (Golwalker 1939).

The post-colonial right's notion of culture is the culture of the indigenous or native elites. The post-colonial right wants to preserve the sacred religious socio-political and economic core of the Hindu religion by reviving the traditional caste-based social hierarchy and gender norms and its caste and class elites. This is a cultural usurpation and consolidation and a politico-cultural and social counter-revolution from above, not a cultural valorisation from below.

Neoliberal capitalism fits only too well in this elitist traditional cultural ensemble because it cannot be challenged by a culturally docile and economically less powerful underclass, and the post-colonial Indian elites can usurp more wealth and gain even more power and control over the labouring classes and the caste subalterns. Naturally, therefore, unlike the post-colonial left, the post-colonial right does not criticise its own class or positions and tries not to talk about how, historically, the caste elites – Brahmin, Baniya and Zamindar – have oppressed the underclass. Because it is basically the remnants of these class and class elites which is at the helm of affairs now under the Hindutva regime.

The Hindutva elites are against what happened during Islamic rule and only partially against colonialism. Their notion is, thus, not really post-colonial but specifically 'post-Islamic-imperialism'. They want to recreate Indian culture not only through 'decolonial' measures but by de-imperializing and de-Islamifying the Indian cultural and socio-political scape. Their goal is to restore the so-called 'sacred, original moment of the true and pure Hindu community in the golden ages in the absence of foreign socio-political and cultural forces' that defiled the Hindu elites and their sacred space (which is itself some form of an utopian imaginary). Only then can religious majoritarian nationalism be forged.

A collective 'imaginary' of 'revenge' and a hidden dream and desire for a new Hindu imperialism underlies this rhetorical 'de-imperialism'. The de-imperialism would take place through the revenge of the subjugated, where the imperial subject and the colonised wants' to take revenge by creating an 'empire' of their own and which would be composed of the 'territorial' notions of *Akhand Bharat* (Savarkar 1923), a territory without the Islamic population (prior to the Islamisation of South Asia and Indian Subcontinent), and *Ghar wapsi* (reconversion of Indian Muslims, who were mainly composed of so-called 'lower castes' who got converted to Islam either under pressure or through Sufi doctrines).

Thus the post-colonial right believes that the people once colonised by the Muslims now have turned powerful, imperialist and expansionist and want to avenge their historical collective defeat and humiliation.

The post-colonial right imagines that they can forge 'national unity' between the elites and the masses by 'othering' Muslims and making them their common enemy. Bringing about the cultural revival of the elites and their nationalist pride, and making the community 'tough' in the mirror image of Islam, would let Hindus pay Muslims back in the same coin. Obliterating the Muslims from India would give the Hindu mind a sense of catharsis, albeit imaginary, and bring about psychological and emotional closure, and make Hindus proud again.

These nationalist ideas of the post–colonial right would not make India a nation of equals but divide the people along the lines of religion, caste and class. As we will be united till we have an enemy other, once the Muslims are gone we will again be divided along caste, class and gender lines. The irony is that united we stand only when we have an enemy, imagined or real, be the external or internal.

Whereas by making a post-national argument, the post-colonial left and subaltern studies clearly speak against the elitist and nationalist ideas of the post-colonial right that have dominated and hegemonised the sundry dissenting nations hidden within the Indian nation and talk about their culture and rights (Chatterjee 1994).

Conclusions

The post-colonial left performs cultural politics from below; the post-colonial right mobilises – for the sake of realpolitik, and conservative religio-cultural nationalism – the cultural resources and capital of the elites from above and tries to form solidarity with the subaltern somehow through vote management, contingency and chicanery to win elections.

The post-colonial left on the other promotes a culture of the subjugated and a post-nationalist and anti-essentialist identity of the subaltern equally. The post-colonial left works with nuances of culture.

Post-colonial left ideas, theory and thought introduce multiple, hybrid and intersectional subjectivities and identities, and accept ideas from all kinds and colours of politics to create a discourse of its own. By fragmenting the border lines and the border itself and the notion of difference, these identities complicate the borders between the left, the liberal and the right. This act of 'border crossing' is ontologically anti-essentialist in nature; it has the potential to stop the 'polarisation' of identities by creating a space in the middle for politics that transcends all partisan divides.

To enable such politics, however, it is necessary to ensure a new 'border gnosis or thinking' (Anzaldua 1999, Mignolo 2000) – or an 'epistemology of exteriority' (Mignolo

BETWEEN THE LEFT, THE LIBERAL, AND THE RIGHT

& Tlostanova 2006: 206) – by critiquing post-colonial theory itself. We must also simultaneously draw ideas from post-colonial theory, and extend its limits, by striving for a 'decolonial' space where theory emerges from the 'lived' dimensions of politics from the 'margin of the margin' (Chaudhury, Das & Chakrabarti 2000).

Recently, dalit movements and ideologies have criticised post-colonialism in India, particularly its reactionary class and caste Hindu origins (Dwivedi & Shaj 2018). This critique has created the possibility for a decolonial space to emerge. However, political action must be rooted in meditative introspection and empathy (Giri 2013), and not realpolitik; it should constantly reposition the margins as the analytical centre and unsettle dominant structures.

Funding

The article was prepared within the framework of the Basic Research Program at HSE University.

References

Anzaldua, G. 1999. *Borderlands/La Frontera: The New Mestiza*, San Francisco: Aunt Lute Books.

Bapu, P. 2012. *Hindu Mahasabha in Colonial North India, 1915–1930 Constructing Nation and History*, London: Routledge.

Bhatt, C. 2001. *Hindu Nationalism: Origins, Ideologies and Modern Myths*, NY: New York University Press.

Burawoy, M. 1989. 'Two Methods in Search of Science: Skocpol versus Trotsky', *Theory and Society*, 18(6): 759–805.

Business Standard. 2022. World benefiting from yoga due to initiative taken by PM. (June 21, 2022) (https://www.business-standard.com/article/current-affairs/world-benefiting-from-yoga-due-to-initiative-taken-by-pm-modi-nadda-122062100624_1.html) (Accessed on 20 July 2022).

Chatterjee, P. 1992. 'History and the Nationalization of Hinduism', *Social Research*, 59(1): 111–149.

———1993. *Nationalist Thought and the Colonial World: A Derivative Discourse, Minneapolis*: University of Minnesota Press.

———1994. *The Nation and Its Fragments: Colonial and Postcolonial Histories, NJ*: Princeton University Press.

———2019. *I Am the People: Reflections on popular Sovereignty Today*, NY: Columbia University Press.

Chaudhury, A., D. Das, and A. Chakrabarti. 2000. *Margin of Margin: Profile of an Unrepentant Postcolonial Collaborator*, Calcutta: Anustup.

Detsch, J. 2015. India's Growing Muslim Population: A Political Challenge? (The Diplomat, May 1, 2015) (https://thediplomat.com/2015/05/indias-growing-muslim-population-a-political-challenge/) (Accessed on 20 July 2022).

Dhanagare, D. N. 1988. 'Subaltern Consciousness and Populism: Two Approaches in the Study of Social Movements in India', *Social Scientist,* 16(11): 18–35.

Dwivedi, D. and M. Shaj. 2018. *Gandhi and Philosophy: On Theological Anti-politics*, UK: Bloomsbury.

Ghosh, J. 2020. 'Hindutva, Economic Neoliberalism and the Abuse of Economic Statistics in India', *South Asia Multidisciplinary Academic Journal* [Online], 24/25 | 2020. (http://journals.openedition.org/samaj/6882) (Accessed on 20 July 2022).

Giri, A. K. 2013. *Knowledge and Human Liberation: Towards Planetary Realizations*, London: Anthem Press.

Golwalker, M.S. 1939. *We or Our Nationhood Defined*, Nagpur: Bharat Publications.

Guha, R. 1998. *Dominance without Hegemony: History and Power in Colonial India*, Ma.: Harvard University Press.

Hansen, T.B. 1999. *The Saffron Wave: Democracy and Hindu Nationalism in Modern India*, New Jersey: Princeton University Press.

India Today. 2014. The Hindu Muslim invasion created Dalits and tribals in India, says RSS, (September 22) (https://www.indiatoday.in/india/story/rss-mohan-bhagwat-hindu-dalits-tribals-muslim-invasion-293816-2014-09-22) (Accessed on 20 July 2022).

Jaffrelot, C. 1996. *The Hindu Nationalist Movement and Indian Politics*, London: C. Hurst & Co. and Penguin India.

Jain, R and T. Lasseter. 2018. By rewriting history, Hindu nationalists aim to assert their dominance over India. (Reuter, March 6, 2018) (https://www.reuters.com/investigates/special-report/india-modi-culture/)(Accessed on 20 July 2022).

Kaviraj, S. 2005 a. 'An Outline of a Revisionist Theory of Modernity', *European Journal of Sociology*, 46(3): 497–452.

_____2005 b. 'On the enchantment of the state: Indian thought on the role of the state in the narrative of modernity', *European Journal of Sociology*, 46(2): 263–296.

_____2018. 'Contradictions of Conservatism', *Studies in Indian Politics*, 6(1): 1–14.

Kulkarni, P. 2018. History Shows How Patriotic the RSS Really Is. (October 7, 2018) (https://thewire.in/history/rss-hindutva-nationalism) (Accessed on 20 July 2022).

Lakshman, N. 2014. Vasudhaiva Kutumbakam' is India's philosophy: Modi. (The Hindu, September 28, 2014) (https://www.thehindu.com/news/national/Vasudhaiva-Kutumbakam-is-India%E2%80%99s-philosophy-Modi/article60344743.ece) (Accessed on 20 July 2022).

Maitra, N. 2022. Why Narendra Modi Presents Himself as a Guru Drawing on traditions of monastic power, Modi's party is trying to promote the image of India as a *vishwaguru*, or teacher to the world. (January 27, 2022) (https://daily.jstor.org/why-narendra-modi-presents-himself-as-a-guru/) (Accessed on 20 July 2022).

Males'evic', S. 2017. 'The Foundations of Statehood: Empires. and Nation-states in the longue dure'e', *Thesis Eleven*, 139(1): 145–161.

Mignolo, W. D. & M.V. Tlostanova. 2006. 'Theorizing from the Borders: Shifting to Geo- and Body-Politics of Knowledge', *European Journal of Social Theory*, 9(2): 205–221.

Mignolo, W. 2000. *Local Histories/Global Designs*. Chichester: Princeton University Press.

Omvedt, G. 1993. *Reinventing Revolution: New Social Movements and the Socialist Tradition in India (Socialism and Social Movements)*, India: Routledge.

One India. 2018. BJP to stay away from imposing beef ban in Northeast, in other parts it might, (March 14, 2018) (https://www.oneindia.com/india/bjp-stay-away-from-imposing-beef-ban-northeast-other-parts-2658402.html?story=1) (Accessed on 20 July 2022).

Panicker, R.S. 2017. BJP Candidate in Kerala Promises Good Beef If Voted To Power Kerala (NDTV, April 02, 2017) (https://www.ndtv.com/kerala-news/bjp-candidate-in-kerala-promises-good-beef-if-voted-to-power-1676398) (Accessed on 20 July 2022).

Pennington, B.K. 2001. 'Constructing Colonial Dharma: A Chronicle of Emergent Hinduism, 1830–1831', *Journal of the American Academy of Religion*, 69(3): 577–603.

Roy Chowdhury, A. 2014. *Subalternity, State-Formation and Movements against Hydropower Projects in India, 1920–2004*. PhD Thesis, Department of Sociology, National University of Singapore.

Roy Chowdhury, A. 2016. Subaltern Studies, in Sangeeta Ray, Henry Schwarz, José Luis Villacañas Berlanga, Alberto Moreiras and April Shemak (eds.), *Encyclopedia of Postcolonial Studies*, Wiley and Blackwell: USA, DOI: 10.1111/b.9781444334982.2016.x.

Roy, B. 2017. Dhormo Ashole Bhalo Itihasher Nothikhana, (April 15 2017 Anandabazar patrika Online) (https://www.anandabazar.com/culture/poila-baisakh/special-write-up-on-ranajit-guha-a-bengali-historian-by-biswajit-roy-1.597807) (Accessed on 20 July 2022).

BETWEEN THE LEFT, THE LIBERAL, AND THE RIGHT

Roy Chowdhury, A and K. Lahiri-Dutt. 2021. 'Extractive capital and multi-scalar environmental politics: interpreting the exit of Rio Tinto from the diamond fields of Central India', *Third World Quarterly*, 42(8): 1770–1787.

Sarkar, S. 2000. Orientalism Revisited: Saidian Frameworks in the Writing of Modern Indian History, in Vinayak Chaturvedi (ed.) *Mapping Subaltern Studies and the Postcolonial*, London, NY: Verso, pp. 239–255.

Savarkar, V.D. 1923. *Essentials of Hindutva*, Mumbai: Hindi Sahitya Sadan.

Scroll. 2019. Western standards of human rights do not apply to India, says Home Minister Amit Shah (2019, 13 October) (https://scroll.in/latest/940344/western-standards-of-human-rights-do-not-apply-to-india-says-home-minister-amit-shah) (Accessed on 20 July 2022).

Singh, J. 2001. Why International Yoga Day is no cause for celebration in India (Down To Earth, 30 November 2001) (https://www.downtoearth.org.in/blog/why-international-yoga-day-is-no-cause-for-celebration-in-india-50269) (Accessed on 20 July 2022).

Spivak, Gayatri Chakravorty. 1988. "Can the Subaltern Speak?" In Cary Nelson and Lawrence Grossberg (Eds.) *Marxism and the Interpretation of Culture*, 271–313. London: Macmillan.

The Hindu. 2017. New education policy soon to correct colonial mindset, says Union minister Satya Pal Singh, (October 23, 2017) (https://www.thehindu.com/news/national/new-education-policy-in-december-says-union-minister-satya-pal-singh/article19906224.ece) (Accessed on 20 July 2022).

_____2019. Expand definition of human rights: Amit Shah. (October 13, 2019) (https://www.thehindu.com/news/national/other-states/expand-definition-of-human-rights-amit-shah/article29669758.ece) (Accessed on 20 July 2022).

The Indian Express. 2022. Secularism in Constitution distorted': Kerala BJP leader PK Krishnadas hints at amendments, (11 July 2022) (https://www.newindianexpress.com/states/kerala/2022/jul/11/secularism-in-constitution-distortedkerala-bjp-leader-pk-krishnadas-hints-at-amendments-2475117.html) (Accessed on 20 July 2022).

The Wire. 2021. In Running as BJP Candidate in WB Assembly Polls, Rajya Sabha MP Swapan Dasgupta Faces Disqualification, (15 March 2021) (https://thewire.in/politics/rajya-sabha-mp-swapan-dasgupta-bjp-mahua-moitra) (Accessed on 20 July 2022).

Truschke, A. 2022. "Decolonizing" Indians Through Hindutva Ideological Control, (May 1, 2022 / Issue 29, *Education*, Magazine) (https://shuddhashar.com/decolonizing-indians-through-hindutva-ideological-control/) (Accessed on 20 July 2022).

van der Veer, P. (1994). *Religious Nationalism: Hindus and Muslims in India*, Berkeley: University of California Press.

Venugopal, V. 2020. Shouldn't minorities, Dalits talk about Indian culture: Kanimozhi asks Centre orities, Dalits talk about Indian culture: Kanimozhi asks Centre. (*The Economic Times*, September 16, 2o2o). (https://economictimes.indiatimes.com/news/politics-and-nation/shouldnt-minorities-dalits-talk-about-indian-culture-kanimozhi-asks-centre/articleshow/78134014.cms?from=mdr) (Accessed on 20 July 2022).

Yadav, Y. 2020. This is no Emergency. Modi and Shah are using democracy to subvert democracy, (The Print, 24 June 2020) (https://theprint.in/opinion/no-emergency-modi-shah-are-using-democracy-to-subvert-democracy/447685/) (Accessed on 20 July 2022).

Notes

1 Associate Professor, School of Sociology, HSE University, Moscow, Russian Federation, Email : achowdhury@hse.ru.

2 There was a revolution in Hungary in 1956. The Soviet Union, invaded Hungary to supress the revolution. Ranajit Guha, already disillusioned with Stalinism, and Communist party

of India (CPI) factionalism left the CPI in protest (Roy 2017). Inspired by on the one hand global geopolitical events, Soviet politics, and the responses of European countries and, on the other, by the experiences of the activists of left political parties in India and Europe (especially Italy), Guha would pen a postcolonial left critique in a series of books and papers. A worldwide group of scholars would carry his legacy forward and add to his work. This school of thought and historiography would come to be known in the 1980s as Subaltern Studies. And Guha would come to be considered the principal theorist of the Subaltern Studies School. The Subaltern Studies School started in Indian academia the postcolonial left stream, which emerged from the experiences of left (Soviet) imperialism, and from protesting the Stalinist party lines, in India, and various postcolonial and contextual realities that the left experienced in Indian society.

Chapter 10

DIRECTIONS: EXIT, VOICE, AND LOYALTY AND THE MODERN HISTORY OF MIGRATION

Ronald Stade

Borders

Over hundreds of millennia, human beings have settled all over the world. For more than two hundred thousand years, *Homo sapiens* moved frequently in search of sustenance and shelter. Then, some 12 to 11,000 years ago, Natufian communities chose a sedentary life in the Levant, even before the rise of agriculture. The investment of labor in agriculture, however, meant that it made even more sense to settle in one place, thereby also creating early forms of property relations between human beings and land. Crossing the boundaries of someone's land could now potentially clash with the unlimited movement and settlement of everyone. With the establishment and expansion of sedentary communities, ever larger territories were thought of belonging to someone until we reach the current age in which we imagine the globe as an absolute map. It is absolute, because, on this map, there are no more white spots. Global space is now "disjunct (no spot can belong to two), categorical (a spot either belongs or it does not), and exhaustive (no spot goes un-belonged)" (Geertz 1995: 21). This means that wherever you are on our planet, you find yourself in a politically defined territory. Standing on the border between Jordan and Syria, for example, you might ask yourself if this particular pebble is Jordanian or Syrian or what might be the nationality of the swallow that is airborne and migratory most its life. The absolute map of the world creates the illusion that our planet and all of its soils, minerals, waters, flora, and fauna belong to someone.

Yet, in reality, the absolute map of the world does not prevent human (and other animal) mobility. A casual glance at the global air traffic at any given time reveals the immensity of human movement across international borders. If we were to add a map that charts every other human border-crossing movement on Earth, we would have a most rich and intricate depiction of travel routes and pathways. What such a map would not show, however, is the profile of those who have permission to cross international borders and those who do not. Other images are needed to expose the many attempts to cross international borders without official authorization. Such images would also uncover how many lives are lost when human beings try to cross oceans, rivers, deserts, and mountains to reach the other side of an international border. A planetary view would disclose that there is a pattern to these efforts. By and large, illegal migrations occur in one direction: they begin in political territories that are ranked low in the Human Development Index and have as their destination political territories that are ranked high, or at least higher, in the Human Development Index. This unidirectional movement across global space is a symptom of an historically evolved world order that, for better or worse, affects the life of everyone. To analyze this world order in simplifying terms as an outcome of earlier colonial relations does a disservice to those who today live under oppressive and destitute conditions. An alternative analysis of the global situation that causes the unidirectional migration of humans across international borders will be presented in what is to follow. Special attention will be given to the interaction between migration and political change. The conclusion will be that only political and social change—which, at times, it might be necessary to fight for using force—will improve the current state of the world.

Exit, Voice, and Loyalty

In his seminal work on individual responses to decline in the quality of private and public services, *Exit, Voice, and Loyalty*, Albert Hirschman (1970) distinguished between three types of reaction: the consumer or citizen quits or leaves (exit), speaks up (voice), or stays quiet and faithful (loyalty). Hirschman's categories have been applied to the study of various political scenarios, as well as to the study of migration, in particular to answer the question of who migrates under what objective circumstances and for what subjective reasons (see, e.g., O'Donnell 1986, Keczkes 1994, Hoffmann 2010, etc.). Lacking in such applications is placing exit, voice, and loyalty in a wider world-historical frame, which will reveal a direct relationship between, on one hand, the political struggle (voice) for the distribution of justice in one part of the world and, on the other, a unidirectional migration (exit) from another part of the world. That is, the historical, often bloody, fight for human and citizen rights, which was about putting the ideas of the radical Enlightenment into social and political practice, resulted in the establishment of liberal democracies and welfare states in some parts of the world. It is these parts of the globe that pull migrants from anocracies (illiberal democracies), dictatorships, and theocracies. What the latter types of regimes have in common is that they perpetuate corruption, injustice, inequality, fragility, conflict, and violence.

At the bottom of the inequality-adjusted Human Development Index (IAHDI) are 40 African countries plus Haiti and Yemen. To classify all of them as poor or "least developed"—and, more perniciously, to blame countries like Norway, Iceland, Finland, and Ireland, that are at the top of the IAHDI, for the lack of development—fails to acknowledge the wealth held by the corrupt elites of these countries and falls short of holding these elites to account. When the people in any of the most inequal countries rise up and demand justice and equity, the elites tend to react with utmost brutality. Scandinavian and some of the other least inequal and developed countries are committed to principled development policies, investing in the promotion of human rights, gender equality, the protection of children, and similar value-driven interventions in the so-called "least developed" and "low-income" countries. In academic debates, this is regularly portrayed as another form of colonialism, rather than as the continuation of the historical struggle for social justice and equity and for human and citizens' rights. It is important to remember that this struggle is neither an inevitable feature of history, as Marxists and "modernists" believed, nor that it is likely to any time soon result in a cosmopolitan order of global equality that provides every individual with the chance to come into their own and to move freely across the planet. Nevertheless, the struggle for equal and universal human rights is necessary to move the countries at the bottom of the IAHDI forward. That this, in effect, is a political fight has been, and will be, concealed by international actors like the UN and NGOs. The most important reason is that these international actors are completely dependent on the good will of the governments in the countries that they are supposed to support. If an African, Asian, and Latin American government decides not to grant entry or residence permits to members of an international actor like UNHCR or Save the Children, that actor is out of the picture.[1] If a national government decides to censor a study or report by an international actor, the actor has no choice but to go along.[2]

The impoverished individual residents of a country that ranks low in the IAHDI tend to be aware of their situation.[3] They know that other lives are possible. In West Africa, for example, it is common to explain differences in wealth with beliefs in witchcraft. Such beliefs center on interpersonal relationships. To acquire magic powers, one has to sacrifice a family member or someone with which one has an intimately close relationship. Powerful men and women are usually suspected of using witchcraft to achieve their riches, superior social status, and political clout (see Geschiere 1997 and 2013). This requires them to literally sacrifice others. To go against the powerful might be dangerous, not only because they control the police, military, and security services, but also because they are likely to have access to supernatural weapons. Consequently, most poor and powerless people will opt for loyalty in Hirschman's analytical triangle of exit, voice, and loyalty. They will endure injustices and poverty and try to get by as best they can.

Hirschman explained that the choice between exit (leaving) and voice (protesting) is not symmetrical. To leave (exit) is a choice that can be made by the individual. To protest (voice), on the other hand, usually requires a number of individuals to coordinate their action and to make their dissatisfaction known. Exit is private, voice is public. The cost of voice can be considerably higher than the cost of exit if protest results in imprisonment, torture, even death. Then again, the kind of exit that involves migrations that are fraught with danger and not rarely end with injury and death—be it drowning in the Mediterranean or the Rio Grande, succumbing in the desert terrains south of the U.S. border, or freezing to death in the Lebanese mountains—can be as perilous as taking to the streets to protest an oppressive regime. More importantly, if exit assumes the proportions of the mass exodus of East Germans in 1989, Syrian refugees in 2015, and Russian men and families in 2022, the act of leaving can itself become a type of protest (voice).[4] For this to occur, the mass exit must be perceived as people "voting with their feet," thereby turning the private act of exit into a public and political act of voice. The discursive battle between those who view migration as a private affair, driven by

142 TOWARD A NEW ART OF BORDER CROSSING

private motives (using cues like "social tourism," "economic migrants," etc.), and those who consider migration as both a private and political act—that is, as private exits that in aggregation reveal deep-seated political problems—defines the political conflict over migration in receiving countries.

Two Types of Hope

The persistent flow of migrants from countries with a poor human development record to countries with a better human development index could—and should!—be interpreted as a public and political act of voice through private acts of exit. At the root of individual decisions to leave a country for another country is discontent, as well as hope. Discontent can function as a great mobilizer. Mass protests, even revolutions, were driven by disaffection. The hoped-for outcome of protests and revolutions remains in most cases unclear. Publicly voicing discontent is first and foremost an act of negation, of negating what is. The poet Andrei Codrescu (1991) wrote a book entitled *The Hole in the Flag*. The title refers to the Romanian revolution that ended the dictatorship of Ceauşescu, in which the revolutionaries cut out the Communist emblem in the middle of the then-used Romanian flag, leaving a hole in the middle of the flag. The philosopher of fancy conjecture, Slavoj Žižek, used the symbolism of the hole in the Romanian flag as an example of pure negation: "It is difficult to imagine a more salient index of the 'open' character of a historical situation 'in its becoming', as Kierkegaard would have put it, of that intermediate phase when the former Master-Signifier, although it has already lost the hegemonical power, has not yet been replaced by the new one" (Žižek 1993: 1). In other words, negation also opens up potentiality; however, without filling the void created by discontent.

The migrant who crosses international borders without official authorization engages in an act of negation as well. But she is also motivated by hope for a better, more secure life. In migration research, this is referred to as push and pull factors. For the individual migrant, it is a matter of traveling toward something that is better. Hope, as the Marxist philosopher Ernst Bloch (1995) explained in his magnum opus, *The Principle of Hope* (which fills 1520 pages in the English translation), is a surplus of material conditions. Hope is the human capability to go beyond what is and to dream about what could be. It is an aspect of the capacity to aspire, as Arjun Appadurai (2013) calls it.[5] While life goes on amid the reality of existing conditions, Bloch argued that human beings also live toward the future, which means living toward that which is not yet. Hope, then, is a surplus of potentiality within actuality. It introduces possibility in actual lives.

The not-yet comes in two guises. One is deeply anchored in actuality. It is a hope for what is possible now. The other is utopian. It is a dream of what might become possible in the future but is not possible now. The pull factor in migrations that involve unauthorized border crossings are most likely energized by the first type of hope for the not-yet, whereas the second type of hope seems more closely linked to utopian aspirations for systemic and regime change. The hope in exit is for what is possible now. The hope in voice might be for what could become possible in the future.

DIRECTIONS
143

As long as international migration is analyzed in terms of private decisions of exit, rather than as political acts of hope, the global migratory pattern continues to be depoliticized. A closer focus on push factors could bring politics back into the debate on migration.

Push Factors

We were sitting in a shell of a building that lacked windows, doors, plaster, paint, plumbing, and anything else that belongs to a finished construction of a residential building. The Syrian refugees that we were talking to offered us sweetened tea and had put out the biscuits and soft drinks that we had brought for them. It was the month of March and in the Lebanese town of Bsharri, that is located some 1,500 meters (4,800 feet) above sea level, there were still patches of snow. Inside the unfinished building, it was freezing, and both the refugees and we were wearing coats indoors. The stories of the refugees who had crossed the border between Syria and Lebanon were familiar by now. We had already talked to hundreds of Syrian refugees in all parts of Lebanon and almost none of them claimed to have escaped to Lebanon because of pull factors. Syria had occupied Lebanon between 1976 and 2005 and only few Lebanese had pleasant memories of this period. Rather, most Lebanese we met expressed their hate for Syria and Syrians and wanted the refugees from Syria to leave Lebanon. There were also widespread rumours about Syrian refugees pretending to be impoverished so they would receive huge sums of money every month from international organizations. Members and supporters of Hezbollah, which is a state within the state of Lebanon, and Amal, the other Shia movement (from which Hezbollah sprang), are champions of, and apologists for, the brutal Syrian regime. To them, the Syrian refugees are traitors, deserters, and potential enemies. In other words, Syrian refugees met and meet few friendly faces in Lebanon.

The families who rented the "apartments" in the shell building in the Christian town of Bsharri—yes, they had to pay rent!—were eager to leave not just the town but Lebanon. One of the men tried to express his desperation by saying that he even would emigrate to Israel (with which Lebanon, at the time of writing, officially still is at war and that is ruled by Jews, who, according to mainstream Muslim ideology, are the enemies of Allah). Another man kept staring at me throughout the conversation until I finally asked him if he wanted to ask me something. In a soft voice, he told me that he, his wife, and son would be moving to Sweden (my home country) in a couple of weeks. They had been selected by UNHCR as so-called quota refugees, that is, as refugees who have been chosen for resettlement in a third country (a safe country that is not the country of current refuge and not the country of origin). In 2020, UNHCR submitted files for almost 40,000 refugees for resettlement in third countries. A little over half of the submissions actually resulted in resettlements. Often this is because third countries have quotas for resettlement that are too low to allow all refugees selected by UNHCR to be resettled. But there are also cases where the refugees turn down the offer to be resettled. Two women we spoke to condensed the reason for refusing resettlement in the phrase "we will lose our children." What they meant was that moving to a

144 TOWARD A NEW ART OF BORDER CROSSING

non-Muslim country would present their children with too many temptations and lead them away from Islam.

The man who with his family anticipated to be resettled in Sweden looked forward to a life in peace and without discrimination. His hope was for his son to be able to get a decent education and make nice friends. He also hoped that he would be able to find work that suited him. We exchanged phone numbers and other contact information, and I was delighted when he sent photos and a message after he and his family had arrived in Sweden. In the years since, life seems to have worked out more or less as he had hoped. The reason is that his hope was for a not-yet that was anchored in actuality. That is, his hope was reasonable. In addition, he understood that Sweden is a country where a wide range of rights are guaranteed and the state protects the common good, as well as individual freedom.

His reason for fleeing Syria, on the other hand, had little to nothing to do with hopes for a better life in Lebanon. As with all other Syrian refugees we talked to, to leave Syria was a matter of not being killed either by the regime's or Russian or Iranian or irregular armed gang's attacks or to be drafted into the Syrian military and be sent to the frontline as cannon fodder or to be "disappeared" by the regime. Finding refuge across the border in Lebanon, Jordan, Iraq, and Turkey was a matter of survival. What in technical language is called prolonged displacement—that is, Syrian refugees living in countries that have a common border with Syria for a decade or more—is at heart a political crisis. For the situation to change, a not-yet that is not possible now, but should become possible in the future, is needed. To put it bluntly, this utopian not-yet involves the overthrow of the current Syrian regime, the expulsion from Syria of the Russian and Iranian mercenaries that preserve the regime, and the disarmament of the militias and gangs that terrorize the Syrian population. No international actor is prepared to bring about such a change and what armed resistance there remains inside Syria is supported by the Islamist regimes of Turkey and Qatar (the major sponsors of the Muslim Brotherhood). The secular progressive forces in Syria have been quashed by the Syrian regime and its foreign allies, as well as by the Islamist militias sustained by Turkey and irregular gangs allowed by the regime to operate with impunity in Syria (the so-called *Shabiha*, شَبِّيحَة). It would have been, and still is, up to liberal democratic nations to rid Syria of its murderous regime and the Russian and Iranian troops without which the regime would not survive.

Because Syria is no exception and the world is full of cruel regimes and illiberal rulers, people choose exit. They risk their own lives and the lives of their children to escape the unbearable conditions in their home countries, which either are among those at the bottom of the IAHDI or are ranked as 'not free' in Freedom House's combined Global Freedom Scores, or both. The lack of human development and of freedom are political issues, as is the struggle for human development and freedom.

Occidentalism and the Radical Legacy

How did the split between the "developed" and "developing" countries come about? One school of thought argues that the colonialism of the late nineteenth and first half of the twentieth century is the single most consequential cause of the split. I hope to convince

DIRECTIONS 145

the reader that this is at best a partial explanation that, again, neglects the political nature of what happened in the eighteenth to twentieth centuries. At the time of writing, the ideology of postcolonialism makes up the mainstream of academic disciplines like anthropology, cultural, and literary studies. It is the latest iteration of occidentalism, that is, the condemnation of what is thought of as a "Western" tradition. Occidentalism is the mirror image of orientalism in that it essentializes one part of the world and its inhabitants and reduces them to stereotypical signs. Whatever the variety of postcolonialism, a common topos is that there is something called "Western" knowledge. There is also a moral master narrative of an asymmetrical relationship between perpetrators ("the West") and their victims ("the Rest"). Selective readings and sources are used to prove this point and story, while other readings and sources that would contradict the topos of "Western" knowledge and a simple dichotomy of perpetrators and victims are ignored. This is why postcolonialism resembles an ideology rather than an academic field of research.

What postcolonialists refer to as "Western" knowledge was in fact an arena of ferocious conflict and far-reaching upheavals such as the French Revolution. The major frontlines ran between three political factions: the radicals, the moderates, and the reactionaries. For example, what is commonly abbreviated as "the Enlightenment" was actually a most fierce conflict between, on one hand, radical and moderate Enlightenment figures and, on the other, between all representatives of the Enlightenment and their common foe, the reactionary detractors of the Enlightenment. The radical advocates of the Enlightenment—people like Denis Diderot, Baron d'Holbach, Mary Wollstonecraft, and Thomas Paine—argued vehemently against slavery, colonialism, racism, monarchy, and religion and defended women's rights and universal and equal rights for everyone. Moderate Enlightenment figures like Montesquieu, Hume, and Voltaire were more interested in having enlightened rulers than an enlightened populace. The existing social order was not their primary concern. The reactionary enemies of any form of Enlightenment simply did not want to have change and were skeptical of human rationality (this skepticism they have in common with poststructuralist and postcolonialist academics).

It is the legacy of the radical form of Enlightenment, with its universalist ambition for equal rights, democracy, and individual freedom, that lives on in the institutions and mainstream values of liberal societies like Sweden, Norway, New Zealand, Germany, and the Netherlands. Unsurprisingly, it is the borders of these countries that millions of migrants try to cross. That fascist leaders, movements, and regimes around the world fight the radical legacy of social-liberal democracy is also not surprising. Universal rights and individual freedom, including legally established rights and individual freedom for women, LGBTQ+ individuals, atheists and apostates, and other free thinkers, are antithetical to fascism's collectivism, communalism, and identity politics. The current global clash between, on one side, social-liberal democracies and, on the other, fascist and other illiberal regimes, would seem to force all of us to choose a side. Occidentalism, either of the postcolonial or the fascist variety, presents an imminent political danger. By creating the illusion that there is a "West," it constructs an enemy that also includes all those who fought for universal and equal human and citizen rights and the kind of individual freedom that allows anyone to come into their own.

146   TOWARD A NEW ART OF BORDER CROSSING

The global migration pattern ought to be taken seriously by scholars. Why is the pattern by and large unidirectional? Why do thousands of Norwegians not cross the ocean in unsafe vessels to reach Mauritania or Guinea? It is a question that requires serious reflection. Some countries, like, for example, Mauritania and Guinea, have a history of military coups and elites robbing the country's wealth. There is little hope that they soon will develop into social-liberal democracies that guarantee universal and equal rights, among them the economic right to a minimal measure of welfare, and individual freedom of all its residents. When the inhabitants of such countries exercise their voice, there usually will be violent crackdowns. Furthermore, even widespread protests in those countries do not address the violence perpetrated against girls, LGBTQ+ individuals, and atheists.[6] The lack of basic rights and individual freedom is not a result of past colonial relations between West Africa and European nations. Both Mauritania and Guinea had more than half a century to introduce universal and equal rights and individual freedom—for example, the freedom not to be genitally mutilated and to be permitted to engage in blasphemous speech and to make public the corruption of the countries' elites. The elites of these countries also had decades in which they could have chosen not to treat the state and its resources as their private property. Instead, they follow the ideological lead of postcolonialism and blame the state of affairs in their countries on their colonial past, thereby hoping to escape accountability for their criminal actions. The impunity granted by postcolonialism to criminal elites in former colonies is perhaps the greatest betrayal of the inhabitants of those countries.

Borders That Need to Be Crossed

What happened in Europe and to a lesser extent in North America, viz. the overthrow of absolute rulers, the separation of Church and State, the gradual introduction of universal rights (which was much too slow because it at every step met with resistance from moderate and reactionary forces), and the spread of the ideal of individual freedom, has either never been replicated in most other countries or is now being rolled back by fascist leaders and their followers. A country like Lebanon, which has been plundered by its elite, attempted to create a lasting peace by dividing political influence and wealth between sectarian leaders. A terrorist organization like Hezbollah even shares a monopoly on violence with the Lebanese police, military, and security forces. The people who take to the streets of Beirut to protest the corrupt sectarian order of Lebanon do not want to be loyal to the identitarian politics of the country. They would prefer to live in a universalist, secular society like France. Islamists and other reactionary groups accuse the protesters of being "Westernized." The terrible contribution of anthropology and cultural studies is that they have legitimized this idea as a valid accusation. "Westernization" is supposed to be interpreted as a bad thing.

Amman's taxi drivers, policemen, and construction workers who stop what they are doing to roll out their mats and pray in the direction of Mecca show the world that they are pious and respectable people. At the same time, they do not easily suffer the people they refer to as "nawar" (نَوَر) or "gypsies." Of course, they also do not tolerate homosexuality and feminism and they ridicule unmanly men and think of women who do not cover up their hair and body as whores. Jordanians and non-Jordanians with dark skin, they call "*abd* (عبد), slave, or '*abusamrah*' (أبوسمراء), an idiom meaning 'father of dark skin', or Karemo," the name of a chocolate-coated marshmallow treat. From afar it might seem that it is the pious, respectable men and women who represent the "true" Jordan. From up close, however, it becomes clear that they are caught in an ongoing conflict, in which they try to contain global influences. Many younger Jordanians wish to escape the confines of the strict norms of their state and society. They have now a number of cosmopolitan spots to choose from in Amman. These spots—cafés, restaurants, malls, university campuses, etc.—allow boys and girls, men and women to meet without supervision. Some of these spots cater to the LGBTQ+ community and facilitate an urban lifestyle. They attract patrons from various social backgrounds and are also popular with Jordan's expats. By providing open spaces (as opposed to the common closed spaces of the home and workplace), they act as wedges between reactionary and progressive forces in Jordanian society. It is these open spaces that bring to the fore the division between the guardians of the status quo and those who hope for a major change that is not possible now but that might become possible in the future (see Lundberg 2018 on open spaces in Amman).

Whose voice will be heard and heeded in the end depends on political circumstances. But history has shown that radical upheavals and profound changes have come about in unpredictable ways. While the Arab Spring and similar widespread protest movements have failed to establish social-liberal democracies in the Middle East and most of Africa and Asia, they should teach us that not just exit but voice too can contain hope. The choice between exit and voice does not always exist for the individual. That the decision to leave or protest is consequential beyond the fate of the individual has hopefully become clear, however.

References

Appadurai, Arjun. 2013. 'The Capacity to Aspire: Culture and the Terms of Recognition', in *The Future as Cultural Fact: Essays on the Global Condition*. London and Brooklyn, New York: Verso, pp. 179–196.

Bloch, Ernst. 1995. *The Principle of Hope*, Vol. 1–3. Cambridge, Massachusetts: MIT Press.

Codrescu, Andrei. 1991. *The Hole in the Flag: A Romanian Exile's Story of Return and Revolution*. New York: W. Morrow.

Geertz, Clifford. 1995. *After the Fact: Two Countries, Four Decades, One Anthropologist*. Cambridge, MA: Harvard University Press.

Geschiere, Peter. 1997. *The Modernity of Witchcraft: Politics and the Occult in Postcolonial Africa*. Charlottesville, Virginia: University of Virginia Press.

Geschiere, Peter. 2013. *Witchcraft, Intimacy, and Trust: Africa in Comparison*. Chicago: University of Chicago Press.

Hirschman, Albert O. 1970. *Exit, Voice, and Loyalty: Responses to Decline in Firms, Organizations, and States*. Cambridge, Massachusetts: Harvard University Press.

Hirschman, Albert O. 1993. 'Exit, Voice, and the Fate of the German Democratic Republic: An Essay in Conceptual History', *World Politics*, 45(2): 173–202.

Hoffmann, Bert. 2010. 'Bringing Hirschman Back In: "Exit", "Voice", and "Loyalty" in the Politics of Transnational Migration', *The Latin Americanist*, 54(2): 57–73.

Keczkes, Robert. 1994. 'Abwanderung, Widerspruch, Passivität. Oder: Wer zieht wann um?', *Zeitschrift für Soziologie*, 23(2): 129–144.

148 TOWARD A NEW ART OF BORDER CROSSING

Lundberg, Arvid. 2018. Openness as Political Culture: The Arab Spring and the Jordanian Protest Movements. Doctoral thesis, Department of Social Anthropology, Stockholm University.

O'Donnell, Guillermo. 1986.'On the Fruitful Convergences of Hirschman's Exit, Voice and Loyalty and Shifting Involvements: Reflections from the Recent Argentine Experience', in Alejandro Foxley, Michael S. McPherson, and Guillermo O'Donnell (eds.): *Development, Democracy and the Art of Trespassing: Essays in Honor of Albert O. Hirschman*. Notre Dame: Universityof Notre Dame Press, pp. 249–268.

Stade, Ronald. 2016a. 'On the Capacity to Aspire. Conversation with Arjun Appadurai', in Thomas Tufte and Oscar Hemer (eds.): *Voice and Matter: Communication, Development and the Cultural Return*. Göteborg: Nordicom, pp. 211–216.

Stade, Ronald. 2016b. 'Debating the Politics of Hope: An Introduction', in Thomas Tufte and Oscar Hemer (eds.): *Voice and Matter: Communication, Development and the Cultural Return*. Göteborg: Nordicom, pp. 203–210.

Žižek, Slavoj. 1993. *Tarrying with the Negative: Kant, Hegel, and the Critique of Ideology*. Durham: Duke University Press.

Notes

1 The Lebanese government under then-president Michel Aoun, represented by his son-in-law and Lebanon's minister of foreign affairs, in 2018, threatened to throw out UNHCR from Lebanon if the organization did not agree to working toward returning Syrian refugees to Syria. UNHCR agreed.

2 These comments are informed by my own experience of conducting a large baseline study for UNICEF Lebanon—All the talk by marginally involved academics about the UN and NGOs behaving like neocolonial actors shows a lack of factual knowledge of operative conditions and who determines what the UN and NGOs actually are permitted to do inside a politically controlled territory.

3 Having lived for the past seven years in the Middle East (in Beirut and Amman), having conducted fieldwork among Syrian refugees in Lebanon, and having visited West Africa on several occasions, has familiarized me with the everyday life and aspirations of marginalized residents of countries that rank low in the IAHDI.

4 See Hirschman 1993.

5 See my conversation with Arjun Appadurai on the capacity to aspire in Stade (2016a), as well as my own discussion of the politics of hope in Stade (2016b). At the time of our conversation, Appadurai had not begun to study Bloch.

6 In Mauritania, atheism, blasphemy, and sacrilegious acts are punishable by death. In Guinea, homosexuality is illegal. Guinea also has one of the highest rates of female genital mutilation in the world.

Chapter 11

CROSSING THE GERMAN–GERMAN BORDER FROM THE END OF WORLD WAR II UNTIL 1990: FROM ESCAPE TO ALIENATION

Detlef Briesen

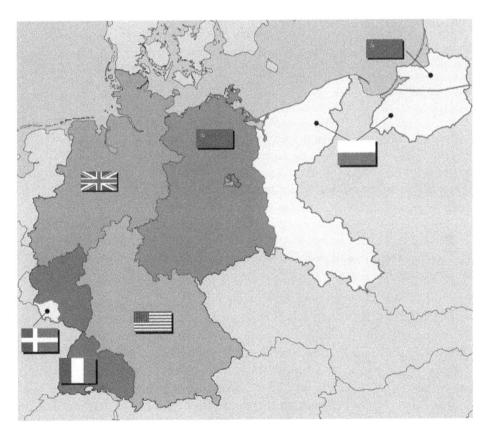

Germany 1945 according to the decisions of the Allied Powers

150 TOWARD A NEW ART OF BORDER CROSSING

1. Preface

Until 1989, massive fortifications along the almost 1,400-kilometre-long inner-German border prevented the inhabitants of the German Democratic Republic (GDR) from visiting the Federal Republic of Germany (FRG) or leaving it permanently for the West. Officially, these fortifications did not include that part of the GDR's border with Berlin, which's western sectors within the city were sealed off from 1961 onwards by the so-called Berlin Wall. Nevertheless, all these border fortifications are generally considered in a common context. The main line of the border separating the Federal Republic and the GDR began in the south at the border triangle of FDR/GDR/Czechoslovakia and ended at the Baltic Sea. During the Cold War, it was militarily and geopolitically a part of the Iron Curtain which separated the occupation zones of the three Western victorious powers (USA, Great Britain and France) including West Berlin from the occupation zone of the USSR and East-Berlin. Not unimportant for an overall assessment was the fact that the Iron Curtain divided Germany mainly in a west-east direction, i.e. contrary to the traditional economic, political, cultural and confessional disparities between northeast and southwest. The border fortifications also cut through the main west-eastern economic axis, which since the industrialisation of the nineteenth century stretched from the Ruhr area via Berlin and Saxony to Upper Silesia. Therefore, the walls cut through the traditional spatial structures of Germany, which initially made the consequences of the division difficult in every respect.

It is hardly surprising that the so-called inner-German border (apart from the Federal German legal concept, however, it had become a national border like any other according to international law in the early 1970s at the very latest) is more suitable than almost any other for studies on the topic of border crossings. However, this actual topic is preceded here, especially for a non-German readership, by a preoccupation with the origin of the border and the legal situation established by bilateral and multilateral agreements up to 1989.[1]

2. The Establishment and Development of the Zonal Border (Zonengrenze)[2]

After a series of war conferences from 1942 to 1945, the countries allied against the Nazi Reich had finally found consensus on the basic lines of a future policy towards 'Germany'. In particular, they had agreed on an unconditional surrender, which finally had to be carried out twice in May 1945 by the High Command of the German Wehrmacht, once to the Western allies, once to USSR. The fact that the German government, unlike that of Japan, was itself refused even a formal surrender, indicates that the Allies originally pursued the debellation (dissolution of a state) of the (Greater) German Empire, which is also confirmed by other measures and declarations up to the Potsdam Conference. However, the Allies increasingly deviated from this original line as early as summer 1945: on the one hand, the United Nations Charter, which contained a general prohibition of debellation, had come into force; on the other, the question of German reunification became a vehicle for the two leading occupying powers, the US

CROSSING THE GERMAN–GERMAN BORDER   151

and the USSR, to seek the support of the German population in the context of the emerging Cold War. Despite this rhetoric of reunification, because of the increasing tensions between the superpowers, a border now emerged, as perhaps otherwise only in Korea, which increasingly separated two power blocs and the very divergent social systems associated with them.

This process did not happen overnight, because the newly erected zonal borders were initially hardly controllable. Since the advance of the Allied troops into the core areas of the Nazi Empire in mid-1944, millions of people from all nations of Europe have been on the move: as war repatriates and released prisoners of war, refugees, displaced persons, bombed-out, as liberated deportees and forced labourers, survivors from camps and prisons, resettled people and many more. This first phase of extremely high mobility lasted until 1950, when many people had found a (provisional) new home and the expulsion of the German population from Ostgebiete and other areas with German population in Europe's east was largely completed.

By then, a border control system had again been established in Central Europe, separating the occupation zones in Germany from neighbouring states and introducing different control systems between the zones themselves. Within the remaining German territories a control system was introduced which was initially based on two pillars: by the general travel restrictions implemented by the Nazi government already and by controls introduced at the respective borders of the four occupation zones. However, these controls were applied in different ways, most strictly for the French zone in southwest Germany which was subject to a general ban on moving in. On the contrary, the borders between the other zones of occupation were initially more open, especially because of masses of expelled persons from Ostgebiete which reached the Soviet Zone first but very often further moved west and south, into the US and British zones.

However, the situation changed decisively in the course of the historical development: as early as January 1947, the American and British Zones were merged to form a United Economic Area (Bizone), and in 1948, France declared its willingness to participate in this association. This process of merging the three Western Zones finally led to the founding of the Federal Republic of Germany (FRG), which was completed by 20 September 1949 at the latest, when the Konrad Adenauer government took office. At the same time, the Soviet Union, also in cooperation with German politicians, pursued the founding of the German Democratic Republic (GDR) on 7 October 1949.

3. From Zonengrenze (Zonal Border) to Deutsch–Deutsche Grenze (German–German Border)[3]

However, the founding of the German states and their increasing integration into the respective block systems of the Cold War soon led to a difficult situation for the GDR: more and more people 'voted with their legs' and went west. From January 1951 onwards, moving from East Germany and East Berlin to the Federal Republic or West Berlin without the permission of the authorities was a criminal offence under GDR criminal law and was punishable by up to three years in prison. By 1968, the GDR had significantly increased the punitive framework for 'Republikflucht' (illegal border

152   TOWARD A NEW ART OF BORDER CROSSING

crossing), including planning, escape assistance and even complicity, as the mass flight caused serious damage to the GDR's economy and its ideologised self-representation. Nevertheless, more than 2.7 million people left the GDR between 1949 and 1961, and this with a total population that fell from 18.4 to 17.2 million between 1950 and 1960.[4] With the construction of the Berlin Wall in 1961, however, the number of refugees decreased; since then, legalized emigration has dominated, and between 1962 and 1990 this number rose to 480,000 persons.[5]

In 1952, 1954, 1964 and 1982, the GDR government issued central ordinances and laws that provided a legal basis for the systematic demarcation line to the former Western zones. The sector borders within Berlin were initially not affected. Since 1952, a 5-kilometre-wide prohibited area has been established along the border with the Federal Republic of Germany; a 500-metre-wide protective strip was created on the GDR side immediately adjacent to the border and a 10-metre-wide control strip at the very edge. Since the border sometimes crossed populated areas, entering the restricted area was only possible with a permit, which the inhabitants of the restricted area had to apply for. However, shortly after the 1952 regulation came into force, thousands of families considered unreliable were resettled in the interior of the GDR as part of 'AktionUngeziefer' (Action Bugs). Since then, the entire restricted area has been controlled by a paramilitary border police force under the authority of the GDR Ministry of the Interior, later the Ministry of State Security. They were allowed to use their firearms not only against armed refugees but also against all persons who did not follow their instructions. This system was continually expanded until 1961, and in August 1961, it was finally extended to the border between the western and eastern sectors in Berlin, thus closing the last remaining open route to the West. On the border between the GDR and the Federal Republic or West Berlin, up to 30,000 border guards were finally stationed since 1961, a special unit of the GDR National People's Army.

By 1989, devices at the border had been increasingly developed into a complex system of fortifications, which made it virtually impossible to escape over the various obstacles. It consisted of:

- a 10-metre-wide (ploughed) control patrol, also known as the 'death strip';
- a chain of concrete towers for the guards of the GDR border troops;
- a protective strip secured with barbed wire, which was systematically cleared of sight obstacles and levelled;
- a system of running installations for chain dogs, barrier fences, metal lattice fences with signal installations and trenches, double barbed-wire fences or concrete walls, minefields and automatic firing ranges and
- a five-kilometre-wide prohibited area in front of the actual border installations.

Moreover, in the 1960s, the security organs of the GDR increasingly switched to so-called preventive border security. Even far outside the actual restricted zone, the Ministry for State Security monitored suspects. In many cases, people wishing to flee were already identified and arrested during their preparations. At the latest when they entered the restricted zones, they were caught in the net of the various persecution

CROSSING THE GERMAN–GERMAN BORDER 153

organs (border troops, transport police, regular police, 'voluntary helpers of the border troops' and border security agents). Thus, 90% of those wishing to escape were detected well before they reached the border fence (Grenzanlagen).

4. Legal Regulations

Between 1949 and 1961, the GDR had made its border with the Federal Republic and West Berlin an almost insurmountable obstacle for those who wanted to enter the West without the permission of its authorities. The West German side, on the other hand, did not recognise the border with the GDR until the agreements at the beginning of the 1970s. As a result, the West always (not at all times in reality) claimed freedom of travel, while the East sought to control the crossing of the border. This did not mean, however, that the border had become impassable. Rather, until 1971/1972, border crossings were regulated by bi- and multilateral agreements and GDR law. But only the international accords from the early 1970s secured a legal framework for improved access until the collapse of GDR in autumn 1989.

Basically, a distinction was made throughout the entire period between November 1953 and the end of 1989 between three groups with varying degrees of freedom to travel: citizens of FRG, citizens of GDR (including East Berlin), and third citizens of West Berlin. The Federal Republic of Germany made no distinction for these three groups, all of whom it regarded as Germans under the Basic Law, either de facto or in exercising their rights. However, the Federal Republic also restricted the freedom of certain groups of people to travel to the East, especially members of the military and the civil service. The GDR, on the other hand, made a sharp distinction between these three groups, which is shown for the first time by an official decree in 1953.[6]

This scheme provided for

- According to § 1, citizens residing in the GDR (including East Berlin) no longer required Interzonenpässe (inter-zone passports) for travel to West Germany; officially issued Personal bescheinigungen (personal certificates) were to be sufficient for passing the checkpoints on the demarcation line. However, the decree did not lay down any criteria for the issue of these certificates.
- For entry into the GDR from West Germany, § 2 required the presentation of an official identity card and a permit from the district administration of the place to be visited in the GDR. This permit had to be applied for by the relatives or acquaintances of the traveller or, in the case of business or official trips, by departments or organisations. This decree was extended to residents of West Berlin in 1956.
- For journeys from West Germany to West Berlin and vice versa, the regulations for inter-zone travel routes and proof of an official identity card applied.

The regulations concealed the fact that the authorities of the GDR were trying to significantly restrict legal travel, for example by refusing entry or exit permits and by obstructing transit traffic between West Berlin and the federal territory. An application to leave the GDR permanently was usually considered illegal. After 1961, travel by

TOWARD A NEW ART OF BORDER CROSSING

GDR citizens under 65 years of age to non-socialist foreign countries was only possible on application, only on specific occasions, and usually only if a return to the GDR was probable. Left behind children or spouses were regarded as guarantees for such a return. From 1964 onwards, all pensioners were allowed to visit relatives in the West once a year. As a result, pensioners sometimes moved to the Federal Republic, where they received significantly better pensions. A high point of the travel restrictions was the Berlin Crisis from 1958 to 1961, that is between the Khrushchev ultimatum and the construction of the Berlin Wall. Since August 1961, travel of West Berliners to the eastern part of the city was no longer possible at all for 28 months. It was not until December 1963 that the Senate Administration of West Berlin succeeded in negotiating the first Passierscheinabkommen (permit agreement) for West Berliners. This was followed by three more until 1966. After the last permit agreement expired at Pentecost 1966, West Berliners were only able to enter East Berlin since October 1966 for 'urgent family matters' due to the decision of a Härtestelle (hardship or emergency centre), which had existed since 1964. Transit traffic to West Berlin also became more difficult: in 1968, a decision by the Volkskammer (GDR Parliament) made passports and visa mandatory.[7]

At the beginning of the 1970s, the intensifying demarcation of the East was put on a different, formal footing within the framework of a new policy of détente and Ostpolitik. In 1972, the governments in Bonn and East Berlin signed a transit agreement for the transport of civilian persons and goods between the Federal Republic of Germany and West Berlin. The accord, which also came into force on 3 June 1972, was the first agreement concluded at government level between the Federal Republic and the GDR. It included ship, car and rail traffic. The Four-Power Agreement and the follow-up agreements changed crossing the borders between East and West. However, a distinction was still made between different groups (citizens of the GDR, German citizens and West Berliners) and travel purposes:

- Travel by West Berliners to East Berlin and the GDR.
- The Transit Agreement confirmed the passport and visa requirements for transit between the Federal Republic of Germany and West Berlin.
- The travel possibilities for citizens of the GDR were also put on a new legal basis by the Decree on the Travel Regulations for Citizens of the GDR of 17 October 1972. These trips had to be applied for by authorities and employers. However, the opportunities were limited to 'urgent family matters' of relatives. In addition, further travel concessions were granted for persons of retirement age and invalids.[8]
- Furthermore, the legal framework for travel by West-German citizens to the GDR changed. On 17 October 1972, the GDR published another decree according to which citizens of the FRG could now undertake visiting trips, either to their relatives and acquaintances living in the GDR for private reasons or on invitation by the competent GDR authorities for commercial, cultural, sporting or religious reasons.[9]
- Finally, in the same year, an additional protocol was agreed for the areas along the border between the Federal Republic and the GDR. Every inhabitant of the Federal Republic of Germany who had his or her main residence in the cities and administrative districts listed individually as 'grenznah' (close to the border) was

CROSSING THE GERMAN–GERMAN BORDER   155

entitled to travel. Only those areas of the GDR could be visited which were also listed in detail as 'border districts of the GDR (city and administrative districts)'. 30 day stays a year were permitted with a maximum of nine visiting days per quarter.

5. Cross-Border Transgressions

What did it mean to cross the German–German border? What experiences were connected with the change from East to West and vice versa? It is hardly possible to give a general picture here, if only because of the large number of 'cross-border' people and the diversity of their motives. However, for the border crossings in the entire period between 1945 and 1989, there are two clear epochs that can be named.

5.1 Crossing Borders between the two Germanies from the 1940s to the 1960s

The first phase, from 1945 to the 1960s, was completed with the construction of the Berlin Wall and the following demarcation of GDR. From this time on, uncontrolled border crossings were virtually impossible: as has already been written, they failed in advance or often ended with the death of the refugees at the border fortifications. For the period prior to this perfection of surveillance, the border crossings took place within the framework of a different horizon of action and experience, which should be central to their contemporary and current assessment: displacement, flight and even voluntary relocation were, until the early 1960s, more in the continuity of a development that had begun in the late 1930s. Their main pull and push factor for migration was the orgy of violence that had escalated ever since. Military violence also initially dominated post-war development, and not only Germany had been forcibly conquered but also occupied (not liberated, as it sometimes seems from today's perspective) until 1945. As a consequence and continuation of this violence, the later GDR and East Berlin had been occupied by the USSR, and the political and social order that the occupying power (in cooperation with German communists) considered appropriate for its zone was established there. Military occupation and sociopolitical reorganisation therefore determined the fate of many European countries from the end of the 1930s to the mid-1950s: first in the context of the expansion of the Nazi Empire, then later in the building of the Soviet Empire, and even, to a different extent, in the formation of the Western Alliance.

Therefore, without being exhaustive about the motives for the period from the end of the war to the middle/end of the 1950s, I will only give a sketchy talk about East–West mobility first: displaced persons from the former German Ostgebiete or other areas of Eastern Central Europe moved further west from the Soviet zone or the GDR for fear of the attacks of the Soviet occupying power or to find better economic conditions. German prisoners of war, who had to commit themselves to work in Soviet industrial enterprises in order to be released from the POW-camps, fled back to their home in West Germany. Those who had long been living in the areas now called GDR moved away because with the SED leadership another totalitarian regime took political measures which had a negative effect on certain groups of the population, now farmers, house and factory

156 TOWARD A NEW ART OF BORDER CROSSING

owners, state employees and the educated. Well-educated, younger people left because they hoped for higher incomes in the West, although income gaps between East and West were not to become more marked until the late 1950s. Politically and religiously committed people, but also former National Socialist activists, set off to escape the threat of arrest or harassment. In contrast to this, from West to East, comparatively fewer people went the opposite way to the East after 1945, convinced communists and pastors, but mainly to reunite families and for professional reasons. Nevertheless, contrary to the main migration stream, half a million people also migrated from the Federal Republic to the GDR before the Wall was built in 1961.[10]

To get back to their experiences: Until the construction of the Berlin Wall, or at least until the mid-1950s, the frame of reference for the main flow of refugees, which went from East to West, was still that of the war and post-war period, with enormous mobility of the population, with roadblocks and checkpoints everywhere, with new forms of political oppression and economic discrimination and the not unfounded fear of being arrested and deported. Above all, however, the refugee existence by no means ceased after arrival in the West, for until the late 1950s, the West was by no means golden: the strange Germans from the East and the later GDR were anything but welcome in the West, especially in the early post-war period. Linguistic and especially confessional differences were great, cultural and mental imprints were too different.[11]

Until the mid-1950s, the Western zones were by no means similar to the affluent society of Western influence that was so striking later on. Although hunger and cold and the worst material hardship in a country largely devastated by the Second World War had been overcome by 1955, the early Federal Republic made a poor and dismal impression overall.[12] It was not yet as fundamentally different from the GDR as it would be hardly more than 20 years later.

5.2 Border Crossings from the 1970s until the late 1980s

This suggests that real experiences of difference when crossing the border from the West to the East, and vice versa should be shifted to the period after the Wall was built, preferably even to the period after the early 1970s. By then, real societal and political differences, divergent lifestyles and levels of prosperity had emerged. Yet the changes in the West since 1950 were greater than in the East: until reunification in 1990, all observers emphasized in a comparison between the Federal Republic and the GDR that the latter had remained 'more German'. The Federal Republic, on the other hand, had become much more involved in international and especially European relations. Therefore, it was not until the 1970s and 1980s that the narratives changed: from the successful escape into an environment no longer marked by direct military-political violence to by far more fundamental experiences of difference, in short, here West, there East. Therefore, until 1989 reports by common people convey the image of two clearly separate worlds that differed considerably in their quality of life. Let us simply take two reports, by East and West Germans, which are typical of the travel experiences of most people since the early 1970s.

CROSSING THE GERMAN–GERMAN BORDER

A journey to the West

Here first the travel experiences of Siegfried Wittenburg, an East German.[13] He received his first direct reports about the Federal Republic of Germany in 1977 from his parents, who had reached their 'Passierscheinalter' (permit age) at the time (they had turned 65) and told him incredible things about their first visit to relatives in the West. He did not believe these stories, especially since in 1977, he would have had to wait until 2017, his own retirement age, and for a passport with an exit visa. Nine years later, a work colleague was granted permission to travel to the West for a silver wedding celebration, and he told similar stories: after crossing the border, the inter-zone train had run more quietly and even the grass became greener. For Wittenburg, this was the trigger to also apply for a visit to the 'enemy of the working class'. Since a close relative in the West celebrated his 50th birthday, he could make an application at his company with for an officially certified document. Wittenburg had to state the period of the planned trip and attach declarations according to which he was taking part of his annual leave for the trip to the west and that he was travelling without his wife. She was therefore deemed to have been deposited in the GDR to guarantee his return.

The application and the assessment initially went on the intra-company journey. This was followed by the approval of the head of department, the technical director and the head of division. Then it was the turn of the SED departmental organizer. The latter found out from his cadre file that he was still subject to a waiting period, that is that he could be a possible confidant of any secrets. Finally, the plant manager signed the informal application with the note: rejected.

Two years later, he made a new attempt. Since he had changed his workplace in the meantime, the internal process progressed rapidly, because his boss was now a heart surgeon, professor and head of a university clinic, internationally active and had often been in the West himself. The chief secretary accepted the application without a comment, passed it on as a matter of routine and after a short time Wittenburg received the clearance certificate requested by the authorities. He filled out the form for a one-week visit to Germany at the registration office of the People's Police District Office. A copy was sent to the district office of the Ministry of State Security where a consultation took place. There were concerns, because his ban period lasted another three months. So he first received an order to be called up by registered mail. The following day he was a uniformed and armed reservist of the National People's Army. The reserve exercise lasted 10 days. An acquaintance said that the three-year suspension period following the draft was now starting all over again, and that Wittenburg could forget his intention to travel to the Federal Republic in three weeks' time.

Nevertheless, he managed to pick up his passport on the day of his planned departure, with already packed suitcases, at the residents' registration office in the People's Police District Office. He received the first passport of his life, sprinted to the Sparkasse (savings bank) to exchange 15 marks of the GDR for 15 DM as 'movement money', reached the commuter train to the main station at the last moment and jumped on the Interzonenzug (train connecting west and east), ready for departure, at the last second.

158 TOWARD A NEW ART OF BORDER CROSSING

There was only one train a day from Rostock to the Herrnburg border crossing and through the Iron Curtain to its destination Essen.

After 90 minutes, it became very quiet in the fully occupied compartment. The train rumbled into the border station, where grey buildings, barbed wire, armed soldiers in uniform and dogs barking dominated the scene. After passport control, the train passed the death strip:

> The rumble turned into a slide. Western car brands, allotments and lawns appeared in the city of Lübeck. And, I couldn't believe my eyes: the grass actually looked greener.[14]

Wittenburg spent the following seven half days and nights as if in a frenzy with flying visits to other relatives and friends in Essen, Cologne, Mainz, Frankfurt and Hamburg. After a good week, the Interzonenzug was back at Hamburg's main station, ready for departure. Heavily loaded travellers from the GDR boarded the train and said goodbye to their relatives in tears. After a 40-minute journey to the east, it became very quiet again in the fully occupied compartment, as the train stopped at the border station. Again soldiers were running around and dogs were barking. Despite passport and customs check, Wittenburg managed to take a whole suitcase full of books, magazines and records to the East.

Then his train started moving again. The houses of the villages passed by, they were grey and worn, plaster crumbled, many windows were without paint: 'I thought that something had to change. Urgently. My wife and I were expecting a child'.[15]

A journey to the East

In August 1984, a group of tutors (tutors were pupils who were about to graduate from high school) from the Wolfgang–Ernst–Gymnasium Büdingen went to the GDR. This original report was published on the Internet.[16] The class trip was typical of a whole series of similar events with almost identical travel programmes, which had probably been organised at the time by the Freie Deutsche Jugend (FDJ, Free German Youth, the youth organisation of East Germany's Communist Party) as standard trip for youth groups from West Germany. The journey led from Büdingen via Hohnstein, Meissen, Königsstein, Dresden and Jena back to Büdingen. Which central impressions did the trip leave with the participants?

The first impressions were obviously striking, as they are described in detail, the border and its crossing and the first views of landscapes and cities in particular. Here, it is worth quoting in more detail:

> We had to gather our first impressions from the bus: A beautiful, sparsely populated landscape and beautiful old houses on the one hand, but on the other hand terribly bad roads, dilapidated houses, grey-monotonous settlements. But above all, the huge billboards and the omnipresent slogans and pithy sayings of socialist propaganda attracted attention. In Eisenach another impression: The air pollution in this area is catastrophic.[17]

The welcome at Hohnstein Youth Hostel was essential that the hostel staff organised a get-together where the staff performed protest songs in English and brandy was served

CROSSING THE GERMAN–GERMAN BORDER 159

(to non-adult persons!). This rather forced international friendship meeting continued on the second leg of the journey, in Meissen, where the group of tutors made contact with a school class from the GDR in the youth hostel's common room. In Meissen, it became clear to the participants that the GDR would not have the materiel shortcomings as often claimed in the West:

> The most important basic foodstuffs, but also goods for daily use, were available in sufficient quantities. We hardly noticed any queues in front of the shops.[18]

In general, the people with whom the group was able to make contact seemed to have a differentiated view of the advantages and disadvantages of life in the FRG and GDR:

> The people were very open-minded and in their statements they gave us their views. We noticed that the FRG was also viewed quite critically. The population of the GDR would like to see more liberalism from their state, but what we perceived as extreme paternalism (insurance by the company, allocation of jobs and company leisure activities, e.g. holidays, etc.), GDR citizens found quite positive.[19]

On the next leg, in Dresden, the negative impressions again dominated:

> The first thing that struck us in the vicinity of the Zwinger were the ruins, which reminded us of the complete destruction of Dresden in 1945 [...] This atmosphere of destruction was further intensified by the heavy air pollution in Dresden. Even the Zwinger was already black and dirty [...][20]

What was striking for the group of tutors was the difference between the opinions of their travel companions from the GDR, which they expressed in official and in private conversations. Very significant for their general attitude was, for example, that in official talks they described the construction of the Wall as a protective measure against the imperialist powers. As soon as one had private discussions with young people, they criticised a lot about their state, but on the whole, they seemed to be satisfied with their lives.

Finally, a highlight of the experience in the GDR was a discussion with young people there, which the group approached with low expectations from the outset. It also turned out that most of the 'young people' were considerably older than the West Germans (almost all were former FDJ'ler). There was also a factory manager and a district secretary of the SED present. They had already prepared an almost opulent buffet for the guests and provided 'western' music, obviously to give an impression of the open-mindedness of our hosts. The following discussion consisted of two parts, here again a longer quotation:

> In the 'official' part, there was one big discussion [...] Especially the "comrade plant manager" tried to present the youth policy of the GDR in as bright a light as possible. In the second part of the meeting, we spoke comparatively casually in small groups. Significantly, the dissatisfaction of the young people from the GDR increased immediately [...] It is clear,

160 TOWARD A NEW ART OF BORDER CROSSING

however, that this last half hour brought us much more for information about the conditions in the GDR than the lengthy "official" discussion before.[21]

What was the lasting impression of the tutor group:

"An outstanding example is probably the way in which the state ideology was integrated into the most ordinary everyday events: No shopping without the image of comrade Honecker, no radio broadcast without reference to the "main task in its unity of economic and social policy" [...] All in all, the study trip has provided valuable, surprising and expected impressions.[22]

6. Summary

The crossing of the border from East to West and vice versa is divided into two clearly distinguishable phases. They both last about two decades each. In the first phase, from the end of the Second World War to the construction of the Berlin Wall, actions and experiences often took place in the context of the orgy of violence that occurred since the late 1930s. Especially with the beginning of the new policy of détente in the early 1970s, actions and experiences shifted towards a normality of 'Germany divided', which had clearly different consequences for the population in East and West: from an eastern perspective, the border expressed personal and social isolation from a West German wonderland; from a western perspective, they separated the Federal Republic from an independent state that was grey, boring, and which's environment was polluted. The border fortifications thus created a piece of European reality in which the people in the West could settle down better and those in the East worse. Only the collapse of the Eastern Bloc and the accession of the new federal states to the Federal Republic of Germany in October 1990 were to change this situation again.

References

Andrea Schmelz: Migration und Politik im geteilten Deutschland während des Kalten Krieges. Die West-Ost-Migration in die DDR in den 1950er und 1960er Jahren, Opladen 2002.

Andreas Kossert: Wann ist man angekommen? Flüchtlinge und Vertriebene im Nachkriegsdeutschland. https://www.bpb.de/geschichte/zeitgeschichte/deutschlandarchiv/238108/fluechtlinge-und-vertriebene-im-nachkriegsdeutschland.

Anordnung über die Regelung des Interzonenreiseverkehrs vom 21. November 1953, ergänzt durch Anordnung vom 3. September 1956.

Anordnung über Regelungen im Reiseverkehr von Bürgern der DDR vom 17. Oktober 1972 http://www.chronik-der-mauer.de/material/180321/anordnung-des-ddr-innenministers-ueber-

Bernd Weisbrod (Hrsg.): Grenzland. Beiträge zur Geschichte der deutsch-deutschen Grenze, Hannover 1993, ISBN 3-7752-5880-9.

Bettina Effner, Helge Heidemeyer (Hrsg.): Flucht im geteilten Deutschland. Erinnerungsstätte Notaufnahmelager Marienfelde. Berlin 2005.

Bettina Effner: Schauplatz bundesdeutscher und Berliner Migrationsgeschichte: Das Notaufnahmelager Marienfelde. https://www.bpb.de/geschichte/zeitgeschichte/deutschlandarchiv/255163/das-notaufnahmelager-marienfelde.

CROSSING THE GERMAN–GERMAN BORDER 161

Claudia Lepp: Wege in die DDR. West-Ost-Übersiedlungen im kirchlichen Bereich vor dem Mauerbau, Göttingen 2015.

Damian van Melis, Henrik Bispinck (Hrsg.): Republikflucht. Flucht und Abwanderung aus der SBZ/DDR 1945–1961. München 2006.

Edgar Wolfrum: Die Mauer. Geschichte einer Teilung. München 2009.

Frederick Taylor: Die Mauer. 13. August 1961 bis 9. November 1989. Berlin 2009.

Gerwin Udke: Dableiben – Weggehen – Wiederkommen. Abwanderung aus Ostdeutschland 1945 bis heute. Motive, Hintergründe, Folgen, Auswege. Mammendorf 2008.

Hans-Hermann Hertle et al. (Hrsg.): Mauerbau und Mauerfall. Berlin 2002.

Hans-Hermann Hertle: Gerhard Sälter: Die Todesopfer an Mauer und Grenze. Probleme einer Bilanz des DDR-Grenzregimes. In: Deutschland Archiv 39, Heft 4 2006, 667–676.

Hans-Joachim Fricke: Hans-Joachim Ritzau: Die innerdeutsche Grenze und der Schienenverkehr. 5., in Teil V ergänzte Auflage mit Berichtigungen und Nachtrag. Zeit und Eisenbahn. Pürgen 2004.

Helge Heidemeyer: Flucht und Zuwanderung aus der SBZ/DDR 1945/49–1961. Die Flüchtlingspolitik der Bundesrepublik Deutschland bis zum Bau der Berliner Mauer (= Beiträge zur Geschichte des Parlamentarismus und der politischen Parteien 100). Düsseldorf 1994.

Henrik Bispinck: "Republikflucht". Flucht und Ausreise als Problem der DDR-Führung. In: Dierk Hoffmann, Michael Schwartz, Hermann Wentker (Hrsg.): Vor dem Mauerbau. Politik und Gesellschaft der DDR der Fünfziger Jahre. München 2003, S. 285–309. https://www.verfassungen.de/ddr/visapflichtbeschluss68.htm.

Ingolf Hermann, Hartmut Rosunger, Karsten Sroka: Lexikon der innerdeutschen Grenze. Das Grenzsicherungssystem, die Folgen und der zeitgeschichtliche Rahmen der innerdeutschen Grenze und der Berliner Mauer in Stichworten, o. O. 2017.

Jochen Maurer: Halt – Staatsgrenze! Alltag, Dienst und Innenansichten der Grenztruppen der DDR. Berlin 2015.

Johannes Cramer: Tobias Rütenik: Die Baugeschichte der Berliner Mauer. Petersberg 2011.

Jürgen Ritter: Peter Joachim Lapp: Die Grenze. Ein deutsches Bauwerk. Berlin 2011.

Klassenfahrt in die DDR. http://www.ddr-zeitzeugen.de/html/klassenfahrt_in_die_ddr.html.

Klaus Schroeder, Jochen Staadt (Hrsg.): Die Todesopfer des DDR-Grenzregimes an der innerdeutschen Grenze 1949–1989. Ein biographisches Handbuch. Berlin u. a. 2018.

Lorraine Bluche: Friedland international? Zur Unterbringung ausländischer Geflüchteter im Grenzdurchgangslager Friedland in den 1970 er Jahren. https://www.bpb.de/geschichte/zeitgeschichte/deutschlandarchiv/259282/friedland-international.

Marion Detjen: Ein Loch in der Mauer. Die Geschichte der Fluchthilfe im geteilten Deutschland 1961–1989. München 2005.

Melanie Piepenschneider, Klaus Jochen Arnold (Hrsg.): Was war die Mauer? Die Errichtung der innerdeutschen Grenzanlagen durch das SED-Regime und ihre Folgen (= Handreichung zur Politischen Bildung, Band 7). Sankt Augustin 2013.

Monatsmeldungen des Bundesministeriums für Vertriebene, Flüchtlinge und Kriegsgeschädigte; Jürgen Rühle/Gunter Holzweißig, Der 13. August. Die Mauer von Berlin, 3. Aufl., Köln 1988, S. 154. Statistisches Jahrbuch der DDR. Staatsverlag der DDR, 1. Auflage, Juni 1989, S. 8 und 17.

Peter Joachim Lapp: Gefechtsdienst im Frieden. Das Grenzregime der DDR. Bonn 1999.

–––––Grenzregime der DDR. Aachen 2013.

Siegfried Wittenburg: Deutschland in den Achtzigern Meine erste Reise zum Klassenfeind. https://www.spiegel.de/geschichte/deutschland-in-den-achtzigern-meine-erste-westreise-a-984773.html.

Thomas Flemming, Hagen Koch: Die Berliner Mauer. Geschichte eines politischen Bauwerks. Berlin 2001.

162 TOWARD A NEW ART OF BORDER CROSSING

Thomas Schwark, Detlef Schmiechen-Ackermann, Carl-Hans Hauptmeyer (Hrsg.): Grenzziehungen – Grenzerfahrungen – Grenzüberschreitungen. Die innerdeutsche Grenze 1945–1990. Darmstadt 2011.

Volker Ackermann: Der „echte" Flüchtling. Deutsche Vertriebene und Flüchtlinge aus der DDR 1945–1961 (= Studien zur historischen Migrationsforschung 1). Osnabrück 1995.

Volker Koop: „Den Gegner vernichten". Die Grenzsicherung der DDR. Bonn 1996.

Notes

1 Bibliographical note: There are a large number of publications on this topic, but they are almost exclusively in German. These publications form the basis of the text and are not referenced in more detail. Footnotes are only included when it comes to details of presentation and primary sources.

2 „Zonengrenze" denotes the border between FRG and GDR with the connotation of not exception it as a legal borderline.

3 Again, the term Deutsch-Deutsche Grenze indicates that FRG's government did not accept its legality as a border and promises to overcome it politically.

4 Quelle: Monatsmeldungen des Bundesministeriums für Vertriebene, Flüchtlinge und Kriegsgeschädigte; Jürgen Rühle/Gunter Holzweißig, Der 13. August. Die Mauer von Berlin, 3. Aufl., Köln 1988, S. 154. *Statistisches Jahrbuch der DDR.*Staatsverlag der DDR, 1. Auflage, Juni 1989, S. 8 und 17.

5 Bettina Effner, Helge Heidemeyer (Hrsg.): *Flucht im geteilten Deutschland. Erinnerungsstätte Notaufnahmelager Marienfelde.* Berlin 2005, S. 27/28.

6 „Anordnung über die Regelung des Interzonenreiseverkehrs vom 21. November 1953, ergänztdurchAnordnungvom 3. September 1956. "(Order on the Regulation of Inter-Zone Travel of 21 November 1953, supplemented by an Order of 3 September 1956) GBl. I. S. 702.

7 https://www.verfassungen.de/ddr/visapflichtbeschluss68.htm.

8 Anordnungüber Regelungen im Reiseverkehrvon Bürgern der DDRvom 17. Oktober 1972 http://www.chronik-der-mauer.de/material/180321/anordnung-des-ddr-innenministers-ueber-regelungen-im-reiseverkehr-von-buergern-der-ddr-17-oktober-1972

9 Anordnung über Einreisen von Bürgern der BRD in die DDR vom 17. Oktober 1972 http://www.chronik-der-mauer.de/material/180321/anordnung-des-ddr-innenministers-ueber-regelungen-im-reiseverkehr-von-buergern-der-ddr-17-oktober-1972

10 Vgl. hierzu Andrea Schmelz, Migration und Politik im geteilten Deutschland während des Kalten Krieges. Die West-Ost-Migration in die DDR in den 1950er und 1960er Jahren, Opladen 2002. Claudia Lepp, Wege in die DDR. West-Ost-Übersiedlungen im kirchlichen Bereich vor dem Mauerbau, Göttingen 2015.

11 Lorraine Bluche: Friedland international? Zur Unterbringung ausländischer Geflüchteter im Grenzdurchgangslager Friedland in den 1970er Jahren. https://www.bpb.de/geschichte/zeitgeschichte/deutschlandarchiv/259282/friedland-international.

12 Andreas Kossert: Wann ist man angekommen? Flüchtlinge und Vertriebene im Nachkriegsdeutschland. https://www.bpb.de/geschichte/zeitgeschichte/deutschlandarchiv/238108/fluechtlinge-und-vertriebene-im-nachkriegsdeutschland.

13 Siegfried Wittenburg: Deutschland in den Achtzigern Meine erste Reise zum Klassenfeind. https://www.spiegel.de/geschichte/deutschland-in-den-achtzigern-meine-erste-westreise-a-984773.html.

14 Siegfried Wittenburg: Deutschland in den Achtzigern Meine erste Reise zum Klassenfeind. https://www.spiegel.de/geschichte/deutschland-in-den-achtzigern-meine-erste-westreise-a-984773.html.

15 Siegfried Wittenburg: Deutschland in den Achtzigern Meine erste Reise zum Klassenfeind. https://www.spiegel.de/geschichte/deutschland-in-den-achtzigern-meine-erste-westreise-a-984773.html.

CROSSING THE GERMAN–GERMAN BORDER 163

16 Klassenfahrt in die DDR. http://www.ddr-zeitzeugen.de/html/klassenfahrt_in_die_ddr.html.

17 Klassenfahrt in die DDR. http://www.ddr-zeitzeugen.de/html/klassenfahrt_in_die_ddr.html.

18 Klassenfahrt in die DDR. http://www.ddr-zeitzeugen.de/html/klassenfahrt_in_die_ddr.html.

19 Klassenfahrt in die DDR. http://www.ddr-zeitzeugen.de/html/klassenfahrt_in_die_ddr.html.

20 Klassenfahrt in die DDR. http://www.ddr-zeitzeugen.de/html/klassenfahrt_in_die_ddr.html.

21 Klassenfahrt in die DDR. http://www.ddr-zeitzeugen.de/html/klassenfahrt_in_die_ddr.html.

22 Klassenfahrt in die DDR. http://www.ddr-zeitzeugen.de/html/klassenfahrt_in_die_ddr.html.

Chapter 12

OVERCOMING THE BORDERS IN SOUTHEAST ASIA? AN ANALYSIS OF TRANSBORDER COLLABORATION IN THE GREATER MEKONG SUBREGION

Detlef Briesen

The crossing or even overcoming of state borders does not depend solely on the efforts of affected individuals or groups. Borders are, as the history of Europe shows, established by institutions such as the state and can also be dismantled through intergovernmental cooperation. Both presuppose that people have something in common within the respective borders and also across borders. If this is not the case, states can dissolve, on the one hand, because their populations cannot be held together even under the greatest duress. Examples of this are historical nationality states such as Yugoslavia, Czechoslovakia, or the Soviet Union or many present-day African states with their fluid borders. On the other hand, traditional state borders can be made more permeable or almost invisible, as is the case with many borders in Western Europe today. However, this in turn presupposes that the respective populations can see advantages in this or are able to build on the same values, cultures, belief systems, etc. on both sides of the borders. Where this is not the case, border crossings that involve more than classic push and pull effects such as labor migration or trade are not easy to manage.

In this respect, the article deals with the difficult attempt to make borders more permeable and to systematically establish transnational cooperation in an area characterized by strong segmentation. For in Southeast Asia, culture, language, economy, and society differ dramatically from country to country, indeed from population group to population group. The article presents this problem, first characterizes the situation in Southeast Asia as a whole and then focuses its attention on the Greater Mekong Subregion. The contribution is based on the results of a scientific congress in 2018 and a recent publication by the author.[1]

I. The Concept of South East Asia and the Diversity of the Area

Let us start with a geographical definition of the region of Southeast Asia which is a part of the Asian continent and includes the countries located east of India and south of China. In the first millennium, the entire region was subject to strong influence from

India; this has been largely replaced by a Chinese one since the eighteenth century at the latest. Individual states, such as Vietnam, Thailand, today's Malaysia, and especially Singapore, are strongly sinicized. Chinese minorities today play a decisive role in the economy of the entire region within the framework of the so-called bamboo networks. Overall, India's role in Southeast Asia is currently rather marginal.

As a rule, the region is further subdivided, for example into the Southeast Asian mainland, traditionally referred to as Farther India (*Hinterindien*), and the insular Southeast Asia or Malay Archipelago. The latter consists of present-day Indonesia, and other states such as the Philippines, Brunei, East Timor, and parts of Malaysia. The term Southeast Asia used today was not created until the Second World War, when the entire area was under the control of Japan. Only until then the USA and its allies began to use the term in the context of re-conquest. Southeast Asia is thus a term that was introduced from the outside to the entire region, similar to other historical terms that are rarely used today, such as British Farther India, French Indochina, Dutch India or New Spain, of which the Philippines was part until the beginning of the twentieth century.

The entire region is extremely heterogeneous in terms of cultures and religions, languages, and political and economic development. Here is just a brief overview: In terms of the predominant religions, the countries of Southeast Asia are more than clearly different from each other. Myanmar, Cambodia, Laos, and Thailand are influenced by Theravada Buddhism, Indonesia by Islam, the Philippines by Catholicism, Vietnam, and Singapore by Confucianism and Hinayana Buddhism. In all states there are indeed diverse religious minorities, but their status is not always guaranteed: Muslims in Thailand and Myanmar, non-Muslims in Indonesia, Malaysia, and Brunei and Christians in Vietnam. Traditionally, all faiths in Southeast Asia have been enriched by numerous elements from other religions, but the most well-known is the mixture of basically mutually exclusive systems such as Buddhism, Confucianism, and animism that prevails in Vietnam. But Southeast Asia has also been affected by the fanaticism of the world religions since the 1970s, especially the influence of Muslim preachers from the Gulf region and fanatical Protestants from the US.

In addition to religious and cultural diversity, there is also linguistic diversity, because Southeast Asia is a mosaic of speakers of the most diverse language families: Sino-Tibetan, Austro-Asian, Tai-Kadai, and Hmong-Mien. So unlike in Europe, there are no dialectal continuums, such as in the Romance languages from Portugal to Italy, but rather sharp transitions from cultural community to cultural community. In addition, different scripts are used for the respective languages: Latin for Vietnamese, Bahasa Indonesia, and Tagalog, Indian scripts derived from the Brahmi script for Lao, Thai and Khmer, and an Arabic alphabet called Jawi, which has official status in Brunei, Malaysia, and Indonesia.

The systems of government of almost all Southeast Asian states are authoritarian throughout, although this has different roots. Country-specific Confucian and socialist influences cross with traditions of rule by monarchs and the military. The respective influence of socialists, state utopists, monarchs, and the military, on the other hand, is due in no small measure to the very different ways in which the countries of South

OVERCOMING THE BORDERS IN SOUTHEAST ASIA?

Table 1: Human Development Index of Southeast Asian States[2]

Singapore	0.932
Malaysia	0.802
Thailand	0.755
Philippines	0.699
Indonesia	0.694
Vietnam	0.694
Laos	0.604
Cambodia	0.582
Myanmar	0.578

Asia have (re)gained their state independence since 1940. While there are similarities in terms of the domestic political situation—hardly any Southeast Asian state can be considered a democracy and constitutional state in the German sense—the states there differ significantly in their economic and social development.

Thus, the region includes states that, according to the appropriate categorization, are characterized by "very high," "high," and "medium human development." The entire region has made an enormous leap in development since the 1970s, which is primarily due to the more intensive interdependence of individual states in the region with the world market, or more precisely with leading economic powers such as the EU, China, the US, Japan, and South Korea. In contrast, regional economic integration still has considerable potential for development, as few data can make clear: In 2015, the ASEAN countries only exchanged 24% of their exports and imports with each other, but 15.2% with China, 10.5% with Japan, 10% with the EU, and 9.4% with the US.[3]

So far, it has already become clear how diverse the states of Southeast Asia are when they are compared with each other. The same diversity also applies to their internal conditions. The situation in Vietnam may serve as an example here. Its population consists of a majority, the strongly sinized Viet or Kinh, as well as a total of 53 other state-recognized minorities. With the exception of the Hoa (Chinese) and Khmer, all these groups have been known as Montagnards since the French colonial period, as they live predominantly in mountainous areas or remote zones of the central highlands. Especially in the mountainous regions of northern Vietnam, the different peoples have developed distinctive forms of economy adapted to the altitude of the mountain regions, such as farmers in valley areas, rice farmers with complex terraced farming on the slopes of the mountains, and hunter-gatherers in higher altitudes. Until colonization by France from the mid-nineteenth century onwards, contacts between the Viet and the Montagnards were rather limited. In the central highlands, for example, the various ethnic groups lived in great isolation under their own legal status, which in colonial times was known as the "crown domain."

All this already indicates that the relations between the various groups or states were generally by no means free of tension and that Southeast Asia was also always far from a multicultural paradise—such a paradise probably never existed anywhere anyway. If, for the sake of simplicity, one looks only at the core area of Southeast Asia, traditionally referred to as Farther India (i.e., today's states Myanmar, Thailand, Laos, Cambodia, and Vietnam), a history becomes visible that is characterized by numerous lines of conflict and wars. They have had both exogenous and endogenous causes, and time and again both causes of conflict have historically been linked. Important lines of tension in Southeast Asia were in this respect:

- Inter-ethnic tensions between minority and majority populations in all the above-mentioned states or their predecessors;
- Rivalries over the position of regional hegemony, for example, between Vietnam, Cambodia, and Thailand;
- Sometimes murderous border wars, for example, between Cambodia and Vietnam or Thailand;
- conflicts with the traditional hegemony of the region, that is, China;
- interventions from outside, by the European colonial powers and Japan up to the end of the Second World War;
- anti-colonial liberation wars fought with greater severity in the region;
- the entire region as victims of the proxy wars between the US, the USSR, and China after the end of World War II;
- recent attempts by the US to use some states in the region for its encirclement strategy against China;
- resource and strategic conflicts, for example, between China and the other countries bordering the South China Sea.

This list is long and could be filled with numerous examples. The traditional animosities are also further fueled by a pronounced nationalism. This has its roots in the anti-colonial liberation movements and, unlike in Western Europe but Britain, has positive connotations, as it is associated in public perception with the liberation of the respective country from the colonial powers and the undeniable economic rise of the entire region, especially since the 1970s. National pride does not necessarily encourage compromise or even the cession of national competencies when it comes to transnational cooperation.

Nevertheless, all the states of Southeast Asia are now members of the ASEAN organization. This Association of Southeast Asian Nations, ASEAN for short, is an international, but unlike the EU, it is not a transnational organization. The headquarters of ASEAN is in Jakarta, Indonesia. The most important institution is the annual summit meeting of the ASEAN states. ASEAN was founded in 1967 by Thailand, Indonesia, Malaysia, the Philippines, and Singapore. It initially had a clear anti-communist orientation during the Vietnam War, but pursued this goal primarily through economic, social progress, and political stability in the member states. The collapse of the Soviet empire enabled reforms in the socialist-oriented states of the region, which became members of ASEAN after 1990. The original goal of improving economic, political, and social cooperation has been supplemented since 1994 by other fields of activity such as security, cultural, and environmental policy. In September 2009, the heads of state and government of the ASEAN countries decided to create a common economic area modeled on the EU.

II. Greater Mekong Subregion as Part of South East Asia

Let us now turn our attention to the Mekong region in more detail. It is also referred to as the Greater Mekong Subregion (GMS) in the context of cooperation within ASEAN. Its fragmentation becomes even more apparent when it is brought into a relationship with China. From a geostrategic and historical perspective, GMS is the open, southern flank of China, traditionally but Japan, the only South-East and East Asian great power. Over the past centuries, China has undertaken great efforts to control its strategic southern flank: from the system of vassal states of the Qing Dynasty and the Indochina wars up to the present, direct and indirect influence on the politics and economy of the countries there. On the one hand, these aspirations to control a strategic hinterland with high economic potential target a region that is profoundly characterized by the traditionally fragmented nature of the countries bordering the Mekong, their ethnic and cultural diversity, and their enduring external and internal conflicts. Since the eighteenth century, the "Balkan" of Asia, on the other hand, has increasingly attracted non-Asiatic powers in their attempt to gain access to China or to limit its influence. Especially since the end of the Second World War, the entire area became subject to American imperial strategies. Today, U.S. foreign policies in GMS can be characterized by the attempt to make the entire region an anchor point of its encircling strategy against a China that is threatening America more and more as the world's leading power. This has created a situation that was believed to have been overcome after the end of the Third Indochina War: The GMS has again become a playing field for the global interests of the major powers. As in the last 200 years, the danger emerges again that the fate of the Mekong region and its inhabitants will not be regulated primarily by the GMS states themselves.

The fragmentation of Southeast Asia is therefore reflected in the Mekong Subregion like a magnifying glass. This becomes particularly apparent when one looks at the structures through which the river that gives its name, the Mekong, determines the entire region. The Mekong region includes parts of China, Myanmar, Laos, Cambodia, and Vietnam. With a length of between 4350 km and 4909 km, the Mekong is one of the 12 longest rivers in the world and with an average discharge of about 15,000 m^3/sec, also one of the most water-rich. However, this discharge fluctuates considerably every year between the dry season and the monsoon season, which is a factor that prevents the Mekong from being used as an international waterway. More importantly, however, the river, like other major river systems, somewhat like the Nile, is divided geographically and hydrologically into clearly distinguishable sections. At least four if not six sections can be distinguished from each other:

- The Mekong originates in several headwaters in the Tibetan highlands and is called Dza Chu there. It originates from the "headwaters of the three rivers" on the Tibetan plateau in the National Nature Reserve of Sanjiangyuan. The reserve protects the upper reaches of the Yellow River (Huang He), Yangtze, and Mekong from north to south.
- Then the Mekong River leaves the Tibetan plateau and enters the Chinese province of Yunnan, whereas a wild mountain river it forms the "three parallel river basin," the Hengduan Mountains, together with the Yangtze River to the east and the Salween

River to the west. In China, the river is called Lancang Jiang.

- At a sea level of about 500 m, the Mekong leaves China and forms for about 200 km, the border river between Myanmar (MekaungMyit) and Laos (Mae Nam Khong). At the end of this stretch, the Mae Nam Ruak flows into the river, forming the Golden Triangle between Laos, Myanmar, and Thailand. This is also the beginning of the lower course of the Mekong.
- Afterward the river first forms the border between Laos and Thailand and then flows in a loop through partly deep canyons and rapids through northwestern Laos to the old capital of Laos. From Luang Prabang on, the shipping traffic decreases considerably, as the course of the river is marked by numerous rapids. Further south, the Mekong River again forms the border to Thailand (here also as Mae Nam Khong) for several hundred kilometers, until all traffic ends at the Mekong Waterfalls on the Lao-Cambodian border. The waterfalls are located south of the Si Phan Don inland delta, from where the river, which is more than 10 km wide there, falls in cascades over 21 m. These falls are therefore the widest waterfall on Earth and with discharge rates of up to 50,000/s, the largest waterfall in Asia.
- After entering Cambodia, the Mekong flows as the TonleMekongk through the wide plains of Cambodia, whereby there is a geographical peculiarity unique in this dimension: Just north of the Cambodian capital Phnom Penh, the Tonle-Sap River flows into the Mekong. This river, which is fed from Lake Tonle-Sap, changes direction when the Mekong floods and its waters push its tributary into the lake. The Mekong thus fills the lake every year for several months. Only when the monsoon recedes, the Tonle Sap also reverses its direction of flow.
- Directly south of the Cambodian capital Phnom Penh the Mekong Delta begins; the river course is divided into two streams, the Bassac and the parallel-running Mekong itself. After crossing over to Vietnam (as Song Me Kong), the river fans out into a delta of over 70,000 km². The nine main arms finally flowing into the South China Sea there also led to the Vietnamese nickname of the Mekong as Song Cửu Long (Nine Dragon River).

To put it in a somewhat striking way, it can be said that the Mekong separates its riparian population rather than connects them. Mekong forms a highly segmented river system, which has only been used in individual sections as an axis of cultural and economic exchange and also serves as a rarely crossed border over long stretches of its course.

III. Relevance of Transborder Collaboration

There is certainly consensus among riparian states about the importance of the Mekong River system for the entire region because the river provides the central resource water for over 60 million people. The control of the water supply is widely considered as an opportunity to influence the further economic development of the riparian states. These ideas are by no means new but can be traced back to the de-colonization of Southeast Asia. Already in 1957, at the initiative of ECAFE, a Mekong Committee was set up, which presented comprehensive measures for river regulation, flood protection, electricity generation, and navigability. These plans were promoted by the U.S.

OVERCOMING THE BORDERS IN SOUTHEAST ASIA? 171

Government as part of its containment policy. The collaboration in the region initially relied primarily on the Mekong Committee (1957–1978) and its successor organization, the Interim Mekong Committee (1978–1995). However, the work of both organizations was made largely impossible by the political antagonisms and armed conflicts that plagued the entire region until the end of the Third Indochina War. Apart from the crisis in Cambodia, the collaboration was also hampered by huge growth differences that existed between the remaining states, Thailand on one side and Vietnam and Laos on the other, in the 1980s and early 1990s.

Since then, various agreements have been concluded, mostly between the riparian states of Cambodia, Laos, Thailand, and Vietnam, to create organizations and instruments for regional collaboration: FCDI, 1993, QEC, 1993, ASEAN, 1994, AEM-MITI, 1994, MRC, 1995, ASEAN-ME, 1996, and first and foremost the Greater Mekong Subregion (ADB-GMS, 1992), as an initiative of the Asian Development Bank. GMS brings together six countries. Cambodia, China (its provinces of Yunnan and the Guangxi Zhuang Autonomous Region), Laos, Myanmar, Thailand, and Vietnam.

The main task of the "Greater Mekong Subregion Economic Cooperation Program" is to support the implementation of high-priority projects in the following areas: agriculture, energy, environment, health and human resource development, information and communication technology, tourism, transport, transport and trade facilitation, and urban development. Under the strategic framework from 2011, the strategy of GMS is based from 2012 until 2022 on the development of economic corridors. Since then, the focus of GMS has shifted from the promotion of conventional infrastructure to multisector investments.

The aim is to create more and stronger cross-sectoral linkages, to involve more stakeholders, and to improve monitoring and evaluation. The program was reviewed in 2017 to set the focus for the remaining five years of its operation. The modification of the program is understood as a response to recent economic trends (such as changes in growth, connectivity, global competition, spatial development, climate change, food security, and finance) and institutional developments (first and foremost G20 and ASEAN). It has recently been integrated into the Hanoi Action Plan 2018–2022. The latter calls for an expansion of economic corridors to improve connectivity: between the member countries, between rural and urban centers, and within rural and urban areas. Thus, the main goal of the Hanoi Action Plan 2018–2022 is to distribute the benefits of economic growth more broadly. The plan has been adopted on 31 March 2018, by the Sixth GMS Summit of Leaders in Hanoi together with a new Regional Investment Framework.

Despite the high level of investment, the activities of the GMS are difficult to assess. On the one hand, the program is based on inter-governmental consultation and dialogue with only a few institutional arrangements. Central institutions are the Leader's Summit, Ministerial Conferences and Working Groups, and Forums in priority sectors. On the other hand, the activities of GMS take place in a region and an area where many other players are active, Greater Mekong Subregion Academic and Research Network (GMSARN), Sustainable Mekong Research Network (SUMERNET), and several organizations of the United Nations involving FAO, UNEP, UNODC, PROFOR, and the Mekong River Commission (MRC) in particular etc.

172 TOWARD A NEW ART OF BORDER CROSSING

The MRC is currently the only regional organization through which the governments of Cambodia, Lao PDR, Thailand, and Vietnam work directly through an inter-governmental organization. The task is the joint management of water resources and the sustainable development of the Mekong River. The aim of the MRC is to work as a regional facilitating and advisory body, which is managed by the Water and Environment Ministries of the countries mentioned, and to ensure the following objectives: to ensure the efficient and mutually beneficial development of the Mekong River and to minimize the potentially harmful effects on the people and the environment in the Lower Mekong Basin. The MRC serves as a platform for water diplomacy and regional collaboration. The member states should benefit from the resources provided by the Mekong river system, and at the same time can claim their legitimate national interests. Therefore, MRC is a knowledge transfer agency for water management, initiating decision-making processes based on scientific knowledge. The MRC has a diverse range of tasks. It includes, inter alia: sustainable fishing, new opportunities for agriculture, freedom of navigation, sustainable generation of electricity, flood protection, and management, preservation, and conservation of important ecosystems. This is also a contribution to the accomplishment of the upcoming tasks. In general, it is expected that the entire Mekong Basin will be exposed to more severe floods and prolonged periods of drought. The delta of the river is also threatened by salinization and global sea-level rise.

Like only a few international organizations operating in the region, technical collaboration within the MRC is governed by established rules. To this end, the 1995 Mekong Agreement established a number of procedures, including Water Quality, Data and Information Exchange and Sharing, Water Use Monitoring, Notification, Prior Consultation and Agreement, and Maintenance of Flows on the Mainstream. In this way, a systematic and uniform implementation of the agreement is to be achieved. The MRC Secretariat has 65 employees in Phnom Penh, Cambodia, and Vientiane, Laos. In addition, each State maintains National Mekong Committees. The riparian states of the upper Mekong, China, and Myanmar are Dialogue Partners of the MRC.

Summing up again, it is noticeable that the previous variety of actors, of which only the two most significant ones have been mentioned here in more detail, makes it difficult to summarize what has been achieved so far. After all, a study by the "StiftungWissenschaft und Politik" concludes: "Although all Mekong residents have enjoyed considerable economic growth over the last decade, both organizations have failed to reduce the development gap between their member countries and to adopt binding procedures to develop a solution to the conflicts that arise from the different ways of accessing the shared resource of Mekong."

IV. The Involvement of Big Powers

The Mekong River system is the geographic backbone of a geopolitical "shatter belt."[4] As mentioned already, it has, therefore, attracted several extra-regional powers since the crisis of China in the nineteenth century. More recently, from the end of the Second to the End of the Third Indochina War, especially the US and Japan were involved, and in the context of the peace process in Cambodia and general development tasks, the UN in particular. Currently, the large number of actors, originating from outside the region,

OVERCOMING THE BORDERS IN SOUTHEAST ASIA? 173

can hardly be overlooked. There is a broad international debate about their aims and procedures, which cannot be described in detail here too.

The most important player today is China. With each passing year, China's influence on Southeast Asia is growing. With investments and infrastructure projects, Beijing chains the smaller nations and thus also operates political agenda setting. The Chinese government recently announced that it would offer Chinese government bonds worth some 900 million euros to the Mekong states of Thailand, Myanmar, Laos, Vietnam, and Cambodia. Over the last few years, China's influence on the five states along the Mekong has grown significantly. China is the largest foreign investor in Cambodia, Laos, and Myanmar. In Thailand, China's share of foreign investment is growing steadily. In exchange for development aid and investment, the People's Republic gains access to natural resources such as oil, gas, and wood. In addition, China is securing support for the ambitious development of hydropower on the upper reaches of the Mekong, which will change the entire ecology of the region.

The rapid changes are particularly visible in Cambodia. For years, the country was financially dependent on Western countries, but in 2016, Beijing spent almost four times as much as the US. Since Cambodia's Prime Minister Hun Sen knows the Chinese at his side, he has criticized the West and accused the US of wanting to overthrow its government. Cambodia is no exception, it is obvious that the whole of Southeast Asia will increasingly be drawn into China's gravitational field. This becomes clear, for example, on the "Belt and Road Initiative" of China's President Xi Jinping. The gigantic infrastructure project aims to connect China with Asia, Europe, the Middle East, and Africa. China's political and economic influence on individual Southeast Asian states also has the effect of successfully blocking joint action by them, especially through ASEAN and the other organizations for regional collaboration; GMS and MRC in particular.

Another factor is playing into the hands of China: the dwindling U.S. involvement in the region. The Trump government's foreign-policy learning course, which has so far failed to present a concept for Southeast Asia, causes mistrust to which the riparian states of the Mekong react with increasing rapprochement with China. In contrast to this, the US has no primary interest in the resources of the region or the river system of the Mekong. Its motive was rather basic geostrategic: The US's China policy has been a mix of confrontational and cooperative elements since Kissinger's détente with Mao Zedong. However, since the turn of the millennium, China's economic and world political growth has been considered by Washington to be the biggest long-term challenge to its national interests. In recent years, the US has found Beijing's foreign policy aggressive, particularly in the South China Sea. In order to curb China's hegemonic ambitions, the Obama administration announced in November 2011 a "sweep" of the U.S. Grand Strategy in order to redirect the attention and resources of foreign policy from Europe and the Middle East to the Asia-Pacific region. As a result, the US increased its military presence in the Pacific—by 2020, 60 percent of U.S. air and naval capacity is to be concentrated here. Bilateral security relations with India, Vietnam, the Philippines, Japan, and Australia have also been strengthened.

In June 2015, Obama obtained the necessary parliamentary authorization to negotiate the large free trade agreement Transpacific Partnership (TPP). The agreement, which was finalized in September 2015 and includes the US, Japan,

Vietnam, Australia, Chile, Peru, Mexico, and Canada, had a clear geopolitical focus through the exclusion of China. This can also be understood as an "encirclement policy." Obama's trade move completed the strategic move to Asia and was one of the few legislative triumphs of his presidency. The TPP, like a future free trade agreement with the EU (TTIP), aims to further order the global economy through rules favorable to the US and the West. This showed the systematic building-up of a frontline against China by the Obama administration. Astonishingly, the Obama administration's geostrategic approaches, which had profound implications for the GMS, were destroyed by the Trump government's vague policies. The resulting insecurity and the worldwide increasing anger among the political elites over the Trump administration in general, have significantly weakened the U.S. position in Southeast Asia.

The third significant player in the region is the European Union and its leading powers France and Germany. The approach followed was neither direct influence (China) nor geostrategic involvement in a "Grand Strategy" (the US). European politics has so far relied on the parallelism of development in Europe and Southeast Asia and on the equality of interests between the two areas. Overcoming the frontlines left by the East-West conflict in Europe as well as on the Southeast Asian mainland puts both regions—despite their many differences—in front of comparable tasks. But it is not just these historical parallels that suggest a strong commitment to European (French, German) politics in the Mekong region. More important are a number of strategic considerations. This region is just as crucial for political stability, economic growth, and interstate cooperation of the whole of Southeast Asia as it is for the relationship of emerging China to its neighbors. The growing integration of this area is therefore in the interests of both, Southeast Asia and Europe as part of a new multipolar world system.

In a number of sectors that the European, German, and French levels have identified as central fields of their work, the Mekong region provides a wide range of tasks for fruitful development cooperation. The Mekong, as the region's largest common resource, represents a particular challenge in this respect. Sustainable use and development of its potential—taking into account the specific needs of the Mekong countries and their various user and interest groups—is indispensable tied to close and trusting cooperation. This target was strongly supported in Brussels, Berlin, and Paris; policymakers there understand such forms of regional cooperation as a means, not only to overcome underdevelopment but also to ensure security. The Mekong region first of all seemed to be a vivid proof of the thesis that the dependence on a common water resource does not cause increasing conflicts, but rather more intensive cooperation between the various beneficiaries. In particular, the Greater Mekong Subregion (GMS) and the Mekong River Commission (MRC) have generated active engagement by the EU and individual European countries.

However, in the European view, the impressive presence of the two organizations often prevents a critical analysis of the depth of impact and the long-term prospects of their cooperation strategies. It is all too easy to overlook the fact that not only the Chinese leadership but also the governments of the other Mekong riparian states are advocating policies that equate development with economic growth and give high priority to the principle of national sovereignty. This places narrow limits on the work of institutions that aim for comprehensive political cooperation and sustainable development.

GMS, which wants to create a common economic area without overarching political structures, is receiving widespread approval in the capitals of the region. It enjoys the support of the Asian Development Bank, which is also funded by contributions from European countries. The fact that GMS gives environmental protection at best a rhetorical value and completely dispenses with the formulation of a binding catalog of principles is seen more as a deficit in Europe. A similarly ambivalent assessment applies to MRC. The approval of this is rather declamatory for the member states too, although the MRC has already advocated in its founding document for sustainable and inclusive development as well as clear rules of procedure in the use of the Mekong resources. The budget of MRC is still largely funded by countries outside the region. At the European level, disillusionment over the possibilities of fostering sustainable growth and security at the same time through the promotion of regional collaboration has become more apparent in recent years.

Another major actor in the region is Japan, notably through the mechanisms of the Mekong Japan Summits, the Mekong-Japan Foreign Ministers' Meetings, and the Meetings of the Japan-China Policy Dialogue on the Mekong Region. However, unlike the EU, Japan pursues a more classical development policy. The means for this are on the one hand the promotion of industrial development in the Mekong region through public–private partnerships. On the other hand, Japan hopes to contribute to the region by utilizing Japan's expertise in areas such as human resources development, health and medical care, and environmental technologies, in addition to the development of "quality infrastructure" that conforms to international standards.

Actors in GMS are, in addition to France and Germany, other European countries such as Denmark, Sweden, Switzerland, Finland, and the Netherlands. A certain role Australia and South Korea continue to play. Recently, India has also propagandizing its "Look-East Policy" for economic integration with ASEAN as part of an initiative to promote India-Mekong Economic Cooperation. Both sides are thus planning for a Mekong-India Economic Corridor which wants to form an integral part of the India-ASEAN connectivity. It remains to be seen to what extent India can mobilize resources to realize this initiative.

V. *Quo Vadis* Mekong?

Southeast Asia, and especially the Mekong region, has certainly made great progress in terms of the transgression of its borders compared with the decades up to 1990. On the other hand, however, the region is still a long way from real cross-border cooperation, for example following the European example. In particular, there is a lack of political will, which is made more difficult by the fact that the people in the region differ too widely from one another along the above-mentioned lines. Also, in contrast to Europe, no permanent coalitions of leading powers are foreseeable, as is the case with the European tandem of France and Germany, for example. For this reason, there is currently a greater danger that those who should institutionally secure the crossing of borders will allow the respective national political classes to be separated from each other by major powers from outside, that is, especially not only the US but also China. It is to be hoped that Southeast Asia has learned from the disastrous consequences of half a century of U.S. intervention and that there will be an urgent need for cross-border cooperation.

Bibliography

Asia Society (2009): *Asia's Next Challenge: Securing the Region's Water Future. A Report by the Leadership Group on Water Security in Asia.* Asia Society Policy Institute: New York.

Asian Development Bank (2016): *Asian Water Development Outlook 2016, Strengthening Water Security in Asia and the Pacific.* Asian Development Bank: Manila. 41.

———(2018): *The Hanoi Action Plan 2018–2022,* https://www.adb.org/sites/default/files/institutional-document/409086/ha-noi-action-plan-2018-2022.pdf. Asian Development Bank.

———(2020): *GMS Program.* http://www.adb.org/sites/default/files/gms-ec-framework-2012-2022.pdf. Asian Development Bank.

Chheang, Vannarith (2016): Tensions and Prospects over the Mekong River. In: *Thinking ASEAN,* Issue 10, April 2016. 2–4.

Cohen, Saul (2003): *Geopolitics of the World System.* Rowman & Littlefield: London.

Council for Security Cooperation in Asia Pacific (CSCAP) (2014): Enhancing Water Security in the Asia Pacific, CSCAP Memorandum No. 23, January 2014. CSCAP.

Hein, Christoph (2014): ASEAN, der übersehene Riese – Essay. https://www.bpb.de/apuz/191924/asean-der-uebersehene-riese. Published under the Creative Commons License "CC BY-NC-ND 3.0 DE - Attribution - Non-Commercial - No Derivatives 3.0 Germany."

Hensengerth, Oliver (2009): Transboundary River Cooperation and the Regional Public Good: The Case of the Mekong River. In: *Contemporary Southeast Asia: A Journal of International and Strategic Studies,* Vol. 31, 2. 342.

International Institute for Sustainable Development (2013): *The Water-Energy-Food Security Nexus: Towards a Practical Planning and Decision-Support Framework for Landscape Investment and Risk Management.* http://www.iisd.org/pdf/2013/wef_nexus_2013.pdf. International Institute for Sustainable Development.

Mekong River Commission (2018): *MRC Procedural Rules for Mekong Water Cooperation.* MRC Secretariat.

———(2017). https://oa.mg/work/10.52107/mrc.ajg6hj.

Memorandum of Understanding between the Mekong River Commission Secretariat and the ASEAN Secretariat, 4 March 2010. MRC Secretariat.

Natalegawa, Marty (2018): Does ASEAN matter? A View from within. Institute for Southeast Asian Studies: Singapore. 228–235.

Pham Quang Minh/Briesen, Detlef (Eds.) (2020): *Collaboration in Water Resource Management in Vietnam and South-East Asia.* Nomos Verlagsgesellschaft Mbh & Co: Baden-Baden.

Renaud, Fabrice G./Kuenzer, Claudia Kuenzer (Eds.) (2012): *The Mekong Delta System: Interdisciplinary Analyses of a River Delta.* Springer: Dordrecht.

Will, Gerhard (2010): Der Mekong: Ungelöste Probleme regionaler Kooperation. 53. https://www.swp-berlin.org/fileadmin/contents/products/studien/2010_S07_wll_ks.pdf. SWP.

World Economic Forum (2011): *Global Risks 2011*: 6th Edition. World Economic Forum: Cologne.

Notes

1 Pham Quang Minh/Briesen, Detlef (Eds.) (2020): Collaboration in Water Resource Management in Vietnam and South-East Asia. Nomos Verlagsgesellschaft Mbh & Co: Baden-Baden.

2 http://hdr.undp.org/en/content/human-development-index-hdi. Human Development Reports.

3 https://asean.org/. The ASEAN Secretariat.

4 Cohen, Saul (2003). *Geopolitics of the World System. Rowman & Littlefield: London.*

Chapter 13

POST OIL MIGRATION FUTURES IN THE *KHALEEJ*: THINKING WITH/OUT BORDERS

Manishankar Prasad

Introduction

Borders are a part of the destiny of the *Khaleej*, (or the gulf) the typology of which is infected by the notions of bordering, as the Persian Gulf was the norm as Persia was a dominant regional player competing for influence along with the Ottoman Empire and the British Raj. The Sheikhdoms of the Gulf from Kuwait City to Muscat to Jeddah, were British-aligned in the imperial chess game. The port town of Muscat had its twin town in Mandvi as per historian Chaya Goswami. The Gulf has the imagination of a desert frozen in time, yet this oriental framing does injustice to the Gulf which has been trading as a part of the Indian Ocean world for centuries. Manama to Muscat were important trading ports for pearling to slavery. Jeddah was known as the 'Queen of the Red Sea' being the eclectic Ottoman port which was the hub of the Muslim Pilgrimage to the twin holy cities of Makkah and Medina (Freitag, 2020).

The pandemic and the years of stagnant oil prices have had a defining role on the migrant lives as many businesses had to reduce as the main employer in the region, the oil sector was contributing to reducing revenues and thus had a cascading impact on the shifting priorities. The region is quickly adapting to a new demographic normal, where millions of migrants who have built the region since oil was struck are being offered hard choices as incomes fall. The realities are reflected in the recalibration of borders externally, and internally as would be fleshed out in the subsequent sections.

Racial '*Kafala*' Capitalism as (B)ordering

Slavery was abolished in Saudi Arabia under pressure from the American administration in 1962 and in the rest of the Gulf in that decade, as the region decolonised (Wald, 2019). The Gulf is a tribal society with many actors aligned in a hierarchy, with power stemming from proximity to the power structure which is the ruling family. Slavery from East Africa to the Gulf was a prominent feature of the Indian Ocean trade till the British outlawed slavery in the 1830s however the trade continued under the mast of the dhow, and enforcement was inadequate. Omani Sultans ruled Zanzibar and port along the Indian Ocean littoral from 1856 till the black nationalist revolution in 1964, when the royal family had to flee to Portsmouth. Zanzibar was connected to the global circuits of capitalism in garments and dates with America, as Oman established the earliest diplomatic contacts with Washington DC in 1840.

The centuries of tribal structuring of society in the Gulf, not unlike the caste system in India or the clan system in Chinese societies creates an internal bordering mechanism which were kept in place during the oil era, as traditions were unchallenged as the Middle East became an employer, a market for goods and an investor in other parts of the developed world. Qatar owns premium real estate in London and is the UAE's major investor in India and Indonesia. The Gulf however is not a monolith with countries such as Oman and Bahrain being under severe budgetary pressures as having limited hydrocarbon income and youth bulge. The Gulf Cooperation Council or the GCC, a collective of Gulf Monarchies is bordered internally with the richer members shadowing the lesser ones.

The tribal dimension of the Gulf society frames the way the bordering within manifests in the way even citizens are tiered. The legacy of slavery plays out in the everyday as gulf citizens themselves are tiered. In the aftermath of the black nationalist revolution in 1964, many Arab families of Omani descent were invited by the late Sultan Qaboos Bin Said to contribute to nation-building after decades of neglect. The Zanzibaris or the 'Zanj's' as they were called in Oman were educated in the East African university system and dominated the civil service in the early years. They have been however perceived as cultural outsiders given their limited ability to speak Arabic, although the generation at present, educated through the Omani school system speak the national language. The Zanzibari identity has been subsumed under the national Omani identity as an Arab country. But is Oman, a purely Arab country?

The Gulf is also home to a dispersed group of South Asians who have been military mercenaries for centuries, the Baluchi who have served in the police forces of the British in Bahrain along with serving in the Omani Armed Forces (Lutfi, 2018). The Baluchi who are divided along the Makran coast along Pakistan and Iran, speak and practice their cultures in the Gulf below the Arabic radar (Murer, 2022). Baluchi musical performances such as the *Malid* are considered Omani at present. However, the Baluchi language is not promoted and there are murmurs of discrimination against Baluchi for public sector employment, and the private sector is where Omani Baluchi fetch employment.

The population of Baluchi have a substantial presence among Omani citizenry, and across the border in the UAE, the Baluchi perform the image of a local citizen by wearing the *'dishdasha'* as they can be often mistaken for a Pakistani by the other *'Muwateen'* or citizens where South Asian communities dominate many a district (Akinci, 2019). The citizen in the Gulf is not an equal entity in terms of valency either, although the passport will be a common minimum and nothing else. The citizenship of a Gulf country is tiered as was demonstrated by Qatar, which stated prior to the partial elections to the Majlis Al Shura, that citizens only a peculiar document called 'the family book' was needed for the citizens who were eligible to vote. The family book

POST OIL MIGRATION FUTURES IN THE *KHALEEJ* 179

is a document that defines the *'nasab'* or the genealogy of the family tree, as a source of legitimacy. The bloodline from the father's side creates the ground of citizenship, as women Gulf citizens married to non-citizens cannot pass on the passport and its associated welfare state privileges to their children.

The Gulf is known for statelessness as well especially in Kuwait and the UAE known as the *'bidoon'* who is without documentation despite being in the country for generations. The family might have missed a deadline to register as citizens as the region was undergoing decolonisation. The stateless might have served in the armed forces or the civil services, but the present generation is without documentation unable to access public healthcare and education (Al Nakib, 2016).

The *Kafala* system has its origins in this genealogical understanding of belonging, as the *'nasab'* configures the hierarchy of belonging even among citizens based on racial purity. The modern origins of Kafala were in colonial roots of monitoring the 'undesirable' in Bahrain in the 1920s (Al Shehabi, 2019). Kafala is effectively a form of migration management as exploitation is embedded in the system, as profits are harvested through the body of the labour, whose destiny is in the hands of the sponsor (Kakande, 2015). The sponsor under the system can cancel the visa of the worker without any due process, and this is a form of structural violence exacted by the sponsor.

Kafala is tantamount to the ownership of people hence a profitable route for gulf nationals is to sell visas in the open market. Migrants run businesses under a local sponsor and pay the sponsor a fixed fee every month as a commission. The figure of the migrant is an extension of the systems of marginalisation triggered by the Kafala system and past origins of racial structuring.

Migrants as Majority Yet Muted and Marginal

Against the backdrop of the Kafala, the migrant is a marginalised entity stripped off agency as the structural oppressions create a human robot to execute a task. In the event of dissent, the migrant is replaced in favour of a similar and often cheaper talent pool looking to replace in a similar role. The global flows of capital have created uneven terrains of development in the global south (Smith, 2008). The paucity of employment opportunities in the home countries has prompted a manpower export industry to send labour to the gulf, as an expression of agency (Rogaly, 2009). Millions of workers from Makati to Mumbai to Mombasa seek jobs in the Gulf, via a set of agents and brokers which comprise a multigenerational migration infrastructure since the late 1940s. Most workers comprise an overwhelming demographic who possess a permanent temporariness build 'temporary cities' of Dubai and Doha are bordered immediately as soon as they arrive here (Elsheshtawy, n.d.; Loong, 2018; Unnikrishnan, 2019).

The act of coming to the Gulf is an expression of worker agency yet, the agency itself evaporates under the desert heat of the region, as oppressive as the Kafala. The migrant worker under the Kafala is not an inanimate entity but a graded hierarchy framed by social capital possessed by the worker, to negotiate with the system. The Kafala impacts all sorts of workers right from a general manager to an office boy. The company's Arbab or sponsor in Muscat where I worked a few years ago, had issued an absconding notice in a prominent national broadsheet to the head of the company by the owner as he had demanded past salary arrears.

The technologies of control under the Kafala have been fine-tuned over the decades, keeping a 'tight leash' on the body of the migrant worker from housing rental agreements to family visas to exit visas for expats in Saudi Arabia that control the movement. These are explicit tools and tactics that are restrictive. Until recently countries such as Oman have removed the Non-Objection Certificate or the NOC when migrants need to move employers, to align with interventional labour conventions and the U.S. Free Trade Agreement between Oman and the US.

Kafala creates a tiered labour market as local citizens operate on different salary scales with minimum salaries for graduate hires than educated migrants who might be their managers initially, but they become their bosses a few years down the line as nationalisation requirements mandate a bias in favour of the local citizen. Migrant worker marginalisation is not exclusively the preserve of the Gulf. Similar systems mirroring the Kafala can be seen in countries that are substantial host countries for migrants such as Singapore and Malaysia. A majority of '3D' labour is performed by 'bachelor bodies' from South Asia from the construction sites building public transportation in Singapore to the palm oil plantations in Johor across the border in Malaysia (Ye, 2014). The migrant labour markets are gendered and racialised as in the Gulf in Singapore as particular jobs in the banking sector prefer women of certain nationalities. The tiering or the bordering occurs even within the migrant worker communities as Foreign Domestic Workers who are women from source countries such as Indonesia and the Philippines are distinct from women who are in service sector jobs. The term 'Sri Lankaniyah' is a derogatory racialised term for a South Asian Domestic Worker in Lebanon given by the local population (Kassamali, 2018).

The migrant communities in countries which host them are tiered and layered, and middle-class expats and the labour compatriots might be at odds with each other. Age, race, ethnicity and language along with income are invisible borders within borders that impact the actual ability to cross borders. The social capital of the migrant is a function of the skill and income but also the identity construct that might create greater acceptability in the host country. Immigrants from Kerala have district-level community associations in the Gulf, which offer social protection to the members of the group in a transnational manner which was in action during the pandemic. There are 30 odd groups of the Indian Social Club in Oman affiliated with the Indian Embassy, as the umbrella organisation was observed by the author during the seven hours of cultural programming prior to the Indian Prime Minister's address to the Indian Community in Muscat on the 11 February 2018 at the Sultan Qaboos Sports Complex in Bousher. Fractures from back home are often transposed to the diaspora, particularly in temporary guest worker communities.

The demographic majority of the migrant workers translates to a spatial configuration of the Gulf City as a mobile common which is not reflected in the 'Visit Dubai' marketing collateral on the digital as the shadow region of the plush Sheikh Zayed Road is relegated and conceptualised as the 'mobile commons' which migrant infrastructure on the scale of a city (Collins, 2016 & 2021). The migrant areas of the city

POST OIL MIGRATION FUTURES IN THE *KHALEEJ*

are a heuristic of spaces which are designed for the low to middle-income migrant, from mini vans to video stores to eateries which are often branches of stores from back home such as Student Biryani from Lahore in the South Asian-dominated Karama district of Dubai, now increasingly gentrified (Mohammed & Sidaway, 2012).

Change and its pace are often not considered while studying the migrant Gulf, as these cities have been the fast-changing skylines in Asia. Along with the rapid development, is also the shuffling of the migrant makeup of the cities particularly in Doha as the old city gives way to the FIFA World Cup Stadium (Mohammed & Sidaway, 2016). The Dubai Taxi was a preserve of the *desi* driver from South Asia, which is now being replaced by Africans from Uganda to Cameroon. Cities in the Gulf have grown more expensive, which makes it harder to save and remit to families back in South Asia.

With the pandemic combined with lower oil revenues since 2014 and greater expectations from the local population, the Gulf has tipped over to a new post oil era. Automation and digitisation have ramped up the prospects of reordering the labour market including reducing migrant workers.

The Post Oil Re-Bordering

The Gulf is a space of flows as a major energy provider over decades. The sands are shifting with time, as decarbonisation and the net zero paradigm are the new zeitgeist of our times. The oil beneath the sands is now fashioned as carbon which is contributing to climate change. The economic edifice of the region is dependent on oil or oil-derived revenues that have been exposed to price shocks, that have had an impact on migrant lived experiences, as jobs dry up or salaries are slashed. The oil shocks were felt from 1998, when oil fell to USD 10 per barrel to 2014 when oil crashed after years of an oil boom. Borders internally for migrants shapeshift as per oil prices, which impacts their lives in a cyclical manner.

The net-zero transition is a major driver for the region, as the oil sector gives way to solar parks and hydrogen manufacturing facilities, retrofitting the existing facilities. China is a major manpower exporter in the region, due to its helming major renewable projects. China has a major diaspora in Dubai which is a topic of a monograph by sociologist Yuting Wang (Wang, 2020).

A major reality of a post oil Khaleej is the greater presence of local citizens in working-class jobs which have been the major social escalator for low-income migrants. When the taxi sector was nationalised in Oman a decade ago, there was a lull, but voids did not exist in the market and a new equilibrium was reached. Even within the local citizenry, the racial and tribal order is at play. The northern emirates are at the periphery of the UAE, while citizens from Abu Dhabi and Dubai capture the best of the opportunities. As the welfare state gets more competitive, the borders internally get drawn sharper.

New Internal Borders?

As the world is in the midst of hypernationalism, a hardening of borders is underway with Brexit and a spate of macho leaders. One region which is embracing the global with a vengeance is the Gulf from Dubai to Riyadh to Salalah. The post oil scenario

182 TOWARD A NEW ART OF BORDER CROSSING

has triggered unprecedented reforms from the opening of theatres to the hosting of the Rea Sea Festival in Saudi Arabia. The opening of the region has created new hierarchies among migrants and citizens, which are internal borders. The formation of the investor class, for whom the liberalisation has occurred will create new problems for the traditional citizenry.

The radical changes can be observed as fresh cartographies are drawn when gauged from the labour lens especially when climate change and the digital are brought into dialogue.

Power/Resistance

The emphasis on worker agency brings to the discussion an examination of the varied typologies of power to resist the hegemonic forces of global capital to shape economic landscapes in the vision of the worker. Worker Collectives of organised labour have been the predominant focus of the empirical case studies to inform worker agency within the subdomain of labour geography has given an impression of the limited range of resistive power that a worker exercises while projecting agency. Collective Bargaining on the part of structured trade unions negotiates with the employer for a set of welfare/workfare benefits for the worker, which the worker also must reciprocate in some tangible manner. Resistance in the form of public strike action (as seen in France and India for instance) at the 'scale' of the plant/company union or a national union opposing privatisation of public sector assets such as the recent Air India sale to the Tata Group.

The range of resistive performances of a worker while affecting agency in particular contexts can be described as Resilience, Reworking and Resistance with a capital 'R', which is a collective effort to recover labour time in the sphere of labour production and social reproduction. As per Katz (2004) in Cumbers et al. (2010), resilience is small actions in the everyday by the worker that does not try to oppose the powers such as networks of care, such as community or faith groups. Reworking attempts to get the structures to align with the worker's objectives to improve his/her situation to carve the middle ground (Coe & Jordhus-Lier, 2011; Gotehus, 2021).

Every articulation of resistance by the worker will span this middle ground as they (the worker) will seek to optimise their presence and utility within the system, as the precarious migrant worker for instance in the Gulf, under the highly discriminatory and lop-sided Kafala System of Labour Governance with work visas tied to the employer will have no scope for redressal, as the nonexistence of labour laws for migrants, entail creative ways of negotiation in enacting 'weapons of the weak' (Scott, 1985). The Sultanate of Oman, where the author grew up (as a second-generation migrant) is one of the poorer Arab Gulf states where low-income citizens are street vendors, drive taxis and have a national trade union (one of the few in the Middle East), albeit only for Omanis. When an Indian owned Steel Mill in the industrial city of Sohar, bordering Al Ain in the UAE, tried to retrench 50 Omani citizens during the pandemic, the trade union brought collective bargaining to the fore with the Ministry of Labour while migrant workers were given a one-way ticket back home.

POST OIL MIGRATION FUTURES IN THE *KHALEEJ*   183

Another set of articulations of power which help in conceptualising resistance is structural power, institutional power, and associational power (Brookes, 2013; Herod, 2018). Structural Power is the ability of the worker to influence the employer, due to the location of the worker within the system. This is further divided into 'workplace bargaining power', which is the location of workers within the strategic sector, and 'marketplace bargaining power', which is the traction achieved from 'tight labour markets' (Herod, 2017). Institutional Power according to Brookes (2013) is the capacity of the worker to influence the interactions and relationship with the employer by formal and informal means. Institutional Power is the agency of the worker to bring the employer within the realm of the law and hold them accountable.

Associational and Coalitional Power is the capacity of workers drawn from the solidarity of civil society associations. However, this type of power is leveraged at various scales from a legal approach to transnational activism. Civil Society associations can be formal and informal, as in the era of neoliberal precarity, privileging the unionised worker, as is the drift from labour geography literature does not capture the worker agency terrain in full especially the precarious worker without access to the same social capital as the unionised worker.

Climate Change: Multi-scalar Game Changer

In light of the global zeitgeist of Climate Change, during the COP26 season, the conversation on energy transitions is dominating the media headlines (Warren & Clayton, 2020). Any energy transition through decarbonisation will entail shifts in the configuration of labour geographies as well (Coe, 2021; Parsons & Natarajan, 2021).

Climate Change is a multi-scalar matter with a global presence with local ramifications for labour. Environmental degradation is known as slow violence, eating away at the planet's capacity to be habitable in the Anthropocene (Nixon, 2018). Yet, when extreme weather events manifest due to climate change such as flooding or droughts, labour at the human scale is impacted as productivity is impacted. At a community level, resource scarcity triggers worker agencies to move. The climate migrant is already a reality as seen with the multiple droughts in the sugar and cotton belt of western Maharashtra State in India which have led to a spate of farmer suicides as well as migration to Pune, Bangalore, and Mumbai in the search for construction labour during the non-sowing season. The precarious climate migrant exercises his/her agency to find employment in an event catalysed by the changing climate (Lambert & Herod, 2016; Strauss, 2020). Similar migrant narratives can be observed in other parts of South Asia such as Bangladesh as well.

Climate Change adaptation literature has utilised risk, vulnerability, and resilience as conceptual anchors to pivot towards the climate era (Bennett, 2016). The green economy paradigm, which is a response to climate change, is uneven terrain, as the old economy where precarity is a constant for communities that have been forced to burden the cost of the transition, such as indigenous people in protected parks or projected GIS experts who are limited time contracts (Neimark et al, 2020). The precarious nature

184 TOWARD A NEW ART OF BORDER CROSSING

of green economy work forms the 'eco-precariat' irrespective of their educational qualifications in this neoliberal transition.

The author would like to extend this notion of 'eco-precariat' in a green economy to any labour who must make sacrifices in the decarbonisation transition and has fallen on the rain shadow side of the energy transition, such as the coal miner in Australia who is facing job cuts as the world transitions away from coal with multiple declarations of no more funds for new coal-fired power plants. The climate change zeitgeist needs to account for worker agency in the conversations towards energy transition. As the analytical focus in the labour geography literature is on the urban, industrial and organised sector worker, the worker agency analytic is a useful measure to rethink how we as scholars think of climate change, from the vantage point of the worker and expand the rubric to other categories of workers.

The oil and gas sector under the climate radar still is the dominant energy provider. The oil and gas workers from the offshore fields of the North Sea in Scotland to Jurong Island in Singapore through the mature oil fields of the Arab Gulf are undergoing a major labour market recalibration. The capacity of worker agencies in the labour geographies of climate change will depend upon the institutional power of the worker unions to voice their dissent. The older worker who is at the tail end of their careers have more to lose than a younger professional who can retrain to a low-carbon skill set. The political economy of the region under study will determine the nature of the reworking/ resilience of the worker while spanning the climate change adaptation objectives.

The availability of global capital towards the climate transition is a key component towards adaptation. Global capital is riding on the climate change transition agenda as climate risk is seen as a value-depleting agent (Barrett, 2013). Insurance companies will charge clients a higher rate of interest if they own a mortgage in a flood-risk-prone area.

The climate financing towards building resilient infrastructure is benchmarked with Environmental, Social & Governance (ESG) standards. The financialisation of the Climate Change paradigm brings about worker welfare measures to the spaces where state-based institutionalised power is weak. These voluntary ESG standards enable worker agency in Global Production Networks, overriding or complementing the role of the place, beyond the container of the nation-state. Worker agency is acknowledged and reflected in multilateral developmental financial agencies linked to social safeguards standards, hence invigorating the worker involved in climate transition projects. The Social aspect of ESG presents an opening into understanding the worker agency through the voices engaged in the stakeholder engagement process in the project-affected area. Although prone to the performance of participation, in the author's lived experience as a social auditor, worker agency does get expressed through established stakeholder management mechanisms. Voicing perspectives through stakeholder engagement platforms in ESG-linked development finance projects can be considered a form of 'reworking' by the employee.

The author was the lead social specialist for an Asian Infrastructure Investment Bank Environmental & Social Impact Assessment report for a USD 400 million syndicated financing for Oman's 500 MW Ibri II[1] Solar Park on the Saudi border. Presence long-term migrant workers from south Asia were identified as camel farmers in the desert

POST OIL MIGRATION FUTURES IN THE *KHALEEJ*   185

on project land as identified on the krookie (land record document), however as the author walked the site on a recce visit, a few temporary camel pens were identified with long-term migrant workers upon speaking to them in Bangla and Urdu (over three visits and spot interviews), were found to be hyper precarious having lived on a solar battery charger for the mobile phone and a bulb with no electricity. These were the very off-grid precarious workers who were being moved off their homes to build a Chinese-funded solar park in relatively prosperous Oman-rich irony indeed. Due to the globally accepted ESG governance norms, the presence of these workers and their voices triggered an independent Resettlement Action Plan for these workers, which would be unlikely given the inadequate legal architecture in Oman as the migrant worker is relegated to a census statistic if at all counted.

Sustainability Reporting is a mandate for many banks and companies listed on public bourses including the Singapore Stock Exchange. Sustainability bonds are being floated by lenders towards achieving a decarbonisation agenda, such as the Nanyang Technological University earlier in 2021. Worker welfare as a metric of ESG performance in the Climate Change finance paradigm brings worker agency to the fore.

It might seem *counterintuitive* that a neoliberal climate finance project is giving voice to worker agency, however geographical scales can be nestled and inverted, with no clear linear narrative. This is the impulse which distinguishes Marxist geography from a broader articulation of labour geography. Singapore has included the reality of a labour geography transition in parliamentary debates, as the low carbon future impacts the oil refining sector as well as the carbon-intensive maritime bunkering space, given the economic weight of the sectoral contribution to the GDP and the jobs which support Singaporean working-class households.

Thinking about worker agency for a worker in an organisation undergoing the climate transition in a direct manner in an oil company is easier than the secondary and tertiary support workers dependent on the core energy sector. The enthusiasm of the oil-producing nations towards pivoting to green and blue hydrogen is linked to the potential of retrofitting the existing oil refining and pipeline infrastructure for the green economy. The political economy of the 'place' and its labour geographies will be coupled with the low carbon transition of the region under consideration.

The informal worker in the 'eco-precariat' impacted by the negative externalities of climate change will have different adaptation modes, including resilience in their everyday lives that is driven by survival.

Reanimating Plural Worker Agencies: Thinking through the Decolonial and Feminist Lens

Herod (2001) writes that the initiative towards thinking about labour geography was not to dispel the geographies of labour but rather to bring the working-class experience as a lens to study the economic geographies of capitalism (p. 48). The political project of labour geography derives its origins from the Western Marxist tradition, which treats the worker as oppressed, rather than with agency needed to have their own spatial fix. The worker agency in labour geography as the *leitmotif* is read from a western-centred, labour union-affiliated worker lens. The worker agency is seen as heroic against the hegemonic powers of global capital that push labour to a corner and squeeze the agentic potential in the process.

Labour is a resource which actively shapes economic landscapes as it also requires them for social and biological reproduction. Worker Agency is not a monolith and is a derivative of the historical and social context of where the worker is located. The Bourdieu-esque 'field' of a worker shapes the nature of the force which it exerts - resistance, rework, or resilience. The agency of the worker is graded and differentiated as per the habitus of the worker which is refracted through intersectional identities of class, race, caste, age and gender (Doutch, 2021). A gendered lens is generative to think through worker agency as it shapes/hinders the capacity to express one's ability to resist in front of the hegemonic structures of power, given the case study of Tirupur Textile manufacturing hub in Tamil Nadu where women situate their own ways of positioning themselves in the labour market (Carswell & De Neve, 2013).

Another layer of identity in India which contributes towards shaping worker identity is caste and religion, as in the case of Dalit Christians (a double minority in terms of socioeconomic vulnerability to render some context) in Carswell and De Neve (2013). Class is a primary preoccupation of labour politics in the West, and thus of Western-centric labour geography, however in the non-west, labour needs to de-centre its obsession with class with other cultural-historical-social imports in shaping worker agency. The decolonial perspective is a popular intellectual movement that seeks to expand the sources of understanding of history, culture, and politics beyond the Eurocentric arena of thought. Decolonisation is a "roomy concept" that provides the leeway for fresh ways of thinking (Clayton & Kumar, 2019; Radcliffe, 2017).

Decolonised perspective is a window into animating worker agency with plural impulses beyond the Marxist class struggle binary. Race is an important layer in configuring worker agency, as can be read from the experience of the uber drivers in Washington DC Airport who used to gather in the parking lot to resist the 'place lessness' of digital labour, and who were predominantly digital drivers of colour (Strauss, 2020).

In the tribal society of the petrostates of the Khaleej, even all local citizens are not considered equal in the labour geographies there, as certain tribes are preferred over the other and citizens of East African or Baluchi descent are considered ineligible for jobs in the state apparatus. Precarious migrant workers are at the bottom of the labour hierarchy with limited worker agency, and there is a graded stratification there as well, with African workers at the bottom while South Asians wrestle it out with other nationalities in a migrant majority region. The migrant labour market in Singapore is stratified, gendered and precarious with male Bangladeshi workers involved in '3D' jobs (male masculinities) while the banking sector hires women expats. They both are precarious in their labour geography coordinates (Ye, 2014). Bringing in Gender, Caste, Race and Tribal Affiliations pluralises the lens towards expanding the notions of understanding Worker Agency beyond class and the informal sector worker with limited potential for worker organising.

Migration Futures

Most of the resident population in the Gulf are foreigners, migrants or expats whose destiny is precarious as per Kafala. During the oil era, the resources to maintain the conservative Kafala system were present in parallel with Petro modernity. Now the populations have increased as well, with oil price fluctuations and renewable energy upsurge in demand the migrant compositions are evolving. The Gulf is transitioning from an investor to one seeking investment. The UAE is upending the playbook with a range of visas offered to the migrants including flexible work options. Pathways to permanent residency in the form of Golden Visas for investors. The borders which characterise the Gulf are dissolved, although new borders are drawn in favour of migrants with economic capital.

The region is opening as other parts of the globe are closing under the waves of right-wing nationalism. Borders respond to the economic realities of the day and migrants are at the frontiers of it.

References

Akinci, I. (2019). 'Dressing the nation? Symbolizing Emirati national identity and boundaries through national dress', *Ethnic and Racial Studies*, 43(10), pp. 1776–1794. https://doi.org/10.1080/01419870.2019.1665697

Al-Nakib, F. (2016). *Kuwait Transformed: A History of Oil and Urban Life*. https://doi.org/10.1515/9780804798570.

Al Shehabi, Omar. (2019). Policing labour in empire: the modern origins of the Kafala sponsorship system in the Gulf Arab States. *British Journal of Middle Eastern Studies*. 48. 1–20. 10.1080/13530194.2019.1580183.

Brookes, M. (2013). 'Varieties of power in transnational labor alliances: An analysis of workers' structural, institutional, and coalitional power in the global economy', *Labor Studies Journal*, 38(3), pp. 181–200. https://doi.org/10.1177/0160449X13500147.

Barrett, S. (2013). 'The necessity of a multiscalar analysis of climate justice', *Progress in Human Geography*, 37(2), pp. 215–233. https://doi.org/10.1177/0309132512448270.

Bennett, N.J., Blythe, J., and Tyler, S. et al. (2016). 'Communities and change in the anthropocene: understanding social-ecological vulnerability and planning adaptations to multiple interacting exposures', *Regional Environmental Change*, 16, pp. 907–926. https://doi.org/10.1007/s10113-015-0839-5.

Clayton, D. & Kumar, M. (2019). Geography and decolonisation. *Journal of Historical Geography*, 66, 1–8. Article 1. https://doi.org/10.1016/j.jhg.2019.10.006.

Collins, F. (2021). 'Geographies of migration I: Platform migration', *Progress in Human Geography*, 45. 030913252097344. https://doi.org/10.1177/0309132520973445.

———(2016). 'Migration, the urban periphery, and the politics of migrant lives', *Antipode*, 48. https://doi.org/10.1111/anti.12255.

Coe, N. M. (2021). 'Afterword: Towards a political ecology of labour?' *Area*, 53, pp. 450–453. https://doi.org/10.1111/area.12727.

Coe, N. M., and Jordhus-Lier, D. (2011). 'Constrained agency? Re-evaluating the geographies of labour', *Progress in Human Geography*, 35(2), pp. 211–233.

Cumbers, A., Helms, G., and Swanson, K. (2010). 'Class, agency and resistance in the old industrial city', *Antipode*, 42(1): pp. 46–73. https://doi.org/10.1111/j.1467-8330.2009.00731.x.

Doutch, M. (2021). 'A gendered labour geography perspective on the Cambodian garment workers' general strike of 2013/2014,' *Globalizations*, https://doi.org/10.1080/14747731.2021.1877007.

TOWARD A NEW ART OF BORDER CROSSING

Elsheshtawy, Y. (n.d.). *Temporary Cities: Resisting Transience in Arabia*. Routledge: UK.

Freitag, U. (2020). *A History of Jeddah : The Gate to Mecca in the Nineteenth and Twentieth Centuries*. Cambridge, United Kingdom: Cambridge University Press.

Herod, A. (2001). *Labor Geographies: Workers and the Landscapes of Capitalism*, New York: Guilford Press.

Herod, A. (2017). *Labor, Polity*. Polity Press: Cambridge.

Gotehus, A. (2021). 'Agency in deskilling: Filipino nurses' experiences in the Norwegian healthcare sector', *Geoforum*. ISSN 0016-7185. 126, pp. 340–349. https://doi.org/10.1016/j.geoforum.2021.08.012.

Carswell, G., and De Neve, G. (2013). 'Labouring for global markets: Conceptualising labour agency in global production networks', *Geoforum*, 44, pp. 62–70, ISSN 0016-7185, https://doi.org/10.1016/j.geoforum.2012.06.008.

Katz, C. (2004). *Growing up Global: Economic Restructuring and Children's Everyday Lives*. Minneapolis: University of Minnesota Press.

Katande, Y. (2015). *Slave States: The Practice of Kafala in the Gulf Arab Region*. Winchester, UK: Zero Books.

Kassamali, S. (2018). *The Migrant Worker Life World's of Beirut*. Columbia University PhD E-Thesis.

———(2012). 'Spectacular urbanization amidst variegated geographies of globalization: Learning from Abu Dhabi's trajectory through the lives of South Asian Men', *International Journal of Urban and Regional Research*, 36. https://doi.org/10.1111/j.1468-2427.2011.01099.x.

Murer, G. (2022). Baloch *Mashkat* (Muscat) and the Sultan Qaboos Era: Cultural Performance, Cosmopolitanism, and Translocal Consciousness. *Arabian Humanities*: 15. Oman Vision 2040 Special Issue.

Lutfi, A. (2018). *Conquest without Rule: Baloch Portfolio Mercenaries in the Indian Ocean*. Duke University. PhD E-Thesis.

Lambert, R., and Herod, A. (2016). *Neoliberal capitalism and precarious work: Ethnographies of accommodation and resistance*. http://site.ebrary.com/id/11202829.

Loong, S. (2018). '"This country, law very strong": Securitization beyond the border in the everyday lives of Bangladeshi migrant workers in Singapore', *Geoforum*, 90, pp. 11–19, ISSN 0016-7185, https://doi.org/10.1016/j.geoforum.2018.01.012. (https://www.sciencedirect.com/science/article/pii/S0016718518300186)

Neimark, B., Mahanty, S., Dressler, W., and Hicks, C. (2020). 'Not Just Participation: The Rise of the Eco-Precariat in the Green Economy', *Antipode*, 52, pp. 496–521. https://doi.org/10.1111/anti.12593.

Nixon, R. (2018). *Slow Violence and the Environmentalism of the Poor*. Johanneshov: MTM.

Parsons, L., and Natarajan, N. (2021). 'Geographies of labour in a changing climate', *Area*, 53, pp. 406–412. https://doi.org/10.1111/area.12737.

Radcliffe, S. A. (2017). 'Decolonising geographical knowledges', *Transactions of the Institute of British Geographers*, 42, pp. 329–333. https://doi.org/10.1111/tran.12195.

Scott, J. C. (1985). *Weapons of the Weak: Everyday Forms of Peasant Resistance*. New Haven: Yale University Press.

Strauss, K. (2020). 'Labour geography III: Precarity, racial capitalisms and infrastructure', *Progress in Human Geography*, 44(6), pp. 1212–1224. https://doi.org/10.1177/0309132519895308.

Smith, S. (2008). *Uneven Development: Nature, Capital, and the Production of Space*. 3rd ed. London: Verso.

Rogaly, B. (2009). 'Spaces of work and everyday life: Labour geographies and the agency of unorganised temporary migrant workers', *Geography Compass*, 3, pp. 1975–1987. https://doi.org/10.1111/j.1749-8198.2009.00290.x.

Unnikrishnan, D. (2019). *Temporary people*. Restless Books: Amherst, Massachusetts.

Ye, J. (2014). 'Migrant masculinities: Bangladeshi men in Singapore's labour force', *Gender, Place & Culture: A Journal of Feminist Geography*, 21(8), pp. 1012–1028, https://doi.org/10.1080/0966 369X.2013.817966.

Wang, Y. (2020). *Chinese in Dubai: money, pride, and soul-searching.* Brill: The Netherlands.

Warren, C., and Clayton, D. (2020). 'Climate change, COP26 and the crucible of crisis: Editorial introduction to the special issue', *Scottish Geographical Journal*, 136, 1–4, https://doi.org/10.10 80/14702541.2020.1874645.

Wald, E. R. (2019). *Saudi Inc.* PEGASUS Books: New York, NY.

Note

1   https://www.aiib.org/en/projects/details/2020/approved/Oman-Ibri-II-500MW-Solar-PV-Independent-Power-Plant-Project.html (information retrieved on 11th November 2021).

Chapter 14

TRANSNATIONAL COMMUNITIES AND THE FORMATION OF ALTERNATIVE SOCIOPOLITICAL OTHERNESS

Abdulkadir Osman Farah

Introduction

In forestalling existing and potential suffering of regressive otherness in the host society, migrant and refugee parent generations often pursue dualistic linear transnational adaptations. They create sociocultural and political spaces under conditions of simultaneous linkages with countries of origin while simultaneously adapting to host societies. Parent generation also combines such endeavors with the task of caring for families. Struggling with such demanding challenges, the parent generations foster and raise the second and third generations—with the expectation of continuity. The youth, however, pursue favorable strategies and connections. While, for instance, witnessing the parent generation in overcoming otherness by sustaining host-homeland community associations, often resting on vanguard charismatic community members with traditional capabilities, the younger generation seeks alternative multi-linear and complex non-traditional adaptations. Though partially adapting aspects of the parent generation's social and cultural upbringing, the youth combine with educational and other sociocultural socialization impulses, mainly from the mainstream society. This makes the youth prefer alternative situational dynamic hybridity. They position themselves as engaging in multiple transformative and transferable fields- often aiming beyond host–homeland connections and community formations. Despite such aspirations, even with the younger generations, challenges regarding otherness persist. Though emerging creative platforms transitionally empower the youth, the shift creates gaps between the youth and parent generations.

Transnational communities generate multiple transformative processes enabling communities to confront prevailing stigma and exclusive otherness. Through diverse activities, members succeed in forming alternative social and political platforms thereby promoting cooperation and solidarities within the community as well as in relation to associated civic networks. Internally, communities remain diverse and heterogeneous resulting in disagreements on vision, ideas, and practical activities and priorities. Externally, communities confront networks and constituents opposing the presence of inhabitants with migrant and refugee backgrounds.

The younger generations differ both from the parent generations and from the wider society. With access to specific community platforms as well as engaging in diverse interactions with the wider society, younger generations navigate through conventions, traditions, and conflicting priorities. In maintaining a respectful position in society, the youth, therefore, assemble resources balancing the past with the present while remaining open for potentialities.

In the following, the paper first discusses conceptions of otherness by presenting thinkers, though having migrant and refugee backgrounds and mainly agreeing on the challenges of displaced and dispossessed peoples, who might disagree on the conception of migrant and refugee otherness and eventual border crossing to overcome such challenges. Secondly, in the empirical section, the paper presents and discusses the Blue Stars, case. This is a creative community formation by youth with an African background in Denmark. The youth mobilized and organized in positioning themselves not exclusively with the past, thereby with their parents, and not necessarily with the present- meaning with the host society- but with the creation of an alternative position of dynamic complex otherness representing not a means to an end for a particular group but for an end itself.

Conceptualizing Migrants and Refugee Otherness

Migrants and refugees belong, among other population groups, to the most politized social groups in the current world (Bojadžijev, 2018). In recent years, societies, both in the wealthier North and in the developing South and beyond, have become politically polarized in relation to understanding and dealing with migration and displacement issues and challenges (Wee, K., Vanyoro, K. P. & Jinnah, Z. 2018). Certain societies advocate for dignified accommodation of immigrants and refugees (Nowicka, Krzyżowskiand Ohm, 2019). Other societies oppose not just the acceptance of new arrivals but also inhabitants with recent migration history and different ethnic affiliations (Follis, 2019; Suarez-Krabbe, Lindberg & Arce, 2018). Despite such intense polarization within host societies coupled with often propagated controversies, migrants and displaced peoples engage and transform political landscapes in influencing diverse regimes, including democracies (Mudde, 2019). Initially, protest movements, mainly from the right, generated intense policy focus on identity differentiation and superiority. In response, counter-movements emerged, in not just resisting constituents portraying outsiders as others and thereby a threat. The movements facilitate dialogue and integration platforms for migrants and refugees seeking opportunities and fleeing from prosecution (Agustín and Jørgensen, 2018).

Such politicizations and controversies existed in ancient periods (Lucassen, 2018). However, processes emerging from the formation of modern political structures and nation-states complicated concepts such as belonging, otherness, and citizenship. Among others, the structures introduced categorized border crossings and sanctuaries for people—especially those exiting from lesser privileged parts of the world (Spijkerboer, 2018).

Conceptions of Otherness and Self-creation

Gadamer conceptualizes otherness, and related solidarities, or lack of solidarities, as processes of historic manifestations emerging from purposeful civic encounters, connections, and dialogues (Risser, 1997). For Gadamer people do not need to have common identities and unified perceptions and meanings in understanding and interpreting existing or emerging sociopolitical conditions. Derrida considers Gadamer's conception of the "fusion of horizons" as an admission of preexisting consensus in identity formation thereby providing limited or no space for differences and thereby otherness (Derrida, 1989). Derrida highlights the need for occasional rupture and discontinuity in the progressive formation of otherness in society. Furthermore, Gadamer also disagreed with Heidegger's conception of otherness as a situated limitation of being- that people might overcome in pursuing temporal sociopolitical adjustments (Gadamer, 2000). This implies, Giri adds, the possibility of overcoming entrenched otherness through creative aesthetic border crossing in moving sociopolitical encounters and connections beyond prevailing dualisms:

> Dualism is entrenched in the heritage of modern anthropology, as in the works of Durkheim and Dumont, for example, and a transformation of modernist anthropology calls for multidimensional strivings for the realization of nonduality, both as an epistemic as well as an ontological engagement is possible to cultivate nondual approaches to understanding our simultaneous condition of nonduality and duality [...] Aesthetics has the potential to cross over boundaries, especially those of entrenched dualism, and now it can be accompanied by spiritual cultivation and transformation (Giri, 2013).

Hannah Arendt, Edward Said, and Abdulaziz Gurnah experienced the challenging livelihoods of being migrants, refugees as well as diasporic persons in exile. In different ways, the thinkers crossed and crisscrossed multiple borders experiencing multiple forms of othernesses. Such experiences let, for instance, Arendt considering refugees as a particular people primarily suffering from the loss of political capital or agency— meaning the absence of proper rights through citizenship acquisition (Stonebridge, 2018). For Arendt, the modern world, consists of nation-states with institutional and legal subordination of subjective societies often referred to as citizenry (Hayden & Saunders, 2019). As soon as such states, more or less legally and ethically determine and designate certain populations, or ethnic groups, as unwelcome, then the excluded and stigmatized constituents risk ending up in public rightlessness combined with persecution. In this regard, Arendt conceptualizes migrants and refugees as primary outsiders of the legal political place and order. The supposedly prime task for refugees, therefore, should be addressing the absence of spaces of rightfulness in relation to existing citizenship platforms (Chiba, 1995). The alternative is continuing suffering from systematic sociopolitical exclusions and exploitations. For Arendt, the most critical occurrence of the human condition is the action related to political existence in which people access legitimate public spaces in advancing purposeful living circumstances (Singh, 2020). This may in certain transitional occasions demand strategies of identity concealment not just through successive planning and thinking but also through concrete mobilizations and actions. Arendt also rejects the nationalists' homogenizing

194 TOWARD A NEW ART OF BORDER CROSSING

claims of authentic superior pregiven historicity—that they insist and expect all should adhere to. For Arendt, citizenship and belonging emerge from actions and exchanges of political commonalities as well as diversities:

> The Minority Treaties said in plain language what until then had only been implied in the working system of nation-states, namely, that only nationals could be citizens, only people of the same national origin could enjoy the full protection of legal institutions, that persons of different nationality needed some law of exception until or unless they were completely assimilated and divorced from their origin (Arendt, 2007).

In situations where such exclusions evolve into sectarian extremism, Authorities mobilize the wider public for exclusive surveillance and oppression of the refugees and other foreigners. Arendt herself on the run from widespread public and state oppression, shares the following:

> Once we could buy our food and ride on the subway without being told we were undesirable. We have become a little hysterical since newspapermen started detecting us and telling us publicly to stop being disagreeable when shopping for milk and bread. We wonder how it can be done; we already are so damnably careful in every moment of our daily lives to avoid anybody guessing who we are, what kind of passport we have, where our birth certificates were filled out—and that Hitler didn't like us (Arendt, 1943/2007)

Such experiences of defenselessness and on the run do not however mean people completely lose options and sense of agency. Struggling people still have the option of joining others in similar situations, as well as with sympathetic constituents in the society, in resisting the often top-down imposed oppressive conditions. The rightlessness condition, for Arendt, represents the bottom of the societal hierarchy and consequently prolongs the suffering of the inflicted victims and related networks. Through speeches and narratives, refugees act and counteract in forming and interpreting prevailing sociopolitical conditions (Arendt, 1970). In remedying such a gross downturn, for Arendt, concerted joint political solidarity and mobilization is the way forward. This has the potential to transform citizenship forms towards the inclusion of marginalized constituents. The current world seems more complex than the one experienced by Arendt and contemporaries. The world today provides migrants and refugees with more concrete and virtual options in pursuing agency and networks across boundaries:

> Arendt's views on refugees and statelessness were undoubtedly influenced by her own experiences […] Without dismissing or diminishing Arendt's personal insights on the horror of the loss of home, or the importance of her observations on the meaning of the refugee problem in Europe [we have] to critically examine the extent to which Arendt's characterisation of refugeehood and statelessness advances understanding of the problems posed by forced migration in the contemporary context […] changes in the international system and the refugee regime, particularly increased focus on voluntary repatriation and the reconstitution of the relationship between refugees and their states of origin, a possibility largely unforeseen by Arendt (Bradley, 2014).

TRANSNATIONAL COMMUNITIES AND OTHERNESS

Edward Said partially agrees with the victimization thesis of migrants and refugees consequently leading to immense desperation and hopelessness. Victimhood, unlike Arendt, suggests, Said suggests emanates from historical imperial frameworks of systematic European colonization and subjugation of peoples and societies across the world. Such imperial efforts not only just restrict to conquering and degrading humans but also overtime also creates more or less legitimized discourses of "orientalism" representing complex mechanisms of manipulations that eventually trapping people into the internalization of specific inferiority consciousness, often sustained through media, literature, and political discourses (Said, 1978). For Said, this can only be overcome with intellectual and practical coordinated civic actions:

> Though Said recognizes the immense suffering of been a refugee, displaced and in exile within or beyond one's homeland, within such imposed existential dispossession refugees and communities occasionally create opportunities for interactions, connections, networks rather giving up in the face of exclusion and alienation (Ashcroft & Ahluwalia 2008: 119).

Said proposed bottom-up civic mobilization approaches coupled with progressive intellectual alertness—supported by civic-minded groups as well as migrant and refugee associations in balanced critical solutions to recurring displacement, subordination, and humiliation.

Though partially agreeing with Arendt and Said in the existence of dialectical processes of historical migrant and refugee victimhood, overall, Gurnah perceives migrants and refugees as resourceful and simultaneous participants and contributors to multiple societies (Nyman, 2009). Migrants and refugees from countering sociopolitical imaginative and practical lives, consequently transforming and impacting not just their immediate social and political conditions but also the wider society—and potentially the wider world. For instance, both Arendt and Said represent good examples of becoming a suffering refugee does not mean the end of history. This is far from a permanent status of marginalization and exclusion. Gurnah proposes migrants and refugees have unique capabilities of multiple consciousnesses in creating their own stories and social lives. In this regard, people continuously transform from traditionally categorized designations of either belonging to their origin or current host society dispositions. For Gurnah what some might consider as endless suffering and powerlessness could equally be an empowering experience, opening up alternative pathways towards genuine transformations and strengthening people's in search of selfhood and recognition. In other words, people can potentially liberate themselves and advance, not just through constant search and struggle for existing formal citizenships, as Arendt and Said imply, through the implementation of public civic mobilizations and resistance within host and homeland environments with the aim of creating statehood for the dispersed communities as well providing dignified life with the host so societies. But also, as Gurnah proposes a situation in which people create stories and justifications for a complex of maneuvering the challenges befalling on communities as individuals as well as in collectivities (Newns, 2015).

Though both Arendt and Said know and acted upon in their daily lives the dynamics of transnational solidarities or lack of solidarities, the two thinkers mainly operate from the boundaries of the formation and reformation of tolerable and inclusive nation-state conditions in which people have to belong to certain geographical, national and citizenship categories.

Gurnah, on the other, suggests communities create an alternative third platform. Through such more or less imaginary platforms, communities through memories and stories through instants and situations create social and political platforms and discourses that could not be categorized as national, state, and unidimensional. It is rather diverse, multidimensional, and complex social, political, and cultural interactions not necessarily reflecting a sense of demoralized victimhood but a forceful articulation combined with the praxis of achieving individual as well as collective liberating and human dignity:

> For Gurnah's migrant characters, witty, humorous interactions afford ways of being that allow for explorations of processes of dis-alienation in the face of hostile environments. At the level of narrative, these interactions also play a role in the representation of race thinking as absurd. Witt thus presents one of the possible responses to an awareness of the kinds of racism and intolerance faced by the characters: it is an effective way to critique and decentre racist assumptions (Steiner, 2021: 126).

Communities and Self-formation/Creation

Studies suggest race differences remain critical in sociopolitical transformations. Similarly, identity formations in accessing or not accessing social, cultural, economic, and political privileges also contribute to social development. Migrants, refugees as well as diaspora groups create complex identities that might conform to or contradict prevailing sociopolitical systems often sustaining otherness. Often marginalized communities eventually respond to such categorizations for instance inventing more or less imaginative categorizations of their own. For Appiah (2006: 16) social and political identifications and categorizations reflect an action rather than a state.

When refugees flee from their homelands they resettle into a new society with its cultural, social, and political priorities. Such new host environments bring new forms of challenges and exclusions- often different from the ones people fled. In coping with such complex challenges, Gurnah proposes, refugees not only adopt but also create alternative social lives through stories. This includes the insistence of not being there and here- and not being us and them. The new platforms help refugees overcome the categorizations of who is fit and thereby deserves recognition and who is unfit and thereby does not deserve recognition and appraisal. Refugees thereby reject victimhood and exclusion through the creation of prospective dynamic identities.

Creating stories and interpreting their own conditions helps refugees to form alternative social and political platforms that more or less function as a kind of restorative aesthetic migrant practice. In normal circumstances, issues such as home, identity, and otherness are linked to nationalism and nation-state formations with embedded privileges and diverse forms of subordination. Refugees with their alternative stories, imaginations, and actions disrupt such platforms. This helps them overcome top-down homogenization and essentialization, confirming the idea of culture as unfixed (Clifford, 1997). Culture is herewith open to reframing and reinterpreting. For many, continuity could be the norm, but for the refugees with the aim of protecting and reframing their identities there are constant discontinuities and repositioning often in contradiction to the dominant discourses that often exclude them- in what Gurnah conceptualizes as "hermeneutics of baggage" (Gurnah, 2002: 7).

Gurnah's approach to refugees is different from for instance Said's. His writing "Reflections on Exile" discusses a romanticized privileged diaspora and exile in which said valorizes the loss associated with exile as intellectually productive and emphasizes the redemptive power of writing for those who are displaced. Though structures often attempt to delay the past—particularly that of the refugees, it is the obligation of the intellectual refugees to sustain the past in their writings and cultural expressions.

Stuart Hall (1994) considers identities as forms of stories narrating people and nations into particular situations. Similarly, communities mobilize identities into multiple forms in overcoming the paradox of "calculating humiliation" asserting themselves as a community of honor—a kind of social empowerment. The emerging refugee stories connect continents and peoples while zigzagging with ease between past and present.

Gurnah rejects homogenization of for instance focusing on African identity. His emphasis is transnational and supranational moving beyond restricted national frames. Gurnah traces the imaginary geography of transregional/transnational movements and encounters. This contradicts the colonial and nationalist ways of mapping. Gurnah seems to highlight how migrants and refugees, among them Africans, are entrapped into situations as well as complex stories of empire and diaspora. He presents multiple forms of hierarchies of dominations, for instance, not just along the well-investigated axes of colonial oppressions, but along multiple intersections and complex interactions between "African, Indian, Arabic, German and British forms of oppressions. He destabilizes notions of nationalism and filiation and the history of crisscrossing relations along multiple spaces, emphasizing intersectionality, relations—and networking.

In Arjun Appadurai's work people are through cultural performances able to create their own "social lives" thereby boundaries of designated otherness (Appadurai, 2006). There are, for instance, tendencies portraying refugees as victims and invoke others (authorities, agencies, and NGOs) to assist them and become a voice for them. Such narrative structures portray the refugee as a victim of a "failed" state and invoke the authority of the international human rights regime to justify the acceptance of the refugee into a host nation. Here the refugee is the ultimate victim of human rights violations and the perpetrators of these violations are corrupt representatives of the rogue state. In turn, the host country that receives the refugee becomes the savior by offering incorporation into a peaceful prosperous society (Song, 2021). Gurnah challenges this narration and framing presenting instead a new structure- dialectic narrative structures that put refugees in dialogue with each other (Helff, 2015).

The Blue Stars: The Second-Generation Transnational African Youth in Denmark

Parent Generation's Dual Approach to Otherness

In Denmark, youth with ethnic minority backgrounds respond to otherness in various ways. They do it in an "intersectional othering" in which the youth capitalize on the otherness they feel thrown to. They also do it through the recognition and articulation of such positions in simultaneously dismissing and insisting on being conventional (Jensen, 2011). Such contradiction emerges from the conditions in which people confront power structures through a dialectical meaning making process. Furthermore, the parent generation's top-down political engagement and priorities might suppress younger generation's activism and civic aspirations (Terriquez & Kwon, 2015). Though an obvious gap exists between the older generations and the younger ones, the younger generation urges the parent generation to be more transformative. In addition, increased emphasis on ethnic diversity, race, and people's origin and history often confuses the younger generations who aim at overcoming imposed otherness. The younger generation of citizens with migrant and refugee backgrounds aims at engagement in the local, national supranational sociopolitical, and cultural platforms. Such dynamic patterns might contradict the priorities of both nationalist-oriented platforms as well as those of skeptical parent generations (Goitom, 2017). For instance, when the second-generation African youth in Canada forge their own identity navigating between the influences of globalization as well as that of calling for cultural diversity in the host society, both national forces and that of their communities respond critically (Goitom, 2017).

This paper partially complements the research identifying existing gaps between the parents and younger generations in which youth pursue alternative complex social connections of overcoming multiple forms of others. The paper presents the Blue Stars case in which parent generations not just restrict but also facilitate and collaborate with the youth in the pursuit of creating alternative progressive otherness platforms. The process started when members of the parent generation and their organizations complained about recruitment challenges, particularly concerning the community's female and youth members. Following successive informal and formal community meetings, community activists agreed to deal with such inclusion and empowerment challenges. This is a community that for decades, filled critical integration and public debate, and perception gaps. Apart from routinely empowering community members, community organizers coordinate workshops, publish editorials, and appear in local, national, and international media, defending community interests. Now community leaders decided to look internally and invite more representatives of women and youth to the community's formal organizational activities. In implementing such a procedure, the community organized successive empowerment sessions in which representatives of the youth, some of them graduates, and some still under education, actively participated. Later the community leadership followed up with additional coaching activities in helping the youth form a new sub-community group called the Blue Stars. The choice indicates the youth preferring the creation of alternative platforms. Eventually, the empowerment sessions, participated by national and international networks, led to the

TRANSNATIONAL COMMUNITIES AND OTHERNESS

authorities inviting the community to concrete collaborative efforts for joint community-authority implementations. Among the approved projects is the Blue Stars project—focusing on the mobilization of the youth constituents within the community.

The Blue Stars Pursuing Complex Alternative Otherness

Certain conceptualizations focus on the demography and age of the different migrant and refugee generations, often dividing them into the first, the second, and the third generations (Portes & Zhou, 1993). Such classifications often refer to countries and the nations from which people originate (Glick Schiller, Çaglar, & Guldbradsen, 2006). Though recognizing the significance of such historical and contextual profiling of migrants and refugees, this paper proposes that the younger generations not just transform relationships with their parent generations as well as with their origin, but also transform existing gaps between their parent generation and the mainstream society. Active members of the younger generation in Blue Stars project an alternative Third Space, altering the prevailing dual hierarchical relationship between their parents and the public in the host society. Concretely, the youth share mixed stories of belonging and complex affiliations with multiple constituents in society. Such narration and story-telling processes enable them to diversify existing traditional categories of otherness that parent generations either ignored or uncritically internalized. The approach also contrasts the low profile in which parent generations kept for accepting a passive co-existence and occasional subordination. With alternative detailed proactive discourses, the youth replace seemingly static linear dialectics with the projection of their own transformative living situational stories, reflecting temporal as well as transformative livelihood conditions.

In the debates of migrants and refugees, the so-called segmented assimilation conception suggests that, unlike the first migrant and refugee generations, host societies incorporate the second and third generations assuming their comparative willingness to adjust to the society. With an expanded host society integration gaps emerge between the generations—meaning that the younger generation moves forward becoming in line with the priorities of the host environment (Zhou, 1997). In combination with such institutional segmentation, younger migrant generations also broker existing boundaries by negotiating and seeking better integration opportunities in the host society (Massey & Sánchez, 2010). Such community negotiations enable the youth to cross boundaries and construct and reconstruct identities questioning and redefining the formation of social groups and interconnected locations at the local, national, and transnational levels (Purkayastha, 2005). This is also in line with the fact that families are unlike in the past scattered due to economic challenges and opportunities that the younger generations pursue—resulting in increased difficulties and conflicts within the generations (Foner & Dreby, 2011). Similarly, contexts and prevailing sociopolitical at a given time also impact how a particular generation adapts and how eventually the younger generation might strategize in dealing with challenges emerging within their own communities and that of the surrounding society (Vedder & Virta, 2005). Consequently, for younger generations, there exist ambivalence and occasional disappointment with parent generations. Most admire their parents' struggle as migrants and refugees but also admit limitations of community mobilization and organization in preparing the communities for the participation of the society's inequally respected terms (Souralová, 2021).

Young people, either born or grown up in Demark, often find themselves caught between diverging cultures and societies (Rytter, 2010). On one hand, the societies they grew up and adapted to might occasionally exclude them. On the other, the youth might fail to accommodate sociopolitical and sociocultural elements from their parents and thereby from their ancestral societies. To address this disjuncture, the youth, combine both consensual and conflictual interactions with both the presumed host and homeland societies. With regard to the complex relationships with their parent generations—through demonstrating respect and admiration, the youth often complain about their parents' priorities and ambivalences (Singla, 2006). Though not directly stating it, the youth also distance themselves from the way in which their parents were treated in the public.

We are tired of been considered as burden—we the youth are in education and work (Safaa, 2017)

They admit that their parent generation was less privileged and thereby less willing to express and assert their positions. They intend to transform such an unbalanced relationship.

Within five years my generation will fill more on the statistics—and our parents will fill the statistics less—then employment numbers will be higher (Amina, 2017).

The younger generations insist on more equal treatment and focus on the real societal problems of prejudice, racism, and other forms of exclusions:

In Denmark we should focus more on prejudice and racism and do something about (Heyfa, 2017).

Since 2017, the Blue Stars succeeded in mobilizing the youth—though some joined the process enthusiastically while others left after a brief membership. Eventually, a core group succeeded in articulating and profiling the concerns and wishes of the youth at the national as well as transnational levels. Among other activities, the youth contacted selected top politicians presenting them with alternative arguments, images, and stories of their communities as well as of themselves and the wider society. The outreach and networking activities enabled members of the Blue Stars to subsequently build up careers and pursue further education. The youth and their working language and culture remain a mixture of African and Danish—suggesting their willingness to place themselves in the middle—not distancing fully from their parent generations—while trying to explain their conditions to the host societies and surrounding environments.

Members of the Blue Stars are born or grown up in Denmark by refugee parents. Estimates show over 35,000 inhabitants originating from the Horn of Africa residing in Denmark. These include migrant and refugee communities establishing organizations with diverse transnational livelihoods and interconnections. In different ways, the younger generations project new demands. Many of them neither fully identify themselves with their parent generations nor fully adapt to the Danish native culture. They often articulate an alternative third position enabling them to overcome current and potential otherness emerging from the past or linked to the present. In addition, the youth also insist on different transnational connections resisting or unwilling, presumably as their parents, to become a means to an end for community elites and politicians in the mainstream society. They consider their identities representing a resource not just for their parents but also for the wider Danish society and probably the world. Specifically, they reject migrant and refugee victimhood as they don't consider themselves as victims. Instead, they project themselves as a plus to the societies and they argue that their stories are unique and should be appreciated.

Despite this self-confidence and energy, the youth cannot claim to fully become independent. On one hand, they will have to build bridges with authorities and institutions and the wider society. On the other, they will have to deal with controversies as well as people from the host societies as well as their parents in maintaining unilinear story presentations. In this regard, under harsh circumstances of otherness, some of the parent generations might become defensive. In contrast, the youth build bridges without compromising their affiliations, identities, and relations. Institutional platforms are therefore necessary for funding opportunities in reaching out to diverse constituents in society—here under the political elite.

The Blue Stars resulted from projects built on successive community round table meetings in 2015 by community activists and representatives of public authorities. This was the product of community empowerment and exchanges with authorities in exploring alternative ways to overcome the otherness. The purpose of the project was to improve the image of the youth among Danes who do not normally meet, talk to, or otherwise have contact with the communities at large. These are Danish citizens who get their information about African communities and their lives in Denmark from the media. The aim was that, as good role models the youth inspire other youth and the wider community in focusing empowerment, education, and participation in society.

Conclusion

Proper integration into a given society takes several generations thereby requiring persistence, resilience, and stability. Despite existing prevailing challenges with systemic exclusions and public designations of otherness, gradual adaptation and adjustment of communities into the society, including the younger generations with host societies, seems possible. Some may in this regard suggest the end of the refugee and traumatic era, in which most of the parent generations long suffered from, is in closer grasp.

Unlike the current more dynamic youth, the elder generations insist on clear distinctions of social and cultural boundaries between host and home environments. For the youth, though not necessarily adopting all impulses from the host society, often reflect and engage in a kind of triangle of multiple transnational dialogues, encounters, and connections. These include interactions between parent generations and the youth, between the youth themselves, and between the youth and the surrounding society.

Among the youth, one also finds differences between those focusing on national platforms and those pursuing more proactive transnational transformations.

The case of Blue Stars confirms the potential of projecting transformative images and stories with mainstream Danish society. Representatives of Blue Stars acted as inspiration for society as well as role models for their communities, particularly the younger ones. In this regard, the youth succeeded, through their openness and storytelling, to overcome the negative sides of the dominant discourse against communities. The activities of Blue Stars additionally confirm the processes of mobilizing and engaging mutual dialogues and sharing stories not just to confront existing static exclusions and otherness, but also to internally enable communities, including the youth, to move beyond perceptions of subordination and victimhood.

References

Agustín, Ó. G & Jørgensen, M. B. (2018) *Solidarity and the 'Refugee Crisis' in Europe* (1st ed.). Springer International Publishing: Cham.

Appadurai, A. (2006) The thing itself. *Public Culture*, 18(1), 15–22.

Appiah, K. A. (2006) The politics of identity. *Daedalus*, 135(4), 15–22.

Arendt, H. (1970) *On Violence*. New York: Harcourt.

———(1943/2007) "We Refugees". In *The Jewish Writings*, edited by Jerome Kohnand and Ron H. Feldman, 264–274. New York: Schocken Books.

———(2007) "The Minority Question." In *The Jewish Writings*, edited by Jerome Kohnand and Ron H. Feldman, 125–133. New York: Schocken.

Ashcroft, B. & Ahluwalia, P. (2008) *Edward Said*. Routledge: London.

Bojadžijev, M. (2018) Migration as social seismograph: An analysis of Germany's 'Refugee Crisis' controversy. *International Journal of Politics, Culture, and Society*, 31(4), 335–356.

Bradley, M. (2014) Rethinking refugeehood: Statelessness, repatriation, and refugee agency. *Review of International Studies*, 40(1), 101–123.

Chiba, S. (1995) Hannah Arendt on love and the political: Love, friendship, and citizenship. *The Review of Politics*, 57(3), 505–536.

Clifford, J. (1997) *Routes: Travel and Translation in the Late Twentieth Century*. Cambridge, MA: Harvard University Press.

Derrida, J. (1989) "Three Questions to Hans-Georg Gadamer," In *Dialogue & Deconstruction: The Gadamer- Derrida Encounter*, edited by D. P. Michelfelder and R. E. Palmer, 52–55. Albany: State University of New York Press.

Follis, K. (2019) Rejecting refugees in illiberal Poland: The response from civil society. *Journal of Civil Society*, 15(4), 307–325.

Foner, N. & Dreby, J. (2011) Relations between the generations in immigrant families. *Annual Review of Sociology*, 37, 545–564.

Gadamer, H. (2000) "Subjectivity and intersubjectivity, subject and person" (1975), trans. Peter Adamson and David Vessey, *Continental Philosophy Review*, 33(2000), 285.

Giri, A. K. (2013) "Kant and Anthropology." In *Philosophy and Anthropology: Border Crossing and Transformations*, edited by A. K. Giri and J. Clammer, 141–146. London/New York/Delhi: Anthem Press.

Glick Schiller, N., Çaglar, A., & Guldbradsen, T. (2006) Beyond the ethnic lens: Locality, globality, and born-Again incorporation. *American Ethnologist*, 33(4), 612–633.

Goitom, M. (2017) "Unconventional Canadians": Second-Generation "Habesha" youth and belonging in Toronto, Canada. *Global Social Welfare*, 4(4), 179–190.

Gurnah, A. (2002) *By the Sea*. London: Bloomsbury.

TRANSNATIONAL COMMUNITIES AND OTHERNESS

Hall, S. (1994) "Cultural Identity and Diaspora." In *Colonial and Post-Colonial Theory*, edited by Patrick Williams and Laura Chrisman, 392–403. London: Longman.

Hayden, P. & Saunders, N. (2019) "Solidarity at the Margins: Arendt, Refugees, and the Inclusive Politics of World-making." In *Arendt on Freedom, Liberation, and Revolution*, 171–199. Edward Elgar Publishing Ltd.

Helff, S. (2015) "Measuring Silence-Dialogic Contact zones in Abdulrazak Gurnah's by the Sea and Desertion." In *Habari ya English? What about Kiswahili? East Africa as a Literary and Linguistic Contact Zone*, edited by L. Diegner and F. Schulze-Engler, 153–176. Oxford: Rodopi.

Jensen, S. Q. (2011) Othering, identity formation and agency. *Qualitative Studies*, 2(2), 63–78.

Lucassen, L. (2018) Peeling an onion: The "refugee crisis" from a historical perspective. *Ethnic and Racial Studies*, 41(3), 383–410.

Massey, D. S. & Sánchez, M. (2010) *Brokered boundaries: Immigrant Identity in Anti-immigrant times*. New York: Russell Sage Foundation.

Newns, L. (2015) Homelessness and the refugee: De-valorizing displacement in Abdulrazak Gurnah's By the Sea. *Journal of Postcolonial Writing*, 51(5), 506–518.

Nowicka, M., Krzyżowski, Ł., and Ohm, D. (2019) Transnational solidarity, the refugees and open societies in Europe. *Current Sociology*, 67(3), 383–400.

Nyman, J. (2009) *Home, Identity, and Mobility in Contemporary Diasporic Fiction*. Brill: The Netherlands.

Portes, A. & Zhou, M. (1993) The new second generation: Segmented assimilation and its variants. *The Annals of the American Academy of Political and Social Science*, 530(1), 74–96.

Nyman, Jopi. (2009) *Home, Identity, and Mobility in Contemporary Diasporic Fiction*. Amsterdam: Rodopi.

Purkayastha, B. (2005) *Negotiating Ethnicity*. Rutgers University Press.

Risser, J. (1997) *Hermeneutics and the Voice of the Other: Re-reading Gadamer's Hermeneutics*. Albany: State University of New York Press.

Rytter, M. (2010) A sunbeam of hope: Negotiations of identity and belonging among Pakistanis in Denmark. *Journal of Ethnic and Migration Studies*, 36(4), 599–617.

Said, E. (1978) *Orientalism: Western Concepts of the Orient*. New York: Pantheon.

Singh, A. L. (2020) Arendt in the refugee camp: The political agency of world-building. *Political Geography*, 77, 102149.

Singla, R. (2006) Intimate partnership formation and intergenerational relationships among ethnic minority youth in Denmark. Outlines. *Critical Practice Studies*, 8(2), 76–97.

Song, J. (2021) The "savage–victim–saviour" story grammar of the North Korean human rights industry. *Asian Studies Review*, 45(1), 48–66.

Souralová, A. (2021) "My parents did everything for us but nothing with us": Parenting and mothering in Vietnamese immigrant families in the Czech Republic. *Asian and Pacific Migration Journal*, 30(1), 39–59.

Spijkerboer, T. (2018) The global mobility infrastructure: Reconceptualising the externalisation of migration control. *European Journal of Migration and Law*, 20(4), 452–469.

Steiner, T. (2021) *Convivial Worlds: Writing Relation from Africa*. Routledge: India.

Stonebridge, L. (2018) *Placeless people: Writings, Rights, and Refugees*. USA: Oxford University Press.

Suarez-Krabbe, J., Arce, J., & Lindberg, A. (2018) "Stop Killing Us Slowly: A Research Report on the Motivation Enhancement Measures and Criminalization of Rejected Asylum Seekers in Denmark." Copenhagen: Marronage.

Terriquez, V. & Kwon, H. (2015) Intergenerational family relations, civic organisations, and the political socialisation of second-generation immigrant youth. *Journal of Ethnic and Migration Studies*, 41(3), 425–447.

Vedder, P. & Virta, E. (2005) Language, ethnic identity, and the adaptation of Turkish immigrant youth in the Netherlands and Sweden. *International Journal of Intercultural Relations*, 29(3), 317–337.

Wee, K., Vanyoro, K. P., & Jinnah, Z. (2018) Repoliticizing international migration narratives? Critical reflections on the Civil Society Days of the Global Forum on Migration and Development. *Globalizations*, 15(6), 795–808.

Zhou, M. (1997) Segmented assimilation: Issues, controversies, and recent research on the new second generation. *International Migration Review*, 31(4), 975–1008.

Part Three

TOWARD A NEW ART OF BORDER CROSSING: RELIGION, POLITICS, ART AND TRANSCENDENCE

Chapter 15

CROSSING BORDERS AND CREOLIZATION: CREATING AND NEGOTIATING NEW WORLDS

David Blake Willis

Creolization and Borders: A Theory of Emergence

One of the objectives of critical social science research is to provide a new kind of cultural critique. In development theory, there has been a focus, first, on the theory of convergence—we are all becoming alike, the implied model being American—and, more recently, on the theory of divergence—we are all very different and unique, the Japanese inspiring this idea in the 1980s. Yet the attempts to understand the process of multicultural relations in our world today have mostly been fraught with the limitations of a simplistic binary opposition that does not reflect the reality of a complex and rich association, a *creolization*.

Viewing culture as a static, monolithic, and homogeneous whole simply makes no sense when seen from the perspective of creolization. Creole cultures accent variation, historical roots, and transitions. Cultural continuity is thus seen as trans-systemic, with the focus being on the interactions and activities of multiple cultures operating on the same stage, rather than on describing the rules and order of some mechanistic conception of a singular culture. Indeed, cultures are sustained and nurtured by this activity of creolization. This creolization is the grammar of shared cultural values. It enables us to understand multicultural relations and border crossings more deeply. As Takeshi Matsuda has called it, this is a new theory of emergence and emerging Creolized cultures (2001). Joined later by adrienne maree brown and her emergent strategy (2017), this is a cultural critique with power and complexity.[1] Emergent cultures have shared values that reveal cultural commonalities that have been subconsciously nurtured during long periods of close association between two or more very different societies (such as the United States and Japan, in the case of my research).

A key concept in understanding these new worldviews and borderlands before us, creolization can be seen as a continuous process whereby distinctive "packages" of cultural signification are braided into new forms (Hannerz 1992, 1996, 2000, 2011; Gundaker, 1998; Eriksen, 1999; Cohen & Toninato, 2010; Cohen & Sheringham, 2016; and others).[2] In the making of Creolized transcultural societies, the creation of shared values and narratives of experiences occur in concrete day-to-day settings.[3] Creolization places us in a process of relationality when crossing borders and creating and negotiating New Worlds.

This process has also been called hybridization,[4] though the creative dynamism and passion associated with the term creolization suggests itself more strongly as the appropriate term. Cultural hybridization in the borderlands, what the Russian literary theorist M. Bakhtin has called "the fundamental condition of all forms of cultural innovation and exchange,"[5] is the locus of creolization. We should be interested in moving beyond dichotomous, essentialized conceptions of hybridization, of course, noting at the same time the particular importance of creolization for multicultural identities and the politics of anti-racism. Moreover, creolization deconstructs the notions of pure, singular cultures and their inevitable assumptions of superiority and sanctioning of human rights violations. Through this concept of creolization, we come to understand culture and cultures in new, more powerful, and more provocative ways.

Creolization is an entirely new way of seeing cultures, not as complex wholes with signs and symbols that we can identify and describe, but as a series of past, present, and future processes. Not as cultural grammars to be deciphered and reconstructed but as a series of transformations, some very grand indeed, some minimal in their impact. We are also entering a territory that is no longer multicultural alone which can be called super diversity (Vertovec, 2007; Meissner & Vertovec, 2015). This accords well with our understanding and view of the planetary as a vast field of active horizontal and vertical links, albeit with clear power differentials (Chakrabarty, 2021).

Culture then becomes one field of action and our roles in interpreting and acting upon this action invariably reflect the degrees of creolization of which we are a part, in some places to a greater and others to a lesser extent. Much of this depends on how, when, and where we cross borders, whether as diaspora by choice as seen by the dean of diaspora studies Robin Cohen (1996, 2023; 2018) or as refugees and other displaced peoples (Papastergiadis, 2000; Schneider, 2011; Schimanski, 2019, Shah, 2020; Cohen & Van Hear, 2020; Laine, 2020a, 2020b; & Cohen, 2021). Language is a critical aspect of creoleness, too, as exemplified in the work of Harris and Rampton (2023), DeGraff (2005), and Ansaldo (2017, 2018, the latter a response to Parkvall, Bakker, and McWhorter, 2018). Language has also been discussed in the work of those on the Mexico–US border, including Anzaldúa, Hicks, and the Saldívars (see Chapter 1). What we need to accommodate is thus a completely different way of seeing the world, where one dimension, be it race, culture, gender, or language (or a package of those dimensions), is no longer so neat and tidy. It is, in fact, in the intersectional messiness between two or more worlds that we find the most creativity.

What is most powerful about the Creole approach is its diversity, its multiplicity, and its pluriversal way of approaching the world. Creolization has the following characteristics according to Glissant (2002):

1. The Lightning Speed of Interaction Among Its Elements
2. The "Awareness of Awareness" Thus Provoked in Us
3. The Reevaluation of the Various Elements Brought Into Contact
4. Unforeseeable Results

CROSSING BORDERS AND CREOLIZATION 209

Glissant sees this cultural interbreeding and its often violent encounter of peoples and cultures as "the condition of a new way of being in the world, of an identity both rooted in a land and enriched by all the lands now related." The key is a relation, which contextualizes the mixture transversally instead of hierarchically, the opposite of the cultural/political domination of the Other or a clash of civilizations that reduces diversity. Creolization is "a process whereby new shared cultural forms, and new possibilities for communication, emerge due to contact. It highlights the open-ended, flexible, and unbounded nature of cultural processes, as opposed to the notion of cultures as bounded, stable systems of communication" (Ibid.).

Borderlands: The "Advancing Boundary of Order-Under-Construction"

The rapid recovery and expansion of the world economy that followed World War II saw a development previously unknown in human history that has had much to do with borders and borderlands: the growth of *transnational cultures*. In Zygmunt Bauman's felicitous phrase, these border-crossing cultures have *served as borderlines for the advancing boundary of order-under-construction* (1997). They are exemplified by those creolized cultures mentioned in diasporic spaces (Cohen & Toninato, 2010; Cohen & Sheringham, 2016; Cohen & Fischer, 2018; Cohen & Van Hear, 2020) and those cultures being created where super-diversity has emerged (Vertovec, 2007; Meissner & Vertovec, 2015). Caught between are individuals, groups, and institutions with various repertoires for addressing this new planetary cultural economy, one characterized by complex, overlapping, and disjunctive cultural crossroads. Diasporic spaces have emerged at the same time in these borderlands which highlight communities, institutions, organizations, and individuals as cultural brokers, as go-betweens for these two powerful cultures.

The late twentieth century discourse which emerged around the themes of transnational and transcultural flows projected new globally informed images of socialization in international contexts.[6] Although it may be too obvious to state that we now live in an intensely interactive world system, the speed at which these interactions are taking place, the transparency of information, and the increasing emphasis on issues of social justice are different from previous eras. As Gloria Anzaldúa, Ulf Hannerz, Arjun Appadurai, Stuart Hall, Clifford Geertz, Takeshi Matsuda, Edward Said, Homi Bhabha, Johan Schimanski, and others have shown us, the quality of the interaction is actually strikingly new.[7] Missing are the authentic voices and reports of those participating in transnational interactions and of transnational contexts and processes that are institutional, societal, and cultural.

What those of us working in the borderlands would like to do is to propose a shift of emphasis, a shift of gaze toward phenomena of relationality and connections, toward creolization. This creolization is reflected throughout the societies in question, historically and in multiple manifestations, which we can approach through a variety of disciplinary lenses. It is a conceptual tool of critical importance for analyzing the interchange that has occurred between people. This context is one of *border thinking*, too, emerging from the cracks between civilization and culture, between what the Creole

210 TOWARD A NEW ART OF BORDER CROSSING

philosopher Édouard Glissant has called globalization and "mondialization," between global designs and local histories (Glissant, 2000 and 2002; Mignolo, 2000; Drabinski & Parham, 2015).

Borderlands and their evocations have been discussed in depth by Michael Agier (2016), who examines migrants and borderlands as spaces for decentering the world, as a center of reflection and what he calls sites of "banal cosmopolitanism." Walter D. Mignolo and Catherine E. Walsh, likewise, have called on us to focus our research through the lens of decolonial border thinking (2018). As Mignolo stated later, "Border thinking (border epistemology) has erupted and can no longer be controlled" (2021, pp. 533–534), and "Border thinking implies the pluriversal" (Mignolo, p. 540).

It is in the spaces of these "encounters" that we find the intersections, networks, and connections of a globalizing world: the transcultural crossroads (Nederveen Pieterse, 2021). Borders are a primary place for intersectionality, too, what Patricia Hill Collins calls a "context of discovery" that resists binary interpretations and that is continually engaged in co-formation (2019, p. 244 and p. 33). Borderlands spaces are spaces of possibility and co-formation, of "heterogeneity, multiplicity, and transgression [...] where ideas co-form via dialogical engagement" (pp. 245–246). As Patricia Hill Collins puts it, too, something captured by the title of our volume, "Because intersectionality encompasses both social sciences and humanities, it can be conceptualized alternately as a social theory that guides the search for truth and as a social theory that guides the search for social meaning." (p. 243). She is of course echoing her fellow scholar Kimberlé W. Crenshaw, too (2017), whose writings on this subject and Critical Race Theory have placed them in the vanguard of new political theorizing.

The communities in these spaces, and especially the individuals living and working there, tell us much about worldviews and how cultural exchange/interchange/ production is enacted. They also open spaces for deeper understandings and the tolerance of difference. We need more exploration of these borders and border crossings, of identity/identities in the context of where societies meet each other, where connections are established and maintained. Relevant scholarship includes Stewart (2007), Cohen and Toninato (2010), Willis (2010), Monahan (2011), Smith (2013), Gordon (2014), and Das et al. (2017). It is, after all, on the subject of boundary construction where much of the world's contemporary discourse is dynamic and fraught with possibilities, alive with the spectacular creation of new forms of human societies and human consciousness. Borders are not where something stops. Borders are where something begins.

Crossing Borders as Mixing: *Mestizaje* as Dance

We should get accustomed to the idea that our identity is going to change in contact with the Other.

—Édouard Glissant (2000)

Mestizaje es grandeza (Mixture is greatness).

—Old Spanish Saying

CROSSING BORDERS AND CREOLIZATION

Creoleness has always been about power, whether the patron was Thomas Jefferson, a cruel Spanish overseer, or an English merchant in the port of Kobe. Unspoken, unspeakable, the taboos and the vivid lure of the relationship with the Other are unmistakable. These relationships may be between women and men, resulting often in Eurasian offspring in the Pacific context, or they could be cultural and social, rather than genetic. Tragic stories of the women on the other side, the Malinche's and the Okichi's,[8] are repeated by those in power because of their fear of the Other. The human obsession with race and blood has meant that we have often overlooked the subtler and ultimately more important miscegenations of cultures in individuals, some of who will never *look* like the Other. Much of this is, indeed, mixing, *Mestizaje* as dance.

Yet, creolization also empowers those who are party to the mixing of cultures. African-Americans, for example, while mastering the conventions and codes of Euro-America, have also drawn on their own knowledge in creating an oppositional repertoire of signs and meanings.[9] Thus, creolization is not entirely, as some would argue about hybridity, simply a re-constituting of another cultural form but a very different contribution to cultural discourse, the intersection of "outsider" conventions with "insider" knowledge and practice.[10] We note the power of double consciousness and the wider range of potential action in this context.

Mixtures of cultures have always been part of cultural landscapes, but what is different today is the breathtaking speed at which encounters and creolizations are taking place as more and more borders are being crossed. Shunya Yoshimi and Sang-Jung Kang, two of Japan's most original thinkers on globalization and its manifestations, have addressed these questions in precise ways (2001), noting the centrality of power while at the same time affirming *ido-sei* (mobility), *junansei* (flexibility), and *ekkyo-sei* (border crossing). For them, flexible identities are embedded in local/global power contexts as multilayered fluctuations of new hybrid identities.

Creolization, hybridization, syncretism, cultural fusion, and mestizaje are thus processes that focus on the interpenetration of different cultures to create new cultural forms. We are entering a new era in the way we describe social processes in transnational settings. The idea of creolized cultures as we see them here, hybrid cultures in the interstices of mainstream cultures, may not be new, but their recognition and prominence are new. What we are seeing now is qualitatively different. What is different about our context is the way this creolization is being enacted. No longer assimilation, it is now a new shared culture, an emergent culture, a culture whose core values include those of liberal democracy, human rights, and open, active communication. This new and broader context for shared cultures is open-ended, eclectic, flexible, and [...] mobile. It is also destabilizing, chaotic, disordered, and random.

Dark sides exist in the context of creolization, too, though in this chaos appears creation, the move to newness. The many new social interactions (and new identities) reflect the importance of Creoles and the processes they are associated with as agents who, to paraphrase Appadurai (1990), continuously inject new meaning streams into the discourses of (their) landscapes. These interactions also highlight a central force in today's world: deterritorialization. The experiences and views from these landscapes can perhaps teach us about the conditions of growing social disjunctures, the permeability of boundaries, and the fluidities of identities.[11] A variety of strategies is produced when creolization takes place, both for relating to outsiders (who are increasingly on the inside) and for re-constituting one's own identity (which is seen to be more and more on the outside, on display to curious Others). Boundaries, cultural and national, are easily re-drawn and even more easily crossed, letting us know in subtle (and some not-so-subtle) ways about the postmodern era we have entered.

We can no longer view culture as having a meaning and form linked simply to territory or of the people of that land as necessarily linked to it culturally. What may be culture for locals (daily interaction anchored around one-on-one relationships in one place, without much moving around) is becoming less and less the norm in the world. The truly dynamic cultures have often been those that transcend space and place. The anchor of their cultural identity is not in a place but in social relationships and interactions.

Those cultures that are territorially defined are literally "losing ground" to those that have collective networks of meaning extending into space and across time. Hannerz has noted that cultures are not the hard-edged, easily separated pieces of a mosaic but phenomena that tend to overlap and mingle (1992, 1996, 2011). The boundaries we draw around them are frequently arbitrary. Another view of one of these boundaries, ethnicity, is now, with the internet and social media, in an era where ethnicity can even be seen as virtual, too.

Hegemony becomes more transparent, surprisingly, particularly in creolized contexts, making it imperative that cultural construction be undertaken in a democratic spirit and form. At the same time, creole histories are replete with inequality, center-periphery relations, and hierarchical ordering (See Eriksen, 1999, for one example). What is different about creolization is that the voices and power of the dispossessed, their resistance and courage, also become part of the story, part of the narrative. In this sense, we are talking about democratization.

Opportunity is also part of this mix, particularly for political and economic entrepreneurship. This entrepreneurship invites powerful adversarial commentary, as too much scrutiny of the central themes of opportunity and power at the heart of the creolization discourse upset the stability and hegemony of the powers that be. The need for secrecy and exclusiveness is great on the part of elites. What creolized situations and creolized people do is blow the cover on what is happening and redefine the discourse in open, democratic ways. The power of creolization for empowering our reflexivity towards ourselves and our contexts is great indeed. We will come to understand the processes of acculturation, diffusion, and transmission better if we locate and focus on those hot spots of meetings, of creolization. Another benefit of studying creolization is that it gives a human face to globalization.

We need to examine human resources as creolization, too. Creolized people are key human resources, both as individuals and as networks, as Zachary has discussed (2000, 2001a, 2001b).[12] With the global movements of millions of people, their cultures, and identities, immigration is a key theme of the twenty-first century (Papastergiadis, 2000; Schneider 2011; Smith, 2013; Horsti, 2019; Shah, 2020; Lassi 2020b; Schimanski, 2019; Cohen, 2021). To be more precise, this is a phenomenon of movement and

CROSSING BORDERS AND CREOLIZATION

mobility *both ways*, not one way. The word immigration itself, encumbered as it is with linear concepts of place and peoples, does not tell us as much as those sites of créolité appearing throughout the world landscape. Now over 100 million people, these moving populations reinforce the idea of diasporic communities in our midst. These are different diasporas, however, from previous times. One of the key differences is the assertiveness and visibility of Creoles and creolizations (Willis, 2001, 2010). Along with Creoles comes a new awareness of the power of indigenous wisdom in crossing borders, a new/old art of crossing borders that has endured despite enormous devastation and cultural deracination.

Negotiating New Worlds, Recognizing Old Wisdoms

The grim prognosis for life on this planet is the consequence of a few centuries of forgetting what traditional Indigenous societies knew and the surviving ones still recognize.

—Noam Chomsky (2013, p. i)

Traditional Indigenous Wisdom in many cultures focuses on a circular logic of renewal and rebirth, returning us to the logic of our past: more matriarchal understandings of life and a more powerful set of tools for our predicament as a species in the Age of the Anthropocene. The extent of the challenges and the rapid timing with which sustainability is teaching us this as a metaphor indicating that the time has come to begin the hard work of balancing human needs with those of other species and our physical and geological home. Yet the powerful dominance of hero-centered narratives continues to be the main image even for luminaries like Greta Thunberg.

We may want to give new attention to Indigenous Wisdom, which reflects the Greek idea of *phronesis*, or practical wisdom, as a way to reveal actionable values and practices (Stillman, 2015; see also the Center for Practical Wisdom at the University of Chicago). The need to move to this vision of border crossings, with the understanding that financial, social, and natural systems are interconnected, has also been foregrounded by Alice MacGillivray (2015). In her work, *boundary* is seen as *the* central concept in systems thinking. The edges of organizations and groups can be seen as places for the mixing of diverse ideas to enable learning and innovation, just as the edges in nature can be places for the mixing of diverse nutrients and species to enable high productivity. It is a new era that has moved us to approaches to social phenomena that are multilateral, multipolar, and multicultural. Indigenous thinking will help us all make better sense of the whole (Davis, 2009; Four Arrows & Narvaez, 2016; Yunkaporta, 2020; Wahinke Topa (Four Arrows) & Narvaez, 2022).

We are of course witnessing the slow dance of a larger imperial decline, not only of the United States but of the structural and political hegemonies of India, China, and Russia as well. Their fates interwoven by pandemic braiding and deep racism or casteism, these nations would do well to heed the teachings of Sri Aurobindo and Mahatma Gandhi, whose wisdom and action give us collective promises for what Anna Lowenhaupt Tsing has called "the possibility of life in capitalist ruins" (2015) and Rebecca Solnit named as *Hope in the Dark* (2016). Like Solnit, Gandhi, Aurobindo, and Indigenous Peoples

214 TOWARD A NEW ART OF BORDER CROSSING

understood the uses of uncertainty and the importance of the stories we tell. People do indeed have the power. "Staying with the trouble," as Donna Haraway calls it (2016) and John Lewis's "making good trouble" are key survival strategies we will need for our "home, our new home." Bhabha (1997a, 1997b, 2013), Rahimieh (2007), and others have spoken of this in terms of our crossing borders to reach new homes as well as, frequently, the 'unhomely moment.'

This suggests a map for global citizenship and border thinking as practice and praxis (Gaudelli, 2016), speaking for a larger movement of crossing borders that is happening: *Decolonization*. Walter Mignolo is especially important on decolonization (2000, 2012, 2021; see also Mignolo & Walsh, 2018), which is also reflected in the controversial presidential address in 2021 to the AAA American Anthropological Association by Akhil Gupta (2021). Indigenous wisdom may be able to help lead the way in healing divides and restoring balance here. This includes what Edgar Villanueva (2018) calls "bringing the oppressor into the circle of healing" with compassion, drawing on Native traditions with the seven steps for how to heal: Grieve, Apologize, Listen, Relate, Represent, Invest, and Repair. I mention again here, too, the critical work of Tuhiwai Smith (1999), Mohanty (2003), Tuck and Yang (2012), Hayman (2018), Bhambra et al. (2018), Alonso Bejrano et al. (2019), and Tuhiwai Smith, Tuck, and Yang (2019).

Such an approach also embraces the deep sense of interconnectedness with all life in the universe that the Lakota sacred prayer invokes when they say *Mitákuye Oyás'iŋ* (All are related).

Dark Hopes and Decolonization: The Way Forward

> We need stories (and theories) that are just big enough to gather up the complexities and keep the edges open and greedy for surprising new and old connections.
> —Donna Haraway (2016, p. 101)

The answers to this need are now seen in the dark hopes offered by such projects as *Decolonizing Methodologies* (Tuhiwai Smith, 1999, 2019) and *Decolonizing Wealth* (Villanueva, 2018). Others have emerged as well, including Mohanty on decolonizing feminism (2003), Alonso Bejarano et al. (2019) on decolonizing ethnography, Bhambra et al. (2018) on decolonizing the university, Gupta (2021) on decolonizing anthropology, Xiiem et al (2019) on decolonizing research, and Radcliffe on decolonizing geography (2022). These, along with practical solutions such as tearing down dams, reveal borders as disappearing, at least the artificial borders installed by man. We are moving beyond decolonization as a metaphor (Tuck & Yang, 2012) to what David Graeber and David Wengrow envisioned as *The Dawn of Everything* (2021). Decolonization has been joined by the incessant drumbeat of the climate crises wrought by the Anthropocene, with fossil fuel companies unlikely to change their operating procedures. Colonial yearnings and displacements continue to be present as older—*scapes* redux (the panoramas of "landscapes" as econoscapes, policy-scapes, and others as imagined by Appadurai, 1990, 2000).

As Amitav Ghosh has reminded us (2022), the present crises we are in have colonial roots, and the scale of these disasters is almost incomprehensible (Loomba, 1998).

CROSSING BORDERS AND CREOLIZATION

We remember the great scholar of colonization, Albert Memmi, too, who saw colonizers as typified by profit, privilege, and usurpation (1991), usually Europeans who often viewed themselves as having crossed too many borders and in exile themselves. Aurobindo and Gandhi themselves both began with projects of decolonization. In some ways, they succeeded spectacularly, and in other ways they were failures. Their activism is echoed by current activists like Harvard's jazz musician Esperanza Spalding, who proposed a decolonial education at Harvard for many months, only to be met with silence (Roberts & Yan, 2022). She resigned her position, noting that to maintain her relationship with the university there would need to be redress of the school's "historical and lingering colonial impacts." This would include rematriation of land and properties, and offering spaces to Black and Native artists, scholars, students, and activists. Colonialism is still with us, as Professor Spalding shared, its hegemony revealing itself in ways that are rawer than before, with large sections of populations in countries like India and the United States internalizing and accepting the "received wisdom" of Othering.

A recent talk by the sociologist Anthony Giddens (2021) pointed the way to other potential directions in the transformation of world politics, some of which have revealed the relative decline in European and American power. This is a huge geopolitical shift. Witness even the authors in this book, few of whom come from colonial, metropolitan powers. Some of these authors, like myself, have in fact spent much of their lives in other cultures in Asia or elsewhere, too. How shall we think about this new emerging world, Giddens asks? Two of the primary impacts, following COVID-19, are AI and the future of work.

We live in what Ulrich Beck called the risk society (1992), though it is now a new form of risk society, especially with AI and ChatGPTentering the picture. The stakes have gotten much higher. Conversely, this may also be a time of high opportunity, especially as the global phenomena associated with the future of work are taking center stage, notably the virtual center stage following the Pandemic of 2020–2022. We are no longer dominated as societies by agricultural labor (from nearly everyone in agriculture to 1% now) or even manufacturing work (from 30% of the workforce to 8%). Embedded in our systems, which are gradually becoming decolonized, are services, the key to resolving the pandemic and other arenas which may come next (Latour, 2018, 2021).

The prospects do give us hope as what seems to be appearing on the horizon is an age of huge creativity. Zoom is a good example, invented by a Chinese remote worker who wanted to see his girlfriend. What followed is of course an extraordinary story of crossing borders, virtual borders, for all of us. Amazon, too, now the world's biggest corporation, thrives on creativity. Although it is a world of unknowns now, dislocations are affecting the professions everywhere with outsourcing (soon to go to AI, rather than Manilla or Bangalore, I might add). It is a huge package of change just as climate crises are arriving everywhere. The Pandemic, again, is a lesson in our own fragility. It is the end of the neoliberal era, which simply couldn't deliver the world that it had promised, and an era of activism is back and growing.

Akhil Gupta noted in his 2021 Presidential Speech to the American Anthropological Association that, *"What would have become of our discipline if it had been constituted as a decolonizing project? Let us offer a few possibilities […] Genocides and Mass Killings; Slavery and Structural Violence;*

216   TOWARD A NEW ART OF BORDER CROSSING

Legal Treaties and the Political Systems That Enable Their Abrogation or Enforcement; Forced Migration and Internally Displaced Populations; Kinship of Humans and Other Nonhuman Animals; Reparations, Landback Initiatives, Truth and Reconciliation, Redistributive and Restitutive Justice, and the Redressal of Historical Wrongs; Critical Approaches to Borders, Nationalism, and Citizenship; and Critical Approaches to the Study of Extractive Industries, Industrial Agriculture, and Monopoly Capitalism."

Something that must be deeply connected to the debate is the future of work in the new borders we are crossing in our societies, what Thomas Berry called the supreme cultural pathology of our consumer society, another result of our external and internal colonialism. As he stated, "The difficulty of our times is our inability to awaken out of this cultural pathology [...]" (1988, pp. 205–206). The anthropogenic or anthropocentric shock that is overwhelming the earth is a logical result of colonialism that now calls for decolonization: "We are the affliction of the world, its demonic presence (p. 209) [...]. Only now have we begun to listen with some attention and with a willingness to respond to the earth's demands that we cease our industrial assault, that we abandon our inner rage against the conditions of our earthly existence, that we renew our human participation in the grand liturgy of the universe." (p. 215). We need to reinvent the human, to remake ourselves. This requires us to further understand that to reinvent means to creolize, to bring the new into existence.

Conclusion: Borderlands Talk

> *The borders are our natural sites of creation [...] the places where we invent, transgress, and create.*
> —Toni Morrison (2007)[13]

We return then to the borderlands, where the crossroads beckon and tell us another future is possible—depending on the direction we choose. We begin with where we are now, but we also imagine a future that will take us to a different place. We need to begin looking at cultures in terms of processes, especially these meeting places of borderlands where we come into contact with each other. Where we are meeting and interacting is where we are articulating a common, shared culture. Sometimes this is visible. Sometimes it is not.

Rev. Martin Luther King Jr. spoke in 1964 at the Nobel Lecture of the "World House," where, because of the powerful twentieth-century scientific and technological revolutions, "all inhabitants of the globe are now neighbors." Dr. King had a vision of what the world could become, not only to survive but to prosper as a human family sustaining the planet. As he said, "This is the great new problem of mankind. We have inherited a large house, a great 'world house,' in which we have to live together—black and white, Easterner and Westerner, Gentile and Jew, Catholic and Protestant, Moslem and Hindu—a family unduly separated in ideas, culture and interest, who because we can never again live apart, must learn somehow to live with each other in peace" (Nobel Prize, 1964).

Creolization and Creole cultures in the borderlands mark a key shift in the human understanding of the world in these contexts. While mixed cultures have been studied before, what we are looking at is different from the older emphasis on the nation and on the limited concepts of nations and societies as boxes. There has not been enough emphasis on the key phenomenon of in-betweenness, of mediators, of bridges.

CROSSING BORDERS AND CREOLIZATION

The liminal condition of the in-between as a fruitful location for border studies, something Anzaldúa (1987) knew all too well, has been followed up on by Aguirre, Quance, and Sutton (2000) as well as Benito and Manzanas (2006). The notion of a culture that we are proposing here redefines culture and society: not the universalism of the West but the *pluriversalism* of the world (Escobar, 2017, 2020; Kothari et al, 2019). We are mapping the grammar of new, shared values by mapping Creolization. This is both a negotiation of difference and a sharing of common ground, noting the need to account for all communities, hybrid or not (Hazan, 2015).

In the planetary space of the twenty-first century, it is the processes of creolization that illuminate cultural spaces and movements. What we thought was America, Japan, Germany, or China we now find to be shifting under our feet as we speak. Sometimes there is reaction and resistance from transient, fleeting cultural structures of supposed authenticity, but more often what we see is interaction and transformation. Culture is not something monolithic or static: the ability to act culturally guarantees the possibility of change, that is, of creolization. It is now changing, not static cultural structures, which captures our attention and interest as researchers.

What we are seeing now are studies of borders and border crossings as a dramatic transformation in the social sciences, a paradigm shift, that is relational and dialogic in nature (Brambilla et al, 2016, p. 1; Konrad & Amilhat-Szary, 2023, p. x). Cultural production has also become deeply tied to border crossings, with themes emerging in art, poetry, literature, music, theater, films, sport, festivals, and of course architecture, one of the premier sites of border crossings (Giudice & Giubilaro, 2015).

Denshō (伝承) is a Japanese term meaning "to pass on to the next generation," or to leave a legacy. Preserving stories of the past for the generations of tomorrow. To learn from our mistakes and missteps, to try new directions, and to find hope in the midst of devastation: all of these involve border crossings. We simply cannot turn our backs on what is happening. The only way to survive is to put ourselves directly into the middle of the borderlands where change and diversity are rapidly occurring. It is there that we notice the power of difference to make the world anew.

Borders and *borderlands* acquire a new power here, too. No longer simply places to go through, to get to the other side, barriers shutting off information, intersection, and interaction, borders and borderlands can now be seen for what they have always been: cultural and psychological sites of crossing. Their potency as physical markers and symbols of demarcation remain, but they are no longer permeable and increasingly questioned. These crossroads and their nearby spaces on either side of the border can now be seen as fertile places of imagination and creation, where the new is found and thrust forth into the world. What has been marginalized and liminal, those entrepôt of people, goods, information, ideas, and cultures, begin to assume center stage.

Borders and other social realities are of course socially constructed, which places culture squarely in the middle of our discourse. It is because of our cultural understandings of what constitutes the nation (or ethnicity, language, religion, or other boundary marker of identity) that borders are where they are. As Jan Nederveen Pieterse has noted for us, "Powerful interests are invested in boundaries and borders, affecting the fate of classes, ethnic groups, elites; while borders and boundaries are a function of

218   TOWARD A NEW ART OF BORDER CROSSING

differentials of power, they are social constructions that are embedded and encoded in cultural claims" (2004, p. 117).

Like James Clifford (1997) and many others, I am interested in the entanglements that occur at the crossroads that are the intersecting regional, national, and transnational levels of human relations, the "minority maneuvers and unsettled negotiations" taking place at what Homi Bhabha (1997a) calls "frontline/border posts." In Border regions, when one side is dominant there are strong demands for acculturation and assimilation, but when the two sides are more closely together in power, even relatively equal, the main form of intercultural relations is *transculturation*. This is the practice of freedom.

Etienne and Beverly Wenger-Trayner have spoken of this new practice as one of the communities of practice in complex systems, where the boundaries are traversed and melded by what they call systems convenors. Their work is important for border studies since it is based and situated in learning communities, with a special emphasis on practice-based learning (Wenger-Trayner et al, 2015), which can of course teach us much about our own and others' identities in the many contexts of border crossings. As they say, "the landscape is diverse [...] relationships between practices are always a matter of negotiating their boundary" (p. 17). Engagement, imagination, and alignment are 'modes of identification' in these landscapes of border crossings (pp. 20–21). Brokers are key personalities in these encounters (pp. 81–90), which they later call 'system convenors.' Respect and challenge are special ingredients for all parties (pp. 101–102). How might we learn from them? Ultimately, this is about "creating imaginative spaces to support bridging boundaries."

Cultural intrusions, which produce a mixing of newer and older cultural forms, may actually be the "normal" state of affairs. "The borderline work of culture demands an encounter with 'newness' that is not part of a continuum of past and present. It creates a sense of the new as an insurgent act of cultural translation," as Homi Bhabha states (Benhabib 2002, p. 23). The importance of change, fluidity, networks, multiple times/spaces, feedback, emergence, and unintended consequences have been shown by physics, too, all of which have had enormous impacts on communications theory and the architecture of social construction. In line with this new thinking, this book has revealed particular societies and imagined communities as networks, rather than as structures (which imply centers, power concentrations, and a vertical hierarchy). This is the new shape of global society/societies.

We now need to respond to the transnational, transcultural characteristics of the new age that has dawned upon us, an era where mobilities, flows, transfers, and circulations are ever-present in the local as well as the global. What we are seeing is thus the global circulation of public cultures. We are now, as the anthropologist Arjun Appadurai reminds us, on a common playing ground, even if from time to time the bumps and pitfalls of past power alignments disrupt this shared space of discourse.

We may, in fact, note the complexity of the present moment, which appears as chaos but is actually notable for its multiple cores and multiple peripheries. The Coronavirus has revealed these multipolarities. We have, in a sense then, a more complicated World Systems Theory, where enclaves of enlightenment clash with peripheries of prejudice and isolation. The back-and-forth flow of powerful centers alternates with times of fragmented states, continually returning, helping us understand that it is indeed the circle, the cycle,

CROSSING BORDERS AND CREOLIZATION

that we are a part of and will always return to as members of human societies. This does not mean that we should accept our fate, a vision nineteenth-century colonials had of Indians and other Asians ("fatalism") that did a disservice to the agency and action that we do have and take part in. Instead, how might we embrace "circulation as a cultural *process*," not only our own "circulation as cultural *practice*" (Lee & LiPuma, 2002, p. 192)?

Rather than seeing culture and its borders/borderlines as an enormous, permanent, and complex social machine, we find the river, with its swirls and eddies, its sometimes swift change and at other times slow, ponderous course, to be an excellent metaphor for presenting this new view of culture, with its flows and changes, some predictable, some not. The river focuses us on processes that are liquid rather than structures that are unmovable. It is no longer the rules but the actions that are taking place in transforming human relations that reveal the importance of cultural activity. It is a view of the river, not from far-off as eternal and unchanging, but up close with change as an implicit aspect of culture. It is a new take on Heraclitus and the River Menander (Meander).

This concept of the flow of cultural complexity shows us that cultural meaning is formed through interaction (Hannerz, 1992, 1997). And it is often in the Borderlands where these meanings and new approaches are formed (Willis, 2018). This is praxis, the action of making meaning, the practice of transnational planetary literacy, which we are pursuing in the essays in this book.[14] Meanings are negotiated directly, and we can no longer describe change as a shift from one cultural system to another, to westernization, americanization, sinicization, sanskritization, or mcdonaldization.

Culture is produced in the form of new habits, the *habitus* of Bourdieu (1984) and Befu (2001), derived from the processes of creolization on the borders of societies. This is not a one-sided assimilation, as some authors writing on hybridity would have it, a process that denies access to the power of defining for some or even many of the parties involved. It is not a discourse of complex wholes but the expression of social and political practice, which our essays in this volume report on in detail. *Culture is not a given but is always being negotiated at the borders of human experience.*

References

Agier, Michael. (2016). *Borderlands: Towards an anthropology of the cosmopolitan condition.* Cambridge UK: Polity Press.

Aguirre, Manuel, Quance, Roberta, & Sutton, Philip. (eds). (2000). *Margins and Thresholds: An Enquiry into the Concept of Liminality in Text Studies.* Madrid: The Gateway.

Alonso Bejarano, Carolina, Lopez Juarez, Lucia, Mijangos Garcia, Mirian A., & Goldstein, Daniel M. (2019). *Decolonizing Ethnography: Undocumented Immigrants and New Direction in Social Science.* Durham: Duke University Press.

Ansaldo, Umberto. (2017). Creole complexity in sociolinguistic perspective, *Language Sciences* Volume 60, March 2017, pp. 26–35.

Ansaldo, Umberto. (2018). Complexity reboot: A rejoinder to Parkvall, Bakker and McWhorter, *Language Sciences*, 66, March, pp. 234–235.

Anzaldúa, Gloria. (1987). *Borderlands: The New Mestiza = La Frontera.* San Francisco: Aunt Lute Books.

Appadurai, Arjun (1990). Disjuncture and Difference in the Global Cultural Economy, *Public Culture.* 2 (2) Spring: 1–24.

———(2000). Guest Editor. *Globalization*. Special Issue of *Public Culture*, Millennial Quartet, 12 (1) Winter.

Bauman, Zygmunt. (1997). The making and unmaking of strangers, in Pnina Werbner & Tariq Modood, eds., *Debating Cultural Hybridity*. London: Zed Books, pp. 46–57.

Beck, Ulrich. (1992). *Risk Society: Towards a New Modernity*. Thousand Oaks: Sage.

Befu, Harumi. (2001). *Hegemony of Homogeneity: An Anthropological Analysis of Nihonjinron*. Tokyo: Trans Pacific Press.

Benhabib, Seyla. (2002). *The Claims of Culture: Equality and Diversity in the Global Era*. Princeton: Princeton University Press. 2.

Berry, Thomas (1988). *The Dream of the Earth*. San Francisco: Sierra Club Books.

Benito Sánchez, Jesús, & Manzanas Calvo, Ana Marie. (eds.). (2006). *The Dynamics of the Threshold: Essays on Liminal Negotiations*. Madrid: Gateway Pres.

Bhabha, Homi. (1994). *The Location of Culture*, London: Routledge.

———(Guest Editor) (1997a). 'Front Lines/Border Posts,' *Critical Inquiry*, Spring, Volume 23, Number 3.

———(1997b). 'Life at the Border: Hybrid Identities of the Present,' *New Perspectives Quarterly*, Vol 14, Number 1.

———(2013). In Between Cultures, in *New Perspectives Quarterly*, Fall, pp. 107–109.

Bhambra, Gurinder K., Gebrial, Dalia, & Nişancıoğlu, Kerem. (2018). *Decolonizing the University*. London: Pluto Press.

Bourdieu, Pierre. (1984). *Distinction: A Social Critique of the Judgement of Taste*. London: Routledge.

Brambilla, Chiara, Laine, Jussi, Scott, James W., & Bocchi, Gianluca (eds). (2016). *Borderscaping: Imaginations and Practices of Border Making*. London: Routledge.

brown, adrienne maree. (2017). *Emergent Strategy: Shaping Change, Changing Worlds*. Oakland: AK Press.

Chakrabarty, Dipesh. (2021). *The Climate of History in a Planetary Age*. Chicago: University of Chicago Press.

Chomsky, Noam. (2013) in "Book endorsements" for Four Arrows, *Teaching Truly: A Curriculum to Indigenize Mainstream Education*: New York: Peter Lang.

Clifford, James. (1997). *Routes: Travel and Translation in the Late Twentieth Century*. Cambridge: Harvard University Press.

Cohen, Robin. (1996, 2023) *Global Diasporas: An Introduction*. London: Routledge.

Cohen, Robin. (2021). *Migration: The Movement of Humankind from Prehistory to the Present*. London: André Deutsch.

Cohen, Robin, & Fischer, Caroline. (2018). *Routledge Handbook of Diaspora Studies (Routledge International Handbooks)*. London: Routledge.

Cohen, Robin, & Sheringham, Olivia. (2016). *Encountering Difference: Diasporic Traces, Creolizing Spaces*. Cambridge: Polity Press.

Cohen, Robin, & Toninato, Paola. (2010). *The Creolization Reader: Studies in Mixed Identities and Cultures*. London: Routledge.

Cohen, Robin, & Van Hear, Nicholas. (2020). *Refugia: Radical Solutions to Mass Displacement*. New York: Routledge.

Crenshaw, Kimberlé W. (2017). *On Intersectionality: Essential Writings*, New York: New Press.

Das, Sukanta, Bhowal, Sanatan, Syangbo, Sisodhara, & Roy, Abhinanda. (eds.). (2017). *Border, Globalization and Identity*, Newcastle-upon-Tyne: Cambridge Scholars Publishing, 2017. ProQuest Ebook Central, https://ebookcentral-proquest-com.fgul.idm.oclc.org/lib/fielding/detail.action?docID=5351396.

Davis, Wade. (2009). *The Wayfinders: Why Ancient Wisdom Matters in the Modern World* (The CBC Massey Lectures). Toronto: House of Anansi Press.

DeGraff, Michel. (2005). Linguists' most dangerous myth: The fallacy of Creole Exceptionalism, *Language in Society* 34, 533–591. DOI: 10.10170S0047404505050207.

Drabinski, John E., & Parham, Marisa, eds. (2015). *Theorizing Glissant: Sites and Citations*. London: Rowman & Littlefield Publishers. Accessed December 23, 2022. ProQuest Ebook Central.

CROSSING BORDERS AND CREOLIZATION

Eriksen, Thomas Hylland. (1999). *Tu dimunnpuvinikreol: The Mauritian creole and the concept of creolization*. Website paper from lecture presented at the University of Oxford, December. DOI: August 20, 2000. (https://www.academia.edu/24749747/Tv_dimunn_pu_vini_Kreal_Creole_and_the_concept_of_Creolization)

Escobar, Arturo. (2017). *Designs for the Pluriverse: Radical Interdependence, Autonomy and the Making of Worlds*. Durham: Duke University Press.

———(2020). *Pluriversal Politics: The Real and the Possible*. Durham: Duke University Press. 4.

———(2021). Reframing civilization(s): from critique transitions, *Globalizations*, to DOI: 10.1080/14747731.2021.2002673.

Four Arrows, & Narvaez, Darcia. (2016). Reclaiming our indigenous worldview: A more authentic baseline for social/ecological justice work in education. In N. McCrary & W. Ross (Eds.), *Working for social justice inside and outside the classroom: A community of teachers, researchers, and activists* (pp. 91–112).

Gaudelli, William. (2016). *Global Citizenship Education: Everyday Transcendence*. London: Routledge.

Ghosh, Amitav. (2022). The Colonial Roots of Present Crises, originally published by *Green European Journal* (https://www.resilience.org/stories/2022-11-07/the-colonial-roots-of-present-crises/), Nov. 7.

Giddens, Anthony. (2021). Covid-19, AI, and the Future of Work, UCSB Global Studies Colloquium Series, April 21.

Giudice, Cristina, & Giubilaro, Chiara. (2015). Re-Imagining the Border: Border Art as a Space of Critical Imagination and Creative Resistance, *Geopolitics*, 20:1, 79–94, DOI: 10.1080/14650045.2014.896791.

Glissant, Édouard. (2000). The Cultural "Creolization" of the World. Interview with Edouard Glissant, 2000 Exchanging. *Label France* – January – No. 38.

———(2002). The Unforeseeable Diversity of the World, in *Beyond Dichotomies: Histories, Identities, Cultures, and the Challenge of Globalization*, Elisabeth Mudimbe-Boyi, ed. (Albany: SUNY Press).

Gordon, Jane Anna. (2014). *Creolizing Political Theory: Reading Rousseau Through Fanon*. New York: Fordham University Press. Accessed December 23, 2022. ProQuest Ebook Central.

Graeber, David, & Wengrow, David. (2021). *The Dawn of Everything: A New History of Humanity*. London: Allen Lane.

Gundaker, Grey. (1998). *Signs of Diaspora / Diaspora of Signs: Literacies, Creolization, and Vernacular Practice in African America*. Oxford: Oxford University Press.

Gupta, Akhil. (2021). Decolonizing US Anthropology, AAA Presidential Lecture, The American Anthropological Association, Nov 2022, available at https://anthrosource.onlinelibrary.wiley.com/doi/10.1111/aman.13775.

Hannerz, Ulf. (1992). *Cultural Complexity*. New York: Columbia University Press. 5.

———(1996). *Transnational Connections*. London: Routledge.

———(1997). *Flows, boundaries and hybrids: Keywords in transnational anthropology*. (https://sites.tufts.edu/anth130fall2012/files/2012/09/hannerz-flows-boundaries-hybrids.pdf).

Haraway, Donna J. (2016). *Staying with the Trouble: Making Kin in the Chthulucene*. Durham: Duke University Press.

Harris, Roxy, & Rampton, Ben (2023). *The Language, Ethnicity, and Race Reader*. London: Routledge.

Hayman, Eleanor, James, Colleen, & Wedge, Mark. (2018). Future rivers of the Anthropocene or Whose Anthropocene is It? Decolonising the Anthropocene! *Decolonisation: Indigeneity, Education, and Society*. 6, 2, 77–92.

Hazan, Haim. (2015). *Against Hybridity: Social Impasses in a Globalizing World*. Cambridge UK: Polity Press.

Hill Collins, Patricia. (2019). *Intersectionality as Critical Social Theory*. Durham: Duke University Press.

Horsti, Karina. (ed.). (2019). *The Politics of Public Memories of Forced Migration and Bordering in Europe*. Cham: Palgrave Pivot.

TOWARD A NEW ART OF BORDER CROSSING

Konrad, Victor, & Amilhat Szary, Anne-Laure, eds. (2023). *Border Culture: Theory, Imagination, Geopolitics.* London: Routledge.

Kothari, Ashish, Salleh, Ariel, Escobar, Arturo, Demaria, Federico, & Acosta, Alberto. (2019). *Pluriverse: A Post-Development Dictionary.* New Delhi: Tulika Books.

Laine, Jussi P. (2020a). Ambiguous Bordering Practices at the EU's Edges. In *Borders and Border Walls: In-Security, Symbolism, Vulnerabilities,* A. Bissonnette & E. Vallet, eds., 69–87. London: Routledge.

Laine, Jussi P. (2020b). Safe European Home– Where Did You Go? On Immigration, B/Ordered Self and the Territorial Home. In *Expanding Boundaries, Borders, Mobilities and the Future of Europe-Africa Relations,* 216–236, eds. Jussi P. Laine, Inocent Moyo, & Christopher Changwe Nshimbi. London: Routledge.

Latour, Bruno. (2021). *After Lockdown: A Metamorphosis.* Cambridge, UK: Polity.

———(2018). *Down to Earth: Politics in the New Climatic Regime.* Cambridge, UK: Polity.

Lawrence-Lightfoot, Sara. (2009). *The Third Chapter: Passion, Risk, and Adventure in the 25 Years After 50.* New York: Sarah Crichton Books.

Lee, Benjamin, & Edward LiPuma. (2002). "Cultures of Circulation: The Imaginations of Modernity," *Public Culture* 14 (1): 191–213.

Loomba, Ania. (1998). *Colonialism/Postcolonialism.* London: Routledge.

MacGillivray, A. (2015). Leadership, Boundaries and Sustainability. In David Blake Willis et al. (Eds.) *Sustainability Leadership: Integrating Values, Meaning, and Action: Volume 5* (Fielding Monograph Series).

Matsuda, Takeshi. (2001). *The Age of Creolization in the Pacific: In Search of Emerging Cultures and Shared Values in the Japan-America Borderlands,* Hiroshima: Keisuisha.

Meissner, Fran, & Vertovec, Steven. (2015). Comparing super-diversity, *Ethnic and Racial Studies,* Vol. 38, No. 4, pp. 541–555, DOI: 10.1080/01419870.2015.980295.

Memmi, Albert. (1991). *The Colonizer and the Colonized.* Boston: Beacon Press.

Mignolo, Walter D. (2000, 2012). *Local Histories/Global Designs: Coloniality, Subaltern Knowledges, and Border Thinking.* Princeton: Princeton University Press.

Mignolo, Walter D. (2021). *The Politics of Decolonial Investigations (On Decoloniality).* Durham: Duke University Press.

Mignolo, Walter D., & Walsh, Catherine E. (2018). *On Decoloniality: Concepts, Analytics, Practice.* Durham: Duke University Press.

Mohanty, Chandra Talpade. (2003). *Feminism Without Borders: Decolonizing Theory, Practicing Solidarity.* Durham: Duke University Press.

Monahan, Michael J. (2011). *The Creolizing Subject: Race, Reason, and the Politics of Purity.* US: Fordham University Press. Accessed December 23, 2022. ProQuest Ebook Central.

Morrison, Toni. (2007). Unpublished speech delivered at the Radcliffe Institute of Advanced Studies, Cambridge, Mass., June 8, cited in Sara Lawrence-Lightfoot. (2009). *The Third Chapter: Passion, Risk, and Adventure in the 25 Years After 50.* New York: Sarah Crichton Books, p. 141 and p. 252.

Nederveen Pieterse, Jan. (2004, 2019). *Globalization & Culture: Global Mélange.* Lanham, MD: Rowman & Littlefield.

Nederveen Pieterse, Jan. (2021). *Connectivity and Global Studies.* London: Palgrave Macmillan.

Nobel Prize (1964). Martin Luther King Jr. Nobel Lecture, https://www.nobelprize.org/prizes/peace/1964/king/lecture.

Ortner, Sherry (ed). (1999). *The Fate of Culture – Geertz and Beyond.* Berkeley: University of California Press.

Papastergiadis, Nikos. (2000). *The Turbulence of Migration.* London: Polity Press.

Parkvall, Mikael, Bakker, Peter, & McWhorter, John H. (2018). Creoles and sociolinguistic complexity: Response to Ansaldo, *Language Sciences,* 66, March, pp. 226–233.

Radcliffe, Sarah A. (2022). *Decolonizing Geography: An Introduction.* Cambridge, UK: Polity.

Rahimieh, Nasrin. (2007). Border crossing, *Comparative Studies of South Asia, Africa and the Middle East,* Volume 27, Number 2, 2007, pp. 225–232.

CROSSING BORDERS AND CREOLIZATION

Roberts, Paton D., & Yan, Eric. (2022). Jazz Musician Esperanza Spalding to Depart Harvard, *Harvard Crimson*, Nov 18, https://www.thecrimson.com/article/2022/11/18/spalding-email-music-departure-baedap/?fbclid=IwAR1jmwJ6LQht5jJQcIMD78bFApXw2vWXUJjqcFw9wK_sFWGFGrrwrV13iZQ.

Said, Edward. (2000). *Out of Place – A Memoir*. New York: Vintage.

Schimanski, Johan. (2019). 'Migratory angels: The political aesthetics of border trauma,' in K. Horsti (ed.), *The Politics of Public Memories of Forced Migration and Bordering in Europe*. Cham: Palgrave Pivot.

Schneider, Dorothee. (2011). *Crossing Borders: Migration and Citizenship in the Twentieth-Century United States*. Cambridge: Harvard University Press.

Shah, Sonia. (2020). *The Next Great Migration London: The Beauty and Terror of Life on the Move*. Bloomsbury Publishing.

Smith, Christopher J. (2013). *The Creolization of American Culture: William Sidney Mount and the Roots of Blackface Minstrelsy*. Bielefeld: University of Illinois Press. Accessed December 23, 2022. ProQuest Ebook Central.

Solnit, Rebecca. (2016). *Hope in the Dark: Untold Histories, Wild Possibilities*. Chicago: Haymarket.

Spivak, Gayatri Chakravorty. (1995). Teaching for the times, in Jan Nederveen Pieterse and Bhikhu Parekh, eds. *The Decolonization of Imagination: Culture, Knowledge and Power*. London: Zed, 177–202. 8.

Stewart, Charles, ed. (2007). *Creolization: History, Ethnography, Theory*. London: Routledge.

Stillman, Paul. (2015). Sustainability as Organizational Culture: Uncovering Values, Practices, and Processes, in Willis, David Blake, Steier, Frederick, & Stillman, Paul, eds., *Sustainability Leadership: Integrating Values, Meaning, and Action*. Santa Barbara: Fielding Graduate University.

Tsing, Anna Lowenhaupt. (2015). *The Mushroom at the End of the World: On the Possibility of Life in Capitalist Ruins*. Princeton: Princeton University Press.

Tuck, Eve, & Yang, Wayne. (2012). Decolonization is not a metaphor, in *Decolonization: Indigeneity, Education & Society*, Vol. 1, No. 1, 2012, pp. 1–40.

Tuhiwai Smith, Linda. (1999). *Decolonizing Methodologies: Research and Indigenous Peoples*. London: Zed Books.

Tuhiwai Smith, Linda, Tuck, Eve, & Yang, K. Wayne. (2019). *Indigenous and Decolonizing Studies in Education: Mapping the Long View*. London: Routledge.

Vertovec, Steven. (2007). Super-diversity and its implications. *Ethnic and Racial Studies*, Vol. 30 No. 6 November, pp. 1024–1054.

Villanueva, Edgar. (2018). *Decolonizing Wealth: Indigenous Wisdom to Heal Divides and Restore Balance*. Oakland: Berrett-Koehler.

Wahinke Topa (Four Arrows), & Narvaez, Darcia, eds. (2022). *Restoring the Kinship Worldview: Indigenous Voices Introduce 28 Precepts for Rebalancing Life on Planet Earth*. Berkeley: North Atlantic Books.

Wenger-Trayner, Etienne, Fenton-O'Creevey, Mark, Hutchinson, Steven, Kubiak, Chris, & Wenger-Trayner, Beverly (eds.). (2015). *Learning in Landscapes of Practice: Boundaries, Identity, and Knowledgeability in Practice-Based Learning*. Routledge.

Werbner, Pnina, & Modood, Tariq(eds.) (1997). *Debating Cultural Hybridity: Multicultural Identities and the Politics of Anti-Racism*. London: Zed Books.

Willis, David Blake (2001). 'Creole Times: Notes on Understanding Creolization for Transnational Japan-America,' in Takeshi Matsuda (Ed.) *The Age of Creolization in the Pacific: In Search of Emerging Cultures and Shared Values in the Japan-America Borderlands*, Hiroshima: Keisuisha.

———(2010). Creolization in Transnational Japan-America, in *The Creolization Reader: Studies in Mixed Identities and Cultures*, edited by Robin Cohen and Paola Toninato. London: Routledge.

———(2018). Resist and Relearn: Comments on Circulations and Escapes in a Barbaric Age, Afterword in Blai Guarné & Paul Hansen, (Eds.), *Escaping Japan: Reflections on Estrangement and Exile in the Twenty-First Century* (2018). London: Routledge.

Willis, David Blake, & Murphy-Shigematsu, Stephen (Eds.) (2008). *Transcultural Japan: At the Borderlands of Race, Gender, and Identity*. London: Routledge.

224 TOWARD A NEW ART OF BORDER CROSSING

Willis, David Blake, & Rappleye, Jeremy (Eds.). (2011). *Reimagining Japanese Education: Borders, Circulations, and the Comparative.* Oxford: Symposium Books.

Xiiem, Jo-ann Archibald Q'um Q'um, Lee-Morgan, Jenny Bol Jun, and De Santolo, Jason. (2019). *Decolonizing Research: Indigenous Storywork as Methodology.* London: Zed Books.

Yoshimi, Shunya, & Kang, Sang-Jung. (2001). *Gurobaru-ka no enkin-ho: Atarashiikokyo-kukan wo motomete. [Perspectives on Globalization: In Search of a New Public Space].* Tokyo: Iwanami, p. 40.

Yunkaporta, Tyson. (2020). *Sand Talk: How Indigenous Thinking Can Save the World.* New York: Harper One.

Zachary, Gregg Pascal (2000). *The Global Me: New Cosmopolitans and the Competitive Edge: Picking Globalism's Winners and Losers.* Washington: Public Affairs.

Zachary, Gregg Pascal (2001a). *Dualing multiculturalisms: the urgent need to reconceive cosmopolitanism. Paper presented at the Conceiving Cosmopolitanism conference, University of Warwick 27–29 April 2000.* Oxford: Transnational Communities Programme.

Zachary, Gregg Pascal (2001b). *A Global Triangle.* October 20, 2000, *The Globalist.* April 15, 2001.

Notes

1   One of the strongest voices on emergence is adrienne maree brown (2017) in her book *Emergent Strategy: Shaping Change, Changing Worlds* [...].

2   Hannerz (1992, 1996) and Stewart (2007) Op.cit., and Ulf Hannerz, *Flows, boundaries and hybrids: Keywords in transnational anthropology.* Website, Transnational Communities Working Paper Series, Oxford: Oxford University Press. January 30, 2011. https://sites.tufts.edu/anth130fall2012/files/2012/09/hannerz-flows-boundaries-hybrids.pdf. The work of Robin Cohen and Paolo Toninato (2010) as well as Robin Cohen and Olivia Sheringham (2016), is especially revealing and powerful in its reporting the place of creolization in our world today.

3   As Eriksen notes in reporting one particular case study, the anthropological use of the concept *cultural creolization* closely approximates actual on-the-ground Mauritian usage. See Thomas Hylland Eriksen, *Tu dimunn pu vini kreol: The Mauritian creole and the concept of creolization.* Website paper from lecture presented at the University of Oxford, December 1999. August 20, 2000. https://www.researchgate.net/publication/228385555_Tu_dimunn_pu_vini_kreol_The_Mauritian_Creole_and_the_Concept_of_Creolization. See also Willis and Murphy-Shigematsu (2008).

4   Hannerz (2000); Pnina Werbner and Tariq Modood, eds., *Debating Cultural Hybridity: Multicultural Identities and the Politics of Anti-Racism* (London: Zed Books, 1997); and Pieterse, Op.cit.; Homi Bhabha (1994), and a host of other authors.

5   Nikos Papastergiadis, *The Turbulence of Migration* (London: Polity Press, 2000), p. 209.

6   Sherry Ortner, ed. *The Fate of Culture—Geertz and Beyond.* Berkeley: University of California Press, 1999; Ulf Hannerz (1992, 1996) and; Stewart (2007); Ulf Hannerz, et.al., *Considering Creolization. A Transnational Communities ESRC Programme of Oxford University, Fall 1999.* October 15, 2000. <https://globaldecentre.org/wp-content/uploads/2020/07/Vertovec-1999.pdf>; Arjun Appadurai, *Modernity at Large* (Minneapolis: University of Minnesota Press, 1996); Jan Nederveen Pieterse, *Globalization as Hybridization.* In Mike Featherstone, Scott Lash, and Roland Robertson, eds. *Global Modernities* (London: Sage, 1995) pp. 45–68; and Iain Chambers, *migrancy, culture, identity* (London: Routledge, 1994).

7   Appadurai, Ibid., Hannerz (1996) Ibid, and Takeshi Matsuda, Ms. for the *Conference on "Exploring Emergent 'JAmerican Culture'"* (San Francisco: 2000). Stuart Hall, utilizing a Bakthinian-Gramscian perspective, saw cultural identity as always hybrid and implicated in the transformation of societies: Stuart Hall, New Ethnicities, in *Race, Culture and Difference.* Ed. James Donald and Ali Rattansi, eds. (London: Sage, 1992) and Who Needs Identity?, in *Questions of Cultural Identity.*Stuart Hall and Paul DuGay, eds. (London: Sage, 1996, 2012). Geertz helped the move away from simplistic essentialism about cultures to *thick description*:

CROSSING BORDERS AND CREOLIZATION 225

See Clifford Geertz, *Available Light* (Princeton: Princeton University Press, 2000); *The Interpretation of Cultures* (New York: Basic Books, 1973); and *Local Knowledge* (New York: Basic Books, 1983). And of course Edward W. Said is an especially potent voice for the mixing of cultures. See his autobiography *Out of Place: A Memoir*(New York: Alfred Knopf, 1999).

8 Malinche was the Aztec woman who became the mistress of Cortez, taught him what he needed to know to conquer Mexico, and is regarded by Mexicans as the Mother of all Mothers of their mestizo nation. Her story is controversial and laced with the innuendo of machismo as she is seen as a *chingada*, a violated woman who invited her own downfall and thus betrayed the nation. The story of Okichi, the mistress to the first US envoy to Japan (Townsend Harris), is seen as a tragic metaphor for purity sullied and the demise of the (male) nation. See also Papastergiadis (2000), Op. cit., pp. 174–175.

9 Grey Gundaker, *Signs of Diaspora / Diaspora of Signs: Literacies, Creolization, and Vernacular Practice in African America* (Oxford: Oxford University Press, 1998).

10 Gundaker, Ibid.

11 Appadurai, Ibid., was one of the first scholars to discuss deterritorialization, but with increasing transnational migrations and mobility this has become a key 21st century term. See Chapter 5, *The Deterritorialization of Culture*, in Papastergiadis (2000), Op cit. Creolizing has also entered the field of literature, with a 'Creolizing the Canon Series' from Rowman & Littlefield (https://rowman.com/Action/SERIES/_/RLICTC/Creolizing-the-Canon).

12 See Gregg Pascal Zachary, *Dualing multiculturalisms: the urgent need to reconceive cosmopolitanism. Paper presented at the Conceiving Cosmopolitanism conference, University of Warwick 27–29 April 2000.* Oxford: Transnational Communities Programme; *The Global Me: New Cosmopolitans and the Competitive Edge: Picking Globalism's Winners and Losers* (Washington: Public Affairs, 2000); and *A Global Triangle. October 20, 2000, The Globalist. April 15, 2001.*

13 From an unpublished speech by Toni Morrison at the Radcliffe Institute for Advanced Studies, June 8, 2007, as reported by Sara Lawrence-Lightfoot (2009, p. 141). This quotation begins a chapter in Lawrence-Lightfoot's book on "boundary crossing" and aging, the next issue taken up by one of the great educators (1978, 1988, 1995, 1997, 2000, 2003). Aging is a signal part of education and crossing borders, with navigating "the borders of new learning" (2009, p. 166) of adult transformative education an especially important challenge and joy. The possibilities and potential for cross-generational learning are especially ripe and potent. See also Willis and Rappleye (2011).

14 Gayatri Chakravorty Spivak, *Teaching for the times*, in Jan Nederveen Pieterse and Bhikhu Parekh, eds. *The Decolonization of Imagination: Culture, Knowledge and Power* (London: Zed, 1995), pp. 177–202.

Chapter 16

VISUAL CONSTRUCTION OF BORDERLANDS: THE CASE OF TOHONO O'ODHAM NATION AT US–MEXICO BORDERLANDS [WITHIN US AND MEXICO] AND THEIR SUBALTERN NARRATIVE

Ahmed Abidur Razzaque Khan and
Abdur Razzaque Khan

1. Introduction

Since the early twenty-first century, the issue of borders, borderlands, and their crossings has become one of the most prominent topics (Gonsior 2014). In recent times, the US–Mexico border has revealed a highly politicized zone. And with the complex reality of illegal border crossing, high petroleum activities, drugs, and human trafficking are the predominating narrative of both countries' borders. Unfortunately, the Native American tribes of the Southwest, the Tohono O'odham Nation,[1] have become a central community for such illegal border crossings due to sloppy enforcement policies on tribal land (Gurbacki 2014: 274–280). Another burning border narrative for both countries and these indigenous people is former president Trump's administration's steps to build a wall around the border to halt unauthorized migration.

Though border historians consider borders as social constructs inside territories and identities, the media's portrayal of borders, particularly in film, must be seen as a form of cultural production that is clearly a potent tool for national territories (Staudt 2014). Since the dawn of commercial filmmaking, the border has been a common backdrop in feature films. The region bordering the US–Mexico border is perhaps one of the most often displayed landscapes in North America. Almost since the inception of the movie business, the filmic depiction of the longest contiguous international boundaries has been a central problem in both national and international films. The U.S. film industry has produced thousands of films about border issues between the US and Mexico. And Mexican movie industry has an almost similar history of representing the US–Mexico borderlands. (Gonsior 2014)

While the film continues to expand as the most popular form of visual entertainment, a stunning body of work on the America-Mexico relationship in

Hollywood blockbuster films to well-known art by well-known directors has formed cinematic borders known as "popular culture." (Dell'Agnese 2005). Surprisingly, the advent of borderlands scholars coincided with the creating of a new type of motion picture known as "borderland films" (Brégent-Heald 2015). This concept is also comparable to the term "border cinema."

This article argues that visual representations of the US–Mexico border in the popular culture of borderland films and documentary films have different politics of representation. This paper is broken into three pieces based on context and actuality above. After a brief explanation of how colonial and nation-states built borderland on Tohono O'odham desert land, and how migration and border security narratives have affected their indigenous narrative of lives and livelihood. The second segment will look at commercial cinema representations of the US–Mexico border. The third and final portion examines the visual architecture of documentary films, focusing on the tribal nation of Arizona's desert, the Tohono O'odham Nation, who today live in Mexico and U.S. borderlands.

2. Methodology

This research aims to investigate the visual creation of borderlands in films and documentaries—specifically at the US–Mexico borderlands. According to John Storey, cultural studies expose the dominant political perspective as a component of popular urban culture (Storey 1996). As a dominant urban culture, the film may not be any different in this regard. Furthermore, the film business in both countries is driven by political economics and globalization, except for documentary films, which have no economic politics other than to visualize the setting, issues, and views.

This research is mostly focused on a critical review of available qualitative studies on borderland films using several qualitative approaches. These studies focus on high-quality films made in Mexico and the US, notably those from Hollywood, across time periods ranging from the 1930s to the 1980s and the most recent two decades. We hope to demonstrate that the dominant narrative of both film industries ignored or obliterated the voice of subaltern people, including non-whites and Indians—the natives of their own soils—through a study of those studies. As a result, such research will shed light on narratives that marginalize and facilitate other exclusion (Cheek 2004).

The investigation then moved on to documentaries and data analysis of existing online documentaries. We opted to limit our documentary film selection to films that were accessible and available on the internet. Those are made in English only (albeit some were obtained through personal communication) regarding Tohono O'odham territory or nation. The study of cultural border formation in documentary films from a subaltern perspective contrasts with the colonial narrative of political dominance, economic exploitation, and cultural oblivion. According to Gayatri Spivak (2003), the theoretical foundation for our research is derived from this political perspective in order to provide a voice to lower-class or oppressed individuals.

3. Literature: Theories and Realities

3.1. The longest borderlands

The longest international border, the US–Mexico border, has produced a zone where economic contradictions are purposely visible. It is the physical location where the First and Third Worlds collide. And according to migration history, the combination of employment in the US and difficult economic conditions in Mexico has resulted in a thriving transnational financial process of the labor movement. As a result, one of the most prominent transborder events in the twentieth century was the migration of Mexicans north across the border. The process is still going strong in the twenty-first century.

However, it is worth noting that the 2,000-mile border between the two states also comprises a population of almost 10 million people. Consequently, this world's busiest land border between the US and Mexico provides all the necessary lawful movement of an estimated 350 million people annually (AFP 2010).

Apart from the realities of cross-border migration, this region has strong family and cultural links, tourism and trade links, and environmental issues. On the other side, the region is commonly referred to as a source of insecurity, threats, and vulnerabilities. A current tendency of militarization of physical territory has also impacted the aesthetic environment (Meza 2019).

According to Jeanette Gonsior, a borderland film scholar, the border has thus become a line of exclusion and conflict, a paranoid defense against the other, and a space of integration and hybridity, a meeting point between cultures. Therefore, it is noman's land, neither American nor Mexican, with a hybrid civilization with its own politics, language, and culture (2014). We can see a similar perspective in cultural theory. The border is a meeting point between cultures; it has become a line of exclusion and conflict, of paranoid defense against the other, but still offers a space of integration and hybridity. We will examine whether such plurality has been reflected in the visuals constructed through films and documentaries.

3.2. The border tribe Tohono O'odham

The Tohono O'odham Nation, whose members own the US' second-largest piece of property (an estimated 2.7 million acres), lives on ancestral territories in southern Arizona's Sonoran Desert. Before any nation-state formed, these aboriginal Americans or indigenous peoples, sometimes known as the "Desert People," resided in the same territory. On the other side of the border, their ancestral lands extend into the Mexican state of Sonora. The irony is that, in the colonial framework of the border and national territory, they are now a border tribe. According to USA Today, the 62-mile international border between the US and Mexico divides 34,000 of their official population (Náñez 2021). Unfortunately, as most tribe members live in poverty, including live below the poverty level, therefore, they are most vulnerable to being involved with negative activities like drug trafficking or smuggling and ending up in prison due to the loopholes unemployment as a consequence of reality on border (Gurbacki 2014: 277–278).

230   TOWARD A NEW ART OF BORDER CROSSING

Since the emergence of the modern period from 1850 to 1880, the economic stride accelerated on both sides of the US–Mexican border and divided their territory (Encyclopedia 2019). The division of O'odham lands has resulted in an artificial division of O'odham society too. The reality pointed out by José Antonio Lucero is that official boundary makers fundamentally overlooked the Tohono O'Odham borderlands in Mexico and the US. We found more as he pointed out the disproportion of boundaries selectively imposed over time and space and the "colonial ambivalence" of borders that place indigenous nations both inside and outside of the U.S. colonial state (2014: 171).

According to the 2019 online encyclopedia, they fought Apaches[2] and Yavapais[3] tribes for Spanish, Mexican, and American conquerors in premodern times. The "Papago" or "Pima" or "Pima Indians" were the names given to them by colonizers when they arrived in their homeland in the 1600s. When the Spanish invaders discovered them in the desert, they dubbed them "Papago," which translates to "tepary-bean eaters." Spanish colonizers referred to such groups living near rivers as "Pima" (Southern Arizona guide, n.d.). Specifically, since the seventeenth century, these indigenous people have been referred to in various ways that have nothing to do with their own identity. The truth is that the tribe and their land have become a key channel for illegal border crossings due to their location, sloppy enforcement of immigration policies, and other realities. Consequently, the community and its people have been through a series of negative impacts, including drug trafficking, violence, and environmental destruction on its reservation (Gurbacki 2014: 274–280). The alarming reality is thousands of migrants have died already and thirsty, tired lost immigrants walking through the heat of the Senora desert in numbers, each day!

3.3. The Borderland cinema and its colonial narrative

During the 1910s, the U.S. cinema industry created and exported over 500 fiction films set on or near the actual borders of the US, according to borderland film researcher Dominique Bregent-Heald. And, according to Brégent-Heald (2015), more than half of borderland films created during this time period are set in the US–Mexico border region. On the other hand, the Mexican cinema industry has a roughly comparable history of portraying the US–Mexico borderlands. For example, between 1936 and 1996, more than 300 border films were created in Mexico, according to Norma Iglesias-Prieto, one of the major historians on the topic of Mexican border cinema. Furthermore, the Mexican Revolution[4] of the 1910s is thought to have inspired hundreds of border films, including a good number of documentaries. This huge film doctrine includes Hollywood mainstream cinema, Mexican commercial cinema, the Nuevo Cine Mexicano, Chicano cinema, independent border films, and videos made and produced by local borderlanders (Gonsior 2014). Therefore, the visual construction of the US–Mexico border in both countries' cinema or film industries has always been highly desirable since its inception.

These productions of cinematic borders acknowledge the variety of film categories, stretching from westerns, Indian dramas, Spanish or Mexican costume pictures, and melodramas to comedies, dramas on crime, and the military(Brégent-Heald 2015: 2–3).

VISUAL CONSTRUCTION OF BORDERLANDS

Border film scholar Iglesias-Prieto notes that her definition of the border genre is as complex as the meaning of the term "border." However, the very border film scholar coined "border cinema" as the following criteria to get a focused view. She claimed that border film must include at least one of these characteristics below.

1. The plot, or a significant part of it, takes place in the Mexico-US border region.
2. The story deals with one or more characters from the borderlands region, irrespective of the setting.
3. The film refers to the population of Mexican origin living in the US.
4. The film is shot on location in the borderlands, regardless of the plot.
5. The story, or a key part of it, refers to the borderlands or problems of national identity. (Gonsior 2014)

Through the study of this scholar (2014) we can see this film genre and cultural industry in Mexico and the US that refers to the following topic and themes below:

The films portray the border as a lawless zone. In fact, Hollywood border films frequently include bandits, villains, and outlaws. Male "race outsiders," such as Mexicans and Native Americans, have often been presented in Hollywood films as renegade figures. Furthermore, the Western genre has been used to establish a criminal sanctuary and inferior "others" since the early film days, with Western heroes vs. greasers, villains, bandits, revolutionaries, and half-breeds. In recent times after 9/11[5] and the change in security narratives, states enhanced the political principle of protectors of citizens. In addition, a linkage between undocumented immigrants and the War on Terror increased the negative portrayal of the "illegal" immigrant.

Major social issues along the US–Mexico border are rarely addressed in Hollywood border films and ethnic minorities and women are often exposed to unfavorable stereotypes. The vast majority of feature films dealing with US–Mexican themes and characters from the eighteenth century to World War II are westerns, according to research. For male characters, the greaser bandit, the lecherous "Latin lover," and the stupid assistant are prescribed and constructed; for female characters, the self-sacrificing young women and the cantina whore are prescribed and constructed.

Secondary characters in borderland films and their existence like War veterans, Mexicans, Native Americans, racially mixed characters, undocumented immigrants from Mexico, illegal aliens, terrorists, bad guys, dominant and domineering women, and drug traffickers from the South all appear on the silver screen of borderlands films as a part of idealizing U.S. borderland regions as part of colonial expansion and U.S. nation-building. Representation of bloodthirsty Indians and Mexican bandits and uncivilized half-naked Indians, cowboy-versus-Indians, Native Americans, and helpless Indian ladies comes as a part of the overlapping colonial narrative (Brégent-Heald 2015: 13–14).

There is no question that border cinema has played a significant role in creating and reinforcing negative border stereotypes. The silver screen of borderlands film is filled with undesirable people such as war veterans, Mexicans, Native Americans, racially mixed characters, Undocumented immigrants from Mexico, illegal aliens, terrorists,

232   TOWARD A NEW ART OF BORDER CROSSING

bad guys, and dominant and domineering women, including drug traffickers from the South. Borderlands film literature finds bloodthirsty Indians and the Mexican bandits, uncivilized half-naked Indians, cowboy-versus-Indians, Native Americans, and vulnerable Indian women as a part of the racialization and othering of the space. Jeanette Gonsior pointed out in her study that from the silent film era to the present, Hollywood films on Mexican migration and the border have followed a basic discursive formula which is a modified version of the western in which the hero struggles valiantly against gangs involved in the trafficking of undocumented workers (2014).

Research found that since the 1960s, several border films have dealt with undocumented immigration. However, the irony is Hollywood immigration films have not revealed much of the human dimension of Mexican immigrants, nor have they reflected or portrayed the substantial contributions that Mexican immigrants have made to the U.S. economy and the social and cultural matrix of the nation. Even though "a new wave of films emerged" in this era, they could not avoid the colonial top-down power structure as the theme of films remains submissive Mexican immigrants being protected by noble English white persons who continued to lead.

It does not mean that the 1977 film *Almabarista!* depicted the harsh realities of life of a Mexican migrant laboring illegally in the fields of the US not being counted in these studies. Though it is a landmark film in portraying the perspective of undocumented aliens and injecting that viewpoint into the national discourse on immigration, its storytelling narrative is a colonial top-down in power structure. The point is the discourse of powerless poor people and how it has been constructed. It is coming from their own perspective of the generations of men coming north for many years, living apart from their families and bearing the personal stress, staying for years as undocumented persons, living as almost second-class citizens without full civil rights?

Staudt stated that the film industry itself brings out the worst of countries in the US–Mexico borderlands. By "worst," the scholar means lawlessness, sexual violence, deaths, and drugs, with "othering" processes alive and well on both sides of the border. In both historical and contemporary films, everyday lives in the borderlands are not well represented. Unfortunately, both countries' borderlands film failed to represent the narratives of aboriginal desert people, though barren deserts have sometimes been presented as a part of the border and landscape. Unfortunately, borderland films in both countries films represent white American men, mostly heroes, some Mexicans, and Apache Indians but not the native people, the Tohono O'Odham.

3.4. The constructed borders on documentary films

From the literature and studies above sections it is evident that the stereotypes representation of US–Mexico border in feature films from the both countries mainstream cinema includes negative images of people around border and "othering" practices alive and well on both sides of the border. Interestingly though the very border tribe Tohono O'odham, the desert people are not present in the feature films however since twentieth century the indigenous community are being started documented on nonfiction films.

VISUAL CONSTRUCTION OF BORDERLANDS

In 1941, the Indian Irrigation Service produced a stock footage documentary on Tohono O'odham, the desert people, made by the University of Arizona, Tucson, and Bureau of Audio-Visual Services, which was produced by the and directed by F.C. Clark. J.R. The 24.65-minute video is available on YouTube with the title "TOHONO O'ODHAM Tribe Native American Indians Tucson, Arizona U.S. Government Film 88304," uploaded by Periscope Film. In the documentary, they are mentioned as "Papago Indians," acknowledging that they called them the desert people and lived there for a hundred years.

Literature reveals that the narrative vulnerability of undocumented migrants and their families was well represented in 1987 by Paul Espinosa in his documentary "In The Shadow of Law." This Chicano filmmaker had the opportunity to examine many key moments in the transborder history of the region. His films were broadcast to a national audience in the US and have also been screened in numerous festivals in Latin America and worldwide.

In 2000 another documentary of this film maker examined Tohono O'Odham reservation in Tucson and the continued land disputes in "The Border." We noticed the literature tracked that the narrative of the desert people and border reality was constructed without influence of colonial narrative.

However, it was part of one of six stories featuring this unique region's slice-of-life in "The Border." It is important to note that the use of documentary films for Chicano rights and human rights movement emerges since 1970s. The attempt to counterbalance the exclusionary discourse of dominant discourse that defines mainstream media and popular culture becomes evident since 2000 through the production of different documentaries.

Since 2005 a number of documentaries been produced on reality of the Tohono O'odham nation and their lands by different filmmakers. Among them "Walking the line" directed by Jeremy Levine, and Landon Van Soest in 2005 on Prophetic politics/activism in the Tohono O'odham Borderlands. In 2006, Joseph Metheo and Dan DeVivo examined immigration through the lives and actions of the people living along the Arizona–Sonora bordering their documentary "Crossing Arizona." This interpretation of filmmakers is people-centric, through the eyes of people directly affected by the policies. These two documentaries examine the issues through the lived experience of the community and practice, and try to expose their voices. The film starts with a hopeful, positive vive as the priest in the church of Altar, Mexico mentions the expectation of receiving the blessing for the journey they are undertaking.

The inside story of immigrants and low-paid workers in borderland was revealed in the experimental documentary "Maquilapolis: City of Factories" in 2006. This exclusive film was the co-funded project of American and Mexican-American filmmakers. The film sheds light on the struggles of women workers in export-oriented industrial zones operating under the shadow of global capitalism.

In 2015, Frances Causey's 17 minutes documentary "Ours is the land" comes up with the accounts of the spiritual, cultural and physical connection of the Tohono O'odham people and their sacred land focusing the controversy of open-pit copper mine in the Santa Rita Mountains. Finally, in 2017, Jason Jaacks interprets the border into Mexico

234 TOWARD A NEW ART OF BORDER CROSSING

with Tohono O'odham tribal members, following a young woman's journey through the environmental and natural discourse by making "Border nations." In the next section of the analysis, we will offer alternative representations of the border by analyzing the US–Mexico border reflected in these documentaries.

4. Cultural Construction of Subaltern Narrative—the Listening Voice of the Community

Media and social change concerning marginalized groups like minorities and indigenous groups have been centered on different social science theories. Through the communication perspective, the premise of Michael J. Fischer that the media, and especially film, can help migrant or marginalized people raise their voices to seek their rights, is one of the hypotheses in this paper (1995: 126–150). This needs a review since, in most cases, mainstream media relies on the theory of nation states based on the theory of Imagined Communities of Benedict Andersor (2016). Furthermore, social theorists and cultural studies scholars have interpreted the media as a popular culture discourse in terms of political communication and civil participation (Aguayo 2005).

Documentary film in the twentieth century has demonstrated effective public engagement and activism tools. Hence, documentary filmmakers are passionate about storytelling to present a narrative from the community or people's perspective mostly. Sometimes documentary on burring issues, especially issues like border crossing could help the undocumented immigrants to find a support from their own countries' foreign missions—policy improvement. For example, the first author's documentary film "The Dreaming Vendors" contributed to developing returning mechanism for the irregular maritime migrants of Bangladesh from Thailand (Abid, 2010).

Recent human rights practice has added observational documentaries, which aim to present the voices of local people by allowing the film subjects, such as an indigenous or local, to tell the story from their own perspectives of their daily lives, activities, and situations that appear in front of cameras (Chanrungmaneekul 2019: 2). Furthermore, as previously said, the political perspective of this article is to investigate if documentaries might provide marginalized people a voice.

However, we cannot assert that documentary films do not have their own politics. We could call the U.S. Government's 1941 documentary about the TOHONO O'ODHAM Tribe, produced by the Indian Irrigation Service, a colonial propaganda tale. It was created as part of a government irrigation service promotional film. Though the film concentrates on their lives and traditions, it also discusses the desert's development, education, and government support. The film's goal was to show how the Indian irrigation agency distributes water to desert dwellers. The documentary also depicts the construction of a dam to help the desert people irrigate and obtain water.

They were also referred to as "Papago Indians" in the film, which is a clear example of a top-down colonial othering narrative. The Papago arts and crafts board, which collects and promotes handcrafted baskets, is an example of this type of work. Finally, the video closes, [...] *and this new generation of desert people, the Papago people, is learning to become an even more important part of the great American dream.* The great American ideal is

VISUAL CONSTRUCTION OF BORDERLANDS

told entirely through the eyes of white men in the US. In that context, this documentary is unquestionably a propaganda film.

Naming them as Papago Indian is the first indication of colonialism and othering as a process of erasing a group's original identity and voice. Thankfully, by the late twentieth century, they had grown bored of being called bean-eaters or beaners, and had adopted the Tohono O'Odham, which means Desert People, as their formal identity in their own language. Unfortunately, their tradition of hospitality had not reflected on the above documentary.

Above types of top-down storytelling altered from Chicano documentary filmmaker Paul Espinosa's work. In "The Shadow of Law," he looked at the daily struggles of illegal families. He also avoided news of bloodshed, illicit border crossings, and border corruption. Rather, he concentrates his stories on current and relevant topics that affect the border region, such as the global economy, water shortages, land disputes, and cultural misunderstandings. It tries to present a different way of thinking about human culture and hybridity locations. His "The Border" presents a new vision of the border that broken negative views. The film showed how many of these people became "poor and powerless" after the US failed to give them the land it promised, he said—as a counter narrative (Johnson, September 15, 1999).

Vicky Funari and Sergio De La Torre have provided critical insight into the suppression and resistance of migrant women factory workers in Maquilapolis as a case study, particularly how marginalized groups negotiate their subject position within hyper-mediated, "de-territorialized" contexts. This film exposes the subaltern narrative of the low-wage, brown female factory workers in Tijuana who must deal with an aggressive foreign imperial presence. The film visualizes that the mass new colonial economic system at borderlands alienates women from the high-tech commodities they produce, treating the women as machine-like, disposable cyborgs without human needs or rights (Bui 2015: 129–56).

The Tohono O'odham nationland's narrative of border crossers has been reflected in Jeremy Levine and Landon Van Soest's documentary "Walking the Line" in 2005. This documentary examines the spiritual and political journey of Mike Wilson, the tribal member of the Tohono O'odham Nation, who puts water out for migrants against the wishes of his tribal council. He has maintained water station in desert since 2001, when he was a Presbyterian lay pastor in Sells, Arizona.

This film also explains the politics or philosophy of this protagonist. Wilson's work is steeped in religious imagery and informed by biblical readings. For example, his original one-hundred-gallon water stations were all named after apostles such as Mark, Matthew, Luke, and John. Later, he began to place the bottles in the form of a cross. This was done both to give migrants some confidence that the water was safe to drink and also to prevent people from destroying the water stations.

In the documentary, Wilson gave a bottle of fresh water to a border crosser. The man had been walking for two days and could barely stand. His paid guide, or coyote, and fellow travelers left him behind when his blistered feet made him too slow and asked him to sit on the ground so that he could treat the man's wounded feet. As he applied iodine to the migrant's blistered feet, he explained in Spanish: "I am a member of this

236 TOWARD A NEW ART OF BORDER CROSSING

tribe, and I have permission, even if the tribe does not like it, to put out water [...]." José Antonio Lucero noted it as the prophetic style of activism (Lucero 2014: 168). To us, it is a subaltern narrative of indigenous people meeting another unknown person—honesty constructed without any exaggeration of information or reality.

Within a 95-minute story, Joseph Mathew and Dan DeVivo presented "Crossing Arizona", a documentary. The film exposes the influx of migrants and rising death toll along the Texas and California borders that funnel an estimated 4,500 undocumented migrants to the Arizona desert on a daily basis. The perilous journey, which can take up to four days, has led to the deaths of thousands of migrants or border crossers. In addition, the documentary film interpreted the complicated feelings about human rights, culture, class, and national security through the eyes of frustrated ranchers, local activists, desperate migrants, former coyotes, and the Minutemen (Mathew & Dan DeVivo 2006).

A person is putting water in the tribal desert of the Tohono O'Odham nation in 95-degree hot weather, eventually meeting someone who is already lost and walking for two days. When the first man gave this person some food and water, the second man shared his narrative that he paid USD 300 or 3000 pesos to find work and his wife needed to do medical surgery. He got a kid. When that man awoke on the road, his shadow moved with him, creating a new reality and narration of his desert. This is Mike Wilson from Walking the Line. Mike becomes a protagonist in two documentaries—as a part of the ongoing narrative of the desert and its people—post-colonial construction of the border and the people that qualify its hybridity.

Finally, Frances Causey presented her film "Ours is the land" that narrates the story entirely from the perspective of the Tohono Nation members themselves, including Legislative Council members and tribal elders who speak about the multi-generational connection between Long Mountain Ce: wi Duag and the Nation today. It is evident since 2005, the topic and style of storytelling focus on the Tohono O'Odham nation. Above mentioned three documentaries presented the voice of the desert, the Tohono O'Odham nation, and their land from their own point of view.

5. Conclusion: The Unseen Narratives

As an indigenous desert tribe in Arizona, the Tohono O'Odham have witnessed the civilizing missions of Jesuits, Franciscans, Spanish colonial rulers, and Mexican and U.S. governments. The Tohono O'Odham nation and lands are literally "at the borders of empires." Both Mexican and American nation-states and militaries dismissed them as "barbarous Indians" aiming to "civilize" their borders (Lucero: 171). In reality, the US–Mexico border has become "an artificial barrier to the Tohono O'odham's freedom" to travel across their land, limiting their ability to obtain foods and commodities necessary for their culture's existence, as well as visit family members and traditional sacred sites. They've also been chastised for their inability to prevent illicit border crossings. Is it true that they have the ability to do so?

And what else could they provide the wandering migrant besides water?

According to this paper, the boundaries established or shown in borderlands movies or fiction films are often a zone defined by the economics of crime and violence.

VISUAL CONSTRUCTION OF BORDERLANDS

According to a critical review of the literature, the exaggerated and amazing stories presented in fiction films have typically eclipsed the cross-cultural voices of the more than 15 million individuals who are simply going about their daily lives, including the narrative of desert people, according to a critical review of the literature.

As a result, both the nation's popular culture and the film industries failed to recognize the Tohono O'Odham people's heritage of hospitality and the tribe members who live along the border. Perhaps it is because to the political economy of the film industry that no selling materials from this group of indigenous people were discovered.

Mike Wilson, a Tohono O'Odham activist, and his pro-human being imaginative action contributed to shaping the subaltern narrative they could deliver in the desert through documentary films. When he forms water into a cross as a sign of hope for migrants, he is sending a message to the neediest and stressed individuals that they have the right to consume water.

He explained his views by saying, "Water is salvation in the desert, water is survival, and I believe that access to water is the essential human right from a universal human rights standpoint" (Human Rights Watch 2015). Mike Wilson's narrative continues to move as he relates his conversion narrative to university audiences, documentary filmmakers, and even social scientists. Thus his voice has been heard through alternative media rather than fiction or feature films.

An insight into what these few documentaries contributed is remarkable. We find a different thought regarding the places of human culture and hybridity, land disputes, and cultural misunderstandings in Chicano documentary filmmaker Paul Espinosa's work. Vicky Funari and Sergio De La Torre's tale takes things a step further by providing essential insight into the oppression and resistance of migrant women industrial employees. "Walking the Line," directed by Jeremy Levine and Landon Van Soest, "Crossing Arizona," directed by Joseph Mathew and Dan DeVivo, and "Ours is the Land," directed by Frances Causey, highlighted the voice of the desert and its people, the Tohono O'Odham.

Over the last two decades, independent documentary filmmakers' subaltern narrative work has made some noise on the visual medium and shared their own voices with global communities.

References

Abid, Ahmed. 2010. *The Demanding Vendors* (50.30 mins).

Aguayo, Angela Jean. 2005. *Documentary Film/video and Social Change: A Rhetorical Investigation of Dissent*. Austin, TX: The University of Texas at Austin.

Agency France Press (AFP). 2010. "U.S., Mexico open first new border crossing in 10 years" *Agency France Press*, January 12, 2010. http://banderasnews.com/1001/to-newcrossing.htm.

Anderson, Benedict 2016 (1983): *Imagined Communities: Reflections on the Origins and Spread of Nationalism*. Verso, London.

Brégent-Heald, Dominique. 2015. *Borderland Films: American Cinema, Mexico, and Canada during the Progressive Era*. USA: University of Nebraska Press.

Bui, Long Thanh. 2015. "Glorientalization: Specters of Asia and Feminized Cyborg Workers in the US-Mexico Borderlands." *Meridians* 13, no. 1: 129–156. https://doi.org/10.2979/meridians.13.1.129.

Cheek, Julianne. 2004. "At the Margins? Discourse Analysis and Qualitative Research." *Qualitative Health Research* 14, no. 8: 1140–1150.

Chanrungmaneekul, Unaloam. 2019. *Use of Observational Documentary to Advocate Human Rights among Youth in Thailand and Myanmar: A Case Study of The Third Eye.* SHAPE SEA Policy Brief, Thailand.

Encyclopedia. 2019. "Pima-Papago". History and Cultural Relations. *encyclopedia.com.* https://www.encyclopedia.com/humanities/encyclopedias-almanacs-transcripts-and-maps/pima-papago. Accessed May 29, 2022.

Fischer, Michael M.J. 1995. 'Starting Over: How, What, and for Whom Does One Write about Refugees? The Poetics and Politics of Refugee Film as Ethnographic Access in a Media-Saturated World.' in *Mistrusting Refugees*, edited by E. Valentine Daniel and John Chr. Knudsen, 126–150, California: University of California Press.

Gonsior, Jeanette. 2014. "Transnational Representations of the U.S. Borderlands. Outlaw Women in Contemporary 'Border Cinema'." Munich, GRIN Verlag, https://www.grin.com/document/502500.

Gurbacki, Karrie A. 2014. "Migration of Responsibility: The Trust Doctrine and the Tohono O'Odham Nation." *Mexican Law Review* 6, no. 2: 273–296.

Johnson, Topper. D. 1999."'The Border' shows unique view of the U.S.-Mexico boundary" *Arizona Daily Wildcat*, September 15, 1999. https://wc.arizona.edu/papers/93/17/06_1_m.html. Accessed May 27, 2022.

Lucero, José Antonio. 2014. "Friction, Conversion, and Contention: Prophetic Politics in the Tohono O'odham Borderlands." *Latin American Research Review* 49: 168–184.

Mathew, J., and DeVivo, D., 2006. *Crossing Arizona.* New York, NY: Rainlake Productions.

Human Rights Watch. 2015. "Life and Death on the Border, in TORN APART: FAMILIES AND US REFORM, Photography by PLATON". Human Rights Watch. http://features.hrw.org/features/Torn_Apart_US_immigration_reform_2014/index.php.

Náñez, Dianna M. 2021. "A border tribe, and the wall that will divide it." *USA Today Network.* https://www.usatoday.com/border-wall/story/tohono-oodham-nation-arizona-tribe/582487001/. Accessed May 27, 2022.

Storey, John. 1996. *Cultural Studies: An Introduction.* New York, NY: Edward Arnold.

Southern Arizona guide. n.d. "Pima and Papago Indians of Southern Arizona" *Southern Arizona Guide.* https://southernarizonaguide.com/pima-papago-indians/. Accessed May 27, 2022.

Staudt, Kathleen. 2014. "The Border, Performed in Films: Produced in Both Mexico and the U.S. to 'Bring Out the Worst in a Country'." *Journal of Borderlands Studies* 29, no. 4: 465–479.

Meza, Mónica Socorro Romero. 2019. "The Power Struggle along the US-Mexico Border: A Space of Dehumanization and of Assertion of Justice." *Geopolítica (s)* 10, no. 2: 185.

Spivak, Gayatri Chakravorty, 2003. "Can the Subaltern Speak?" *Die Philosophin* 14, no. 27: 42–58.

Notes

1 It is a federally recognized tribe that includes approximately 34,000 members. It is located in south central Arizona's Sonoran Desert and borders the Mexico–US border for 74 miles (119 km) on its southern border. The nation is organized into 11 local districts and employs a tripartite system of government. The Tohono O'odham Nation occupies four separate pieces of land for a combined area of 2.8 million acres (11,330 km²), making it the second largest Native American land holding in the United States. And the majority of tribe members live off of the reservations.

2 A group of culturally related Native American tribes in the Southwestern United States that speak variations of the Athapascan language and are of the Southwest cultural area. The tribes fought the invading Spanish and Mexican peoples for centuries. The first Apache raids on Sonora appear to have taken place during the late seventeenth century.

VISUAL CONSTRUCTION OF BORDERLANDS

3 Another Native American tribe in Arizona. The Yavapais speak a dialect of the Yuman language. Historically, all Yuman tribes lived near the Colorado River, sharing a common creation myth that locates their origins at Spirit Mountain along the Colorado River near modern-day Bullhead City, Arizona.
4 An extended sequence of armed regional conflicts in Mexico from 1910 to 1920.
5 September 11 attacks, also called 9/11 attacks, series of airline hijackings and suicide attacks committed in 2001 by 19 militants associated with the Islamic extremist group al-Qaeda against targets in the United States, the deadliest terrorist attacks on American soil in U.S. history. (Source: Britanica.com).

Chapter 17

HIGH TECH FOR THE EXTERNAL BORDER

Ralf Homann and Manuela Unverdorben

'High Tech for the External Border' is based on a radio documentary by Ralf Homann and our collaborative art-based research project The Better Think Tank Project – BTTP. The radio documentary 'High Tech for the External Border' was aired by German Radio ARD in a podcast for deep investigative approaches. The global border security market is prospering, and BTTP is always at the pulse of time! High Tech for the External Border deals with the externalization and outsourcing of border control from national governments to private firms. The absurdity of this concept is emphasized by using voices and quotes from the key actors. These actors are profiting from migration control and technologized borders but only as long as this form of officially unauthorized migration will continue as a threat to national security. In this respect, we can pose the question: does the European border regime conform more to the economic demands of a border security industry than a border police requirement or a humanitarian request?

Whether you are securing an international boundary or securing the perimeter of a facility, being able to remotely monitor a border is important. Because wireless technology can solve some of the challenges inherent in securing a border, wireless networks are increasingly playing a key role in the overall security design system.

Rely on BTTP as your partner in border security!

BTTP was founded in Stockholm in 2006 and is currently based in Munich.
TAKE G4S security check [Setting: Author and two guards]
[Author] Sir, is it possible to go to Security and Policing? [Guard] Do you have a pass? [Author] No [...]
DRONE (UAV) DOWN
'Security and Policing'. One of the world's leading high-level meetings of the security industry. In Farnborough, Greater London. March, 2016.
TAKE G4S security check
[Guard] E-mail? [Author] Yes, I have my email. [Guard] Could you show me the e-mail, please. [Author] Er, no, you mean this code, no, no, I didn't get it. [Guard] You should have it, otherwise you would not be able to get in. [Author] Ah, really?
DRONE UP

242 TOWARD A NEW ART OF BORDER CROSSING

In front of the shuttle bus running between the station and the fair tents, the author is having a discussion with a security guard. His uniform has yellow reflective stripes.

TAKE G4S security check

[Guard] You need to have either your e-mail or your actual badge. [Author] Ah-ja, the badge! Ja. Ja. But the badge, I will pick up there, but I didn't get the e-mail till now.

DRONE DOWN

The organizer of the fair is the government. Farnborough is a traditional site of the British arms industry. The biggest European defence group, BAE Systems, has a headquarters there. Its portfolio includes not only military classics for external defence but also various product offers where internal security is concerned: cyber-security. The industry is adapting. 'Security' is the politically acceptable way of describing something that used to be called defence.

TAKE G4S security check

[Guard] Are you working on a stand? [Author] Yeah, yeah, yeah. [Guard] What stand? [Author] Its, in German it's Jenoptik [Guard] Jenoptik? [Author] Yeah, but I didn't get the [...] [Guard] I'm just gonna need your full name, yeah, your first name and surname [...] You're an exhibitor, yeah? [Author] No, I'm a journalist and want to meet them.

DRONE UP

Farnborough is a good trade fair site for customers in the security industry. It has its own business airport. That would have spared the author the security check on the bus.

DRONE DOWN

The airport apron is right beside the exhibition site. Short and fast access, therefore. The trade fair is like a sort of duty-free shop for all James Bonds, or rather, for everyone named 'Q' worldwide.

ORIGINAL SOUND Max Bank (LobbyControl)

So here we are at the heart of the EU quarter in Brussels. Over here we can see the European Commission, with the central building where President Juncker also presides, the Berlaymont building.

DRONE LEFT

Max Bank. He keeps an eye on what is happening in Brussels for LobbyControl. The Cologne-based organization is committed to transparency in politics.

ORIGINAL SOUND Max Bank (LobbyControl)

If we look up Avenue Cortenbergh from Rond-Point Schuman, that's also where the lobby office of the French arms company Thales is located. A little further back is Europe's biggest employers' association, BusinessEurope. So we actually have a centre of lobbying here, very close to the EU institutions.

DRONE UP

The employee of LobbyControl and the author cross the street, heading over to the Council building. This is where conferences of the EU interior ministers are held. Their daily agendas are divided into work areas: the EU external border, migration, and terrorism.

DRONE DOWN

HIGH TECH FOR THE EXTERNAL BORDER

In the public eye, these separate responsibilities tend to become blurred. Refugees are frequently classed with terrorists, who in turn arrive via the borders. Illegal migration as a 'threat scenario'.

ORIGINAL SOUND Bernd Kasparek (migration researcher)

Historically, when we go back to the 1970s or even earlier, migration was always an issue dealt with, say, by the Federal Ministry of Labour and Social Affairs. Migration was primarily seen as a question of work, a question of social integration. That's where it belonged. Then in the 80s, we suddenly saw it being shifted to the interior ministries. And that's actually the main modus operandi in the EU today. All migration issues, all border issues and all asylum issues are discussed by the Council of Interior Ministers and decided there.

DRONE LEFT

Bernd Kasparek. The Munich-based mathematician and migration researcher is the founding editor of the first-ever journal in the German-speaking countries for migration and border regime research. The scientific journal appears online and is open-source.

ORIGINAL SOUND Bernd Kasparek (migration researcher)

And then, of course, there's Schengen too, which basically invents a European external border for the first time – before then, no one had any notion of a European external border, each member state had its own ones of course. And in 1985, they threw it all together and said they would now construct a common territory with a common border, and that its protection was a shared responsibility.

DRONE UP

The most important German EU external borders are the airports. For example, the major hubs of Frankfurt or Munich. That is where the Federal Republic assumes its share of responsibility for border policing.

DRONE RIGHT

More precisely: it discarded all responsibility long ago and placed it in private hands. The legal processes here are called 'carrier sanctions'. The sanctions punish airlines that fly irregular passengers into Europe and burden companies with possible deportation costs.

ORIGINAL SOUND Bernd Kasparek (migration researcher)

This entry check on whoever is authorized to enter the European Union has been carried out at airports outside Europe for a long time now. At the airport in Nairobi, say. These carrier sanctions compel refugees to take the dangerous land route, on foot or by bus, or in small ships, because there's basically no other way of crossing the European frontier.

AMBIENCE airport

OVER

DRONE RIGHT

The carrier sanctions are currently focusing migration paths on Greece and Italy.

DRONE DOWN

Are carrier sanctions the reason why the Mediterranean has become a mass grave? Off Lesbos and Lampedusa? The Pope travelled there – and the enlightened West is averting its gaze.

DRONE UP

When the EU external border gets discussed, this usually refers merely to the green land border or the blue sea border. Regions that can handle a lot of armoured equipment: Drones, offshore sensors and satellite monitoring.

DRONE RIGHT

If this unmanned technology turns out to be inadequate for defence against refugees, then warships arrive, or Frontex follows with new coastguard forces.

DRONE LEFT

The EU external border: Munich Airport. The author meets a group of young scientists. The thesis of the research group:

QUOTE research group

In the field of border policy in particular, with its current focus on technologisation and militarization, organized lobby interests are in full swing. Especially from the defence and security industry.

AMBIENCE UP

DRONE LEFT

The scientists want to oppose militarization of the border with their militant research.

DRONE LEFT

The term comes from the Italian and French. Militant there means activist. Not research on behalf of the state, nor of industry, but from below. Field research for a genuine debate on the benefits and risks of EU policy.

AUTHOR

Who ultimately stands to gain financially from this fixation on the EU's external border as a territorial boundary around an area?

ORIGINAL SOUND research group [voice distorted]

The smugglers, clearly, are the major beneficiaries, and they're not even being taxed [...].

DRONE UP

Pending the outcome of its investigations, the research group wants to remain anonymous.

ORIGINAL SOUND research group [voice distorted]

[...] and then there's the military-industrial technology complex in Europe. Clearly. So, it involves billions. And that's just for starters.

DRONE UP

Farnborough, near London. The author is still standing in front of the shuttle bus to the Security and Policing trade fair.

TAKE G4S control

How yer doin' Rachel, it's Dillon here from G4S. I've got another gentleman here with no e-mail or badge, he says, he's went to working on one of the stands. So I just wanna confirm with you his name?

DRONE AHEAD

The guard is making a phone call, because of the author's accreditation. The guard is from G4S. The world's largest private security provider. They work in 120

HIGH TECH FOR THE EXTERNAL BORDER

countries: security and surveillance services, money transporters, and security at major events such as the Olympic Games in London. But they also manage police stations and run privatized prisons.

TAKE G4S security check

It's Ralf, Homann, R-A-L-F, no, it's a-l-f, yeah, and then it's Homann, it's H-O-M [pause] A-N-N.

DRONE UP

The G4S Group accepts jobs from European border management: during his deportation from England by the G4S, Jimmy Mubenga died. That was in 2010. The British Home Office promptly withdrew from the private deportation agreement.

Since 2014, the G4S has organized the deportation centre in Vordernberg, for the Austrian state. The monthly transfer to G4S: Nearly half a million euros. Contract period: 15 years.

TAKE G4S security check

OK. Wonderful!

DRONE UP

The guard steps back, and gestures towards the door of the shuttle bus to the technology trade fair 'Security and Policing'. The author is given back his permit.

TAKE G4S security check

[Author] Thank you very much. [Guard] Hi. [Steps, change in ambience from outside to inside the bus]

OVER

DRONE RIGHT

In Farnborough, the future of the European external border becomes visible. The full range:

DRONE UP

Smart software solutions, highly complex radio and communication technology, the latest drones, and satellite radio and radar technology are required for their remote control – detectors for the fluoroscopy of shipping containers all the way to bulk detection of car number plates. Ground sensors, night-vision goggles and body scanners. The very best in high technology – absolutely anything that promises security along the border.

DRONE RIGHT

There's only one thing that Farnborough appears not to be offering: simple barbed wire.

DRONE UP

The Spanish ESF, the European Security Fencing, has no stand at the fair. It is the main producer of NATO wire. Those are the fences with the razor blades.

ORIGINAL SOUND Bernd Kasparek (migration researcher)

There's a popular concept of what the border's like, it has a lot to do with fences, or with security architecture, along with barriers, and of course always the border guards, the border police, exercising their sovereignty there, and making a very clear distinction between inside and outside. But when you actually look at the

European external border, you see that this concept was abandoned as early as 2005 by the institutions that think ahead.

DRONE AHEAD

Bernd Kasparek. Migration researcher.

ORIGINAL SOUND Bernd Kasparek (migration researcher)

And meanwhile, the border itself in Europe has become very different indeed. The border relies an incredible amount on databases, for example. That means that long before anyone reaches the border post that most people imagine, the border check has long since been carried out at some server farm or other – in Strasbourg, for example – using computer algorithms that determine whether an entry permit can be issued or not.

AMBIENCE European Parliament, Bruxelles

OVER

DRONE UP

Brussels. European Parliament. Block F. This is where decisions are made about EU research and development projects. Since 2009, 21 border management projects have been funded – for example, by the current research framework program 'Horizon 2020'. The scope of Horizon 2020 is roughly 80 billion euros. For example, for subsidies that attract more funds. Both private and state funds. Such as subsidies for the EU program Copernicus.

DRONE RIGHT

Europe's eye on the globe. Satellites for more knowledge about what is happening on the planet. Air quality data in Europe, for example, or the melting of the polar ice caps. These are examples of the civilian use of the Copernicus programme. Military use is possible too. This is a so-called 'dual-use technology' – an elegant way of circumventing the old distinction between unpopular military research and publicly acceptable civil research.

AMBIENCE UP

DRONE UP

Before it was renamed, Copernicus was called GMES: Global Monitoring for Environment and Security.

DRONE DOWN

The author leaves the lift in Block F and walks past some ornamental plants:

DRONE AHEAD

There are programmes – such as Copernicus, for example, from the European Union – which appear to be in place for climate protection but are also used for border surveillance. Is this some kind of marketing strategy – an easier way of selling something to the population by saying that it also helps the environment?

ORIGINAL SOUND Ska Keller (MEP)

I'm more inclined to see it this way: some of these monitoring projects were first established with just a relatively neutral or positive aim. Involving environmental monitoring, for instance, or checks on illegal fishing. Satellite data are used for that too. And then someone notices, hey, we want to monitor the borders too, and we also need to see which refugees are sitting inside which boats. And don't we have

HIGH TECH FOR THE EXTERNAL BORDER

those satellites that we actually wanted to use for checks on illegal fishing – so why don't we use those?

DRONE AHEAD

Ska Keller. Member of the European Parliament

She is Vice-President and Migration Policy Spokesperson for the group of the Greens/European Free Alliance.

ORIGINAL SOUND Ska Keller (MEP)

We see this trend not only with satellites and monitoring but also with databases. We can see there's a huge expansion. First, it's only about a small group and a small target, and then it gets successively expanded.

AUTHOR

So, who benefits from such a huge volume of data, and from the enrichment of that data?

ORIGINAL SOUND Ska Keller (MEP)

The beneficiaries are companies with the capacity to actually manage databases of that size, and also the very people who manufacture the devices to produce these databases. Those could be fingerprint devices – or now, for this so-called Smart Borders package, they need so-called ABC gates – those are the border kiosks that can already be seen at numerous airports.

DRONE ASTERN

In Germany, ABC, the Automated Border Control, is known as 'EasyPass'. The market leader is the Federal Printing Office in Berlin. It has long been a big player in the border business. In April 2016 it secured frontier clearance in Morocco.

DRONE UP

Throughout Europe, the EasyPass reader terminals from the Federal Printing Office and the ABC kiosks by other manufacturers are supposed to directly access the Schengen Information System SIS in Strasbourg. It is useful for manhunts.

Further databases are about to be launched: The 'exit-entry' system is aimed at the data acquisition of all authorised border crossings at the EU external border. So that means at least 650 million border movements.

ORIGINAL SOUND Ska Keller (MEP)

If we now equip all airports, all external borders in all European member states plus the Schengen states with border machines like those, and there are so many of them, and they need to be serviced and all the rest – well, that is a seriously major stimulus package.

AUTHOR

A stimulus package for the security industry?

ORIGINAL SOUND Ska Keller (MEP)

Exactly.

AMBIENCE airport

DRONE UP

The author meets the research group again.

DRONE DOWN

248   TOWARD A NEW ART OF BORDER CROSSING

As a first step, the scientists try to clarify the cash flows within European border management. Which of the EU budget funds are responsible for border security? Which ones are for refugee policy? And which companies and organizations get the money?

AMBIENCE UP

DRONE UP

What is the source, for example, of the quarter-of-a-billion-euro annual budget for the EU border agency Frontex? What is the money used for? How are the roughly two billion euros for the Schengen database SIS financed? Or the quarter of a billion euros for EUROSUR – Frontex's border surveillance system?

ORIGINAL SOUND research group [voice distorted]

There's no border without a border crossing. The moment we have a border, we can assume that it will be crossed. The border is always a passage, and always designed as such.

DRONE DOWN

Illegal border crossings in Europe in 2015, the year of the so-called 'welcome culture': 1.8 million. That is nearly three per mil of all border crossings. Billions are being spent on that tiny fraction.

DRONE DOWN

Are these only snowflakes on the tip of the iceberg? EUROSUR alone will continually require updates for its control centres, along with new space-based communications, and better drones [...]

ORIGINAL SOUND Matthias Monroy (German Parliament)

However, it must be said that Frontex also processes private satellite data. And the large defence firms have satellites in orbit themselves that they market – or they also enter into joint ventures and participate in public programmes with their own funds, in return receiving the licence for evaluation of the resulting data, that is, for sale of the resulting data, for the next ten, twenty or thirty years, depending.

DRONE UP

Matthias Monroy. The Berliner writes for the police-critical magazine 'Bürgerrechte und Polizei' (Civil Rights and the Police) about surveillance and data protection and is a research associate of the Left parliamentary group in Germany's Bundestag.

ORIGINAL SOUND Matthias Monroy (German Parliament)

The increasing digitalisation of policing is happily equated with looking for a needle in a haystack – in the old days when things were analogue, the haystack was carried off so that the needle could be found, whereas now the routine seems to be that we enlarge the haystack with as much data as we can gather, and then try and give it a structure using statistical methods, that is algorithms, and then make things easier for police officers on the basis of that data.

DRONE UP

The Munich migration researcher Bernd Kasparek and the author walk past a bar with a coffee machine. Hanging from a nail on the wall is a large, old school map, with a black wooden rod at the top and bottom of it, enclosing the printed canvas in between.

HIGH TECH FOR THE EXTERNAL BORDER

ORIGINAL SOUND Bernd Kasparek (migration researcher)
This map dates from 1958 and is entitled 'Paths to European Unity'. And it gives us quite a good idea of how things were back then – almost sixty years ago actually – and of how things were envisaged at that time.

AUTHOR
On this beautiful teaching map on the wall, "Paths to European Unity', Ireland still wasn't a member of the European Community, or whatever it was called back then. However, today, Dublin is a very important keyword in the European Union's migrant policy. What role does the so-called Dublin Regulation play?

ORIGINAL SOUND Bernd Kasparek (migration researcher)
The regulation refers of course to deportation within Europe. If the person has an interest in preferring to apply for asylum in Germany and being granted it there, it's obvious that the person won't necessarily say that they entered via Greece. Then little tricks were developed – roaming messages on mobile phones, for example. 'Welcome to Vodafone Greece'. But that doesn't scale, as they say, these days, it's not universally applicable. That's why in 2003, together with Dublin Two, they decided on the so-called Eurodac regulation and also implemented it. Eurodac is the big Europe-wide database in which the fingerprints of all asylum-seekers, and anyone apprehended at the border, get stored. And by using fingerprints – and this is the reason why fingerprints play such a major role in the whole Dublin issue – they can now prove, aha, the person was picked up five months ago on the Turkish–Greek border, in other words, Greece is responsible.

DRONE UP
Connected to the Eurodac management database are the so-called hotspots, with their fingerprint capture terminals. The hotspots are mobile management facilities. They track the various routes taken by refugees across the EU's external border. If data collection at these key collection points for refugees fails to function, the Schengen system is 'suspended'.

DRONE DOWN
The result: a huge fuss about the external border. Checks and traffic jams at long-forgotten internal borders, barbed wire, and military action. Talk of an emergency situation, and of borders having to be made secure. Laws are being tightened. And the market for border technology is booming.

ORIGINAL SOUND Ska Keller (MEP)
Refugees are not a security issue. The problem is when the registration process is not thorough enough, or when the asylum procedure takes too long – and of course with inclusion, too, and that again is a social issue.

DRONE UP Ska Keller. Member of the European Parliament.

ORIGINAL SOUND Ska Keller (MEP)
Uncertainty only really arises when refugees are obliged to arrive irregularly, because there is no other way, and a normal border check cannot be carried out. That's why legal entry would be desirable, also for reasons of security.

AMBIENCE airport
DRONE UP

TOWARD A NEW ART OF BORDER CROSSING

At a German European Union external border once more. The author meets the militant research group.

DRONE RIGHT

Who blocks legitimate travel routes – a humanitarian visa, for instance? Who benefits from rigid adherence to the escape routes across the Mediterranean?

QUOTE research group

The operation as well as the development and use of new border defence technologies require a significant financial commitment. All of these developments are very expensive.

ORIGINAL SOUND research group [voice distorted]

Well, the first big suitability tests, practicability tests, and also tests to check the acceptance of such technological interventions in the everyday lives of the general population, as it were – historically, those tests have always been carried out on minorities.

QUOTE European Commission

Over the past ten years, the volume of the global security market has increased almost tenfold – from around 10 billion euros to about 100 billion euros in 2011, whereby annual sales in the EU amounted to about 30 billion euros. In light of recent market developments, however, there are signs that the global market shares of European companies could experience a significant drop over the next few years, insofar as no measures are taken to improve their competitiveness.

DRONE UP

Commission proposal for a programme to promote growth in the security industry. Brussels, July 30, 2012.

QUOTE European Commission

European companies still number among the world's leading players in the security market. The creation of favourable internal-market conditions and a strengthening of the position of the EU security industry in emerging markets are prerequisite for maintaining and extending its technological lead.

AMBIENCE Demonstration outside British Home Office

OVER

TAKE Demonstration outside the British Home Office

Today they've invited 350 arms and security companies to talk to 79 delegations from some of the worst countries in the world. Places like Saudi Arabia, Bahrain and Qatar to buy policing and security products.

OVER

DRONE UP

Demonstration outside the British Home Office.

Against the government trade fair for 'Security and Policing'. Candles are burning in the square, with banners hanging beside them. Slogan: 'They don't make us safer' – 'Their security is not our security'. Signs protesting against the arms trade.

A light drizzle.

TAKE Demonstration outside the British Home Office

HIGH TECH FOR THE EXTERNAL BORDER

You can be executed in Saudi Arabia, for protesting the government. And people have been.

DRONE RIGHT

The biggest customer for British defence and security products is the Kingdom of Saudi Arabia. German know-how has been in demand there for a long time now. For example, in 2007, the German Federal Police began training Saudi border guards. That was followed in 2008 by EADS-Cassidian, today Airbus, selling border technology. According to press reports, the order was worth at least two billion euros; later, the magazine Handelsblatt reported more than three billion. In 2011, official assistance arrived from the German army to integrate German drone technology into the Saudi border security system.

ORIGINAL SOUND Max Bank (LobbyControl)

[sound of roller suitcase] Now we already have a far better view of the European Parliament, and we're also approaching the Solvay Library, which is actually a very short distance away from the Parliament building.

DRONE UP

The two people pass a park – the Park Leopold. In the middle is a pond, and a sports ground. Shimmering through the mighty trees is the windowed façade of the European Parliament. On a small rise, the author and Max Bank arrive at an Art Nouveau building.

AUTHOR

Library – is that an actual library containing books then?

ORIGINAL SOUND Max Bank (Lobby Control)

The Solvay Library was a library with books once, yes. The key thing is that lobbyists reside here as well, including the think-tank Security and Defence Agenda – a kind of exchange forum if you like between arms lobbyists and policy-makers. Such think tanks often organize events both inside and outside Parliament – for instance, in the library we're now standing in front of. A fine building for receptions, to bring lobbyists together. It's always very pleasant of course – a think-tank is considered as something neutral, aimed merely at stimulating discourse and initiating political discussion.

QUOTE: Brussels. October 13, 2014.

Dear Trade Commissioner Malmström,

The CEO of Airbus Group, Mr Tom Enders, will be arriving in Brussels on the morning of November 6. On his behalf, I would like to ask you politely for an appointment.

The European Union is extremely important to us and we actively support European policy, in projects such as Copernicus, Galileo and SESAR.

Mr Enders would be honoured to welcome you to the annual reception of the Airbus Group at the Bibliothèque Solvay. We have already sent your office an invitation in this regard.

DRONE UP

Letter from the Brussels office of the Airbus Group to a Member of the European Commission; Online publication by the European Commission under the reference number 3397972.

DRONE UP

Think tanks form networks. And at the end of 2014, the think-tank 'Security and Defence Agenda' was integrated into the think-tank 'Friends of Europe'. Also linked with the 'Friends of Europe' was the so-called 'Group of Personalities' (GoP).

ORIGINAL SOUND research group [voice distorted]

The European Commission once wanted a research programme. And for that, they appointed a group of personalities, a group of experts, so to speak. And the majority of its members were people from the defence industry.

DRONE UP

The author skypes with the research group. They have studied the history of the Group of Personalities (GoP). The 28 personalities involved designed the cornerstones of European security research policy. That was in 2003.

ORIGINAL SOUND research group [voice distorted]

You can also see that in the entire research framework program FP7, which ran until 2013, and now in the current research programme 'Horizon 2020': private interest groups were constantly invited to occupy seats within these expert groups, and they actually have a very strong say in what the policies will be like.

DRONE UP

Represented in the group of personalities: EADS, now Airbus, the French company Thales, Spain's Indra, and Italy's Finmeccanica. They provide the ideas for the orders they later receive.

DRONE RIGHT

The main recommendation of the GoP: Politicians should earmark at least one billion euros each year for security research. A further recommendation is a 'European Security Research Advisory Board' (ESRAB).

DRONE UP

Which was duly established on 22 April 2005, following a decision by the European Commission.

QUOTE Frankfurter Allgemeine Zeitung

Equipment suppliers such as Airbus, but also their French rival Thales, are increasingly sensing long-term business opportunities in this sector, and realigning themselves strategically as providers of 'smart systems' for these politically sensitive projects.

DRONE UP Frankfurter Allgemeine Zeitung, 17 February 2016.

DRONE UP

Strategies like these are developed by bodies such as the European Organisation for Security (EOS). The Brussels lobby group with its neutral-sounding name was founded in 2007.

OVER DROWN DOWN

The work of the EOS was entrusted to two working groups: the working group for border surveillance, and the working group Smart Borders. The latter deals with smart border checks at border crossings, the former with monitoring the border between the border crossings.

DRONE UP

HIGH TECH FOR THE EXTERNAL BORDER

The European Organisation for Security (EOS) styles itself as follows:

The members of the Brussels lobby organisation come from 13 European countries. In addition to the major players such as Airbus, Thales, Indra, Finmeccanica and G4S, they include the Fraunhofer VVS, Saab, Edisoft, 3M, Eustema, Almaviva, Altran, Atos, CEA, Centric, Cobalt, Corte, DCNS, Kromek, LArea, Multix, Posteitaliane, Safran, Securitybrokers, Visionware [...]

OVER DROWN DOWN

We believe that a European security industry policy could be a driving force, and for that reason alone, the European security industry deserves a chapter of its own in the forthcoming EU strategy for internal security.

DRONE UP

That is what the EOS propagates, and it has achieved its goal. Internal security as a product of the products in the security industry. A privatized domestic policy.

DRONE RIGHT

The think-tank acts on behalf of its member organizations but also assumes coordination of EU programmes. Here, the EOS is pursuing an objective that amounts to nothing less than the renewal of the continent:

QUOTE EOS

The creation of a single European security market would indeed provide a secure basis and reinforcement for the re-industrialization of Europe.

DRONE UP

The Chairman of the European Organisation for Security, Santiago Roura, on September 29, 2014.

AUTHOR

[car driving past, French voices] There's no doorman, so we could even take a brief look inside, and look at the company nameplates [...]

ORIGINAL SOUND Max Bank (LobbyControl)

Sure, why not. We are now in the Rue Montoyer 10, this is where the European associations of the defence industry are headquartered: The Aerospace and Defence Industry Association of Europe, or ASD for short, a key lobbyist [...]

AUTHOR

And of special interest to me [...]

ORIGINAL SOUND Max Bank [interrupting author]

[...] And the European Organisation for Security, EOS. They're both based here in, yes, the same building. We're six, seven minutes away from the European Parliament. So the EU institutions aren't all that far away from the defence industry. Hmm. Interesting.

DRONE UP E-mail to the press office of the EOS:

QUOTE mail German Radio (BR)

I would very much appreciate an interview with you about the recommendations of the EOS with regard to the development of smart borders, and improvement of migration control.

DRONE UP Answer received from communication management:

QUOTE EOS

Thank you for your inquiry. The EOS does not wish to make any statement on this matter. At the moment we are still working on a common position.

DRONE UP

Later, the author gives the EOS a second opportunity to comment. Yet again, the lobby of the security industry prefers to work under the radar.

DRONE RIGHT

The ideas of the EOS are high-flying ones, however. For example, they circle around the special summit of EU interior ministers on the terrorist attack in Brussels on March 22, 2016.

DRONE UP

Council building. Rond-Point Schuman. The vehicle entrance for state limousines. On his way in, the German interior minister stops in front of German cameras. As a response to the terror attack, he calls for further expansion of the entry-exit system. – That is the procurement contract for Europe-wide detection technology for entry and exit operations.

DRONE DOWN

A good deal, and a part of the Smart Border concept. High-tech at the external border.

ORIGINAL SOUND German Federal Interior Minister

We have separate data resources for travel, migration and security. It is imperative that, in the interests of safety, we should be able to link these data. To do that, we need changes in the law, and we also need technological solutions. I urge the Commission to make a proposal in this regard without delay. And we also need an entry-and-exit register, so that we can detect all those who enter the Schengen area as third-country nationals and then leave again.

DRONE DOWN

In front of the television cameras, it's a pretty impressive call to action. But it remains illogical.

DRONE UP

The terrorists from Brussels and Paris did not enter from outside. They were EU citizens. They grew up here.

DRONE DOWN

So why post intelligence at the border, if there is far more need of it locally?

ORIGINAL SOUND Ska Keller (MEP)

I also find it striking, especially with the Smart Borders package, that it just doesn't help with any known problems. I mean, if we collect the data of everyone who crosses the border, that won't help us – it won't help us prevent crime, or terrorism.

DRONE UP Ska Keller. Member of the European Parliament.

ORIGINAL SOUND Ska Keller (MEP)

Originally, the Commission said it was important for us to be able to find out who was staying for longer than allowed. And that's true – then we know for instance that John Smith did not leave the country as planned after three months unless he just happened to be at a border crossing where the machine wasn't working or whatever else. But where is he then? Even if I want to deport him, I can't find him.

HIGH TECH FOR THE EXTERNAL BORDER

And if John Smith now commits a terrorist attack, then I know where he crossed the border, but that knowledge didn't help me at all. That's why it's completely unclear what problem if any this Smart Borders solution is addressing.

TAKE Demonstration Home Office

[Speaker] What starts here? What starts here? Repression starts here [Chorus]: Let's stop it here. [Speaker] What starts here! [Chorus] Let's stop it here [Speaker] Repression starts here [Chorus] Let's stop it here. [Speaker] Together we can stop war and repression at the source [...]

OVER

DRONE UP

A typical red London bus briefly blocks our view. The author stays at the edge of the demonstration, talks, rummages in his sports bag, and pulls out a microphone with the blue ARD logo on it.

ORIGINAL SOUND Wael Kassim (Speaker)

On the one hand, we see that the state wants nothing more to do with search and rescue operations at sea. We've had to experience the cutting back of search and rescue operations, such as those carried out by the coastguard or the armed forces in Europe. On the other hand, we're seeing an unconditional willingness to privatize tasks on the external and internal borders. And it's lobbying that ensures that new areas are contracted out to private security firms.

DRONE UP Wael Kassim.

Speaker at the demonstration outside the British Home Office against the government trade fair for Security and Policing.

ORIGINAL SOUND Wael Kassim (Speaker)

I'm from a campaign called 'Defend the Right to Protest'. The sort of lobbying I'm talking about doesn't just take place here in the UK, but also when our politicians accompany private security firms on trips to various countries around the world, and then sell the products side by side with them in Saudi Arabia or Qatar, for example.

AUTHOR

What influence do the security industry or companies in the security industry have on European Union policy?

ORIGINAL SOUND Ska Keller (MEP)

I'd say that security companies have a great influence on policy. It all starts with them organising conferences on security issues, where politicians invite guests and the companies are there too and demonstrate their products, for example. And those are the networks. Or [...]

DRONE UP Ska Keller. Member of the European Parliament.

ORIGINAL SOUND Ska Keller (MEP)

[...] Or: Frontex holds conferences that are all about how we can use drones. That has nothing whatsoever to do with basic rights or human rights.

QUOTE EOS

In 2016, Frontex 2016 will be organizing joint days of action for the first time: one on the territorial EU external border in the Western Balkans, and a further one on the external borders at airports.

DRONE UP From the event overview of EOS.

QUOTE EOS

Frontex has also invited the industry to attend three workshops, in September, October and December 2016 respectively.

ORIGINAL SOUND Bernd Kasparek (migration researcher)

Yes, but that would presuppose that one accepts that these migrations take place. Then you could formulate a policy for example, and say, okay, how can we as a society handle migration? But we're nowhere near that stage as yet.

AMBIENCE airport

OVER

DRONE UP

On the German EU external border. Munich Airport. The author meets the militant research group.

It seems that they have reached their scientific limits. Confusing contracts, unofficial bodies, and a lack of neutral observers. No concrete results.

ORIGINAL SOUND research group [voice distorted]

Put it this way: The border and migration control technologies have always been areas of technological application where the aspect of democratic control was minimal.

AMBIENCE Farnborough S & P Fair

OVER

DRONE UP

Farnborough. Greater London. Cramped stands at the trade fair covering only two square metres each, and more representative ones with far more space. VIP lounge atmosphere. Violet carpeting, blue partition screens.

A private dining room for relaxed informal meetings.

At the back of the exhibition tents, is a special zone for the future of the border.

DRONE DOWN

Know what will happen. Fresh high-tech products will soon be demanded by politicians. To make the border safer still. A comfortable business model. The current refugee crisis is facilitating sales, says Airbus. That would be Stand F39. The Italian Finmeccanica, doing good business keeping out Libyan refugees, would be Stand D42.

DRONE (UAV) UP

The author walks around two advertising islands, with trade fair gimmicks piled high on them. Paper bags bearing the logo 'Security and Policing'. He joins the queue for the cloakroom. Mr. S. from G4S addresses the author:

TAKE G4S Farnborough

[Mr. S] Sorry, can I just have a word with you […] it says here, that you do broadcasting, and [Author] Ya, Yes. [Mr. S] No media are allowed in the show. So. [Author] Ah. [Mr. S] This is a general regulation? [Mr. S] Yeah. [Author] No media? [Mr. S] No media at all. [Author] Also, if we do not publish something?

[Mr. S] No. No media at all. I'm afraid, I have to take your badge back from you, because you [...]

OVER

CLOSING TITLES AND CREDITS

aired by German Radio (BR, WDR, SWR, NDR, RB) in 2016, shortlisted as a German contribution to Prix Europa (section current affairs); rebroadcasting by Deutschlandradio Kultur, Berlin 2020.

Chapter 18

JOURNEYS AND MYTHS: TRANSCENDING BOUNDARIES IN AMITAV GHOSH'S *GUN ISLAND*

Amrita Satapathy and Panchali Bhattacharya

A traveler, unlike the tourist, goes beyond the confines of boundaries. These boundaries can be actual or metaphorical, or more or less man-made constructs—some geopolitical, some social, and some psychological. Hence, the very act of traveling or crossing borders and traversing boundaries is often related to meaning-making. It becomes a site where multiple semantic possibilities are produced, giving access to various ways of thinking and interpretation. The idea of crossing boundaries and borders, for that matter, can have several inferences—from visiting, learning to relocating to challenging its stifling and limiting sociopolitical agendas and agencies. As Culbert (2019: 346) puts it, travel reflects "both powerful vested interests and myriad alternative possibilities of resistance and contestation." Social scientists and geographers (cultural and political) are of the view that borders since they also create differences, are more like processes because they help us to understand how the differences, thus created, are established and renegotiated. In his essay, "Boundaries, Inequalities, and Legitimacies: A Conceptual Framework for Border Studies Collaboration," Bernd Bucher (2018: 12) sees, "borders and boundaries as a process, rather than as any kind of static entities, they are never ontologically implicated, that is, they do not begin by merely 'existing' as entities, rather, they are continuously drawn and redrawn: in a constant state of becoming over time, they in fact precede nation states." Andrew Abbott (2001: 263) further elaborates this idea by pertinently commenting, "These points us towards boundaries and borders as processes (rather than stable and natural things) that constitute and relate 'things' as functions of their performance: 'Social entities [...] come into existence when social actors tie social boundaries together in certain ways. Boundaries come first, then entities'." It will be useful, at this juncture, to first understand the difference between the two terms,

> The border is a political concept, which identifies the territorial limits of the state and beyond where movement is limited to those with the necessary permits and documents. The boundary is a looser term, which signifies the territorial margins of the state, reflecting other social and ethnic characteristics of the population on either side. (Newman 2017: 1)

260 TOWARD A NEW ART OF BORDER CROSSING

In a globalizing world, the idea of travel, borders, and boundaries is often a hybrid one. With an increase of disruptions in lives on the borders, their dislocation, the consequent upsurge of intrusions, the nomadic state of humanity in the fringes, and the rising precarity of human lives, terms like "romantic," "escape," "imaginative" to travel is no more applicable. And in a society prone to a constant state of flux, the idea of journeying across borders, the immobility and stability of these borders and boundaries is certainly not a straitjacketed one. There has now come into existence a space called "transition zones," where there is a "straddling both sides of the boundary where peoples from both sides can interact as part of the border opening process, and where, over long periods of time, ethnic and political hybridity may emerge." (Newman 2017: 1). Similarly, myth, mythical tales, and legends have the capacity to offer multitudinous interpretations of this state of in-betweenness. Myths are essentially theories of culture, of the mind, and hence the society: "Myth is essentially a cultural construct, a common understanding of the world that binds individuals and communities together" (Pattanaik 2003: xiv), and may be read symbolically because in many cultures and societies, myth, folktales, and legends represent either natural phenomena or human attributes because myths, as Susan Stanford Friedman states, can represent "a polylogue of languages, cultures, viewpoints, and standpoints" (2010: 494). Also, "myth concerns the human experience of the world, not to say the deepest anxieties experienced in the world [...]" (Segal 2015: 104). Where transition zones and myth overlap, we find a form of shared space, which holds multiple possibilities of resolutions of oppositions. When coalesced with the idea of a journey, the meaning-making becomes more cyclical in nature than linear. Moreover, the meaning-making becomes recurrent rather than progressive (Segal 2015: 105).

As a process, myth involves rationality. Similarly, borders and boundaries, as processes possess an inherent plurality and multidimensionality, rendering the space fragile and unstable. This instability of borders and boundaries becomes obvious, as Kate Roy suggests, due to the involvement of different actors, states, individuals, and literary and artistic works. These variables are contributing to the shaping and reshaping of the idea of borders and boundaries yet again. Borders and boundaries are no more fixed and solid, they are rather, fluid, and permeable-

> What was some time ago dubbed (erroneously) 'post-modernity' and what I've chosen to call, more to the point, 'liquid modernity', is the growing conviction that change is the only permanence, and uncertainty the only certainty. A hundred years ago 'to be modern' meant to chase 'the final state of perfection'—now it means an infinity of improvement, with no 'final state' in sight and none desired. (Bauman 2012: xiii–ix)

According to Van Houtum and Naerssen, borders are now dynamic in nature. They are no more,

> [...] ordering, othering and negotiating difference: The process through which borders are demarcated and managed are central to the notion of border as process and border as institution. [...] Demarcation is not simply the drawing of a line on a map or the construction of a fence in the physical landscape. It is the process through which borders are constructed and the categories of difference or separation created. (Van Houtum & Naerssen 2002: 35)

The concept of "transition zones" is illustrated powerfully in Amitav Ghosh's *Gun Island* (2019). On one level we see people from various cultures, nations, and nationalities, crisscrossing across borders and countries, crossing over, and straddling boundaries to form new modes of interactions and forging new identities. On the other level, we have the mythical tale of the Gun Merchant which literally becomes a synonym for the concept of shared space. Myths symbolically represent the shared space positing a reconciliation or mediation of issues. Myth precisely tempers a contradiction 'dialectically,' by providing either a mediating middle term or an analogous, but more easily resolved contradiction. (Segal 2015: 101). In other words, myths most often thrive in borderlands, where cultures, languages, and traditions converge. These liminal spaces can foster the development of unique hybrid identities and narratives. By exploring borderland myths, people can appreciate the richness of cultural exchange and challenge rigid notions of national or cultural boundaries.

It can be argued at this juncture that Amitav Ghosh's *Gun Island* illustrates two aspects. Firstly, the "permeability between genuine and fictional travel," as said by Matthew Coneys (2018: 363) in his analysis of late medieval travel writing like Mandeville's or Marco Polo's. And secondly, the novel demanding "[...] not so much an erasure of the boundaries as a complex narrative negotiation with textual traditions and readerly expectations of verisimilitude and fiction." (Culbert 2019: 348). The inclusion of the mythical motif of the *Bonduki Sadagar* or the Gun Merchant, into the fabric of the narrative heightens this aspect. Borders and boundaries are constantly under reaffirmation and negotiation. We see this exemplified and brought to life through the characters in the novel—in Dinanath Datta or Deen, the rare book dealer; the pair of teenage boys—Tipu and Rafi (denizens of the Sundarbans); Piya Roy, an Indian American professor of marine biology; and the vivacious Professor Giacinta Schiavon, an internationally acclaimed scholar in History. All of them are travelers "investigating the fraught and ambiguous boundaries between the life and the text, fiction and veracity, the personal and the political." (Culbert 2019: 344). The journey motif in *"Gun Island"* is multifaceted and serves as a powerful vehicle for exploring mythic, environmental, and cultural themes. Deen's physical and spiritual odyssey drives the novel's plot forward while highlighting the interconnectedness of human lives and the impact of storytelling on shaping our understanding of the world. The characters go a long way to prove that if a traveler is restricted by such a border or boundary, the process of meaning-making stops altogether because no more is there a finality or fixity to it. As noted, travel writer Pico Iyer informs in his essay, "Why We Travel?" (2000), "And we travel to fill in the gaps [...]" Travelling is thus metaphorical in nature; one must sense a place in order for it to evoke experiences and "[...] to bring what little we can, in our ignorance and knowledge [...]" (Iyer, 2000). This intertwining of the traveler's experience and its myriad interpretations has made possible the understanding of the complexities and the homogeneity of the postmodern world's mobility and interconnectedness. This enables the traveler to sense the porosity that underlies borders and boundaries, thereby turning the exercise of going beyond it into a quest for not just the unknown, but the unknowing thus familiarising one with situations that he/she would normally ignore. It will not be fallacious to state that crossing borders and boundaries is not so much an anathema at this juncture of time, having moved beyond its conventional nomenclature, i.e., physical, and geographical. Although applied to the tourist gaze, the idea of the novel as a 'global hybrid' holds credibility since Amitav Ghosh has used "an assemblage of technologies, texts, images, social practices and so on, that together enable it to expand and to reproduce itself across the globe." (Urry & Larsen 2011: 28). Borders, boundaries, and margins are no longer impenetrable territories or inactive contact zones. Rather they are permeable spaces of interaction that continuously shape and reshape events, communities, and identities in the global sociopolitical arena. In these contemporary times, it defines our lives in ways more than one. It can bring myriad openings, or it can hint at a suitable closure.

Interestingly, the use of myth and folklore can also assist in the reinterpretation of boundaries, borders, and margins as it forges a vital link between the past, present, and future. Besides, it encourages a more inclusive and compassionate worldview by drawing on the wisdom and insights embedded in these narratives. Through them, individuals and societies can challenge rigid divisions and embrace a more interconnected, borderless understanding of humanity and the world we inhabit. The application of this trope can enable a deeper understanding of how the once-tight limits of borders and boundaries are being revised. The function of myth and folklore is to present alternative ways of thinking. They act as narratives of enquiry. As narratives of enquiry, they show ways by which the rigidity of borders and boundaries can be transcended. And this is enunciated subtly by the boatman who informs Nilima di that, legends and stories "[...] open a world that we cannot see" (Ghosh 2019: 17). When applied to fiction writing, myth and folklore turn the narrative from popular fiction to factual fiction. This hybridization of the novel form has its echoes in the semiotic notion of 'intertextuality' introduced by Julia Kristeva, associated primarily with poststructuralist theorists. Reflecting and concerning itself with the trending phenomena and conditions of contemporary times, stories are blurring the lines between fiction and non-fiction. As Amitav Ghosh states through his character Giacinta Schiavon, a story is never over, it can always reach into the future in a new form. Factual fiction is highly referential in nature as it communicates about possibilities by creating/constructing an imaginary world drawn solely upon facts; thereby, giving the reader the opportunity to discern between the real and the imaginary. Such narratives also use myth and folklore to show how 'the borderscape can be an ambivalent space of both power and resistance' (Schimanski 2015: 41–43, as quoted in Schimanski and Wolfe 2017: 9), because "there is something in them that is elemental and inexplicable" (Ghosh 2019: 127)

Amitav Ghosh's *Gun Island*, using an age-old archetype and folklore, stands at the cusp of fact and fiction, certainly multitasking between the two oeuvres. As a border-crossing narrative, it "depict[s] individuals and communities negotiating with placelessness, language, ethnicity and sexualities in hybridized discourses of resistance and ambivalence." (Rosello & Wolfe 2017: 12). Ghosh tells us about contemporary global crises and phenomena like human migration, climate change, and dying marine eco-system. The novel also becomes a significant meeting point of fiction and reality. Using the twin tropes of travel and myth, the book shows how the lines literally blur and the two intertwine just as they do in our lives, sometimes. This is deftly done through

JOURNEYS AND MYTHS

the exploration of universal boundaries prevalent between fiction and reality and the aesthetics governing the age-old myth/ urban myth dichotomy. This idea is aptly summed by Giancinta Schiavon when she explains,

> In the seventeenth century, no one would ever have said of something that it was "just a story" as we moderns do. At that time people recognized that stories could tap into dimensions that were beyond the ordinary, beyond the human even. They knew that only through stories was it possible to enter the most inward mysteries of our existence where nothing that is truly important can be proven to exist—like love, or loyalty, or even the faculty that makes us turn around when we feel the gaze of a stranger or an animal. Only through stories can invisible or inarticulate or silent beings speak to us; it is they who allow the past to reach out to us. (Ghosh 2019: 127)

Deen, during his flight to Italy, observes, "From that height it was possible to mistake the Venetian lagoon for the Sundarbans." (Ghosh 2019: 147). Venice reminds him of Calcutta. He finds both the places sharing a geophysical and topographical affinity— the estuarine landscape of lagoons, marshes, and winding rivers. The fading of various geographical boundaries becomes more pronounced as each character traverses continents (from India to Bangladesh to the Middle East to America to Europe) effortlessly. Each character's journey reveals the uniformity of the human situation and psyche. The sense of the 'other'—that individual or syndrome on the other side of the border is fast disappearing. Deen's observation that Venice and Varanasi "[...] are like portals in time" reinforces this idea further. The kinship between the two cities for Deen is because, "in both cities, as nowhere else in the world, you become aware of mortality. Everywhere you look there is evidence of the enchantment of decay, of a kind of beauty that can only be revealed by long, slow fading." (Ghosh 2019: 151).

The novel becomes an ideal example of how the normative constructs of borders and boundaries in the twenty-first century can be challenged by presenting a narrative that embraces interconnectedness, fluidity of identity, and shared global challenges. It is just like switching between two states of mind, as Deen mentions. As posited by Kate Roy, borders and boundaries "can crack, they can rupture, and be fuzzy around the edges— there is always 'a degree of movement within [our] border zones'" (Roy 2018: 3). This can be seen as an offshoot of what sociologist and philosopher Zygmunt Bauman terms as "liquid modernity," which emphasizes on the fact of the rapid change that society is undergoing. Liquid modernity has become a sort of metaphor to explain the condition of constant mobility and change in relationships, identities, and the global economy within contemporary society. The coming of age of factual fiction and the blurring of borders and boundaries are in fact a result of constant fragmentation and mixing of styles, genres, narratives, and oeuvres. The use of myth and folklore, especially in factual fiction like *Gun Island* showcases the crossing of boundaries on multifarious levels. As Jopi Nyman points out the 2000's have seen both "a 'cultural turn' in border studies and a 'border turn' in cultural studies." (2021: 5).

Gun Island becomes representative of the hyperreality of borders and boundaries. It is symbolically exemplified through the internet's geo-physical omnipresence— "The Internet is the migrants' magic carpet; it is their conveyor belt. It does not matter whether they are travelling by plane, or bus or boat: it's the Internet that moves the wetware-it's that simple, Pops" (Ghosh 2019: 61). Tipu's precocious statement defines the idea of going beyond borders and boundaries rightly as something that signifies "spatial distance, marks progress, promises the future" (Bhabha 1994: 6). Tipu and Rafi both prove that rural India is no longer "backward" when it comes to modern gadgets. As Deen corroborates, "[…] in India, as in many other poor countries, there were great numbers of people whose digital skills were completely disproportionate to their material circumstances and formal education." (Ghosh 2019: 85–86).

Weaving myth and folklore into the fabric of its travel narrative, it deals with global issues that often challenge the idea of borders, territories, and boundaries. It can be seen as donning the mantle of a new-age narrative that aids the reader to comprehend the limits of science and technology, the limitlessness of humanity, and the potency of the mythos. It also serves as the perfect vehicle to show how globally humans are grappling with crises like xenophobia, climate change and natural disasters, immigration, and human trafficking. As Homi Bhabha opines in *The Location Culture* (1994), "The wider significance of the postmodern condition lies in the awareness that the epistemological 'limits' of those ethnocentric ideas are also the enunciative boundaries of a range of other dissonant, even dissident histories and voices" (Bhabha 1994: 6). Although from a postmodern point of view, it can be critiqued as championing "mini-narratives which are provisional, contingent, temporary, and relative", providing "a basis for the actions of specific groups in particular local circumstances" (Barry 2017: 88), but the intertextual and hybrid nature of the novel seeks to show how myth, folklore, and legends are powerful "glocalising" forces that foreground the idea of converging and overlapping boundaries and borders—ethically, metaphysically, geographically, linguistically, politically, and socially. As posited aptly by Cinta, "a story is never dead; it is alive and talks about the here and now." She hints at the mobile nature of folktales and stories, that are syncretic in nature and have the ability of going beyond the place of their origin, by undergoing "periodic revivals after long intervals of dormancy" (Ghosh 2019: 7). The narrative hints at the rhizomic nature of borders and boundaries that are constantly in a state of movement and change. The blurring of boundaries and the existence of a shared space across boundaries is further emphasized through the verse—"*Kolkataey tokhon nachhilo lok na makan/ Banglar patanito khonnagar-e-jahan*" [Calcutta had neither people nor houses then/ Bengal's great port was a city-of-the-world] (Ghosh 2019: 16). The idea of "city-of-the-world" becomes the leitmotif of a world that is witnessing the steady merging of boundaries. It hints at the confluence of cultures as well as the limitlessness of glocalization. The shrine of the snake goddess Manasa Devi becomes emblematic of the idea—"the dhaam was revered by all, irrespective of religion: Hindus believed it was Manasa Devi who guarded the shrine, while Muslims believed that it was a place of jinns, protected by a Muslim pir, or saint, by the name of Ilyas." (Ghosh 2019: 15). Ghosh, very subtly brings out the recurrent nature of the myth throughout the narrative to illustrate the blurring of boundaries—imaginary and man-made, political, and geographical, mythical and rational.

JOURNEYS AND MYTHS

Gun Island has an a-linear, multiple, and all-proliferating narrative structure that traverses space and time. It gives us the possibility of perceiving how the peripatetic and mobile nature of the postmodern traveler reinterprets boundaries, center/margins, or limits of borders and boundaries and the subsequent reterritorialization/deterritorialization that they undergo in the present times of liquid modernity. One sees in Deen, Cinta, and Piya, and even Tipu for that matter, the markings of this postmodern being that is caught in "a moment of transit where space and time cross to produce complex figures of difference and identity, past and present, inside and outside, inclusion and exclusion" (Bhabha 1994: 2). Their sense of belongingness lies at an intersection where multiple social boundaries transect. Thus, it proves that the postmodern traveler is culturally hybrid and without settling into a state of primordial polarity. Amitav Ghosh, through his characters and his use of folk narrative, has vividly brought out the liminal nature of the myth that acts as a border-crossing catalytic agent and the postmodern being acquiring the extrinsic quality of mythical deities, who manages to transition "the interstitial passage between fixed identifications." (Bhabha 1994: 5).

For Deen, the protagonist, his life, his identity, and the geographical spaces that define him merge through the legend of the Manasa Devi, The Gun Merchant, and The Gun Island:

> What amazes me in retrospect is not the youthful hubris that allowed me to make these arguments but rather the obtuseness that prevented me from recognizing that the conclusions I had reached in relation to the legend might apply also to the history of its existence in my own memory. I never asked myself whether the legend might have surfaced in my mind because I was myself then living through the most turbulent years of my life: it was a period in which I was still trying to recover from the double shock of the death of a woman I had been in love with, and my subsequent move, by grace of a providential scholarship, from the strife-torn Calcutta of my youth to a bucolic university town in the American Midwest. When at last that time passed it left me determined never to undergo that kind of turmoil again. (Ghosh 2019: 7)

Deen finds himself journeying from India to Los Angeles to Venice, physically and also, each trip becomes for him a voyage down memory lane replete with characters from life and legends. For Deen, just like Chand, the Gun Merchant, life becomes a "fragile resolution" (Ghosh 2019: 6)—an in-between space—inactive and contested, that provides him "the terrain for elaborating strategies of selfhood—singular and communal—that initiate new signs of identity, and innovative sites of collaboration, and contestation, in the act of defining the very idea of society itself." (Bhabha 1994: 2). Contradictorily, through Deen one, sees that "crossings do not always bring answers, nor do they promise resolution." (Roy 2018: 3). Nevertheless, he becomes an embodiment of "the increasingly mobile, because disrupted, nature of academic life; scholars in the corporatized university embody 'nomadic' states that reflect broad economic conditions of displacement and heightened precarity." (Culbert 2019: 346).

Myths and legends have always flouted the laws of geography because the intrinsic porosity of the mythoi form often resonates with the story of the human condition across time and space. In Amitav Ghosh's *Gun Island*, the novel's exploration of myth and migration further exemplifies the porous nature of mythoi, as the protagonist's journey navigates the fluid boundaries of cultures and continents, echoing the universal quest for identity and belonging amidst the complexities of a globalized world. This has been further substantiated through the legend of the *Bondooki Sadagar* or Gun Merchant, the folklore around which Ghosh's narrative revolves. It clearly shows how stories especially folktales often have their connections to times of upheavals and disruption in human history. This is made palpable through one of the seminal characters of the novel, Nilima Bose's reference to legends and how they "may open up a world that we cannot see." (Ghosh 2019: 17). The legend in *Gun Island* tells the tale of a merchant who refuses to obey the goddess of snakes, Manasa Devi, who wants to make him a devotee. As a consequence of this refusal, the goddess pursues him with a series of catastrophes so that he is compelled to flee from the Sundarbans. Even after that, the merchant falls prey to the goddess' wrath when he gets bitten by a poisonous snake and is then held captive by pirates in the *Gun Island*. The merchant finally frees himself only after promising to build a temple for the goddess in his homeland, thereby coming to be popularly known as the *Bonduki Sadagar*.

The legend further cuts across boundaries and finds a strong resonance in Cinta's closing speech at the conference in Los Angeles where she narrates almost a similar tale of a merchant who went to Venice in the seventeenth century. A unique modern interpretation of this folklore describes how the merchant's homeland, in eastern India, got struck by drought and floods brought on by the climatic chaos that occurred back then. He lost everything including his family and decided to travel overseas to Venice to recoup his fortune in trade. The Mediterranean region was experiencing unseasonal weather with ferocious storms and devastating floods back then. When the merchant reached Venice, the city was a haunted place, and "its best days as a commercial power were over [...] this was, after all, the calamitous time of the Little Ice Age." (Ghosh 2019: 220). As a liminal deity, "a crosser of boundaries," the snake goddess, Manasa Devi blurs the border between fact and fantasy as the lore revolving around her reverberates with the Venetian Basilica of Santa Maria della Salute:

> Inside this church, there is a 'gilded icon of a dark-skinned Madonna and Child'. This goddess-like figure surprisingly recalls Manasa Devi in as much as '[s]he is the Black Madonna [...] Madonna the Mediator: it is she who stands between us and the incarnate Earth, with all its blessings and furies'. In a similar way as Manasa Devi, she is an intermediary between human beings and the nonhuman in a certain way, and therefore she has the status of 'Mediator' and is the 'Minoan goddess of snakes.' (Dutrieux 2021: 56)

This porousness of an ancient myth that transcends boundaries thus reveals how myth has the ability to undermine the established belief system that stability, fixity, and emplacement are typical, whereas travel and displacement are considered anomalies. The porousness of boundaries is further substantiated when Rafi narrates how his father once remarked that, "[...] the rivers and the forest and the animals are no longer as they were [...] things were changing so much, and so fast." (Ghosh 2019: 86).

JOURNEYS AND MYTHS

Further, by decoding the myth of *Bonduki Sadagar* in the context of the twenty-first century, it also becomes evident how an old legend has been intertwined carefully by the novelist to show the apocalyptic repercussions of climate change—floods, droughts, famines, and storms. Each layer of this story emerges as an allegory of human hubris and global environmental collapse and shows how, just like a folktale, the fundamental and inextricable connections between human actions and environmental change permeate spatial-temporal boundaries. Ursula Kluwick in her essay, "The global deluge: floods, diluvian imagery, and aquatic language in Amitav Ghosh's *The Hungry Tide* and *Gun Island*" (2020), claims that the tale of the Gun Merchant functions as a review of climate change. It determines the consequences of human reluctance to recognize the underlying and inextricable links between human actions and environmental alterations (Kluwick 2020: 9). Climatic cataclysm is not a thing of the distant future; it is an impending crisis that can potentially eradicate life on earth. Dylan M. Harris notes,

> [...] the way we largely come to know about climate change is through the language of science, but this is not a universal language. Telling stories, however, is a shared experience. Stories make the symbolic visceral, the unknowable known [...] With regards to climate change and our perceived inability to address it, stories—when listened to—provide not only a roadmap for understanding where we are but are also a point of departure from the status quo. (Harris 2020: 312)

The universality of the myth of the Gun Merchant and its relevance in the contemporary geo-political context is thus documented through its inescapable connection with the global climate realities. In her work, Kluwick (2020) pertinently corroborates that in the myth of the Gun Merchant, Manasa Devi, the snake goddess is the incarnation of Mother Earth, and the Merchant represents the entire humanity constantly seeking profit. Driven by the desire to acquire materialistic goods by any means, the entire life of the wealthy *Bonduki Sadagar* exemplifies the absurdity of mankind's obsession with wealth and its pursuit of profits at the cost of wreaking havoc on nature. The connection between the mythical Gun Merchant's global odyssey and the devastation that is being inflicted on the climate throughout the world under the pressure of consumerism attributes a universal appeal to a distinctly local folktale and thus crosses boundaries in more ways than one:

> The legend like a voice from the past reminds the world about, "the limits of human reason and ability become apparent not in the long, slow duration of everyday time, but in the swift and terrible onslaught of fleeting instants of catastrophe". A rereading of the legend in the present times brings out the eco concerns of the Goddess who understands that the driving nature of human beings is "quest for profit." (Gupta 2020: 123)

The novelist shows the legend of the Gun Merchant travel across the globe, from his homeland in eastern India to the Maldive Islands and then to the 'Land of Palm Sugar Candy', 'Land of Kerchieves', '*Gun Island*' and the 'Island of Chains'. As the story unfolds, Deen, with the help of Cinta and Rafi, unravels the mysteries of the legend, only to find that these are historically documented places. The places evoked in the

268   TOWARD A NEW ART OF BORDER CROSSING

legend remind one of the journeys of the refugees like Tipu and Rafi. The Merchant's route thus parallels the places crossed by the migrants.

Human migration, a major theme addressed by Ghosh in *Gun Island*, is considered more than a local issue as it is now premised "on ties to territories and systems that are understood to encompass the planet as a whole" (Heise 2008: 10). Ghosh explores the theme of human migration as a complex and interconnected global issue. By linking individual stories of displacement to broader environmental, economic, and technological forces, he challenges readers to consider migration beyond local contexts and recognize its implications for the entire planet. The novel invites contemplation on the need for a collective response to address the challenges faced by migrants in an increasingly interconnected world. However, there is an element of paradox linked to immigration as far as it involves crossing borders. There is a clear distinction between various categories of refugees—those who migrate within the country and others who cross the geo-political borders. Nonetheless, in the discourse of the migrants, the notion of borders in both categories appears to be futile, and as a consequence, the definition of refugee based on the notion of frontier also seems to be irrelevant since the refugees themselves flout the construct of borders and boundaries. The story of Tipu and Rafi's migration resonates with the predicament of the migrants the world over who seek to "[…] redefine the ways in which "space matters" and borders are crossed or reshaped altogether […]" (Roy 2018: 5). The problematics of borders and boundaries and their intersections thereof are brought to the limelight through Tipu and Rafi's crossing over. Tipu confesses to having crossed borders, particularly the one between India and Bangladesh, without any legal documentation. This disregard for official papers is significant in the journey of migrants, as clearly the validity of these documents can be negotiated in exchange for money: "Who need to spend all that time in government offices? There are easier ways of getting a passport, and if you've got the money, you can choose whichever kind you want" (Ghosh 2019: 64). This theme of the arbitrariness of national boundaries is significant in Ghosh's narrative since he argues that these borders are the result of political decisions (Hawley 2005). In one of his most recent interviews with Raghu Karnad, Ghosh explained how during his research on migrants, he identified the futility of international passports, thereby problematizing the entire idea of border crossing (The Wire 2019: 00:07:32). Nizar Messari (2018) further elaborates on this idea by discovering "how migrants in and of the region of North Africa and the Sahel themselves narrate their 'push and pull' factors and their journeys, and how their resultant narratives (and the commonalities between them) shape their world around them and encourage them to continue 'acting and moving'" (Roy 2018: 5). This idea is also applicable to understand the dilemma of Tipu and Rafi and the porous nature of boundaries and borders. Their story of going beyond the social borders and overstepping the political boundaries highlights the production of inequalities and simultaneously challenges the normative assessment of the legitimacy of their situations. It can also be stated that both become voices for those who have been destabilized, socially, politically, or geographically.

Gun Island has, in the words of John Stephens and Robyn McCallum, "a global or totalizing cultural narrative schema which orders and explains knowledge and experience." (1998: 21). It is a frame narrative incorporating and elucidating other short

JOURNEYS AND MYTHS

narratives within conceptual models that accumulate them all into one holistic account. The juxtaposition of the folklore with the migrants' issue brings into perspective the myriad stories of hope, suffering, hardships, and resilience. In a world that is fraught with ever-increasing displacement and transition, *Gun Island* presents hypothetically a space where the modern and the ancient collide, where the east meets the west, the human and the non-human interact, where the lines between natural and supernatural merge, and where narratives overlap to suggest the possible collapse of all borders and boundaries. Throughout the novel, Deen navigates between belief and skepticism, oscillating between accepting the mythic narratives he encounters and questioning their validity. This internal journey reflects the tension between tradition and modernity, myth, and rationality. Thus, the novel endorses the political scientist Emmanuel Brunet-Jailly's view that "borders are no longer only about territorially bounded authorities" and "they are not just sea and air ports of entry, or border crossing," but "[…] also increasingly virtual or simply impalpable" (Kurkii 2014: 1056). One sees in the broad spectrum of the narrative the intermingling of diverse disciplines also—magic, myth, history, science, zoology, etymology, climate change, global politics and human migration, transcending space, and time. The characters of the book represent a class of people in whom one perceives the amalgamation of the corporeal and the imaginative notion of the margin. They are a set of hybridized individuals with multiple identities coinhabiting a liminal space. Thus, the process of the vanishing of boundaries and borders is further accentuated by the presence of hybrid and mobile entities with a sense of *risveglio* (a kind of awakening) as Cinta points out, who add new scopes and dimensions to the discourse of transcending boundaries. Amitav Ghosh through his book brings to light not only the fluidity of the margins through the mythical, imaginative, and physical crossing of borders and boundaries but also through, as Pico Iyer identifies, "an entirely new breed of people, a transcontinental tribe of wanderers […]" (Urry 2021: 4). *Gun Island* brings to the fore "the authors' benign vision of tolerance and respect in the intercultural encounter ("live and let live") (Culbert 2019: 6). The book can be described as a "complex bundle of coordinated processes" (Bucher 2018: 10), where one sees the vanishing of known and unknown boundaries and reformation of new shared spaces. The novel through its infusion of myth into the narrative brings to the fore the osmotic nature of the journey in a globalized world.

References

Abbott, Andrew. 2001. *Time Matters. On Theory and Method*. Chicago and London: The University of Chicago Press.

Barry, Peter. 2017. *Beginning Theory: An Introduction to Literary and Cultural Theory*. Manchester, UK: Manchester University Press.

Bauman, Zygmunt. 2012. *Liquid Modernity*. UK: Polity Press.

Bhabha, Homi K. 1994. *The Location of Culture*. Oxon: Routledge Classics, Routledge.

Bucher, Bernd. 2018. Boundaries, Inequalities, and Legitimacies (BIL) –. A Conceptual Framework for Borders Studies Collaboration. *Intervalla*, 6: 7–18. https://www.fus.edu/intervalla-files/vol6/2_Bucher_Boundaries_Inequalities_and_Legitimacies.pdf.

Coneys, Matthew. 2018. Travel Writing, Reception Theory and the History of Reading: Reconsidering the Late Middle Ages. *Studies in Travel Writing*, 22(4): 353–370, doi: 10.1080/13645145.2019.1612148.

Culbert, John. 2019. *'Theory and the Limits of Travel', Studies in Travel Writing.* Routledge. https://doi.org/10.1080/13645145.2019.1624072.

Dutrieux, Mathilde. 2021. Climate Change in Amitav Ghosh's *The Great Derangement, The Hungry Tide,* and *Gun Island.* Unpublished MA thesis, Liege University. https://matheo.uliege.be/handle/2268.2/12071.

Friedman, Susan Stanford. 2010, September. Planetarity: Musing Modernist Studies. *Modernism/Modernity,* 17(3), 471–499. http://doi.org/10.1353/mod.2010.0003.

Ghosh, Amitav. 2019. *Gun Island.* India: Hamish Hamilton: Penguin Random House.

Gupta, Shaveta. 2020. Ecocide: A Study of Climate Change in Amitav Ghosh's *Gun Island. Language in India,* 20(5): 115–124.

Harris, Dylan M. 2020. Telling Stories about Climate Change. *The Professional Geographer* 72(3): 309–316. doi: 10.1080/00330124.2019.1686996.

Hawley, John C. 2005. "The Writer, his Contexts, and his Themes". In *Amitav Ghosh: An Introduction.* Cambridge, UK: Cambridge University Press. doi:10.1017/UPO9788175968172.002.

Heise, Ursula K. 2008. *Sense of Place and Sense of Planet: The Environmental Imagination of the Global.* Oxford: Oxford University Press.

Iyer, Pico. 2000. Why We Travel. Pico Iyer Journeys. https://picoiyerjourneys.com/2000/03/18/why-we-travel/

Kluwick, Ursula. 2020. The global deluge: floods, diluvian imagery, and aquatic language in Amitav Ghosh's The Hungry Tide and *Gun Island,* Green Letters, doi: 10.1080/14688417.2020.1752516.

Kurkii, Tuuliki. 2014. Borders from the Cultural Point of View. *Culture Unbound,* 6: 1055–1070. Linköping University Electronic Press: http://www.cultureunbound.ep.liu.se.

Messari, Nizar. 2018. Challenging State-Centered Geopolitics with Migrant Narratives: Reflections on a Moroccan Conversation. *Intervalla,* 6: 60–71. https://www.fus.edu/intervalla-files/vol6/5_Messari_Challenging_State-Centered_Geopolitics_with_Migrant_Narratives.pdf.

Newman, David. 2017. "Borders, boundaries, and borderlands". In *International Encyclopedia of Geography: People, the Earth, Environment and Technology: People, the Earth, Environment and Technology.* Wiley Online Library. 1–13. https://doi.org/10.1002/9781118786352.wbieg1039.

Nyman, Jopi. 2021."Introduction: images and narratives on the border". In Johan Schimanski and Jopi Nyman (eds), *Border Images, Border Narratives: The Political Aesthetics of Boundaries and Crossings.* Manchester: Manchester University Press. https://doi.org/10.7765/9781526146274.00006.

Pattanaik, Devdutt. 2003. *Indian Mythology: Tales, Symbols and Rituals from the Heart of the Subcontinent.* Vermont, USA: Inner Traditions International.

Rosello, Mireille, and Stephen F. Wolfe. 2017. "Introduction". In J. Schimanski and S. F. Wolfe (eds.), *Border Aesthetics: Concepts and Intersections.* New York: Berghahn Books, pp. 1–24.

Roy, Kate. 2018. Introduction: Beyond Borders? Interrogating Boundaries in our Twenty First Century World. *Intervalla,* 6: 1–6. https://www.fus.edu/intervalla-files/vol6/1_Roy_Beyond_Borders_intro.pdf.

Schimanski, Johan, and Stephen F. Wolfe. 2017. *Border Aesthetics: Concepts and Intersections.* New York: Berghahn.

Segal, Robert A. 2015. *Myth: A Very Short Introduction.* Oxford, UK: Oxford University Press.

Stephens, John, and Robyn McCallum. 1998. *Retelling Stories, Framing Culture: Traditional Story and Metanarratives in Children's Literature.* New York: Garland Pub.

The Wire. 2019 Jun 19. *In Venice, I Heard Bangla Everywhere: Amitav Ghosh on 'Gun Island'.* [Video]. YouTube. https://www.youtube.com/watch?v=r5RbdChKMv4&ab_channel=TheWire.

Urry, John. 2021. *Mobilities.* USA: Polity Press.

Urry, John, and Jonas Larsen. 2011. *The Tourist Gaze 3.0.* New Delhi: Sage Publications.

Van Houtum, H., and Ton Van Naerssen. 2002. Bordering, Ordering, and Othering. *Tijdschrift voor Economische en Sociale Geografie,* 93(2): 125–136. https://henkvanhoutum.nl/wp-content/uploads/2013/05/TESG2002.pdf

Chapter 19

TRANSGRESSING BORDERS AND BOUNDARIES: RELIGION, POLITICS, AND ART FROM THE PHARAOH KHAFRA TO THE WORK OF SIONA BENJAMIN

Ori Z. Soltes

This essay begins with a discussion of religion and the inscriptional origins of the notion of a sacred-profane border (the *lapis niger* in pre-republican Rome) before turning to a particular image of the Egyptian Pharaoh Khafra (ca 2450 BCE) in which his political agenda is furthered by the interweaving of religion and art. Following, by way of brief descriptive references of five key works of art in the Greek, Roman, medieval, and renaissance worlds—the *Anavysos Kouros*, Polyklitos' *Doryphoros*, the *Augustus of Prima Porta*, a thirteenth-century Byzantine Virgin and Child, and Raphael's *Tempi Madonna*—the discussion will turn to modernity, by way of the shifting concepts of sacred-profane, process-product, and Jewish-Christian boundaries in works like Monet's series of paintings of the Rouen Cathedral and Barnett Newman's *The Name II*. The discussion will culminate with reference to the work of three contemporary artists, Mako Fujimura, Asim Abu-Shakra, and Siona Benjamin. Each of these painters transgresses religious and/or cultural and/or ethnic and/or political and visual borders simultaneously; the work of Benjamin, in particular, is intended to eradicate traditional borders with new art, literally, of re-imagined transnational, transcultural, interfaith realities with, as its purpose, the repair of a world very much fractured by its traditional sense of borders and boundaries that separate diverse groups of human beings from each other in their own self-conceptions.

Religion, art, politics, Egypt, Greece, Byzantine, Renaissance, Impressionism, Holocaust, Monet, Barnett Newman, Siona Benjamin, Krishna, Fixing the World, Japanese screens, triptych form.

* * * * *

I. *Religio, sacer,* and *profanes*

One might begin this narrative by considering the ultimate boundary within human understanding, that between divinity and humanity. Religion's purpose is to transgress this boundary under careful conditions. While English refers to the two realms separated

272　　　　TOWARD A NEW ART OF BORDER CROSSING

by this boundary as "sacred" and "profane" we may understand boundary, realms, and religion more clearly by reference to the Latin antecedents of all three terms (*sacer, profanus,* and *religio*) and specifically, the inscription in which the term *sacer* first appears.

The root of the Latin word *religio*—"-lig-"—means a "binding."[1] *Religio* binds a community to (its sense of) divinity. More precisely, *"re-"* means "back" or "again," so religion binds a community *back again* to that which *created* it. (The "-io suffix" indicates that the term is, grammatically speaking, a feminine noun.) That creative source is the *sacer.*

Whereas "sacred" and "profane," particularly in juxtaposition, tend to offer positive and negative connotations respectively, *sacer* and *profanus* are both inherently neutral—and offer a wider range of meaning than that connoted by "sacred" and "profane." The Romans used the term *profanus* to refer to the realm of the *known:* the community, daytime, being awake, life, the human realm; the realm where things happen according to what we might term normal patterns of expectation. In the *profanus,* 1 o'clock is reliably followed by 2 o'clock, and the distance between Cleveland and New York is different from that between Los Angeles and Paris.

The *sacer* is the *unknown* realm in all its aspects. It is beyond the edge of the community—wilderness, forest, desert, ocean, or outer space; it is nighttime, sleep, and dreams; it is before birth and after death; it is the realm of divinity. It operates unpredictably in relation to our understanding, in time, space, and circumstance, according to its *own* patterns. In dreams, for instance, one can be in Cleveland one instant and in Paris the next; one can converse with people not only thousands of miles away (without a telephone), but with those who have died and thus moved altogether beyond normal (*profanus*) reach.

When we sleep, we may have no dreams or dreams that are sweet or horrific. When we go out into the forest nothing unusual may happen—or we may be torn apart by wolves, or our fairy godmother may appear and offer to fulfill three wonderful life-altering wishes. When we pray to divinity for rain there may be no response, or the gods may respond with a deluge that drowns half the community or with sufficient rain for our crops to flourish so we survive.

The term *sacer* can also apply to an individual, in which case it also implies being apart from the community, the familiar, and the everyday. Some individuals are inherently connected to both the *sacer* and the *profanus.* Thus a prophet or priest is separate, in part, from the community. Such a figure, in turn, guides the community (the *profanus*) in its relationship with the *sacer;* hence that figure is termed, in Latin, *sacerdos*—"one who gives the *sacer* [to us]," (and "one who gives us to the *sacer*").[2] Other sub-categories of *sacerdos* (plural: *sacerdotes*) include poets, artists, pharaohs, shahs, kings, heroes, and heroines.

So, too (in the negative sense), one who has transgressed a *boundary* between *profanus* and *sacer* space—for example, a border between a grove devoted to a goddess and hallowed by the goddess's protection—becomes *sacer.* That individual becomes estranged from the community (the *profanus*)—and must be *exiled* into the *sacer,* because he *is sacer.* Why? For three related reasons. First, simply: since he is no longer part of the *profanus,* he is no longer protected by that which binds the community together: *leg-es*—laws—and *re-lig-io.*[3] That loss of protection means that the individual who is *sacer* is at risk should anyone in the community wish to harm him.

TRANSGRESSING BORDERS AND BOUNDARIES

His exile into the *sacer* is also necessary to protect the community. To transgress the boundary between the community and the divine grove may *potentially* anger that goddess and bring catastrophe upon the community. More specifically (and this is the third reason), this potential danger obtains because of the analogy between *sacer-profanus*, grove-community boundary, and the *ultimate* boundary between the predictable, known *profanus* and the potentially dangerous, unpredictable *sacer*—the realm of gods and *daimons* that can be as malignant as they can be beneficent in their interaction with the *profanus*.[4] As long as the one who has potentially offended the *sacer* is part of the *profanus*, everyone is in danger.

So the offender must leave not only to protect himself from the community but to protect the community from potential divine wrath—like Oedipus, who was cast out of Thebes, carrying with him the curse of plague with which Thebes had been afflicted through his offense to the gods. So, the one who has engendered that potential for disaster by disturbing any boundary, departs, like Oedipus, carrying whatever malignancy from the *sacer* with him/herself out into the *sacer*.[5]

How might the offending one return from apartness, estrangement, exile, curse, and *sacer*ness back to the *profanus* of the community? He would seek out someone who could guide him in what actions to take: a *sacerdos*, whose inherent nature enables him to answer such a question. And the *sacerdos*—in this case, say, a priest—will no doubt suggest a specific action.

That action will inevitably be to offer a gift of expiation to the offended powers. Most commonly, the offender offers a surrogate—a lamb, a goat, a cow, an ox, a bouquet of flowers, a bowl of fruit; to which his *sacer*-inducing sin is transferred—to the *sacer*. In Roman culture, this sort of action must have been common enough, since the Latin word "make"—*facere*—and the term *sacer* were ultimately combined in a one-word configuration: *sacrificare*—"to sacrifice."

Nor, of course, is this principle unique to Roman religion. It is precisely what occurred at the Israelite-Judaean Temple at the annual time of expiation called *Yom Kippur* (Day of Atonement/Expiation): the High Priest (*sacerdos*), bearing a year's worth of sins from the community (*profanus*) on his shoulders, would place his hands on a goat (the *scapegoat*) and transfer that pollution onto the animal that, cursed (*sacer*) by bearing all the sins of the people on its shoulders, was thereafter cast out into the wilderness (*sacer*)—or actually thrown from the heights of the Temple mount to the valley below—and thus sent to its death (*sacer*).

While the English word "sacrifice" is derived from *sacrificare*, the latter does not necessarily mean slitting the surrogate's throat and/or burning it (although it certainly *can*), reminding us that the Latin term, like the term *"sacer"* itself, has a broader meaning than the one that its English equivalent possesses. It means "to make *sacer*": the one who has offended a divinity makes the animal *sacer* in his/their stead. When in Genesis 22, Abraham in the end does not slaughter his son, he still makes him *sacer*, for both are now active parties to the Covenant with God.[6]

Precision defines the sacrificial ritual. It must be accomplished at a precise time and place and according to a precise method. Moreover, the time and place will themselves be sacerdotal: they will be borders/boundaries, underscoring further that aspect of the *profanus-sacer* relationship.

274 TOWARD A NEW ART OF BORDER CROSSING

Thus the offering will be made precisely at midnight, at dawn, at sunrise, at sunset, at high noon—natural or conceptual border times between day and night, or between the rise and fall of the sun in the sky. It will be made at a place that the *sacerdos* knows is propitious for *sacer-profanus* contact—typically thanks to some event that once marked that location as particular. It might be, say, an unusually large oak tree (in the Roman or Druid tradition, for instance) that was once struck by lightning, that still stands tall while possessing a significant hole or crack, blackened by that lightning bolt that emerged with a roar from the *sacer*.

Or the location might mark an event such as that recorded for the Israelites in Genesis 28: 10–22. There the *sacerdos* Jacob, fleeing the *profanus* of his family's encampment and the murderous anger of his brother, Esau, was out in the *sacer* wilderness where, during the *sacer* nighttime, he slept and had the *sacer* experience of a dream—in which a ladder-like element connected heaven (*sacer*) and earth (*profanus*), and sacerdotal beings—for convenience's sake we may refer to them as angels—were moving up and down along its "rungs." The text explains that when Jacob awoke he expressed astonishment at what he understood to be a communication to him from the *sacer*—"the God of my fathers Abraham and Isaac."

So he took the stone on which he had laid his head, together with other stones in the area, and built a marker of that experience: a "high place," which is what an altar is—from Latin, *altus*, meaning "high." The site was subsequently referred to as *Bet El*—meaning "House of God" in Hebrew, underscoring its sacerdotal role not only for Jacob but for his many descendants who would bring their offerings to this site over time. So the *sacerdos* guiding the one who has offended (or potentially offended) a god or goddess would instruct that offender with regard to a precise, border/boundary time and place: transgression of the *sacer-profanus* boundary is atoned for by way of a sacrifice offered at a boundary time and place. The mode of sacrifice will also be prescribed along precise lines.

Two paradoxes are inherent in all this. First, the *sacer* is—to repeat—an intrinsically neutral and potentially positive or negative concept. On the one hand, every religion assumes that the divine aspect of the *sacer* is, on the whole, benevolent. So to be *sacer*—to be what the gods are, to be with the gods—must mean to be *blessed*. Thus, for example, in dying, one may come to reside with the gods—a blessed state of existence concerning which there is ample discussion in Greco-Roman and other traditions. Yet in the case of a *scapegoat*, that animal, *sacer*, is clearly understood to be *cursed*. The bilateral, self-contradictory nature of the *sacer*, then, is clear—and is essential to Western religious history. For Christianity, Jesus in earthly death, becomes *sacer*. He who bears humanity's sins on his shoulders is, one might say, as cursed as one can be; he who returns to the realm of God-the-Father is as blessed as one can be.

The second paradox pertains to the space-time quality of the *sacer*. It is boundless, yet, in addressing it, we do so in precisely bounded places, at precise times, by way of carefully prescribed rituals—as if, in defining precise boundaries about the aspects of our relationship to the *sacer*, we can render its unfathomability accessible; its intrinsic unpredictable chaos ordered to our limited understanding. And how do we know what time, place, and procedure to observe? The *sacerdos*, to whom the *sacer* has revealed this information, will guide us.

TRANSGRESSING BORDERS AND BOUNDARIES 275

These aspects of precision will apply, of course, not only to an individual who has inappropriately transgressed the boundary between *profanus* and *sacer* and/or offended the power(s) of the *sacer*. Every *religio* will prescribe precise times within precise spaces for the precise rituals which, on a periodic basis—be it daily, weekly, monthly, or annual— define the relationship between the *profanus* of each such *religio* and its sense of the *sacer*. In the Jewish tradition, for instance, *Shabbat* (the Sabbath) begins *precisely* at sunset—set off from the amorphous *profanus* of the rest of the week. One enters (and exits) this *sacer* time by means of precisely prescribed rituals: candle lighting, the blessing and consumption of wine and bread of a special sort.[7]

The *sacerdotal* spaces where one celebrates religious rituals are, moreover, analogues of an ultimate centering point for the cosmos. A centering space within the bounded and yet amorphous *profanus* is understood to be connected (by analogy) to the centering point assumed (by further paradox) to be found within the boundless, shapeless *sacer*. When the Temple in Jerusalem still stood, it was the bounded center of the Israelite-Judaean community, and within it was the Holy of Holies (*sacer sacrorum*); the central stone marker at Delphi was known as the *omphalos* (so-called because of the belief that it marked the centering umbilical connection between heaven and earth).[8] Different traditions offer a variety of accounts of time *before* our own time and space, as *centered*: around a tree in a garden as in Sumerian Dilmun or biblical Eden, or as the tree, *Isdril*, is found at the center of the Norse conception of the universe, or as a mountain such as Indra's mountain at the center of the Vedic cosmos.

All of this is so—to return to the beginning of this discussion—because religion, which presupposes the dichotomy between *sacer* and *profanus*, addresses itself most particularly to that aspect of the *sacer* called "divinity." That aspect of the *sacer* is by far the most disturbing one, because of the assumption that it has the power to determine the extent and patterns of our lives: the *sacer* that created the *profanus* can destroy it. It can help or harm us, bless or curse us, and it is the purpose of religion and its sacerdotal leadership to assure that we realize the positive.

Religious rites and rituals govern the boundaries between ourselves and the *sacer*, regulating their traversal when appropriate, structuring the process with minutely detailed care in order to ensure as much as possible a positive response from that realm toward our own. *Sacerdotes* are those who are believed to possess thepeculiar knowledge (granted by the *sacer*) of what rituals and rites to prescribe and of how properly to accomplish them. So, in their respective traditions: Abraham, Moses, Jesus, Muhammad, Buddha, or the Baha'ullah; the priest in the Israelite Temple, in the Sumerian Great Ziqqurat, or in the Temple to Jupiter Capitolinus in Rome.

II. Religion, Art, and Politics

One of the most obvious complications of religion and its concerns is that, in addressing a reality so different from our own human *profanus* reality, the terminology for transgressing the border into exploration and explanation of the *sacer* necessarily derives from the *profanus*. In practical terms, everything that we say regarding divinity—particularly as God is understood, for example, in the Jewish, Christian, and Muslim traditions—is

276 TOWARD A NEW ART OF BORDER CROSSING

a metaphor. If God is termed "all-powerful" or "all-good" or "all-knowing," these are all concepts derived from and understandable in the context of the human *profanus*. They are metaphors when used with reference to God, however: we cannot know what "power" or "goodness" or "knowledge" truly *mean* in divine *sacer* terms.

One consequence of this is that humans have always multiplied the languages in which such vocabulary is shaped. In order to cross the boundary between *profanus* and *sacer*, we have not only used words formed into prayers and hymns; we have *transcended* words by means of non-verbal instruments, such as music, dance, and visual art. The visual language that humans have been inspired to shape, moreover, has assumed its own dialects: naturalistic and abstract; direct, literal depiction and indirect representation by way of symbols: colors, shapes, numbers, or natural features of our own *profanus* reality that are intended as stand-ins for aspects of the *sacer*.

One among the many places where one may see symbols operating within a visual context is ancient Egypt, where diverse gods and goddesses were, for millennia, represented as possessing human, animal, or combined human and animal forms. Divinities offering, say, a human body with an animal head offered an inherent transcendence of our *profanus* reality—by virtue of combinations never found within the *profanus*—yet each of the individual elements themselves derives from the *profanus*. Thus a human body with the head of a falcon–hawk would have been understood by every Egyptian to represent Horus. The image of the falcon–hawk in its entirety, without human parts, could and did also come to represent Horus—and every Egyptian would understand that the "falcon–hawk" Horus is inexpressibly more majestic and powerful than the everyday falcon–hawk that represents the god.

The image of a sphinx, such as the gigantic one in Giza, in combining the body of a lion and a human—pharaonic—head, adds another, specific twist to the manner in which visual art articulates the *sacer-profanus* border-transgression. The Great Sphinx represents the pharaoh, Khafra (ca 2570–2480 BCE). Its intention, in turning the Egyptian ruler into a border creature—one that straddles the human and the *animal* realm—is to present him, by metaphor, as a border creature who straddles the human and *divine* realm. For non-human animals—wild, fierce, and unpredictable animals in particular—can serve as a metaphoric stand-in for the divine realm: animals and divinities are both *sacer*. The pharaoh is thus another sort of sacerdotal border-creature.

Moreover, this particular image crosses another border—from religion into an aspect of human enterprise: politics. As art helps religion to address the *sacer*—so that artists are analogues of prophets, priests, and pharaohs—religion often serves politics in articulating and validating the agenda of its leaders who would be understood as *sacerdotes*: the pharaoh straddles the border—is himself the border—between two realms. Anyone who opposed the pharaoh would be opposing a god, the gods, with inevitably bad consequences for that opposition.

Khafra's artists also expressed this idea in other media, using a different dialect of the same conceptual and visual language. In one of these, a statue repeated in several iterations, the pharaoh sits on his throne, with every detail of his body and face perfect, supernaturally regular—even his shaved head and face on which, in lieu of hair and beard that are naturally irregular, he offers a false, regularized, "beard" and

Figure 1. *Pharaoh Khafra* with Horus Falcon Hawk 2570 BCE, Egyptian Museum, Cairo.

"hair"—suggesting his eternal, unchanging, and therefore divine qualities. In the statue to which I refer, moreover, the added exclamation point is the placement of a falcon–hawk with its wings outspread around the back of the head and onto the shoulders of Khafra (Figure 1). The favor of the god Horus rests literally upon him.

There are thus variations on the theme of crossing the *sacer-profanus* border in the Egyptian crisscrossing of the boundaries of religion, art, and politics. The specifics of this threefold transgression will undergo multiple transformations as one follows it through the nearly 25 centuries between the time of Khafra and our own time. Greek culture, as it begins to emerge in the eighth and seventh centuries BCE, encounters and is inspired by Egyptian culture, particularly where statuary is concerned, and the Greeks begin to produce full-size naked male images in the sixth century BCE by adopting and adapting the sort of pharaonic style that continued in Egypt with little change between Khafra's era and that of such Greek statuary.[9] Thus a succession of *kouroi* (sing. *kouros*), present idealized male youths intended to suggest Apollo, and are reminiscent of the Egyptian pharaonic figures in their perfect symmetry and the manner in which they stride ever so slightly forward, still compositionally trapped in the stone block (Figure 2).

Rather than representing gods as animals (or partial animals), Greek gods are completely anthropomorphic. However, the Greeks rapidly became interested in adjusting their representations of such figures—in crossing an aesthetic, conceptual border—in order to move to idealized representations of Hero-warrior-athletes who are god-like in their perfection but in motion and thus not to be mistaken for unchanging

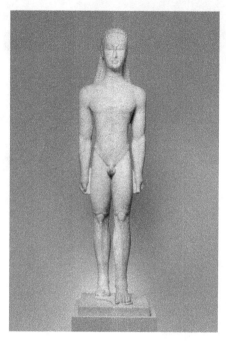

Figure 2. *Attic Kouros*, ca 590–580 BCE, Metropolitan Museum of Art, NYC.

Gods. Among the more famous such images was the *Doryphoros* ("Spear-bearer") of ca 440–430 BCE sculpted by Polyklitos (we only possess Roman copies).

In shifting the representational border this work also transgresses other boundaries. The figure is shown striding forward, shifting his weight from one leg to the other, and thus the sculptor has depicted him with one leg tense (weight-bearing) and the other relaxed (weight-relieved); one is bent and the other straight. The arms offer a similar dialogue between straight and bent and between tensed (holding the—now-missing—spear) and relaxed by the figure's side. This offers a dynamic balance made up of carefully calibrated, systematic imbalances (Figure 3).

Thus the Greeks transformed the Egyptian interest in art for religious and political purposes into an interest in art for art's sake, and the border of interest is one that itself shifts away from that between divinity and humanity toward one between different states of human being in the world. Later Greeks looking back at the *Doryphoros* considered it to be a portrait of Akhilleus—the consummate athlete-warrior, whose preternatural abilities derived from the fact that his mother was a goddess (the sea nymph, Thetis).

Akhilleus is understood to be the ultimate *sacerdos*-as-hero, straddling the border between that most *profanus* aspect of human experience—mortality—and that most *sacer* feature of gods: immortality. Humans in general and the Greeks, in particular, express an obsessive concern for the question of whether we mortals can achieve immortality, and part of the answer to that question is that, while all of us cross the border from life to death, we can somehow achieve the paradox of immortality while dying through not only the garden-variety means of producing offspring in whose DNA and memories we live but beyond that, by acts that are outstanding and remembered beyond the confines of family.

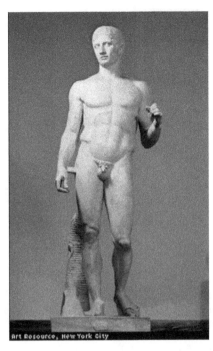

Figure 3. Polyklitos: *Doryphoros*, 450–430 BCE (Roman copy), National Archaeological Museum, Naples, Italy.

The hero Akhilleus knows that if he participates in the Trojan War, he will die in his youthful prime, but his actions on that battlefield will earn him *kleos aphthiton*: undying glory. While he has a choice—to die obscurely, of old age, or to go to Troy—he really has no choice, because the essence of Akhilleus is to be the consummate hero-athlete-warrior, and not to participate in the greatest of wars and commit the greatest of hero-athlete-warrior acts would be to fail to be Akhilleus. If the *Doryphoros* is indeed a portrait of Akhilleus, then it transgresses not only borders of stasis and action and their concomitants (bent and straight, relaxed and tense limbs), but that most significant of *sacer-profanus* borders, life and death, and its concomitants: mortality and immortality and therefore humanity and divinity.

This array of shifting borders and boundaries addressed by art can be seen to move forward toward the Roman culture that emulated the Greeks as well as the Egyptians in many ways. Thus the famous sculpted image of the first Roman Emperor, Augustus—the *Augustus of Prima Porta* (its original location was in the back garden of the villa of Augustus' wife, Livia, at Prima Porta)—offers a distinct adaptation of the *Doryphoros* with regard to bent and straight, tensed and relaxed limbs and shifting weight (Figure 4).

The most obvious difference between this work and the sculpture by Polyklitos is that, instead of an ideally muscled athlete, Augustus is attired in a military uniform—and his figure is both placed and proportioned slightly differently from the placement and proportions of the *Doryhporos*, facilitating a broader torso for the low-relief-carved decoration of the breastplate that offers the viewer a statement of Augustus' accomplishment as a "warrior": reclaiming the Roman standards from the Parthians

Figure 4. *Augustus of Prima Porta*, ca 15 CE, Vatican Museum, Vatican City, Italy.

that had been taken in the defeat of a Roman army led by Augustus' colleague, Crassus, at Carrhae, more than two decades before Augustus became Emperor.

Moreover, the image suggests a divine connection for the emperor. At his side, there is a dolphin—a symbol of Aphrodite-Venus—with a Cupid-Eros figure (the son of Aphrodite-Venus) straddling the sea creature's back. The Roman viewer—like the Egyptian recognizing the meaning of the falcon–hawk associated with Khafra—would be reminded that Augustus claimed linear descent from the Trojan hero, Aeneas who, after an extensive journey from the burning city in which he had been a key hero-warrior, led a band of refugees to Italy, with the assistance of his mother, the goddess Aphrodite-Venus, where his descendants would found the Roman Republic of which Augustus would be the savior more than 11 centuries after Aeneas.

Whereas Aeneas was semi-divine—like the Akhilleus who played the key role fighting against the Trojans and who earned undying glory—Augustus might be said to possess a lower percentage of divine blood flowing through his veins, but that percentage is emphasized along with the fiction of his military accomplishments (it was his friend, Agrippa, who actually fought and won the battles). Augustus is also reminiscent of Khafra in another way: he is depicted here—and always—in the prime of his youthful manhood. Whereas for the most part, Roman portraiture reveled in depicting people as they were, including aging emperors, Augustus was always portrayed as ageless and thus god-like. This is particularly true of this sculpture: he is shown in full military regalia but barefoot, and the fact of his shoeless condition has long been believed to symbolize the fact that he is dead. If this is indeed a posthumous portrait (and Augustus died at the age of 77, in 14 CE), then the youthful image emphatically connotes his transgressive divine aspect.

III. Stylistic and Symbolic Continuity and Change

Both the sense of the divine *sacer* and how it engages with us, and the sense of what sort of immortality is available to humankind shifts with the arrival of Christianity onto the stage of history and the transformation of the Roman empire from a polytheistic pagan to a monotheistic Christian world. The process is gradual, its most crucial timeline extending from Constantine's Edict of Milan in 313 CE, which legalized Christian practice, to Theodosius' decree, around 380 CE, which rendered Christianity the official religion of the Empire.

The crossing of that all-important conceptual border will have, among other consequences, the politicization of the Church as it asserts its hegemony and struggles with diverse forms of spiritual disagreement or pushback—from an array of forms termed heretical to major schisms in 1054 between the Western and Eastern Churches and subsequent schisms within the Western Church that culminate with the era of Reformation and Counter-reformation, and with it, an Age of Religious Wars that dominate the sixteenth and seventeenth centuries. Additional crises included the struggle between church and state (as exemplified by the Investiture Controversy of 1075–1077), the arrival on the scene of Islam in the seventh and eighth centuries, and Judaism. Both Islam and Judaism share the Christian view of the divine *sacer* in broad terms but diverge from Christianity most obviously in not embracing the concept of Jesus as God.

The concept of a being that is both fully divine and fully human took many centuries to develop. Not until the Council of Chalcedon of 451 was the unequivocal Christian understanding of God as triune asserted—and the initial form that heresy took was to deny that view.[10] Thus there were those who did not accept the divinity of Jesus, those who argued that Jesus was only divine—that his "human" nature was an illusion—and those who believed that he was half-divine and half-human, rather than fully divine and fully human.[11] In addition to disputes regarding how to engage the boundary between the human *profanus* and the divine *sacer*, there were controversies regarding *how* precisely to understand Jesus as a border-straddling *sacerdos*.

The struggle to define correct belief engendered a series of evolving convictions regarding how to visualize Jesus. Whereas Jewish and Muslim art turn primarily to abstraction and when figurative, to a limited vocabulary of subjects and styles—since the invisible God Itself cannot be depicted—Christian art can and freely does depict God, figuratively, in His human form. The eastern part of the Roman Empire, its capital in Constantinople (later called Istanbul), continued until 1453, and also came to be known as the Byzantine Empire. The art of Byzantium included depictions of Jesus and his Virgin Mother who, as both a virgin and a mother, straddles a border analogous to that between the human and divine straddled by her son. Typical Byzantine representations of the Virgin and Child include a thirteenth-century image in the National gallery of Art in Washington, DC, that, on several levels, reflects the double boundary-transgression.

Both figures are stylized in their flatness and in the manner in which, instead of irregular shadows, their garments are highlighted by regularized gold leaf striations; their exposed faces and hands are flattish, her fingers preternaturally elongated and his head, particularly his forehead, simultaneously large and adult-like in mien. Their gestures are entirely toward the viewer, not toward each other: her right hand guides

Figure 5. *Virgin and Child*, Thirteenth Century, National Gallery of Art, Washington, DC.

the viewer's eyes toward the child and he holds the scroll of his New Covenant with one hand and with the other, offers a benedictory gesture (Figure 5).

The haloed Virgin doesn't quite *sit* within a kind of *cathedra* (a bishop's throne) that is as much edifice as chair and the haloed Christ Child neither quite stands nor sits on what are barely her arm and lap. Mother and Son are placed against a background that it is not naturally *profanus*, but gold leaf, creating a spaceless space; and the faces and torsos of two angelic figures, each within a circular frame, simultaneously suggest a pair of portrait-tondos hanging on this golden non-wall and apertures through it into another—*sacer*—realm, from which these two sacerdotal beings peer.

The colors are all intended to speak an abstract symbolic language to reinforce the figurative elements: white, the color of virgin purity; red, the color of blood and thus of the sacrifice anticipated three decades beyond this "moment"; green, the color of spring and rebirth; blue, the color of the sky and thus of God's Truth—the entirety framed in the gold that in its material value symbolizes the spiritual value of the message being conveyed regarding the divine-human, *sacer-profanus* relationship.

The image functions as a visualization of the border-crossing necessary in both directions for that relationship to flourish. Everything about the figures, the setting, and the angelic beings beyond them, suggests that the viewer stands at a portal through which the *sacer* may be partially viewed, just as elements of the *sacer* look toward our *profanus* realm. Interestingly, Byzantine religious politics, beginning with Emperor Leo III the Isaurian in 726 and continuing until 842, yielded a conflict—known as the iconoclastic ("image-breaking") conflict—in which images like this were banned by Byzantine emperors because of the conviction that the icons were being worshipped, promoting a form of idolatry. Ultimately Icons survived and continued to be painted because the side of the argument that won contended successfully that they were not

Figure 6. Raphael: *Tempi Madonna*, 1508, Alte Pinakothek, Munich, Germany.

being *worshipped* but *venerated*—as one venerates the Bible as an instrument that guides one over the border into a potential understanding of and relationship with the divine *sacer*.

As the Byzantine artistic tradition continued to follow fairly unchanging stylistic guidelines for many centuries—which, in the ethereal depiction of its subjects and their contexts, emphasizes their *divine*, rather than human qualities—in the West, as medieval art yielded to the Renaissance, those proclivities changed; they crossed another border, into a style that reflects a desire to emphasize the *human* qualities of the Virgin and Child. Thus, for instance, the *Tempi Madonna* (1508) by the Umbrian painter, Raphael (1483–1520)—while utilizing virtually the same vocabulary of symbolic colors—transforms its figures into a lovely Umbrian peasant woman and her plump and robust baby, both with barely-visible haloes. They press their cheeks together lovingly, as she looks at him and he looks off winsomely, and they are placed within a naturalistic landscape that includes a bright sky (Figure 6).

Raphael's painting is one among many reflections of a humanistic revolution—both in the sense that, conceptually, human responsibility for the shaping of the *profanus* is being promoted; and that, visually, the emphasis is on the human side of Jesus, rendering him more like you and me than was the case for the Byzantine-style Jesus. One can see this issue—of crossing borders into new ways of visualizing the divine *sacer* and in conceiving of the borders themselves in new ways—in myriad developments in religion and art (and politics) as we continue into modernity and toward our own time.

IV. Border- and Boundary-Crossing in Modernity

One might fast-forward to Impressionist painting, created in a late-nineteenth-century cultural context that referred to itself as post-Christian (in Nietzsche's words) and/ or secular—in which the teleological understanding of the *profanus* as profoundly influenced by the divine *sacer* has been supplanted by a mechanistic perspective for which a metaphysical superstructure is at least irrelevant and at most nonexistent—and ask what Impressionist paintings are about. There are several parts of the answer to that question, beginning with the newly conceived border between process and product. Where a painting by someone like Raphael was intended to give the viewer the illusion of looking into volumetric space—through a window or a doorway, as it were, with flesh-and-blood figures within that space, and with the evidence of the painter's brush eliminated—the Impressionists shifted the border between viewer and painting and thus between viewer and painter. By intentionally leaving the rough-hewn evidence of the paintbrush on the canvas—including horsehairs still embedded in the paint—the artist intended for the viewer to "complete" the painting by deciding how far or close to the canvas s/he must stand in order for the almost sketch-like brush-stroked pigments and forms to coalesce into the subject the artist was depicting.

In other words, the completed work is dependent in part on the optic nerve of the individual viewer, the amount of sleep, perhaps, that s/he had before looking, the light of a particular time of day or season of year—a range of factors beyond what the painter actually did with his paintbrushes and pigments and his own visual and mental perception of his subject. One may recognize this issue in the over 30 depictions of the Rouen cathedral that Claude Monet (1840–1926) produced in 1892–1894. Painted at different times with different light under changing conditions affecting the appearance of the building façade, its color changes (because both light and also shadows are composed of a spectrum of colors) and its edges feel sharper or more blurred, clearer or more obscure (Figure 7).

Figure 7. Claude Monet: *Rouen Cathedral in Morning Light*, 1894, JP Getty Museum, Los Angeles, CA.

TRANSGRESSING BORDERS AND BOUNDARIES 285

What makes this particular series so compelling, aside from its aesthetic attributes and their relationship to optics and spectroscopy, is the significance of the subject: a structure that, when it was built, was regarded as an important sacerdotal border where the human French Catholic *profanus* and the Christian divine *sacer* met in mutual exploration. As a Gothic cathedral, one of the important aspects of that exploration was understood to be light, a symbol of God's presence within the edifice, entering through the array of stained-glass windows that replaced substantial swathes of stone walls. For Monet, the cathedral is merely a man-made object not dissimilar in aesthetic significance from the haystacks of which the artist also painted a series—yet the same element, light, is the quintessential aspect of reality (part of nature, which may be understood as divinely generated whereas the building is man-made) which is the real focus of the paintings. God may be ignored or may still be understood to be present—but light is the feature enveloping the structure and changing the appearance of its façade (even as light itself is unchanging—like the eternal and unchanging divine *sacer* whether it be ancient Egyptian or medieval Christian).

As Western art entered the twentieth century, one of its creative adjustments was the growing inclusion of non-Christian—specifically Jewish—artists made possible because of European self-definition, up to a point, as secular or post-Christian. If the spiritual-political Christian boundaries that marginalized Jews for 15 centuries began to dissipate on a purely religious basis, it turns out that they didn't disappear, but—in another instance of border-transformation—they shifted toward concepts with new shapes in the Western world: race and ethnicity. Jews often found themselves marginalized, albeit along non-traditional grounds, and the unhappy culmination of this unchanged change was the Holocaust that eliminated one-third of the Jewish population across Christendom in the mid-twentieth century.

One of the consequences of that catastrophe is that the Jewish painters who shaped the Chromaticist side of the American Abstract Expressionist movement, the leaders of whom were mainly Jews like Mark Rothko, Adolph Gottlieb, and Barnett Newman, found themselves asking how they fit, as Jewish artists, into the history of Western art that had been primarily Christian during the previous more than 15 centuries—and how they might respond to the Holocaust. For both Christians and Jews, the question of God's presence or absence during that debacle arose.

The paradox of God's presence/absence is the central idea behind Newman's 1950 *The Name II* (Figure 8). This all-white painting is marked by two thin, vertical gold strips that in effect reduce it to a stylized triptych. Newman (1905–1970) offers a version of that most Christian of forms in Western painting—which in its threefold presentation has long offered the symbolism of the Christian concept of God as triune, simultaneously three-fold and singular. Moreover, in that tradition God occupies the central panel: Christ on his Virgin Mother's lap, flanked by saints; or on the Cross, flanked by the two thieves. But Newman has offered a Jewish re-vision of that figurative representation, an imageless image of the imageless God. Indeed, anyone conversant with the Jewish tradition would know that the very *name* of God is not uttered by traditional Jews outside of the context of prayer (and even the name uttered in prayer is a circumlocution for the unknown, ineffable *real* Name of God); instead they substitute the (double) circumlocution, "*HaShem*," meaning "The Name."[12]

Figure 8. Barnett Newman, *The Name II*, 1950, National Gallery of Art, Washington, DC.

So Newman's title has announced to the viewer exactly what he is doing: presenting God but through a Jewish visual vocabulary: as imageless—and using white, the absence of color. Further, he has addressed that consummate post-Holocaust theodicy question. The Holocaust was the proof of the *absence* of God for some, but for others the certainty of God's *presence* saved them (Berkovits 1973: 3–6). And white is not only the *absence* of color, but—both chemically and in its traditional role as symbolizing light— the *totality* of color: the merging of all colors. So by way of visual circumlocution—color is both absent and present—God may be "seen" as both absent and present. The artist-*sacerdos* straddles the border between Jewish and Christian art and between positive and negative responses to theodicy.

Boston-born (1960), New York-based painter, Makoto Fujimura straddles related but different borders. He draws on his Japanese heritage and its long tradition of screen paintings together with elements echoing Chromaticist Abstract Expressionism. Influenced particularly by Mark Rothko and Barnett Newman, his work offers a calm, meditative *Presence* that gently surrounds the viewer. His work bridges East and West, and is suffused with faith (Tryon Center 2001: 40–42).

In his triptych entitled Trinity, Fujimura uses color symbolism that reverberates from throughout medieval and Renaissance Western and Eastern Christian art. The left-hand panel is inundated with gold leaf. Various shades of green bleed through the gold—alluding both to spring and rebirth and, in its bleeding through, to the oxidation process by which green undertones sometimes show through the gold surface of Byzantine icons and medieval and early Renaissance paintings. The right-hand panel is dominated by red. The central panel is various shades of blue. Each panel is actually a pair of panels, suggesting Japanese screens or the folding doors to the sacred associated with Shinto shrines. So this work is both cross-cultural and interfaith in the syncretism of the inspirational and intentional borders it bestrides (Figure 9). The spiritual

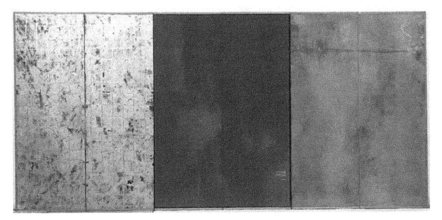

Figure 9. Makota Fujimura, *Trinity*, 1997, Private Collection.

underpinnings are underscored by the artist's references to his work as offerings rather than as personal aesthetic expressions (Walstedt 1997: 5).

One might twist the re-casting of boundaries another turn by considering the painting of Asim Abu-Shakra (1961–1990). An Israeli Muslim from the city of Umm al-Fahm (had he lived just beyond 1993 and the Oslo Accords he would have called himself a Palestinian Israeli), Abu-Shakra studied in the Avni Art School in Tel Aviv; his visual vocabulary reflects on Israeli identity as heterogeneous. He repeatedly depicts the Israeli cactus—the *sabra*—and its fruit. What had become the quintessential symbol of (Jewish) Israelis native-born Israelis are commonly called Sabras—has been repurposed as a symbol of the Palestinians (Figure 10).

Figure 10. Asim Abu Shakra, *Cactus with City in the Background*, 1988, Private Collection (Courtesy of Sultan Sooud Al Qassemi).

288   TOWARD A NEW ART OF BORDER CROSSING

The sabra plant is difficult to uproot; bulldozers may tear it up, but it somehow emerges again from the soil. If that has been said historically of the Jews, it is intended by Abu-Shakra to refer to Palestinian Muslim and Christian Arabs, who use sabra bushes to mark building plots and the boundaries of villages from which they cannot be uprooted. Even if it is removed from natural soil and potted—many of Abu-Shakra's images are of potted sabras—it remains what it is. Wherever they are located or mislocated, Palestinians remain Palestinians. The sabra bush separates as a hedge; as a shared symbol, it connects, reflecting a common interest in return and renewal: for Jewish, Christian, and Muslim—Israeli and Palestinian—communities on both sides of the religious, cultural, ethnic, and political border.

V. The Boundary-Crossing Art of Siona Benjamin

Barnett Newman and the other Jewish Chromaticists—gathering in each others' studios to discuss "Jewish art," visual responses to the Holocaust, and similar issues— expressed ongoing interest in Jewish mysticism. They were particularly obsessed with the sixteenth-century Safed-based kabbalist, Isaac Luria. Prominent among Luria's teachings was his prescription to engage in improving the world—*tikkun olam* in Hebrew. It turns out that the overall schema of the Chromaticists was to create paintings—large, unframed, and offering a visual field that draws the eye toward the center—that put the world back together on the microcosm of the canvas: each painting is a small act of secularized *tikkun olam*; each painter plays the role of *sacerdos*, in mediating between the inscrutable *sacer* and the post-Holocaust, post-Hiroshima *profanus*.

That sense of using one's art as an instrument to transgress boundaries between religions, ethnicities, races, and nationalities as part of an overall act of furthering *tikkun olam* is nowhere more extravagantly expressed than in the work of Mumbai-born and-raised Siona Benjamin (b. 1961). Growing up Jewish in a Hindu and Muslim community, attending Catholic and Zoroastrian schools, and eventually settling in the United States, Benjamin evolved a style that crosses diverse boundaries: she is inspired by Persian and Moghul-era miniatures, Islamic abstractions, Russian Icons, Bollywood posters, Amar Chitra Katha comic books, and the American Pop Art style of Roy Lichtenstein.

For Siona, the question of where her "Jewish" art fits into "Christian" art intersects other questions: where do I as a non-Westerner fit in? Where do I as a person of color fit in? Where do I as a woman fit in? Particularly in her series called *Fereshteh* (Urdu for "angels"), part of a larger series called *Finding Home*, Siona applies this wealth of stylistic input to subjects derived from a combination of Hindu, Moghul Muslim and Jewish subjects upon each of which she has imposed her own sense of *midrash*—a Hebrew word referring to the rabbinic habit of digging beneath the surface of a (usually biblical) subject to extract more meaning from it than a surface reading provides.

Her *Fereshteh* figures have blue flesh, like many Hindu deities, particularly Krishna. For Siona the color alludes both to Krishna,[13] and to the sky and oceans that hover over and support all of us—eradicating borders. Because of their blue skin, Siona's figures are associated with Kraishnavite *bhakti* (love and devotion) and with broad-mindedness with respect to religious perspectives and the embrace of paradox.[14] Since these figures are typically female, she has carried the idea of spiritual embrace to that of gender-diversity embrace.[15] Her heroines embody *Ardhanareshwara*, the composite image of the god Shiva and his female consort, Parvati. She has also synthesized the Hindu idea of *Ardhanareshwara* to the Jewish kabbalistic idea of the *Shekhinah*: the paradoxically female aspect of the genderless God that resides in both men and women when we are "gender-balanced" in our thoughts, words, and actions.

Moreover, she notes that skin color, even within the context of feminist solidarity, often marks "Otherness." "Well-intentioned Western feminists often direct a Eurocentric gaze elsewhere. I have noticed and experienced myself that (regarding) non-western women […] very often assumptions are made before we can open our mouths: 'do you speak English?' 'Are you educated?' 'Do you have our level of sophistication?' 'Were you timid, oppressed, uneducated before you came to live in the West?'" So even within the feminist world, race (and religion) can offer an unwitting marker to those whose perspective is insufficiently global. "Blue skin has become a symbol for me of being a *Jewish woman of color*" [emphasis added], underscoring a triple perspective—religion, gender, and race—connecting the personal to the universal. For, "very often I look down at my skin and it has turned blue. It tends to do that when I face certain situations of people stereotyping and categorizing other people who are unlike themselves."[16]

Each of her figures is thus a kind of self-portrait even as her art is not about *her*, but about all of *us*. One of the things all humans share is a love of stories, and Siona's images are bearers of story—they entertain as they educate. In one image of the biblical character, Miriam (*Fereshteh;#72; 2006*)—the sister of Moses dances at the center of a web of multiple pasts and futures, her angel wings not only part of her figure, but repeated on the side panels—the wings—of the triptych form of which she is a part (Figure 11).

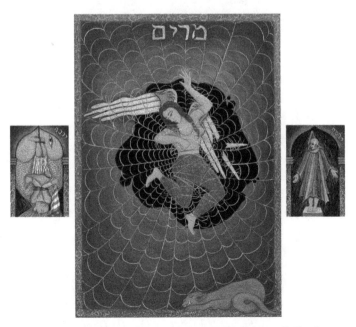

Figure 11. Siona Benjamin, *Fereshteh #72: Miriam*, 2006, Private Collection.

Siona places her blue-skinned heroine in the heart of a gold-drenched, Icon-like image that emulates centuries of Christian-styled devotion toward God. Miriam, singer of God's praises (Ex. 15: 20–21) and bearer of life (finding water in the wilderness), is ambiguously the spider (a female, inherently suspect, inherently dangerous to the males interpreting God's word across history; and ancestor of Jews suspected as poisoners of wells and devourers of Christian children)—and the fly (caught in the web of those hostile interpretations). She is trapped, moreover, in the web of Middle Eastern oil—a black blob behind her suggests this. But we are all trapped: the image of Jonah, near her, in a fish, is an American who was hanged several years back, and opposite him, as "Joseph," is a prisoner from Abu Ghraib, standing on a box, with a conical hat and Christ's *stigmata* on his hands and feet.

The point is to push the viewer to think about these and other ways in which we are separate and joined. Ultimately, Siona's goal, aside from making beautiful art, is to use art as part of the process of *improving* the world, and not merely *observing* it, by obliterating diverse visual/conceptual boundaries. A small gouache and gold leaf work on paper from the year 2000—*Finding Home #46*—articulates her overall intentions concisely. It is called "*Tikkun ha-Olam.*" (Figure 12). A Krishna/Kali-like figure dances on a lotus that is also a burst of light, her multiple arms raised upwards. There are seven arms—six extending from her two sides and a seventh directly from her head, all raised to the same precise height so that their termini—stylized Muslim art-style *hamseh* hands

Figure 12. Siona Benjamin, *Finding Home #46: Tikkun Ha-Olam*, 2000, Private Collection.

yielding to stylized flames—create a seven-branched *menorah* form: the most persistent symbol in two millennia of Jewish art.

In the colorfully spaceless space within which this figure hovers, the words *tikkun ha-olam* are written in Hebrew on one side; on the other they also appear, transliterated into *devanagari* script. Boundaries and borders dissipate within this image in which a range of aspects of the artist are held in perfect balance by a figure that is at once a self-portrait and the portrait of everywoman—and everyman—and a prescription for rethinking the borders between us all.

Bibliography

Ankori, G. 2006. *Palestinian Art.* London: Reaktion Books.
Asad, T. 2003. *Formations of the Secular: Christianity, Islam, Modernity.* Stanford, CA: Stanford University Press.
Bal, M. 2007. "Lost in Space, Lost in the Library," in *Essays in Migratory Aesthetics: Cultural Practices Between Migration and Art-making.* Edited by Sam Durrant and Catherine M. Lord. Amsterdam and NYC: Rodopi, pp. 23–36.
Berkovits, E.1973. *Faith After the Holocaust.* NYC: KTAV Publishing House, Inc.
Bourriaud, N. 2010. *The Radicant.* Translated by James Gussen and Lili Porten. NYC: Lukas &Sternberg.
Chidester, D. 2014. *Empire of Religion: Imperialism and Comparative Religion.* Chicago: University of Chicago Press.
Fleischner, E. (ed.). 1977. *Auschwitz: Beginning of a New Era?* NYC: KTAV Publishing House, Inc.
Fuhrer, R. 1998. *Israeli Painting: From Post-Impressionism to Post-Zionism.* Woodstock: Overlook Press.
O'Neill, J. P. (ed). 1990. *Barnett Newman: Selected Writings and Interviews.* NYC: Alfred A. Knopf.
Shaw, R. D. 2018. "Beyond Syncretism: A Dynamic Approach to Hybridity," *International Bulletin of Mission Research,* 42(1), 6–19.
Soltes, O. Z. 2016. *Tradition and Transformation: Three Millennia of Jewish Art & Architecture.* NYC: Canal Street Studios.
Tryon Center for Visual Art. 2001. *Like a Prayer: A Jewish and Christian Presence in Contemporary Art* (exhibition catalogue). Charlotte, NC: Tryon Center.
Walstedt, E. 1997. *Hours: Makoto Fujimura.* NYC: Dillon Gallery.

Notes

1 One finds this root in "lig-aments," that bind muscle to bone, and "lig-atures," that bind up wounds, for example, or that bind phonemes together in certain writing systems, such as Egyptian hieroglyphs or the Devanagari system used to write Vedic, Sanskrit and their linguistic descendants.

2 A slightly different theory derives *sacerdos* from *sacer* + an Indo-European root **dhe*, meaning "do," thus: "do, make *sacer.*"

3 In this particular linguistic context, it is the consonants that count; thus the Latin root for "binding" is properly "l-vowel-g." It is variously expressed as "lig-" or as "leg-," since vocalic alternation is not uncommon, for various reasons under various conditions, but that discussion is well beyond the scope of this narrative.

4 As the *profanus* and *sacer* are both realms with a large number of analogic aspects or subcategories, so the notion of analogues, that is endemic to religious sensibility, and is observable across the panoply of human cultures, applies here: all boundaries are analogues of each

292   TOWARD A NEW ART OF BORDER CROSSING

other and of the ultimate *profanus-sacer* boundary and thus all boundary-crossings are both potentially dangerous and/or potentially propitious. Moreover, as noted above, the divine aspect of the *sacer* in particular can only be described by analogy and metaphor, using terms that derive from the *profanus* realm.

5   Note that Oedipus saved Thebes from the plague of the sphinx when he met her and solved her riddle at a *crossroad* (where two paths meet and cross: a *boundary* zone) and met and killed the one he did not know was his father at a second crossroad.

6   While in Genesis, that son is Isaac, in the Muslim tradition there is a long debate as to whether it is Isaac or Ishmael and most Muslims today believe that it was Ishmael.

7   Go to any American city with a reasonably sized Jewish community and the local Jewish newspaper will come out on Thursday and on the top or bottom of the front page the precise time to kindle the Sabbath lights will be indicated. The bread, incidentally, alludes to the shewbreads in the Temple in Jerusalem, and the wine to the blood-sacrifices. Because of the preciousness of the Sabbath and the reluctance to leave it behind and get back to the *profanus* of the work week, its endpoint offers a paradoxic exception to the rule of precision: the appearance of three stars is a precise formulation, but seeing precisely three stars is virtually impossible: by then there are many more than three that are visible. So in waiting for three stars one is waiting for *more* than three and therefore waiting for a moment that is actually imprecise but in any case well beyond sunset and the end of the Sabbath day.

8   "*Omphalos*" is the Greek form of the Latin "*umbilicus*."

9   The exception to this lack of change was the brief period of Amarna art and its un-idealizing naturalism. I would suggest, however, that even the Amarna style reflects the conviction that the Pharaoh and his family, marked by somewhat extraordinary physical deformities, deliberately promoted the imaging of those deformities as a sign that they were marked out by the God, Aten, as special and divinely connected.

10   The idea was first formally articulated at the Council of Nicaea in 325.

11   These forms of heresy were referred to as Arianism, Monophytism, and Miaphytism, respectively.

12   Even when (in Hebrew) one says "*Adonai*," one is uttering a succession of phonemes that do not correspond to the actual phonemic content of the letters that make up the Name that one is "reading." This is further complicated by the fact that the letters on the page would have, until the ninth century or so, been limited to consonants, so in fact the full sense of how to vocalize them would not have been present on the page before the reader.

13   The word "*krishna*," in Sanskrit, literally means "dark" or "black" or "dark blue." Krishna is depicted early on as dark or black but eventually blue prevails as the pigment of choice in Hindu-tradition miniature paintings. The Bhakti tradition refers to his pigment as "tinged with the hue of the blue clouds."

14   If for Vaishnavite Hindus, Krishna is merely an avatar of Vishnu, for Kraishnavite Hindus— at least by the medieval period and the advent of the *bhakti* tradition—all gods, from Vishnu to Shiva to Brahma to Devi, are manifestations of the single, supreme godhead, Krishna.

15   The color is also associated with some female figures, notably Kali (and also with other male deities), but the image of Krishna is the most familiar and is in any case Siona's intended referent.

16   All of these quotes come from remarks made by the artist in conjunction with a 2007 exhibition of her work—*Blue Like Me: Paintings by Siona Benjamin*—at the Brooklyn Museum of Art.

Chapter 20

TRANSGRESSION, TRANSCENDENCE, AND MEANING CREATION IN ART: MYSTICO-ARTISTIC ROUTE FOR RE-ENCHANTING THE WORLD

Muhammad Maroof Shah

There is, monks, an unborn, not become, not made, uncompounded; and were it not, monks, for this unborn, not become, not made, uncompounded, no escape could be shown here for what is born, has become, is made, is compounded.
But because there is, monks, an unborn, not become, not made, uncompounded, therefore an escape can be shown for what is born, has become, is made, is compounded.

(Gawtama the Buddha—Udāna, 80–81)[1]

The world is miserable because men live beneath themselves; the error of modern man is that he wants to reform the world without having either the will or the power to reform man, and this flagrant contradiction, this attempt to make a better world on the basis of a worsened humanity, can only end in the very abolition of what is human, and consequently in the abolition of happiness too. Reforming man means binding him again to Heaven, reestablishing the broken link; it means tearing him away from the reign of the passions, from the cult of matter, quantity and cunning, and reintegrating him into the world of the spirit and serenity, we would even say: into the world of sufficient reason.

Frithjof Schuon—*Understanding Islam*, p. 26

"Homo Sapiens have always been homo religiousus" and "a human existence bereft of transcendence is an impoverished and finally untenable condition."

Peter Berger—"Secularism in Retreat"

Eric Voegelin in his monumental work *Order and History* has shown how man is a creature who stands in tension with what transcends him and his felicity or flourishing and redemption lies in keeping this quest alive. Transcendence is understood here as what transcends the familiar notion of man as an individual ego who resists or negotiates non-self/Other, as what summons the self to an ethical and supra-individual spiritual end is a sort of transgression of ego boundaries. The modern project of maintaining or securing the life of man as an ego against all kinds of forces or prerogatives to find self by losing it in the service of others as Gandhi would put it given "I" is a lie as Simone Weil put it has been an evasion of this transcendence. The notions of mystery, beauty,

294 TOWARD A NEW ART OF BORDER CROSSING

wonder, cognizance of death, love, charity, and compassion have all been traditionally nurtured in the ambience of transcendence.

According to world religions and wisdom traditions, modern man has fooled himself into pretending that he needs no transcendence. He needs it because he is still man and he finds it though in impoverished versions here and there in broken images. What sustains the very act of writing, the act of choosing to live, the will to speak and stand by the truth of one's experience, to be oneself is, in last analysis, transcendence. Where all is mystery and nothing comprehensible to reason how can we veto transcendence. "[...] all existence, change, or genesis is unintelligible." We are a mystery. "To execute the simplest action we must rely on fate: our own acts are mysteries to us." What is transcendence but the mystery of existence? God is the name of this Mystery. The tradition of the negative divine that is traceable in all religious/mystical traditions is an expression of this mystery of existence, mystery in things phenomenal as Stace has argued in his *Time and Eternity*. Rising of the sun is a perpetual mystery as Santayana remarked. Science itself has increased rather than decreased the mystery and wonder of the universe. Philosophy owes its origin to wonder according to Plato. Mysticism and religion celebrate mystery. God is Mystery according to the Quran and Stace similarly sums up the mystical view of God with the phrase "God is Mystery." Certain modern trends in philosophy have forcefully shaken the claims of reason to divest mystery out of court. What is the source of animal faith that allows us to live? "[...] animal requires no special philosophical evidence for its validity. All experience, all knowledge, all art, are applications of it, and reason has non competence to defend this faith because it is based on it" as Schillipohas pointed out. Why does man love his family and why is he driven to seek beauty and why is he never willfully bad? Why does man wish to be liberated from illusions and to live in truth? What compels man to stand for justice? Nothing will ever drive a man to revolt against the Platonic triad of truth, goodness, and beauty. Man can't live in revolt against God who grounds these things and if he believes he revolts, he does so in the name of another God, the God of truth, purer truth. IbnArabi has made a profound observation that even atheists worship God. To be a man is to be oriented toward that which transcends merely human.

Dostoevesky's Father Zossima's conviction that paradise is here with us, all around us if we only knew is laughed away but there is a counter assertion regarding the omnipresence of hell from which there is no exit. Encounter with life is nauseating. Modern literature depicts absurdity, alienation, horror, and angst. It knows how to mock and not how to love and praise or celebrate. Catharsis, purification, joy, and bliss are characteristically absent in modern literature. Resentment, lamentations, vain revolt, stinking atmosphere of guilt, sordid, and squalor are seen. Reconciliation and sense of peace, fulfillment and contentment and joy of discovery, and adventure are more or less absent. The god powerless to be born and modern man's vain search for the same absent God despite his resolute claim to lucidity is the motif of modern literature. Man can't live without the ideal of the Absolute. He is made for the Absolute, for knowing the Absolute or he perishes according to religious traditions. He has to invent counterfeits at least. Man searches for the impossible, for the unattainable, the unreachable and it is that seeking alone that gives meaning to life. It is in the light of Absolute alone that

TRANSGRESSION, TRANSCENDENCE, AND MEANING CREATION   295

contingent gets justified. The light that is neither in the heavens nor in the earth, the light that never was in the land or the sea is to be sought. Postmodernism rightly exposes counterfeits and idols of reason. It shows how the light that man seeks is not in this world. But then it is lost in abyss. It stops short of outbraving the brave. The moon that Camus' Caligula seeks in order to transfigure everything is there and man has to get it. The moon is the light that guides travelers in the night of existence. It is the far of light that man must find in his bosom. But the postmodern man is despaired of finding the moon. For him, it is absolutely unattainable.

Modern man's distrust of the traditional theological and metaphysical narratives and postmodernism's incredulity toward all metanarratives—in short, the absence or death of traditional God in the post-Nietzschean world implicates the death of traditional man and his world of meaning and consequent alienation, pessimism, nihilism, and relativism. Modern literature is a painful record of modern man's agonizing search for a (lost) soul, for alternative gods, for meaning in a supposedly meaningless universe, for dealing with the absences, the silence, and nothingness at the heart of existence, and reconciling with his absurd Sisyphean predicament.

Mysticism is the art of remaking man, the art of deweeding the primrose Garden of life. It is the art of beautifying life, of enjoying life, of contentment, of peace and celebration, and of seeing heaven in a flower. To achieve this end, it engenders certain transgressive moves—transgression of bounds of ego, reason, senses, mind, and language. This transgression collapses their delimiting, dividing, or alienating roles. Transgression is, in short, a route to transcendence—transcendence of ego, reason, sensory epistemology, the empire of mind, and linguistic representational constructions.

God mysticism, soul mysticism, and nature mysticism—these three mysticisms exhaust all possible approaches to reality that man could possibly make. Who is not moved by the starry heavens above and who can afford to refuse the call of love, to give love and receive love? No age can afford to live by bread alone. All ages are seeking the feast of the senses and the spirit. Mysticism is time tested path for getting this feast. It is an invitation to join the grand feast. If a modern man feels unable to join with all his senses, heart, and mind he is to be pitied. He suffers from dyspepsia perhaps. His philosophy itself is a product of impoverished senses and hardened heart and crippled intelligence. Intelligence to perceive essences, to see into the heart of things, and vital spirits to enjoy life at its hilt, modern man lacks. His loveless heart finds everything as deserted. Mysticism is, in truth, "a temper rather than a doctrine, an atmosphere rather than a system of philosophy." As man retrogresses with the passage of time, as the *kaliyuga* spreads its dark wings, and as man falls lower and lower into the abyss this temper is increasingly lost.

Here, we explore how artistic or aesthetic route to transcendence is more universally accessible—Abhinvagupta called art or drama the fifth Veda. The treasured place for art in integral traditions both Semitic and non-Semitic needs to be reclaimed today to fight nihilism. Essentially theological and salvific function of art is a traditional thesis—Zen religion is akin to art; Sufi poetry sessions are mass mantra/*wazeefa* and God is Beauty; the beauty of the face of Buddha is an *upaya* of salvation; the world of a saint is not some airy abstraction or supraterrestrial other world but this world seen

TOWARD A NEW ART OF BORDER CROSSING

subspecies aeternatatis. Heideggerian argument for poets showing the path of fugitive gods and Nietzschean-Foucaultian emphasis on making life a work of art becomes better understandable in light of the metaphysics of beauty and function of art in general and sacred art in particular. Beauty, as the splendor of truth or attractive power of perfection, is a noetic and not just an aesthetic notion and satisfies that longing to know the Real or what is considered absolute. Invoking the theology of the aesthetic and emphasizing reading art as a ritual for purification and support to contemplation one could counter pervasive nihilism that keeps haunting the postmodern world.

Art is premised on making things beautiful or deciphering beauty in the other and while accomplishing it one is transformed and the anxiety to hanker after this or that project of will is laid to rest. Art achieves releasement, letting go and that is a redemption that comes from surrender of will as insisted by religions as well. Here is how one can get hold of the essences—the heart of things and the reality behind the appearances and see how livelier and beautiful is this vision of the "beyond," the world of ideas. This answers (post)modern skepticism regarding the vision of essences. As Underhill notes it is not by turning to mystics but to artists—universally recognized priests of art—that essences are revealed to all those who purify perception.

Following William James, it was wrongly believed that mysticism is about the altered states of consciousness which come and go and depend on certain factors which ordinarily are quite difficult to access. Mysticism is extraordinary or special things and thus the prerogative of special (chosen) extraordinary people. It is disjointed from other day-to-day experiences. Many have expressed the view that they had no mystic experiences and thus the worldview of mysticism is based on faith for them or they find this reason for rejecting it. But the reality is that we are all, by virtue of being human, mystics to a certain degree. All experiences can be channels to transcendence. Mysticism is everyone's prerogative. Even if we relegate mysticism to certain extraordinary experiences, it still is an open thing as these extraordinary experiences are too common and at one time or the other perhaps happen to all if we are attentive enough. What is needed is not something which man is unable to do—otherwise, there would have been no such thing as a mystical path found in all religious traditions. Mystic experience is akin to "aesthetic experience." In fact, all experiences can become means to it or partake of mysticism.

For mystics, nothing is closer to man than God. But we are not allowing Him to enter our world. Grace is always present but man may be absent to receive it as Schuon says. Man is not prepared to open up to God. It is not easy to leave illusions and veils that obstruct the light of God from us. Eternity is with us, inviting our contemplation perpetually,

> but we are too frightened, lazy, and suspicious to respond: too arrogant to still our thought, and let divine sensation have its way. Yes finding God who is every leaf and every stone needs 'industry and goodwill' 'a veritable spring-cleaning of the soul, a turning-out and rearrangement of our mental furniture, a wide opening of closed windows, that the notes of the wild birds beyond our garden may come to us fully charged with wonder and freshness' Very few strive in the way of God as they should and those who do this discover that 'they

TRANSGRESSION, TRANSCENDENCE, AND MEANING CREATION 297

have lived in a stuffy world, whilst their inheritance was a world of morning-glory; where every tit-mouse is a celestial messenger, and every thrusting bud is charged with the full significance of life' (Underhill, 2004).

Different varieties of mysticisms—nature mysticism, theistic mysticism, monistic mysticism, or to adopt Stace's classification extrovertive and introvertive mysticisms make a common claim to take us to the beyond, to the heart of things, to the world of wonder and beauty. The key thesis of nihilism that we have no reports from the other world, that we have no access to peace that passeth all understanding, and that the heart of reality is ever veiled to us are belied by consideration of the work of great artists and poets, leaving alone mystics.

Underhill in her classic studies has made a connection between aesthetic or artistic and mystical perceptions. Underhill observes that the vision of the world presented to us by all the great artists and poets perpetually demonstrates the hierarchical character of human consciousness. To quote her illustrations:

> Leaving on one side the more subtle apprehensions which we call 'spiritual', even the pictures of the old Chinese draughtsmen and the modern impressionists, of Watteau and of Turner, of Manet, Degas, and Cezanne; the poems of Blake, Wordsworth, Shelley, Whitman—these, and countless others, assure you that their creators have enjoyed direct communion, not with some vague world of fancy, but with a visible natural order which you have never known[…]. They prove by their works that Blake was right when he said that 'a fool sees not the same tree that a wise man sees' (Underhill, 2004).

Mysticism asks us to remember what we are rather than search for something, some object out there. No extraordinary experience or vision is sought. In fact, all seeking has to drop. There is nothing subjective, nothing extraordinary, nothing "mystical," nothing misty about mystics. God is the Light of the World, the Manifest Truth, and the ground of everything. Mystics are children. It is children who go to heaven. Only those who can afford to be children again—innocent, pure in heart, unprejudiced, nonjudgmental get access to the kingdom of God. Nietzsche too conceives the child to be the highest stage in the transformation of man to superman. We must be open to truth and for that, a pure heart, a child's innocence, and a humble soul, are needed. A receptivity to truth that excludes nothing, prejudges nothing, withholds nothing, and contemplates with absolute disinterest and total detachment. Modern man despite his claim to objectivity is far from achieving such humility. Perception of truth needs superhuman virtue of attention and disinterest. Seeing things in truth or in God is very different from seeing things in themselves. Things in themselves are not, nonbeing. It is the Spirit which adopts the veil of forms but it shines and shines in them with such heavenly brilliance that man can hardly afford to see them in all nakedness. Man can't see God and live. This is what Moses was told. What superhuman beauty and grandeur are in the world can't be expressed in human language.

Achieving a new way of perceiving things is what mystical discipline brings. Mystical discipline is directed to train our will and our mind so that we see but don't see—it is

298   TOWARD A NEW ART OF BORDER CROSSING

God who sees in us. It is not seeing with the eyes of the self. It is seeing without seer, experiencing without experience.

When we believe things to be mere things, brute facts, as gratuitous entities that just are, we may take them to be absurd. This belief is based on a truncated epistemology and is rejected by mystics on empirical grounds. The world is far more colorful than our limited senses that respond to few frequencies in the electromagnetic spectrum would have us believe. The mystic is adept in that art of cleansing of perception and his radars receive all kinds of signals from a variety of realms. What the mystic especially emphasizes is the mystery of existence and mystery is sacred, it shows there is more to a thing than meets the eye. Mystery means not a mere fact but something more. It is symbolism that seeks to clarify and decipher the infinite signification of this mystery. For mystics, all facts are "projections of timeless forms on a time-space forms" or symbols. In R. L. Nettleship's words, true mysticism is "the consciousness that everything which we experience, every 'fact,' is an element and only an element in 'the fact'; i.e. that, in being what it is, it is significant or symbolic of more." That is why everything is meaningful and not absurd.

In the world of mystics, "nothing in the world is trivial, nothing is unimportant, nothing is common or unclean." It is the feeling that Blake has expressed in the lines:

> To see a world in a grain of sand
> And a Heaven in a wild flower,
> Hold Infinity in the palm of your hand
> And Eternity in an hour

This is the view echoed by Mrs. Browning in Aurora Leigh:

> There's not a flower of spring,
> That dies in June, but vaunts itself allied
> By issue and symbol, by significance
> And correspondence, to that spirit-world
> Outside the limits of our space and time,
> Whereto we are bound.

"The mighty abstract Idea I have of Beauty in all things stifles the more divided and minute domestic happiness," Keats writes to his brother George; and the last two well-known lines of the *Ode on a Grecian Urn* fairly sum up his philosophy "Beauty is truth, truth Beauty, that is all Ye know on earth, and all ye need to know."

What else than beauty and love does one need to know according to different traditions and mystics? Do we need to argue rationale of kiss as Augustine asks? Mystics find earth as heavenly and praise every blade of grass.

Nothing extraordinary is needed to see the world in a different light transfused with light and glory that is God. All things are His messengers. The Beloved smiles in everything. Men of God, as Wordsworth tells us,

> Need not extraordinary calls
> To rouse them; in a world of life they live,

TRANSGRESSION, TRANSCENDENCE, AND MEANING CREATION   299

By sensible impressions not enthralled,
[...] the highest bliss
That flesh can know is theirs—the consciousness
Of Whom they are.
Prelude, Book xiv. 105, 113.

The Supernatural, the Traceless is manifesting everywhere and in all things phenomenal but we need to see its portents. Here I am tempted to quote Rumi, the great Sufi poet, who reiterates the importance of our worthiness to receive the heavenly messages and messengers.

The Caravan of the Unseen enters the visible world, but it remains hidden from all these ugly people
How should lovely women come to ugly men, the nightingale always comes to the rosebush [...].
Like cream hidden in the soul of milk, No-place keeps coming into place
Like intellect concealed in blood and skin, the Traceless keeps entering into traces.
Diwan, 30789–94

For Rumi everything veils and unveils God. The supernatural, the beyond, the true world is manifest everywhere. The Beloved for whom a Sufi lives is manifest everywhere and if He were not he would die in a moment. As Rumi says: "All the hopes, desires, loves, affections, the saint knows are desires for God and all these things are veils."

Tahrene reiterates, in company with all the mystics, that "'Tis not the object, but the light that maketh Heaven: 'tis a purer sight." Here is a famous description from his *Centuries of Meditation*.

All appeared now, and strange at first, inexpressibly rare and delightful and beautiful. I was a little stranger, which at my entrance into the world was saluted and surrounded with innumerable joys [...]. The corn was orient and immortal wheat, which never should be reaped, nor was ever sown. I thought it had stood from everlasting to everlasting. The dust and stones of the street were as precious as gold: the gates were at first the end of the world. The green trees when I saw them first [...] transported and ravished me, their sweetness and unusual beauty made my heart to leap, and almost mad with ecstasy, they were such strange and wonderful things. The Men! O what venerable and reverend creatures did the aged seem! Immortal Cherubims! And young men glittering and sparkling Angels, and maids strange seraphic pieces of life and beauty! Boys and girls tumbling in the street, and playing, were moving jewels. I knew not that they were born or should die; but all things abided eternally as they were in their proper places[...]. The city seemed to stand in Eden, or to be built in Heaven (Traherne, 2007).

But he remembered enough of those early glories to realize that if he would regain happiness, he must "become, as it were, a little child again," get free of "the burden and cumber of devised wants," and recapture the value and the glory of the common things of life. Indeed, the mystic doesn't devalue this world but he alone knows its value and sees its supernatural beauty. He needn't believe in some beyond; he tastes it here and now when he disciplines his attention and opens up to the depth of things. Being unveils to those who are not servants of calculative thought but are capable of what Heidegger calls meditative thinking, a thinking which is "more rigorous than the conceptual" and that "contemplates the meaning which reigns in everything that is" (Heidegger, 1966: 46) and that can consist simply in "dwell[ing] on what lies close to us and meditate[ing] on what is closest[...]". (Heidegger, 1966: 47). He proposes for accessing the Truth of Being something like "learned ignorance" of the mystics, attention to something that is too close to require "building complicated concepts." Instead "it is concealed in the step back that lets thinking enter into a questioning that experiences [...]" (Heidegger, 1977: 255). His call is essentially Iqbalian one for opening up the human spirit, standing naked before the Mystery, perfecting the faculty of attention, and forgetting the manipulating, willing, technological self that modern man has been reduced to. Truth/the Real is more an ontological than epistemological issue. The Being Heidegger invites us to "is not conceived of as a thing, but as that which 'transcends' things thinking and talking about it in traditional terms becomes impossible." Such a goal is strikingly similar to the goals of many of the world's most prominent mystical traditions, as Jeff Guilford has pointed out (Guilford, 2011). The metaphysics which Heidegger labels as nihilism is concerned with representing Being instead of "thinking" it as Being isn't a being or a thing. Heidegger, as paraphrased by Marmysz, protested that "We are guilty of nihilistic thinking any time that we fail to recognize the fact that language, and the rational and logical tools it utilizes, necessarily chops up what 'is' into fragments, and so falsifies and 'covers over' Being-itself" (Marmysz, 2003: 77).

How could God be dead or absent when beauty is not absent in the world, neither is love, nor are visitations and intimations of divine, nor conversations between God and his friends? The world is filled with the messengers of God though few heed them. "For the sage every star, every flower, is metaphysically a proof of the Infinite" as Schuon noted. The light of the dawn is enough proof for a man of the Friend as Josh says. For the mystic who has cleansed his perception, everything speaks of Him as everything is Infinite. Nothing appears to the mystic as opaque, dense, or inhuman. There are no brute and mute facts, no gratuitous entities.

Carlyle has expressed this mystic intuition in Sartor Resartus in these words: "Rightly viewed no meanest object is insignificant; all objects are as windows, through which the philosophic eye looks into Infinitude itself" (Book i. chap. xi). The universe presents to mystics as the "living visible garment of God," and "matter exists only spiritually," "to represent some Idea, and *body* it forth." This is the "divine madness" of which Plato speaks, the "inebriation of Reality," the ecstasy which makes the poet "drunk with life."

This experience of the transcendent is far too common to humanity than usually recognized and in fact, the supernatural, the beyond, is far too real for traditional man, for all those who have not closed their faculties of souls, who have loved with great abandon and who have died to their selves than anything tangible in the world of senses. We have, arguably, experiences of a transcendent world of meaning. In fact, our

TRANSGRESSION, TRANSCENDENCE, AND MEANING CREATION   301

apprehension of beauty is one glaring example. Cottingham has beautifully presented the evidence:

> As simple an experience as that of seeing the colours of leaves in autumn discloses the world around us as resonating with an astonishing harmony and richness; it reveals objects as qualitatively irradiated in modalities which even the most sober of analytic philosophers have agreed are not fully capturable in the language of physics. When Blake urges us to see heaven in a wild flower, he was pointing to something that few humans could honestly deny: our ability, in those lucid moments that Wordsworth called 'spots of time,' to see the world transfigured with beauty and meaning. Human beings can't live wholly and healthily except in responsiveness to objective values of truth and beauty and goodness. If they deny those values, or try to subordinate them to their own selfish ends, they find that meaning slips away. (Cottingham, 2002: 103).

What Caligula longs for—the moon—countless people (and not only mystics) have found.

Focusing on Sufis we can assert that they breathe in the supernatural. Angels are at their deck and call. IbnArabi, one of the greatest Sufis and Sufi metaphysicians, used to tell that angels are his faculties. God's wish for attention from the Buddhas. There are countless tales narrated in the lives of mystics and by those who have known them—many of them skeptics to begin with—which clearly demonstrate that there are higher orders of being that transcend what we ordinarily call the natural world with which man can communicate. In fact, certain prophets and sages are reported to have talked to animals and stones. The universe is not indifferent but our very home for those who have learned to attune themselves to its rhythms. "If you could maintain God-consciousness angels will meet you and shake hands with you," the Prophet of Islam told his companions.

Mysticism demands nothing but the art of being here and now, the process of deconditioning from bondage to past and future, the demand to be open, and receptive excluding nothing from the sphere of consciousness or perception. To be here now is what is to transcend the mind because reality is not in thoughts, in the past and future but in the present. Nothing is colored by human thought or sentiment which should distort the perception of what is or Reality. To see truth is to see phenomena with unclouded eyes. For the East, self-knowledge is a prerequisite of all knowledge and without it, nothing is really known about the world. Self-knowledge is synonymous with bliss and the conquest of sorrow. With self-knowledge comes knowledge of everything. No more is anything outside oneself and neither are we strangers to the world. Things reveal their secrets, their essences to the sages. But because one doesn't know oneself one doesn't know anything and it is knowledge which saves according to traditions. To quote from "Ode: Of our Sense of Sinne" a poem by a poet who belonged to the metaphysical school:

> But we know our selves least; Mere outward shews
> Our mindes so store,

TOWARD A NEW ART OF BORDER CROSSING

That our soules, no more than our eyes disclose
But forme and colour. Only he who knows
Himselfe, knowes more.

In a prose passage of great beauty Traherne thus describes the attitude toward earth which is needful before we can enter heaven.

> You never enjoy the world aright, till the Sea itself floweth in your veins, till you are clothed with the heavens, and crowned with the stars: **[...]** Till you can sing and rejoice and delight in God, as misers do in gold, and Kings in sceptres, you never enjoy the world.
> Till your spirit filleth the whole world, and the stars are your jewels; **[...]**. till you love men so as to desire their happiness, with a thirst equal to the zeal of your own: till you delight in God for being good to all: you never enjoy the world [...]. The world is a mirror of infinite beauty, yet no man sees it. It is a Temple of Majesty, yet no man regards it. It is a region of Light and Peace, did not men disquiet it. It is the Paradise of God [...]. It is, the place of Angels and the Gate of Heaven (Traherne, 1908: 20–21).

He is forever reiterating, in company with all the mystics, that "It is not the object, but the light that maketh Heaven: It is a purer sight."

Mysticism is the experience of the transcendence of belief and all mental or ideological constructs about experience. "It is not belief in fate or belief in God or even belief in transcendence." Dostoevsky was pointing to this. "It is through love of life (rather than any means to deny it based on a fear of suffering) that we are able to transcend our beliefs about it. This doesn't require upholding the absurd, merely an acceptance of it" as Solomon says. Once fully accepted, it can be transcended. This is how Nietzsche' does by constantly overcoming. Nietzsche's key term Will to Power is defined by Solomon as "the enthusiastic vitality to act on the world (rather than reacting to it)."Here mystics and artists in their call for being open or receptive rather than judgmental about the other join hands with Nietzsche.

Let it be made clear that the mystical vision is based on Intellect, shaper and more intense senses, and thoroughgoing empiricism.

> I can't say cogito truly, but only cogitator. "I" neither think nor see, but there is Another who alone sees, hears, thinks in me and acts through me; an Essence, Fire, Sprit, or Life that is no more or less "mine" than "yours," but that never itself becomes anyone, a principle that informs and enlivens one body after another [...] one that is never born and never dies, though present at every birth and death [...] that can only be known im-mediately (Coomaraswamy, 1977: 426).

That immanently transcendent non-being, affirming which the world becomes enchanted garden, is envisaged by the whole human tradition:

> Our whole tradition everywhere affirms that "there are two in us"; the platonic mortal and immortal "souls", Hebrew and Islamic *Nefesh (Nafs)* and *ruah (ruh)*, Philo's "soul" and "Soul of the soul", Egyptian pharaoh and his *ka*, Chinese Outer and Inner sage, Christian Outer and Inner Man, Psyche and Pneuma, and Vedantic "self" (*ātman*) and "self's Immortal

TRANSGRESSION, TRANSCENDENCE, AND MEANING CREATION

Self" [...] one the soul, self, or life that Christ requires of us to "hate" and "deny", if we would follow him, and that other soul or self that can be saved (Comaraswamy, 1977: 428).

This distinction between soul and Spirit, outer and inner man is crucial to mystical understanding of freedom and ontology of art.

By way of conclusion, we may sum up by stating that artistic and the mystical are one or can be integrated in a single vision and for both the condition is transgression of ego boundary and its expansion or better dissolution in love. Mysticism may be simply defined as a remembrance of God or God consciousness which means other/ non-self-consciousness. It means one is not conscious of one's self or ego and the misery associated with the ego and the mind. Absurdism arises from the confrontation of the individual/ego/mind with the universe divested of transcendence. The impoverishment of intelligence, senses, beauty, empirical sense, sense of proportion and measure and misdirected relationship with the mysterious or the sacred, lack of such intellectual virtues as attention and such moral virtues as humility, privileging finite over the Infinite, gravity over grace, object and objective to subject and subjective contribute to the formation of pessimistic absurdist worldview. Taking art seriously one is redeemed from the self that asks the question of what is it for as one basks in the sunshine of Spirit which is its own reward.

References

Coomaraswamy, A. K., 1977, "The Meaning of Death," in *Coomaraswamy*, Vol. 2, ed., Roger Lipsey, London: Princeton University Press.
Cottingham, J., 2002, *On the Meaning of Life*, London: Routledge.
Guilford, J., 2011, "Was Heidegger a Mystic?" *Explorations*, 6, 86–93.
Heidegger, M., 1966, *Discourse on Thought*. New York: Harper & Row Publishers.
_____1977, "Letter on Humanism," in *Basic Writings: from Being and Time to The Task of Thinking*, ed., Krell, David Farrell. New York: Harper & Row Publishers.
Marmysz, J., 2003, *Laughing at Nothing: Humour as a Response to Nihilism*, New York, SUNY.
Spurgeon, Caroline F. E., 2019, *Mysticism in English Literature*, Good Press. (It is from Spurgeon that quotations from English literary figures have been reproduced in the paper).
Traherne, T., 1908, "The Third Century," in *Centuries, Poems, and Thanksgivings*, Vol. 1, ed., H. M. Margoliouth, Oxford: OUP.
_____2007, Centuries of meditation, Cosimo Classics.
Underhill, E., 2004, *Practical Mysticism*, New Delhi: Abhishek Publications.

INDEX

A
African communities 201
America-Mexico relationship 227
American Abstract Expressionist
  movement 285
American Academy of Religion (AAR) 105
American Anthropological Association
  (AAA) 28, 214, 215
American Philosophical Association
  (APA) 105
anachronistic 115, 125
Anglo-American world 128
Anthropocene 27, 28, 183, 213, 214
Anthropocentrism 28
anthropology 18, 21, 139, 145, 146, 193,
  214, 224n2
anti-colonial critique 79
anti-colonial mobilisations 129
anti-racism 27, 208
Ardhanareshwara 289
artistic representation 8, 9
Arya Samaj 127
Audio-Visual Services 233
Australasian Association of Philosophy (AAP) 105
*Australasian Society for Asian and Comparative
  Philosophy* (ASACP) 105

B
Better Think Tank Project (BTTP) 241
Bharatiya Janata Party (BJP) 125
Black freedom movement 61
Black Lives Matter 26, 27, 62
Black Lives Matter movement 62
Black, Indigenous, People of Color
  (BIPOC) 63
Border Studies Collaboration 259
Borderlands film literature 232
boundary transformation 4, 46

British colonialism 132
burgeoning movements 16

C
Capitalocene 16
charismatic community 191
civic mobilization 195
colonial administration 79
colonialism xi, xiv, 16, 78, 79, 126, 128, 129,
  132, 133, 135, 141, 144, 216, 235
commercial filmmaking 227
communist movements 117
communitarian dimensions 126
community welfare 28
Comparative Philosophy 29, 98–105
contemporary reflections 5, 7
conventional nomenclature 262
creolization xvi, 28, 29, 207–9, 211, 216, 217,
  224n3, 224n6, 225n9
creolized cultures 207
creolized transcultural societies 207
Critical Race Theory 210
critical social science 207
cross-cultural communication 117
cross-cultural mediation 114, 116–19
cultural collision 63
cultural continuity 207
cultural dissemination 118
cultural hegemony 27
cultural hybridization 208
cultural identity 212, 224n7
cultural mediation 116
cultural misunderstandings 235, 237
cultural valorisation 133

D
Decolonizing Methodologies 214
de-imperialism 133

Deleuzian ontology 7
democratic electoral mechanism 128

E
ecclesiastical organization 71
eclecticism 130
ecological ontology 8
emasculated imperialism 129
empiricism 302
Euro-Marxist movements 132
evolutionary transmutation 65

F
Federal Housing Administration (FHA) 62
Federal Republic of Germany (FRG)
  xv, 150, 151
fictive ethnicities 51, 62, 63, 65
Finnish-Russian border 18
fragile resolution 265
freedom movement 116
French Revolution 145

G
geo-physical omnipresence 263
German Democratic Republic (GDR)
  xv, 150, 151
Giri, Ananta Kumar xi, xii, 3, 17, 46, 51
global economy 174, 235, 263
global movements 212
global sociopolitical arena 262
globalization xi, 15, 25, 28, 139, 198, 210,
  211, 212, 224n6, 228
Gramscian theories 130
Gramscian war 131
Great Green Wall 19
Gun Island xvii, 261–63, 265–69

H
Home Owners Loan Corporation
  (HOEC) 62
homophonic pairing 60
Hongladarom xii, xiii, 41, 44
Human Development Index 140, 167
human history xi, 79, 209, 266

I
identitarian politics 146
illiberal democracies 140
Indian Irrigation Service 233, 234

inequality-adjusted Human Development
  Index (IAHDI) 140
intellectualism 115
international networks 198
international organizations 143, 172
international politics 64
internationalism 117

J
Jewish-Christian boundaries xvii, 271

K
Kyotophonie Borderless Music Festival 23

L
Little Ice Age 266

M
Mexican immigrants 232
Mexican-American filmmakers 233
migratory movements xvii
modernist ideology 59
mondialization 210
monotheistic Christian world 281
most-awarded film 24
Mukerji, Dhurjati Prasad 76
multiculturalism 112
multidisciplinary border 21
multi-generational connection 236
mysticism 29, 294–97, 301–3
mythopoetic imagination 59

N
National Archaeological Museum 279
National Immigration Forum 25
Nationalistic democracies 3
Native American tribes 227, 239n4
neo-imperialist logic 128
neoliberal capitalism 130
nihilism xvii, 295–97, 300
Nixonian diplomatic gamble 69
nonfiction films 232
non-monolith Nature 77
non-sovereignties xii, 4, 5, 16
nonviolent resistance xiii, 83, 84, 87, 88, 92

O
occidentalism 145
oral literature 74

INDEX

307

P
Papago Indians 234
parochialisms 9
personal companionship 77
pharmaconic 65
pharmacopeic potentials 60
philosophical traditions xiv, 97, 100,
   103, 109n6
plural personality 64
pluriversalism 217
political mobilisation 116
post-Islamic-imperialism 133
post-Christian 283, 285
postcolonial right xiv
post-colonial theories 113
postcolonialism xiv
post-Holocaust theodicy question 286
Postinternational Environment 5
Post-Marxian tradition 111
pre-eminent voice 17
pre-republican Rome 271
psychic chasm 63

R
rationalistic schemes 115
rational-ritualistic 65
religio-cultural nationalism 134
Roy, Ram Mohan 73
rural Indian society 132

S
sanitorium 61
Santa Rita Mountains 233
Santiniketan 70, 72, 80n19, 80n22
sectarian extremism 194
secularism 126
segmented assimilation conception 199
semiotic system 18
social boundaries xii, 3, 41, 259, 265
social tourism 141

social-liberal democracies 145, 147
Society for Asian and Comparative
   Philosophy 105
Southeast Asian countries xv
spiritual-political Christian boundaries 285
Spivak, Gayatri 228
structural isomorphism 130, 131
Subaltern Studies Collective 113
Susan Stanford Friedman 260
Swaraj 70, 72
system convenors 218
systematic European colonization 195

T
Technocratic solutions 115
techno-human condition 26
Thapar, Romila 71
Traditional Indigenous Wisdom 213
transition zones xvii, 260, 261
Transnational communities 191
transnational cultures 209
trans-national organisations 117

U
University of Norway (UiT) 22
US–Mexican themes 231

V
Vasudhaiva Kutumbakam 129
Vatican Museum 280
Vivekananda, Swami 127
Voegelin, Eric 293

W
Westernization 146
Wolastoqey Nation 61, 64
working-class organisations 118–20
World Systems Theory 218
World War II xv, 25, 168, 209, 231

www.ingramcontent.com/pod-product-compliance
Lightning Source LLC
LaVergne TN
LVHW091714070225
803225LV00002B/47